RESEARCH METHODS FOR APPLIED LANGUAGE STUDIES

Routledge Applied Linguistics is a series of comprehensive textbooks, providing students and researchers with the support they need for advanced study in the core areas of English Language and Applied Linguistics.

Each book in the series guides readers through three main sections, enabling them to explore and develop major themes within the discipline:

- Section A, **Introduction**, establishes the key terms and concepts and extends readers' techniques of analysis through practical application.
- Section B, **Extension**, brings together influential articles, sets them in context, and discusses their contribution to the field.
- Section C, **Exploration**, builds on knowledge gained in the first two sections, setting thoughtful tasks around further illustrative material. This enables readers to engage more actively with the subject matter and encourages them to develop their own research responses.

Throughout the book, topics are revisited, extended, interwoven and deconstructed, with the reader's understanding strengthened by tasks and follow-up questions.

Research Methods for Applied Language Studies:

- provides an advanced introduction to quantitative and qualitative research methods used in second and foreign language learning, teaching and assessment
- takes readers step by step through the processes of research, from formulating research questions to writing up a dissertation or report.
- employs a wide variety of carefully structured tasks and discussion points to guide the reader through the key themes, frameworks and procedures of applied language research, including ethnography, conversation analysis and quasi-experimental designs
- engages students in readings and tasks on articles from leading names in the field, including Alison Mackey, Roy Lyster, Angela Creese, Junko Mori, Rod Ellis and Diane Larsen-Freeman
- is supported by a Companion Website, including data sets for practice and guides to writing a proposal, making recordings, conducting interviews, producing questionnaires and organising a dissertation.

Written by experienced teachers and researchers in the field, *Research Methods for Applied Language Studies* is an essential resource for students and researchers of Applied Linguistics.

Keith Richards is an Associate Professor in the Centre for Applied Linguistics at the University of Warwick.

Steven J. Ross is Professor of Second Language Acquisition at the University of Maryland College Park.

Paul Seedhouse is Professor of Educational and Applied Linguistics at Newcastle University, UK.

ROUTLEDGE APPLIED LINGUISTICS

SERIES EDITORS

Christopher N. Candlin is Senior Research Professor in the Department of Linguistics at Macquarie University, Australia. At Macquarie, he has been Chair of the Department of Linguistics; established and was Executive Director of the National Centre for English Language Teaching and Research and was the founding Director of the Centre for Language in Social Life. He has written or edited over 150 publications in the fields of language education, discourse analysis, and professional communication and co-edits the *Journal of Applied Linguistics and Professional Practice*. From 1996–2002 he was President for two terms of the *International Association of Applied Linguistics (AILA)*. He has acted as a consultant and as external faculty assessor in over 30 universities worldwide.

Ronald Carter is Professor of Modern English Language in the School of English Studies at the University of Nottingham. He has published extensively in the fields of applied linguistics, literary studies and language in education. He has given consultancies in the field of applied linguistics and English language education, mainly in conjunction with the British Council, in over thirty countries worldwide and has been a regular linguistic adviser to UK government organizations. He is a Fellow of the British Academy of Social Sciences and has been a recent chair of the British Association for Applied Linguistics.

TITLES IN THE SERIES

Translation: An advanced resource book
Basil Hatim and Jeremy Munday

Grammar and Context: An advanced resource book
Ann Hewings, Martin Hewings

Second Language Acquisition: An advanced resource book
Kees de Bot, Wander Lowie and Marjolijn Verspoor

Corpus-Based Language Studies: An advanced resource book
Anthony McEnery, Richard Xiao and Yukio Tono

Language and Gender: An advanced resource book
Jane Sunderland

English for Academic Purposes: An advanced resource book
Ken Hyland

Language Testing and Assessment: An advanced resource book
Glenn Fulcher and Fred Davidson

Bilingualism: An advanced resource book
Ng Bee Chin and Gillian Wigglesworth

Literacy: An advanced resource book
Brian V. Street and Adam Lefstein

Language and Interaction: An advanced resource book
Richard F. Young

Intercultural Communication: An advanced resource book for students, Second Edition
Adrian Holliday, Martin Hyde and John Kullman

Research Methods for Applied Language Studies

Keith Richards, Steven Ross and Paul Seedhouse

Routledge
Taylor & Francis Group
LONDON AND NEW YORK

First published 2012
by Routledge
2 Park Square, Milton Park, Abingdon, Oxon OX14 4RN

Simultaneously published in the USA and Canada
by Routledge
711 Third Avenue, New York, NY 10017

Routledge is an imprint of the Taylor & Francis Group, an informa business

British Library Cataloguing in Publication Data
A catalogue record for this book is available from the British Library

Library of Congress Cataloging in Publication Data
Richards, Keith, 1952-
Research methods for applied language studies / Keith Richards, Steven Ross, Paul Seedhouse.
p. cm. – (Routledge applied linguistics)
1. Language and languages–Study and teaching. 2. Applied linguistics–Methodology. I. Ross, Steven, 1951– II. Seedhouse, Paul. III. Title.
P129.R55 2010
407.2–dc22 2011003876

ISBN: 978-0-415-55140-3 (hbk)
ISBN: 978-0-415-55141-0 (pbk)

Typeset in Akzidenz Grotesk, Minion and Novarese
by Keystroke, Station Road, Codsall, Wolverhampton

MIX
Paper from responsible sources
FSC www.fsc.org FSC® C004839

Printed and bound in Great Britain by
TJ International Ltd, Padstow, Cornwall

Contents

Contents cross-referenced

Illustrations

FIGURES

TABLES

Series editors' preface

The Routledge Applied Linguistics series provides a comprehensive guide to a number of key areas in the field of applied linguistics. Applied linguistics is a rich, vibrant, diverse and essentially interdisciplinary field. It is now more important than ever that books in the field provide up-to-date maps of what is an ever-changing territory.

The books in this series are designed to give key insights into core areas of applied linguistics. The design of the books ensures, through key readings, that the history and development of a subject is recognized while, through key questions and tasks, integrating understandings of the topics, concepts and practices that make up its essentially interdisciplinary fabric. The pedagogic structure of each book ensures that readers are given opportunities to think, discuss, engage in tasks, draw on their own experience, reflect, research and to read and critically re-read key documents. Each book has three main sections, each made up of approximately ten units.

A: An **Introduction** section: in which the key terms and concepts which map the field of the subject are introduced, including introductory activities and reflective tasks, designed to establish key understandings, terminology, techniques of analysis and the skills appropriate to the theme and the discipline.

B: An **Extension** section: in which selected core readings are introduced (usually edited from the original) from existing key books and articles, together with annotations and commentary, where appropriate. Each reading is introduced, annotated and commented on in the context of the whole book, and research/follow-up questions and tasks are added to enable fuller understanding of both theory and practice. In some cases, readings are short and synoptic and incorporated within a more general exposition.

C: An **Exploration** section: in which further samples and illustrative materials are provided with an emphasis, where appropriate, on more open-ended, student-centred activities and tasks designed to support readers and users in undertaking their own locally relevant research projects. Tasks are designed for work in groups or for individuals working on their own. They can be readily included in award courses in applied linguistics or as topics for personal study and research.

The target audience for the series is upper undergraduates and postgraduates on language, applied linguistics and communication studies programmes as well as teachers and researchers in professional development and distance learning programmes. High-quality applied research resources are also much needed for teachers of EFL/ESL and foreign language students at higher education colleges and universities worldwide. The books in the Routledge Applied Linguistics series are aimed at the individual reader, the student in a group and at teachers building courses and seminar programmes.

We hope that the books in this series meet these needs and continue to provide support over many years.

THE EDITORS

Professor Christopher N. Candlin and Professor Ronald Carter are the series editors. Both have extensive experience of publishing titles in the fields relevant to this series. Between them they have written and edited over one hundred books and two hundred academic papers in the broad field of applied linguistics. Chris Candlin was president of AILA (International Association for Applied Linguistics) from 1996 to 2002 and Ron Carter was chair of BAAL (British Association for Applied Linguistics) from 2003 to 2006.

Professor Christopher N. Candlin
Senior Research Professor
Department of Linguistics
Division of Linguistics and Psychology
Macquarie University
Sydney NSW 2109
Australia

and

Professor of Applied Linguistics
Faculty of Education and Language Studies
The Open University
Walton Hall
Milton Keynes MK7 6AA
UK

Professor Ronald Carter
School of English Studies
University of Nottingham
Nottingham NG7 2RD
UK

Acknowledgements

The publishers would like to thank the following for permission to reprint their material:

1. Oxford University Press journals and the author for permission to reprint material from Andrea Golato (2003) 'Studying compliment responses: A comparison of DCTs and recordings of naturally occurring talk', *Applied Linguistics* 24(1): 90–121.

2. John Wiley & Sons for kind permission to reprint Larsen-Freeman, D. and Cameron, L. (2008) 'Research methodology on language development from a complex systems perspective', *The Modern Language Journal* 92(2): 200–213. Copyright © 2008, John Wiley & Sons.

3. Oxford University Press journals for permission to reprint material from Basturkmen, H., Loewen, S. and Ellis, R. (2004) 'Teachers' stated beliefs about incidental focus on form and their classroom practices', *Applied Linguistics* 25(2), 243–272. Copyright © 2004, Copyright © 2006 by the Oxford University Press. Reprinted with kind permission of the authors.

4. Oxford University Press Journals for permission to reprint Table 2 on page 422 from Mackey, A. (2006) 'Feedback, noticing, and instructed second language learning', *Applied Linguistics* 27(3), 405–430. Copyright © 2006, Copyright © 2006 by the Oxford University Press.

5. Taylor & Francis Ltd for kind permission to reprint extracts from Koshik, I. (2002) 'Designedly incomplete utterances: A pedagogical practice for eliciting knowledge displays in error correction sequences', *Research on Language and Social Interaction* 35(3), 277–309. © 2002 Routledge. Reprinted by permission of the publisher (Taylor & Francis Ltd, http://www.tandf.co.uk/journals).

6. *TESOL Quarterly* by Toohey, K. (1998) 'Breaking them up, "taking them away": ESL students in Grade 1', *TESOL Quarterly*, 32(1): 61–84. © 1998 by Teachers of English to Speakers of Other Languages. Reproduced with permission of Teachers of English to Speakers of Other Languages in the format Other book via Copyright Clearance Center.

7. Oxford University Press journals for permission to reprint one table on p. 313 of DeRidder, I., Vangehuchten, G., and Sesena-Gomez, M. (2007) 'Enhancing

automaticity through task-based language learning', *Applied Linguistics* 28(2): 309–315. © 2007 Oxford University Press.

8. Sage for permission to reprint extracts from Gao, X. (2007) 'Strategies used by Chinese parents to support english language learning: Voices of "elite" university students', *RELC Journal*, 37(3): 285–298. Copyright © 2006 Sage Publications. Reprinted with permission.

9. John Wiley & Sons for kind permission to reprint Appendix B from Kitano, K. (2001) 'Anxiety in the college Japanese language classroom', *Modern Language Journal* 85(4): 549–566. © 2002, 2001 *The Modern Language Journal.*

10. John Wiley & Sons for permission to reprint material from Seedhouse, P. and Almutairi, S. (2009) 'A holistic approach to task-based interaction', *International Journal of Applied Linguistics* 19(3): 311–338. © 2009, John Wiley & Sons, journal compilation.

11. Cambridge University Press for permission to reprint Table 4 in Lyster, R. (2004) 'Differential effects of prompts and recasts in form-focused instruction', *Studies in Second Language Acquisition* 26(3): 399–432. 2004 © Cambridge Journals, reproduced with permission.

12. Taylor & Francis Ltd for kind permission to reprint extracts from Mori, J. (2003) 'The construction of interculturality: A study of initial encounters between Japanese and American students', *Research on Language and Social Interaction* 36(2): 143–184. © 2003 Routledge. Reprinted by permission of the publisher (Taylor & Francis Ltd, http://www.tandf.co.uk/journals).

13. Taylor & Francis Ltd for kind permission to reprint extracts from Creese, A. (2003) 'Language, ethnicity and the mediation of allegations of racism: Negotiating diversity and sameness in multilingual school discourses', *International Journal of Bilingual Education and Bilingualism* 6(3 and 4): 221–236. © 2003 Routledge. Reprinted by permission of the publisher (Taylor & Francis Ltd, http://www.tandf.co.uk/journals).

14. Cambridge University Press for permission to reprint Table 7 in Ellis, R. (2005) 'Measuring implicit and explicit knowledge of a second language: A psychometric study', *Studies in Second Language Acquisition* 27: 141–172. 2005 © Cambridge Journals, reproduced with permission.

15. Brown, A. (2003) 'Interviewer variation and the co-construction of speaking proficiency', *Language Testing* 20(1): 1–25. © 2003, Sage Publications. Reprinted by permission.

16. Oxford University Press journals for permission to reprint material from Sheen, R. and O'Neill, R. (2005) 'Tangled up in form: critical comments on "Teachers'

stated beliefs about incidental focus on form and their classroom practices"' by Basturkmen, Loewen and Ellis, *Applied Linguistics* 26(2): 268–274, pp. 270, 271, 272.

Every effort has been made to trace and contact copyright holders. The publishers would be pleased to hear from any copyright holders not acknowledged here so that this section may be amended at the earliest opportunity.

We would like to thank our students for the contribution they have made to our understanding of issues in the teaching of research methods over the years. Particular thanks are due to Fatos Eren Bilgen and Maneerat Tarnpichprasert for giving us permission to include extracts from their work in this book.

CHAPTER 1
Introduction to research in language teaching and learning

Overview

This text aims to provide an advanced introduction to a mixed-methods approach in which quantitative and qualitative research methods are used in common themes in second and foreign language learning, teaching and assessment. The assumption we make is that readers will be at the postgraduate level but may not have had much first-hand experience doing original research in the domain of language teaching and learning or applied linguistics. A chief goal of the text is to introduce research in a mixed-methods framework – one which seeks to use the best of ethnographic, conversation analytic and hypothetical-deductive research approaches. To this end, a number of research themes are exemplified in the text.

Each theme is organized according to the Routledge Series structure. The *Introduction* describes a research theme from a qualitative or quantitative perspective, with tasks designed to orient readers' attention to possible options and choices available in addressing the research topic. The *Extension* section features selected published studies corresponding to the theme presented in the *Introduction*. Research themes in the *extension* section are approached qualitatively or quantitatively, featuring the research strategies used by the studies' authors. Tasks and discussion points orient readers to examining the topics from a mixed-methods approach. The *Exploration* section introduces readers to specific research methods with data samples for both quantitative and qualitative analysis. The research methods in some of the chapters correspond to the *Extension* section by 'reverse engineering' the designs used in the featured studies. The design and analysis procedures treated in the *Exploration* section include topics such as randomized and quasi-experimental designs, selection bias, quantitative data analysis, and approaches to the micro-analysis of interaction, and ethnographic observation and interviewing. In *extension* sections focused on quantitative methods, a sample data set describing the file organization, analysis strategy, assumptions and interpretation of each analysis specimen are included to give readers a opportunity for a 'hands on' experience in performing sample analyses. For qualitative data analysis practice, focused tasks are provided for data analysis, practice and discussion. A series of appendices on the accompanying website provide guidance on dealing with the practicalities of your own research project. A glossary defines the technical terms employed in the book.

Our approach to mixed-methods research is based on the premise that in order to understand how different methods can be brought together into a coherent research project, it is first necessary to understand each method in its own right. We have therefore deliberately avoided the temptation to draw together from the start the different approaches covered in the book; instead we have addressed each topic from the distinctive perspectives these approaches offer, but in a way that should allow you to see connections and complementarities. Many of the tasks are designed with this in mind, and as the book progresses you should find that you are developing a sense of how the same research topic can be approached from different standpoints in a way that allows a deeper and broader understanding of its nature and the issues associated with it.

If our approach succeeds, by the time you reach the final chapter with its discussion of key concepts and description of mixed-methods research, the content should seem like a natural drawing together of material with which you are already familiar. One of the things we will ask you to do in that chapter is to return to this introduction in order to revisit the concepts introduced here and interpret them from the different perspectives with which you will then be familiar, establishing relevant connections for yourself.

Another decision we have made, arising from our wish to preserve and reflect the authenticity of the different approaches covered in the book, is that we should allow their distinctive characteristics to emerge from the outset. Ethnographic, conversation analytic and hypothetical-deductive research approaches are different – and they are different in quite fundamental ways. They involve not just different procedures and processes but different ways of thinking, and this has implications for how they are written. We could have attempted to smooth over these differences in order to produce a more homogeneous text, but this would have been an artificial and ultimately, we believe, unconvincing exercise, so instead we have sought to preserve as far as possible a sense of what is distinctive about these approaches in terms of not only content and procedure but also style and representation.

It might be said of qualitative approaches that the greatest challenge lies in appreciating the rigorous demands made by the complexity of what appears to be familiar and straightforward, while the challenge in hypothetical-deductive research is to be found in understanding what is unfamiliar and manifestly complex. In both cases, the best way of responding to these challenges is to engage with tasks that reflect the sort of work that research demands, and in the case of hypothetical-deductive research, where so much is new and unfamiliar, this can seem at first sight a very daunting prospect. We have chosen what might be described as a 'deep end' strategy because we believe that this is the only one consistent with our commitment to authenticity, but this does mean that some readers will find aspects of this first chapter particularly daunting. This book is foundational but it is not a primer, so readers new to hypothetical-deductive research may need time to adjust to the work associated with this. In order to respond to this need we have provided a number of additional tasks on the associated website that offer the opportunity for further practice.

Section A
Introduction to research

Research is a process which normally involves a) identifying a research focus, research questions or a problem b) gathering appropriate data c) providing answers to a) on the basis of b). If you keep this structure firmly in your mind at all stages of your own research project and do not diverge from it, you stand a good chance of completing it successfully. From this perspective it seems quite a simple and straightforward enterprise. Of course, language teaching and learning research is a complex process and the reason for this is that language learning and conducting research with human subjects are both highly complex, multidimensional processes. As we will see, basic concepts and procedures are contested, debated and constantly evolving.

By the end of this chapter you should be able to have a basic understanding of:

- language teaching and learning research and the processes involved;
- key terms and concepts in language teaching and learning research;
- how research studies are designed to answer research questions;
- core issues in relation to how to conduct a quantitative study and how to do ethnographic and conversation analytic research;
- how to begin designing your own study;

To start with in this chapter, we look at the phases involved in the process of research and outline some of the options involved in each phase. The diagram below showing a flow chart of the processes of research is one we will be using throughout the book. It is of course not the only way of thinking about research, but it should help keep you focused and ensure all elements of your research are pointing in the same direction. Clough and Nutbrown (2007) have a very useful guide to developing research design in the social sciences. The Research Planning Audit (Appendix 1) in their book is particularly useful as a point of reference: it is based on a list of questions you will need to answer in the process of planning your research.

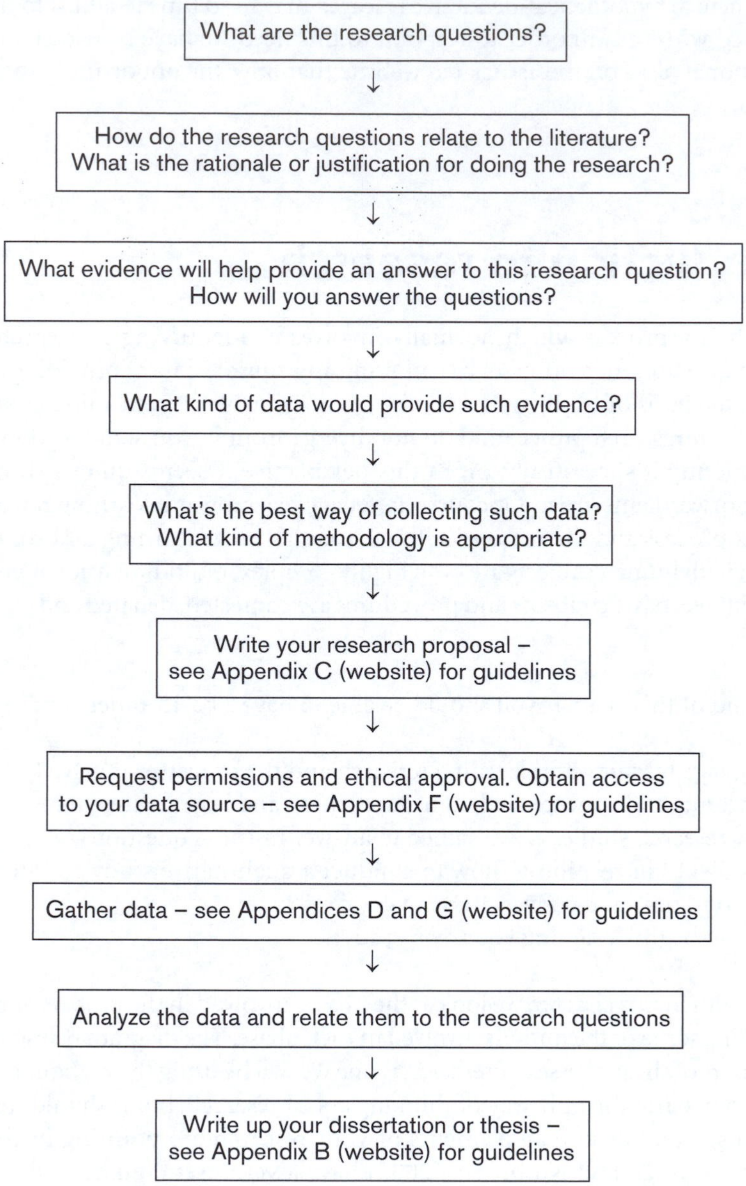

Figure 1.1 Research design flow chart

We now go through these stages in turn.

WHAT ARE THE RESEARCH QUESTIONS?

Producing a viable research focus and research questions is a vital part of the research process. It is often a good idea to start with a problem with which you are familiar in your own teaching context. For example, you notice that students are very reluctant to say anything in the foreign language. Alternatively, you could identify an interesting phenomenon which requires explanation. For example, you observe a number of speaking lessons conducted by communicative teachers and notice that they appear to be avoiding using words like 'no' or 'wrong' in their feedback when students make mistakes; you decide to investigate why they might be doing that. You may, on the other hand, identify an interesting research question from reading the literature. It is good practice to state where your research questions have originated.

It is important to be realistic about what you can achieve. Your research questions must be answerable by one person during the time period available. This varies across countries and universities, but typically a master's dissertation will take six months to a year of full-time study and a doctoral thesis three to five years. A typical error is to try to do too much, to pose questions which would take a team of experienced researchers many years to answer. An example of a research question in this category (for a master's) is as follows:

> How to design effective classroom activities to motivate students in language learning. How to estimate inputs and learning outcomes, as well as make maximal use of resources in classroom language acquisition.

A common mistake in framing research questions is to ask questions which are impossible to answer or which are so vague that an answer will similarly be very vague. An example of a research question in this category is as follows:

> How can I give evidence suggests that this learning material has benefits in learners' better command of registering with doctors? (sic)

Another common mistake is to include in a research question several concepts which are not on the same level of analysis and therefore cannot easily be related to each other. An example of a research question in this category is as follows:

> Are learners more motivated to produce long and high-quality speaking with authentic models and materials to simulate? (sic)

Another frequent mistake is to include unproven assumptions in a research question. These often display biases on the part of the researcher. An example of a research question in this category is as follows:

> How does a test influence how learners learn speaking? To what degree and extent, does the test influence how learners learn? (sic)

In the above case, it has been assumed that the test influences how learners learn. Yet another common mistake is to ask too many research questions, or to have too many elements in the same question, which means that it is difficult to tell what the main focus is. An example of a research question with too many issues and factors is as follows:

> My proposed research question will mainly focus on classroom activities, exploring the participation and communication in communicative approach in English listening and speaking classrooms to investigate some useful methods to assist schools to make improvement in teaching listening and speaking.

So in a well-framed research question you should include concepts which are on the same level of analysis and which can easily be related to each other. The question should not include assumptions which are not proven. It should be clear from the question that it is possible to answer it and you should have a clear idea of how you will go about gathering evidence to answer it, which is the next stage of the process. It is important to spend time framing research questions and there is a helpful guide to this in Clough and Nutbrown (2007).

Some examples of well-framed research questions are as follows:

> What role do teacher gestures play in vocabulary explanation sequences? (Lazaraton 2004)

> Can a synthetic phonics package increase the English reading and spelling ability of children studying in schools operating in a slum area of India?

Task A1

➤ Examine the research questions below. Having read the discussion above, which would you say are well framed and which are not? If they are not well framed, which common mistakes have been made?

- a With respect to pedagogical functions, what are the interaction structures and the relationship between the NS teacher's teaching pedagogies and interaction? Can the structures and relationship, to some extent, reflect the concepts of sociocultural theory, such as mediation, ZPD and scaffolding?
- b Why do the teachers believe the way of their feedback could facilitate the learning?
- c Do EFL students perform significantly better on a test of listening comprehension when the speaker shares the students' native language or not?
- d Which strategies do parents use to support English language learning of their children?
- e How can autonomy be realised in a concrete learning situation with the integration of an online learning management system into an English course?
- f What writing processes do Libyan university students use while composing in L1 (Arabic) and in L2 (English)?

It is possible to organize research questions so that there is a main research question, which is broken down into a series of sub-questions. By answering the sub-questions, an answer will be provided for the main research question. Having a main research question is generally a good idea because it can give a strong, clear focus to the research. An example of this is provided below.

The main question is:

> How is a speaking test organized in interactional terms?

Sub-questions are:

> What is the organization of turn-taking?
> What is the organization of sequence?
> How is the topic developed?
> How and why does interactional trouble arise and how is it repaired by the interactants?
> What types of repair initiation are used by examiners and examinees and how are these responded to?

So by answering the sub-questions, a basis is provided for answering the main question.

Originality

At master's level, most universities do not require originality in research, but in doctoral studies this usually is a requirement. A doctoral thesis may be original in a number of ways and what this might mean is open to interpretation. You need to check with your supervisor(s) whether your research is likely to have an appropriate degree of originality. It is important in a doctoral thesis to state explicitly what you consider to be original about the thesis, so that this is evident to the examiners. According to Pearce (2005), the following can provide a thesis with an element of originality:

1. Setting down a major piece of new information in writing for the first time;
2. Continuing a previously original piece of work;
3. Carrying out original work designed by your supervisor;
4. Providing a single original technique, observation or result in an otherwise unoriginal but competent piece of research.

Your methodology may have a degree of originality. For example, you may take an existing model or methodology from the literature and modify or extend it by adding a new means of gathering data. One example is Algarawi (2010), who used the model employed by Lyster (2004) (see Chapter 5) of pre-test/post-test quasi-experimental design in which parallel classes each received a different form of spoken error correction. Algarawi employed this design in a Saudi context, but also recorded the interaction in all of the classes. Through conversation analysis (CA) she tried to show how the interaction was organized differently in each class and how this created different learning environments which could then be related to variations in test scores. Rather than merely replicating the research design, the addition of CA added a new dimension.

Task A2

➢ For students wishing to develop an element of originality in their methodology:

Choose a well-known research study from this book, or one you have encountered during your studies and which you admire. Consider whether you could modify or extend the methodology, model or research design. Note that this modification or extension has to be appropriate and add a useful new dimension to the methodology, model or research design.

If you do not require originality in your methodology, then you could consider replicating an existing research design in your project. Appendix A contains guidelines for conducting replication, from the journal *Language Teaching*. The advantage of this is that you have an existing framework on which to base your research, although this will typically not appeal to those who wish to create their own knowledge. Replication of an existing research design in a particular local teaching context can still produce results and implications which are helpful in a local context.

Task A3

➢ For students *not* wishing to develop originality in their methodology:

Choose a well-known research study from this book, or one you have encountered during your studies and which you admire. Consider whether you could replicate this study in your own teaching context. Write a plan of how you would do this and of the logistics and time frame involved. Note that the original study may have been carried out by a team of researchers over several years and may need to be scaled down so it can be managed within your time frame. For example, Lyster's (2004) project took five years from start to finish.

You may also develop an element of originality in your work by obtaining data which are original in some way. For example, it may be that a particular teaching technique or a particular technology has not been researched before. New forms of communication in relation to language teaching and learning are springing up due to globalization and developments in communication technology. For example, Sukutrit (2010) looked at voice-based Skype chat rooms for beginner-level learners of English wishing to practise speaking with each other.

She asked the following research questions:

1. How do participants in voice-based chat rooms open their participation?
2. How do participants in voice-based chat rooms manage their topics?
3. How do participants in voice-based chat rooms close their participation?

There is sometimes scope for an element of originality in relation to geographical areas and cultures. For example, there have been many research studies of Communicative Language Teaching. However, it may be that no-one has studied its introduction and use in your particular country and you may want to see whether it is appropriate to your culture and educational system. Nonetheless, you should be wary of taking this principle too far. For example, we are now seeing examples of students covering topics which have already been heavily researched (e.g. learner strategies) and which have been already been researched in their own country and culture. However, these student then claim originality on the grounds that this has not been studied in their particular town; examiners are unlikely to be impressed by such a claim.

NOTE

It is of course possible to design research studies in other ways than on the basis of research questions, and a number of studies in this book do not employ research questions. We are employing research questions as the basis of research design in this chapter as we believe this to be an appropriate and effective way of helping master's and doctoral students through the process. Other ways of organizing a study are:

Stating hypotheses which are then to be proved or disproved by data. An example in this collection is Ellis (2005) in Chapter 7, for example: 'Tests of implicit knowledge will elicit more certain responses from learners than tests of explicit knowledge.'

Identifying a problem. The aim of the research is to find a solution to the problem. An example in this collection is Seedhouse and Almutairi (2009) in Chapter 5. This presents a technological solution to the problem of how to analyse task-based interaction.

Stating a research focus. A focus may be stated which is not formed as research questions. An example is Koshik's (2002) study in Chapter 2. Koshik states that she intends to analyse an interactional/pedagogical practice used by teachers, namely designedly incomplete utterances.

HOW DO THE RESEARCH QUESTIONS RELATE TO THE LITERATURE? WHAT IS THE RATIONALE OR JUSTIFICATION FOR DOING THE RESEARCH?

There is a 'chicken and egg' relationship between the research questions and the literature and phases 1 and 2 of the process really need to be considered simultaneously. In order to form good research questions, it is necessary to know the literature in a particular area.

The two questions 'How do the research questions relate to the literature?' and 'What is the rationale or justification for doing the research?' are generally closely related. Ideally, if you require originality, you will locate what is called a 'research gap'. This means that you find something that has not been researched before and is worth researching; this implies there is a rationale or justification for it. It is often worth thinking of a problem, issue or need of which you are aware in your own teaching context. For example, it may be that in your particular teaching institution you find that students are lacking in motivation to learn a language. No one has ever tried to establish what their needs are, whilst the curriculum and teaching materials and guidelines on teaching methods are produced centrally by the government in a city a long way away and you think they are totally unsuitable for your students. On searching the literature, you find there are lots of studies of motivation, needs analysis, curriculum, teaching materials and teaching methods. However, there are none which relate to the specific problems you have identified in your institution, and this is your research gap. Your rationale or justification is that you hope to improve the situation, for instance by trying out new teaching methods or materials. So far, so good, but be warned that it is quite common for governments or institutions to block permission for research which might show them in a negative light, so you need to proceed cautiously! A good place to look for an existing research gap is in the latest articles in the area. These often have suggestions for future research right at the end of the article.

You need to make to clear which literature you think is relevant to your research area and remember that often a number of rather different research literatures may be relevant to your project. For example, Rababah's (2001) thesis reviews literature on communication, SLA, language teaching and communication strategies in order to cover all areas relevant to his research questions. When you write your research proposal, you should include a brief literature review, so that your supervisor can see whether you are familiar and up to date with the relevant literature. When you write your dissertation or thesis, you will need a whole literature review chapter. Look at Appendix B (website) for guidance on how to write a literature review.

In order to locate relevant literature for your proposed research area, you should do a search using an academic database. In order to do a search of the literature for your area it is best to use an electronic database such as ERIC or MLA. Using an academic database is better practice than doing a normal Internet search as all publications in an academic database have been checked for quality. Normally, your university library will show you how to search for literature by using one of these databases. Your library may also give you access to electronic journals, which means you can instantly obtain, read or print articles. If you do not have access to university database facilities, Google Scholar offers an alternative. Good online guides to literature searching are available at http://www.shef.ac.uk/library/libdocs/ml-rs17.html and http://www4.rgu.ac.uk/library/howto/page.cfm?pge=25989

HOW WILL YOU ANSWER THE QUESTIONS?

The next stage in the process is to consider how exactly you will go about answering the research questions. If your research questions have been well designed, it should be fairly clear what the best ways of answering them will be. We can break this stage down into two phases, by asking:

- What evidence will help provide an answer to this research question?
- What kind of data would provide such evidence?

When considering what kind of evidence will help provide an answer to a research question, it is important to check whether the evidence is on the same level of analysis as the research question.

For example, research was once reported in the media that concluded that people from country X are more intelligent that people from country Y. The evidence was a comparison of the average number of educational qualifications achieved per head of population in country X and country Y. However, the evidence is not on the same level of analysis as the conclusion, i.e. it is not proven that having more educational qualifications relates directly to greater intelligence (no doubt readers can think of many counter-examples of this!). There is a further challenge to validity in that for a valid comparison, the two countries would have to have exactly the same system of educational qualifications with the average student taking exactly the same number of qualifications at the same age; this was not actually the case with the two countries concerned.

Task A4

➤ Now consider the two research questions below:

1. What do people say in response when someone pays them a compliment?
2. Can a particular teaching method improve the ability of students to learn a particular grammatical form?

➤ For each research question, write answers to the two bulleted questions below **without looking at the discussion below!**

- What evidence will help provide an answer to this research question?
- What kind of data would provide such evidence?

For question 1, evidence of actual human behaviour is required. Data which provide evidence of actual human behaviour are generally of two types. One involves asking people what they do (or would do) in a particular situation. This can be in the form of a questionnaire, an interview or a discourse completion task (DCT) (see Golato [2003]). The second type is by observing and/or recording people actually doing something, e.g. responding to a compliment. Observation and recording actual behaviour can be subdivided into a) recording or observing people in a naturalistic situation without giving them any instructions whatsoever, b) providing a script, instructions or roles for participants. All of these methods of gathering data have inherent problems. In the first type, one is asking people what they would do, which is not necessarily the same as what they actually do. One may try recording or observing people in a naturalistic situation for many hours without the targeted behaviour ever occurring, e.g. a compliment is never paid or responded to. Scripted behaviour may still not be the same as actual behaviour. Of course it is possible to collect more than one type of data, which is exactly what Golato (2003) does.

For question 2, evidence of a different type is required. Evidence of whether one teaching method is better than another implies a) a comparison between at least two groups, b) testing all students' knowledge of the targeted grammatical form before and after the teaching (known as pre-test and post-test), c) ensuring that there are no other factors (variables) which could lead one group to get a better score than another group. The evidence required by the question tends to push researchers to what is called a quasi-experimental design, which is quantitative in nature. The basic evidence required is of test scores of both groups in the pre-test and post-test of the targeted grammatical form. Often there is a control or comparison group which receives 'normal' teaching and one or more experimental or treatment groups which receives the innovative method. A comparison of test scores is the evidence which demonstrates which teaching method has been more effective, provided there has been control of variables. Examples of this kind of design are in Lyster (2004) in Chapter 5 and in De Ridder *et al.* (2007) in Chapter 3.

It is a good idea to produce a chart for each research question in your proposal to show the kind of evidence and data you will use in relation to them, as in the example below:

The sub-questions	The instruments to be used
1 Do personal traits, such as qualifications and experience, affect the performance of teachers of English in Saudi intermediate schools?	Questionnaires with teachers of English in the intermediate schools Interviews with some selected supervisors of English in the intermediate schools

This chart will enable your supervisor(s) to see easily whether your proposed means of answering the questions are appropriate and feasible or not.

WHAT'S THE BEST WAY OF COLLECTING SUCH DATA? WHAT KIND OF METHODOLOGY IS APPROPRIATE?

It may be evident from the previous sections what the best way is of collecting data and which kind of methodology is appropriate. For example, we saw above that if one asks the research question 'Can a particular teaching method improve the ability of students to learn a particular grammatical form?', then this tends to push one towards a hypothetical-deductive type of design, because it can possibly provide evidence as to whether the teaching methods make a difference to learning the grammatical form of interest. Similarly, if one asks the research question 'How is a speaking test organized in interactional terms?', then a methodology for analysing naturally occurring spoken interaction is required which is able to produce a description of interactional organization, and so CA is an obvious candidate.

However, it may not be obvious in the case of some research questions which research methodology is most appropriate or what the best way is of collecting data. There may be a number of possible methodologies, with a choice of qualitative, quantitative or mixed methods, together with a variety of data collection instruments.

First, we need to be clear about the difference between a data collection instrument and a research methodology. According to Cryer (2000), a research methodology is an overarching concept, 'A rationale for the methods used to gather and process data, in what sequence and on what samples, together constitute a research methodology. This is not a grand term for "list of methods", but an informed and properly argued case for designing a piece of research in a particular way.' In this chapter we introduce the reader to three research methodologies which are frequently employed to research language teaching and learning, namely quantitative approaches, CA and ethnography.

A data collection instrument is a means of collecting data, for example questionnaire or video/audio recording of interaction. Mackey's (2006) study in Chapter 2, for example, employs learning journals, stimulated recall, written responses and questionnaires as data collection instruments as part of an experimental research methodology. It is important to note that the same data collection instrument can be employed in a range of methodologies. For example, interviews are also employed in Toohey's (1998) and Creese's (2003) ethnographic studies. Taken as a whole, the articles cited in this book introduce the reader to a range of research methodologies and data collection instruments.

Task A5

➤ For each article in this book, identify the authors' stated research methodology and the data collection instruments which they employ.

Task A6

➤ For the research questions below, which research methodology is most appropriate and what are the best data collection instruments?

1. How do teachers practise a particular teaching approach?
2. What beliefs do teachers hold about this particular teaching approach? To what extent are these beliefs internally consistent?
3. To what extent are teachers' beliefs about this particular teaching approach in harmony with their observed practices?

➤ When you have completed the task, turn to Basturkmen *et al.*'s (2004) study in Chapter 8 and see how they collected data and which type of methodology they used.

Task A7

➤ Here we provide you with two different sets of research questions. Choose either a) or b) and complete all of the frames below to make decisions on the research process you will go through to answer them.

a Which strategies do parents use to support the English language learning of their children?

b 1. Is the anxiety level of an individual college-level Japanese learner related to his/her dispositional fear of negative evaluation?
2. Is the anxiety level of an individual college-level Japanese learner related to the self-perception of his/her speaking ability in Japanese?
3. Do fear of negative evaluation and self-perception of speaking ability in Japanese interact to relate to the anxiety level of individual Japanese learners?

➤ When you have completed the frames, read the text of Gao (2007) and Kitano (2001) in Chapter 4. You will then see how the authors themselves designed their research process to answer these research questions.

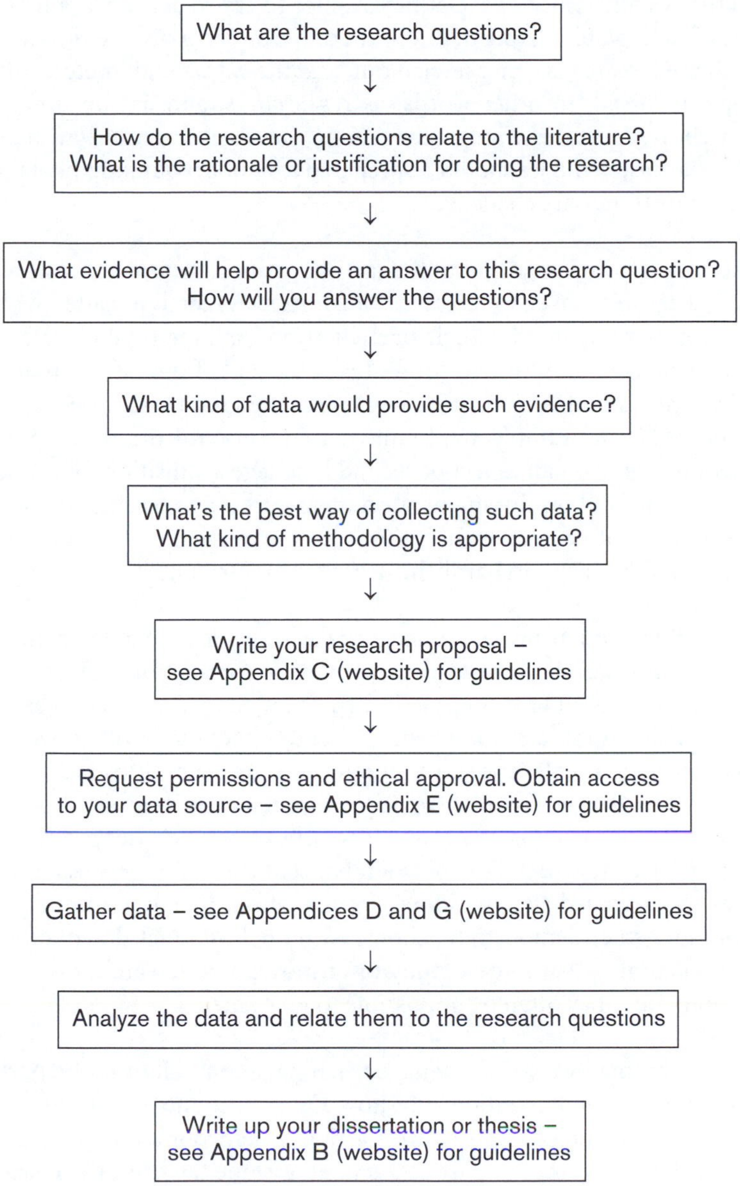

Request permissions and ethical approval. Obtain access to your data source.

No research should be undertaken without giving due consideration to ethical issues, something which should take place from the start and continue through to the completion of the project (and sometimes beyond). What Hammersley and Atkinson (1995: 285) have to say about ethnography applies equally well to all forms of research:

> It is the responsibility of the ethnographer to try to act in ways that are ethically acceptable, taking due account of his or her goals, the situation in which the research is being carried out, and the values and interests of the people involved. In other words, as researchers, and as consumers of research, we must make judgments about what is and is not legitimate in particular cases. And we should be prepared to support our judgments with arguments if they are challenged.

This description draws attention to the fact that ethical conduct in research is not something that can be taken for granted or dismissed as merely a matter of obtaining consent from participants for their participation. As Fine (1993/2001: 372) has observed, '[t]he grail of informed consent is at the end of the twisted road of most ethical discussions' and the journey down the 'twisted road' has to be a careful one. It is all very well, for example, to obtain written consent from participants in an experiment focusing on an aspect of second language acquisition, but if they have not been informed of how this might affect their studies and teachers in the relevant institution have not been consulted about how arrangements might affect their work, then the approach can hardly be described as ethical.

It is not possible to do justice in the short space available here to the complexity of ethical issues in research, so instead we provide a checklist of important considerations, a guide to useful reading and information on two valuable websites. First, though, we wish to draw attention to an aspect of ethics that is often neglected but which has particular relevance to ethnographic or even conversation analytic research in our field: anonymity. Novice researchers tend to see this as unproblematic, a matter of changing names and places, but more experienced practitioners (e.g. Nespor 2000) regard it as a considerable challenge. One researcher (Walford 2005) has even argued that in some circumstances it may be better to reject anonymity altogether, demonstrating how easy it can be to track down 'anonymised' groups and claiming that in case study or ethnographic research involving small groups anonymity may often be impossible to guarantee.

In the relatively small world of language teaching, anonymity may be particularly problematic, as a brief illustration will show. One of the authors of this book, who had researched a group of teachers in a particular staffroom, presented an extract from one of his recordings as part of a talk at a venue far from the research site. All names and places had been changed, but one of the audience approached the speaker afterwards and insisted he knew one of the participants (and hence the school) because of a single expression one of them had repeated. Although the researcher refused to confirm or deny this, it made no difference to the challenger, who insisted, 'It can only be him – he's the only person I know who uses it like that.' There are no easy solutions to problems like this, but the example underlines the need to approach ethical considerations with due seriousness.

With this in mind, we offer the following list as no more than guidelines for your consideration when wrestling with the ethical implications of your research:

General

- Is the information on which informed consent is based adequate for the needs of the participants and the purposes of the research?
- Who are the different parties involved in the research and are there any potential conflicts arising from their relationships?
- To what extent and in what form is disclosure required in order to complete the research successfully and what are the requirements in terms of relevant permissions?
- Are there sufficient safeguards in place to ensure that anonymity is maintained?
- Are there any power relationships that might undermine efforts to control disclosure and anonymity?

For qualitative (especially ethnographic) research

- How and to what extent will those involved in the research have a say in the content and/or form of any future representation of it?
- Are there any issues relating to the researcher's own right to privacy?
- Are there any ongoing ethical issues that the researcher will need to keep in mind once he or she has left the field?

Although there are now plenty of book-length treatments of research ethics available, Oliver (2003) offers a particularly readable and thorough introduction. Its division into two parts (stages in the research process and themes) means that it can be approached either from the perspective of the research stage you have reached or in terms of an issue that concerns you. Readers wishing for a briefer introduction should find Kent's (2000) treatment of informed consent very useful.

Perhaps predictably, most discussions of ethical issues are written with qualitative research in mind and there is no shortage of advice here, though the advantage of Burgess (1989) and Fine (1993/2001) is that they are very engaging. Burgess uses personal research experience as a point of departure and Fine offers a well-written treatment of 'ten lies of ethnography', though much of the discussion has wider relevance. While quantitative researchers are less well served, Jones (2000) provides a useful introduction. For anyone wrestling with issues of anonymity, Nespor (2000) and Walford (2005) provide outstanding treatments, while confidentiality is explored very thoroughly in a provocative treatment by Baez (2002), written from a critical perspective.

Excellent documentation on what is required in terms of ethics for applied linguistics research projects can be found on the BAAL website http://www.baal.org.uk/about_goodpractice_stud.pdf and the TESOL Quarterly website http://www.tesol.org/s_tesol/seccss.asp?CID=476&DID=2150. However, your university will probably have its own ethical guidelines and procedures and you must follow these. The accompanying website contains a model consent form for use with informants.

It is important that you check all of the above points with your supervisor(s) and your university's regulations, so you are clear on the regulations within which you must conduct your research.

GATHER DATA

The studies in Chapters 2–8 provide concrete examples of the kind of data which you could gather in your own study. Appendix D (website) has guidelines on how to make recordings and Appendix G (website) has a checklist for conducting interviews.

ANALYSE THE DATA AND RELATE THEM TO THE RESEARCH QUESTIONS

Appendix B (website) has guidelines on procedures for analysing data and relating them to the research questions. The studies in Chapters 2–8 provide concrete examples of data analysis using the three different methodologies.

WRITE UP YOUR DISSERTATION OR THESIS

Appendix B (website) provides detailed guidance on writing up and organizing your final dissertation or thesis.

TIMESCALE

It is vital to develop a realistic timescale for all stages of your project and this must correspond to the requirements of your university. You can write your projected dates on the blank flow chart for research design on the final page of this book.

Task A8

➤ Now you should chart your own research design, going through all of the stages outlined above. Turn to the final page of this book, where you will find a blank flow chart to complete to show how you intend to carry out your research project. This will help you to complete your research proposal (see Appendix C, website) and you will be able to check you are following your design as you progress through your project.

Section B
Quantitative and qualitative research

One of the most common distinctions made in research is that between quantitative and qualitative approaches. In its simplest terms, this boils down to drawing a distinction between the sort of research that is based on statistical measurement of some sort (experiments, large scale surveys, etc.) and research that tends to avoid quantification, relying instead on verbal description (observation, interviews, etc.). Reduced to its simplest, this boils down to 'words' versus 'numbers'. As a broad categorization that might be fairly harmless, but unfortunately there is an associated history of disputes about the advantages of one approach over the other, often based on attempts to undermine the value of the 'alternative' position. Such disputes have produced a great deal of heat but no light and are best avoided.

There is, says Dörnyei (2007: 25), an 'almost irresistible urge to contrast qualitative and quantitative research'. He goes on to offer an illuminating explanation how this might have arisen, but perhaps the terms themselves are partly to blame, appealing as they do to a fundamental distinction in everyday affairs. We are enjoined not to sacrifice quality for quantity, for example, or directed to 'never mind the quality, feel the width'. The distinction between worth and quantity seems fundamental, but for researchers the issue is not whether there is a distinction between the two but whether the distinction, framed in this way, is helpful. In our view it is not and in what follows we suggest why, before going on to consider other ways of thinking about these two aspects of research. The tasks in this section invite you to think carefully about a relationship that is often treated rather simplistically and it therefore prepares the way for our introduction to mixed-methods research in Chapter 8. In order to obtain maximum benefit from our discussion there, we suggest that you work through the intervening chapters, but you might find it helpful to return to the following tasks when you have completed that chapter, reconsidering your responses in the light of what you have learnt from the book. We have deliberately avoided attempting at this stage to suggest how the different approaches might be brought together, though you may wish to reflect on how the same concept (e.g. validation) is treated in different ways.

Task B1

- How might you distinguish qualitative and quantitative research without making any reference to numbers?
- How might the following feature in making such a distinction: theories, categories, groups?

It would be wrong to suggest that there is something fundamentally misguided in the standard terminology and that considerations of value and quantification should be set aside, so we begin with a perfectly sound characterization in these terms. It appears in an editorial in a medical journal and follows a paragraph highlighting the complementarity of qualitative and quantitative traditions in medical research:

> A form of qualitative research, for example, would be desirable when asking questions about meaning, human value, or the understanding of social processes not previously explored or when searching for new theory grounded in the perceptions and traditions of social groups. Questions of magnitude, rate, incidence, or prevalence, on the other hand, generally yield only to quantitative methods.
>
> (Inui 1996: 770)

What is of most interest here is that the writer does not work from the distinction but from research questions. If we begin here, rather than with more abstract concerns about numbers and words or value and measurement, our inquiry will provoke considerations that go well beyond such a straightforward characterization and address aspects that will have a bearing on the whole research process.

A fundamental consideration in all research is the sample on which the research will be based, and a naive approach might assume that quantitative research involves large numbers while qualitative research is directed to much smaller numbers of participants. This may be generally true (though it is by no means universally the case) but in terms of addressing a specific research question it is unhelpful. Instead, the researcher needs to consider their relationship to the relevant group. If the aim is to understand the behaviour, beliefs, understandings, values, etc. of a particular group (or individual), to explore aspects of a world in its context, then the approach may best be described as qualitative. On the other hand, if this relationship is not particularly important and the researcher is more interested in the group as representative of a population, with a focus on common rather than individual features, the approach is likely to be quantitative. This is why qualitative research often involves immersion in a natural context, while quantitative research tends to focus on establishing the parameters or conditions relating to a specific group or situation. Dörnyei (2007) captures the two strategies particularly memorably in his distinction between 'meaning in the particular' (qualitative) and 'meaning in the general' (quantitative).

Task B2

- Brown and Rodgers (2002: 16) have argued that survey research 'provides some common ground between the qualitative and quantitative approaches.' Consider the following comments from a paper on qualitative survey research in the light of the above discussion (the full paper is available online):

> While the statistical survey analyses frequencies in member characteristics in a population, the qualitative survey analyses the diversity of member characteristics within a population.
>
> (Jansen 2010: Abstract)

> The qualitative type of survey does not aim at establishing frequencies, means or other parameters but at determining the diversity of some topic of interest within a given population.
>
> (Jansen 2010: 6)

All research connects in some way to concepts or theories as part of a web of understanding. However, the part that theory plays in the research process can be very different depending on the nature of the approach. In qualitative research, for example, although the researcher will be aware of the theoretical context in which the research is set and may go to considerable lengths to elaborate this, there is no sense in which this is treated as determining the nature of the research. Theory may influence this but if the researcher closes off the possibility that new theoretical dimensions might emerge as the research progresses, this would be seen as an illegitimate; in fact in some ('grounded') research, theory is expected to emerge directly from the data. In quantitative research, on the other hand, theory informs the design of the research and great care is taken to link the two. In research designed to test a hypothesis, for example, it is theory that enables relevant predictions to be made and the results of the research will contribute directly to that theory. It may be that this leads to a proposed refinement of the theory or in rare cases even a new theory, but in neither case can this be said to have 'emerged' from the data.

Categories (or codes) feature in a very similar way. For obvious reasons, in quantitative research these need to be determined with great care at the outset. Researchers define the variables with which they will be working as part of their research design and these will eventually inform the numerical analysis on which claims will be based. Qualitative researchers, however, tend to work from the data, developing and refining verbal categories until an adequate description is achieved.

The distinction between qualitative and quantitative research we have developed here has focused on a few fundamental features and other writers have proposed more extended lists. Bryman (2008: 393–395), for example, offers a useful table, together with a brief gloss, while Creswell and Clark (2007: 29) represent the differences in terms of stages in the research process. However, we conclude this section with an invitation to think more carefully about one of the aspects we have introduced.

Task B3

- The following extract, from a paper on narrative inquiry, has been chosen because it expands on our brief comments on categorization and because it refers to a topic (anxiety) that will feature in Chapter 4 of this book. Read the extract and try to form a picture of what research from each of these perspectives might look like in terms of how it might be represented in an academic paper (think particularly in terms of the findings). Then compare your picture with the research discussed in Part B of that chapter.

In the quantitative approach to research, categories often are selected prior to the collection of data. Researchers spell out in advance the operations of measurement and observation that determine whether an event or thing is to be considered an instance of the categories of interest. In most quantitative inquiries, the researcher's concern is not simply a nominal interest in which category an item belongs, but for categories that vary in the extent or amount its instances have of it, they seek to determine this amount. For example, a researcher could be interested in not only determining whether a particular emotional response belongs to the category *anxiety*, but also in how intense is the anxiety of the examined instance. Computational analysis can provide mathematical descriptions of the relations that hold between and among nominal or interval categories. A type of computational analysis, factor analysis, identifies the possibility of common categories underlying combinations of the researcher-identified categories.

In contrast with the preselection of categories of quantitative approaches, qualitative researchers emphasize the construction or discovery of concepts that give categorical identity to the particulars and items in their collected data. Qualitative researchers examine the data items for common themes and ideas. The coding schemes of qualitative analysis are designed to separate the data into groups of like items. The grouped items are inspected to identify the common attributes that define them as members of a category (Strauss 1987). Most qualitative analytic procedures emphasize a recursive movement between the data and the emerging categorical definitions during the process of producing classifications that will organize the data according to their commonalties. The analysis builds the categorical definitions by continually testing their power to order the data. The categories are revised and retested until they provide the 'best fit' of a categorical scheme for the data set. Although the general practice of qualitative analysis follows this description of developing a categorical schematic out of the data, some researchers follow a practice similar to the quantitative approach in which they come to the data to determine whether they fit with a predetermined network. Often these conceptual networks reflect previously developed theoretical systems.

(Polkinghorne 1995: 10)

Section C

C1 Introduction to quantification

Language teaching and learning research is often concerned with establishing *that* particular phenomena occur systematically in relation to other **phenomena**. Testing whether such relations occur in a non-random manner frequently requires a quantitative analysis with representative samples rather than individual cases. Other research questions may be concerned with possible causes of language learning phenomena. In such research, the question is focused on *why* there are particular outcomes under certain conditions, but not under others. Research focused on establishing that relations exist systematically, and tests of possible hypotheses as to why language learning outcomes evolve as they do are the primary motivations for addressing language teaching and learning research quantitatively. The goal of quantification in research is generalization beyond the specific circumstances of the sample. For research intended to be potentially representative of a population, rather than a specific individual or context, quantitative research is often preferred.

A primary goal of the quantitative approach to research is to arrive at a macro-level generalization supported by empirical evidence. Samples from a specific population are typically taken, and are summarized numerically, related to other samples of data or are tested for statistically to determine the extent to which they differ from other samples. Quantitative methods are generally abstract, and aim to fulfil one of three inferential goals: to describe, to relate or to make causal inferences. In these ways, the quantitative approach to research can provide evidence about what the current state of affairs is, that there are relations among different phenomena, and provide tests of theories why specific samples from a population differ from each other. These objectives correspond to description, relation and causal inference.

The philosophical basis for quantitative research is predicated on *critical realism* (Phillips and Burbules 2000), which seeks to differentiate between phenomena that are possibly the consequence of cultural convention or construction and those that can be construed as part of a natural system. The choice of research methods is generally dependent on researchers' assumptions about the existential basis of the objects of research. Those that are based on values and beliefs, for instance, are often approached qualitatively. Some objects of research such as interaction, turn-taking in discourse, identity and embodied actions during talk-in-interaction, are also usually not in the purview of quantitative research methods. There are, however, some descriptive similarities across qualitative and quantitative approaches.

Quantitative research uses the tools of inferential reasoning based on probability theory. In contrast to static description, many quantitative methods seek to examine the likelihood of observed relations and possible causes of phenomena. Most quantitative research follows the principle of *falsification*, which seeks to find **empirical evidence** to support claims of relations among phenomena, and their possible causes. The falsification approach frequently uses hypothetical-deductive reasoning, which formulates research questions in terms of hypothesized relations and possible causes. Evidence supporting any particular hypothesis serves at best as a token of non-refutation. The cumulative mass of research on a particular theory will point toward its current validity, but is generally assumed not to provide certain proof. Claims not supported by cumulative weight of empirical evidence are thus eventually weakened until they are recognized by the research community as unlikely to be valid. Claims corroborated by repeated tests survive as the 'best explanation' (Lipton 2004) until overturned by the weight of new evidence. The modern quantitative approach is thus largely **probabilistic** and **post-positivist**, and seeks mainly to test claims of relation and causation against representative samples from the real world – and strives to be critically aware that research is undertaken in a social world with agendas, motives and incentives which can inject bias into the research enterprise.

Quantitative research methods have evolved to serve three main purposes. The most general is for the purpose of *description*, which is also a primary goal of the CA and ethnographic approaches to research. A descriptive statistic provides a summary estimate of the 'state of things', primarily as an average or mean, the extent of variation around the average or the relative frequency with which a phenomenon occurs. **Descriptive statistics** are essentially estimations of what may be representative of a larger population or may be limited to a particular sample. The circumstances of the sampling limit possible inferences about a descriptive statistic.

As a case in point, researchers may be interested in the relation between hours of study and examination outcomes. If the average number of hours of study outside of class is estimated at a particular university, the average arrived at from the sampling of students would validly represent the school mean only if all possible students enrolled at the school were randomly sampled and surveyed about their out-of-class study time. The generalization would be limited to that particular university context. If the sample were, however, based on a survey of students conveniently found on a Friday night at the library, the descriptive statistics derived from the sample would not be a likely estimate of the actual university mean. Descriptive statistics are thus highly sample-dependent. Population estimates are assumed to sample all possible members of the population (Trochim and Donnelly 2007). For quantitative summaries and inferential interpretations of data, the method of sampling is crucial.

Task C1.1

➤ Formulate a descriptive research question about a context you are familiar with. Consider how the sampling would be conducted, and the possible limits to the generalisability of the descriptive statistics.

Much of applied research seeks to establish the relations among phenomena that are observed to vary across individuals. Many individual differences in language learning constructs such as motivation, willingness to communicate, anxiety, aptitude, attitude, etc. are frequently the objects of *relational* research. Relational research is essentially a quantitative test of the extent to which two variables co-relate. Two variables can be positively correlated such that as one is relatively higher, the other corresponding becomes higher. An example of a positive correlation would thus be hours of study and test performance. Variables can also be negatively correlated. As one increases, the other decreases. An example of a negative correlation might be anxiety and the quality of a performance. As individuals manifest more anxiety prior to an event such as a class presentation, their performance quality may correspondingly decline. When a negative relation is observed across many studies, the cumulative weight of the evidence will point to the **inference** that the relation is real in the population. An example from SLA research is the negative relation between post-critical period language learning and the speed of information processing. If the speed of language processing is indeed constrained by neurological changes over time, a realist inference is that this particular phenomenon would not be a social construction or convention, but is a universal and natural consequence of ageing.

Researchers may also hypothesize that there is no relation between two variables. If there is no plausible reason why two phenomena would co-vary, the expectation may be that they are unrelated in nature, and would thus yield a correlation coefficient approximating zero.

Task C1.2

➤ Construct a list of language learning phenomena you would hypothesize to be a) substantially correlated, b) negatively correlated and c) uncorrelated. Discuss why these relations would or would not exist in a sample of learners.

Relational research seeks to establish replicable patterns of relations among phenomena hypothesized to be interrelated. The relations may be assumed to be natural or may be limited to particular circumstances. Patterns of correlations that are circumstantial will not be constant across different samples from a larger population. Patterns of replicable correlations across samples from a population imply a **nomological** network (Cronbach and Meehl 1955). A nomological network indicates a set of relations that recur across samples with sufficient regularity to warrant a claim of their representing a rule-governed system. Many quantitative methods have evolved to test the replicability of interrelated phenomena to confirm their nomological status.

As an example of modern relational research, a covariance structure analysis examines covariances between or among latent variables, each of which is implied in a measurement model. **Covariance structure analysis** seeks to test whether latent variables are themselves correlated with each other to create a more complex nomological network. An example of a simple covariance structure analysis is represented in Figure 1.2

When groups of variables are collected from a large sample of individuals, clusters of correlations among particular subgroups of variables imply there are latent variables which are possible reasons why the correlation clusters form. Such clusters are usually referred to as factors. A group of variables that are strongly inter-correlated can be gathered into a set to create a **measurement model**. A measurement model is thus a set of indicators of a hypothesized latent variable. For example in Figure 1.2, three measures of listening, self-assessed confidence to understand a second language and willingness to engage in interaction with target language speakers are hypothesized to co-vary among themselves and thus indicate

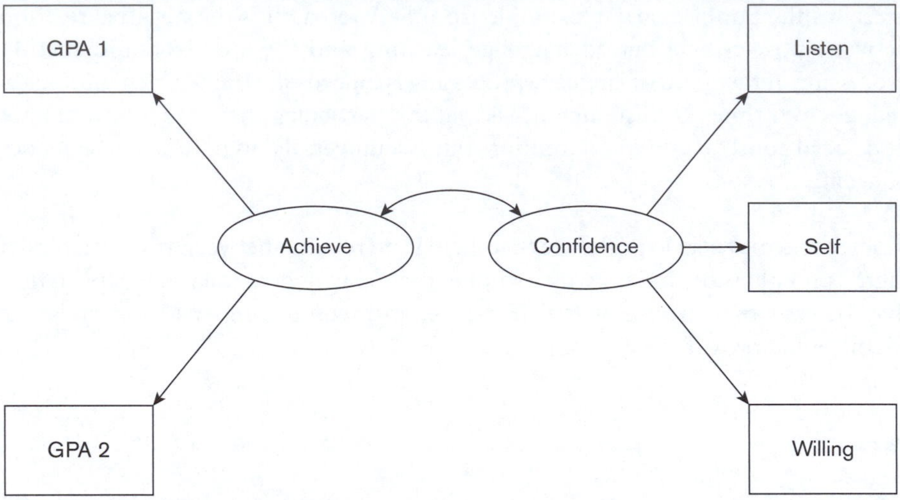

Figure 1.2 Covariance between two latent variables

a latent variable called 'confidence'. Evidence that the three indicators all indicate the latent variable *confidence* would be observable through the magnitude of the relations each measure has with the latent variable. A possibly valid measurement model would thus need **indicators** that co-vary with each other so as to imply a latent variable, and the magnitude of the relations would need to be replicated across many samples for a claim that they indicate a stable nomological system.

The measurement model indicating the latent variable *confidence* is hypothesized to co-vary with another measurement model comprised of two indicators of a latent variable *achievement*. The indicators of achievement are grade point averages over four foreign language courses in each of two semesters of study. The double-headed arrow specifies that the two **latent factors** are hypothesized to be correlated with each other but are not in a causal relation. The hypothesized model would be tested against a representative sample of data. To the extent that the relations postulated in the model fit the data adequately, the model would be considered plausible. A covariance structure turning out not to match the data sample would be falsifying evidence against the validity of the model. Much of applied linguistics research concerning individual differences variables involves testing hypothesized models against representative data in order to gather confirmatory or corroborating evidence.

Relational research uses many variants and methods. Basic relations are different types of **correlations** between individual variables. When many variables are involved, linear regression models allow for the combination of sets of variables which are hypothesized to cumulatively account for variation in a particular outcome or dependent variable. Regression models can be linear or non-linear, and thus can predict particular values of an outcome, or the probability that an outcome of interest will or will not occur. Both linear and non-linear regression methods aim to reduce the redundancy that can build up when many different possible **independent variables** are hypothesized to influence variation in an outcome of interest.

Task C1.3

➤ Sketch out a small measurement model with at least three measures you would hypothesize to co-vary with each other highly. Discuss what latent factor would be a plausible reason for the measures to co-vary. What name would you give to the latent variable?

Task C1.4

➤ Expand your previous measurement model with a second one. What relation would you hypothesize to exist between the two latent variables? Discuss what sampling strategy would be appropriate to test the covariance structure.

The third main goal of quantitative research methodology is to test hypotheses about possible *causation*. A putative cause of a phenomenon is possibly an agent of causation only if it is present in the condition under which the phenomenon of interest evolves. Absence of the hypothesized causal agent is manipulated contrastively to verify the difference between presence and absence of the putative cause and a hypothesized outcome. The classical approach to testing causation is the randomized experiment. In the true experiment, all participants have an equal chance of exposure to either the causal agent (X) or the **counterfactual** condition (~X) in which the causal agent is absent. If an authentic randomized experiment is used, the design reduces to an isolation of the hypothesized cause affecting the outcome.

R	X	Y
R	~X	Y

Difference between the randomly assigned groups (X and ~X) yield mean differences on Y that are attributable to differential exposure to the causal agent X, which is often referred to as the '**intervention**' or 'treatment'. Randomization (R) is assumed to equally distribute all possible **moderating** variables affecting Y equally into the X and ~X groups – thus eliminating any potential bias. Assuming that randomization has succeeded in distributing all other possible causes of the differences between the two groups on the outcome Y equally, the mean difference observed on Y would be attributable to the presence of the causal agent X.

An example of such a design might be a study to test the hypothesis that exposure to classical music during class causes a reduction in anxiety and increase in concentration, which consequently increases the processing of visual input. If the research designers could randomize individual students into the two conditions, and control for the exposure to the classical music in class over a sufficiently realistic time period during foreign language reading classes, which would be identical other than exposure to the classical music, the outcome, reading comprehension, could be tested. The hypothesis would be that the X condition (classical music exposure during all reading class meetings) will be the causal agent in increasing facility in input processing. Since X only occurs in one of the groups, the mean differences on the Y **dependent variable** (a reliable and valid reading proficiency test) would provide evidence in support, or counter-evidence against, the claim that classical music is a causal agent in enhancing reading comprehension. The test would be against the **null** (no difference) hypothesis. If the null hypothesis were not rejected, the inference made would favour falsification of the theory of anxiety reduction and concentration enhancement through classical music. A single experiment would not, however, constitute definitive evidence one way or another. In quantitative relational and causal research, the results of many similar studies are frequently collected into **meta-analyses** (Ross 1998; Norris and Ortega 2000), which provide a summary of the average effect and homogeneity of research outcomes on a particular theory.

Causal research using true experimental designs is relatively rare in the domain of applied linguistics and language teaching and learning. The main constraint is the logistical requirements for authentic randomization to take place, and the fact that most research is locally conducted within institutions where researchers rely on convenience sampling. When randomization is not used, there is a threat to the **interval validity** of a study if groups are preformed or differ in ways unknown to the researcher prior to the use of an intervention. The alternative to experimental research is quasi-experimental research design (Shadish, Cook and Campbell 2002). A typical quasi-experimental design uses a number of **covariates**, which are measures of individual differences prior to the deployment of the intervention in one of the groups. A quasi-experimental design might look like:

W Z Y1 X Y2
W Z Y1 ~X Y2

Here, **W** might be a survey of learner motivation, **Z** a self-report of extra-curricular contact with the target language and **Y1** a pre-test of the dependent variable **Y** prior to the intervention **X. Y2** would be the post-test of the dependent variable (outcome) after the intervention. The purpose of the covariates is to statistically isolate likely causes of group differences on **Y2** existing prior to the intervention, so that the difference between **X** and ~**X** can be assessed without ambiguity. When successful, the quasi-experimental design can provide the basis of causal inference, though it is generally found to be less valid than the true randomized experiment.

Task C1.5

➤ Sketch out a quasi-experimental design. What pre-intervention covariates would be most relevant?

Causation and relation can simultaneously be examined if the element of time is included into the design. For both static and dynamic phenomena, hypothesized causal influences can be tested as long as an evolutionary order can be established in such a manner that consequential phenomena post-date earlier states or processes. Covariance structure analyses can be integrated with time-varying processes to test causative hypotheses empirically rather than solely in a metaphorical sense (cf. Larson-Freeman and Cameron 2009).

Covariance structure models can be constructed to capture the dynamics of change across individuals (Singer and Willett 2003, Raudenbush and Bryk 2002), and the variation across individuals in the change process can be hypothesized to fit into a causal relation with states that evolve after the change process. A common theme in applied linguistics research should illustrate this application of covariance structures over time.

Motivation is currently held to be a dynamic phenomenon among language learners (Dornyei and Ushioda 2009). Changes in motivational state over time would potentially co-vary with individual differences in an end-state such as language proficiency if variation in motivation has a causal relation with success in learning. In order to test such a dynamic model, a longitudinal design would be needed in which the motivational states of learners are measured repeatedly as they evolve in a particular socio-cultural context. The expectation would be that each learner would have a possibly unique trajectory of change in motivation. To control for individual differences in proficiency prior to and after the putative motivational change, two measures of language proficiency would be needed. One would be at the outset of the change process and the other would be at the end of it. The hypothesis that motivational dynamics have a causal relation with consequential differences in proficiency could then be tested while controlling for pre-existing variation in proficiency.

Figure 1.3 illustrates this design. The four measures of motivation are collected at the beginning and end of each of two semesters. Prof 1 is a pre-instruction test of individual differences in proficiency and Prof 2 is tested after the end of the second semester of instruction.

The measurement model on the right side of the diagram captures individual differences in motivational change over four semesters. All possible trajectories of change are allowed at the individual difference (learner) level. The relational and causal hypotheses are formulated in the path coefficients. Prof 1 → Level tests the hypothesis that initial proficiency co-varies with concurrent individual differences in starting motivation (level). Prof 1 → Change tests the hypothesis that initial proficiency accounts for changes in motivation over time. Level → Prof 2 tests the hypothesis that the initial state of motivation accounts for the end-state of proficiency. The main hypothesis would be the Change → Prof 2, which would test the unique causal relation between changes in motivation over time and developed proficiency, which post-dates the change process, controlling for all other relations

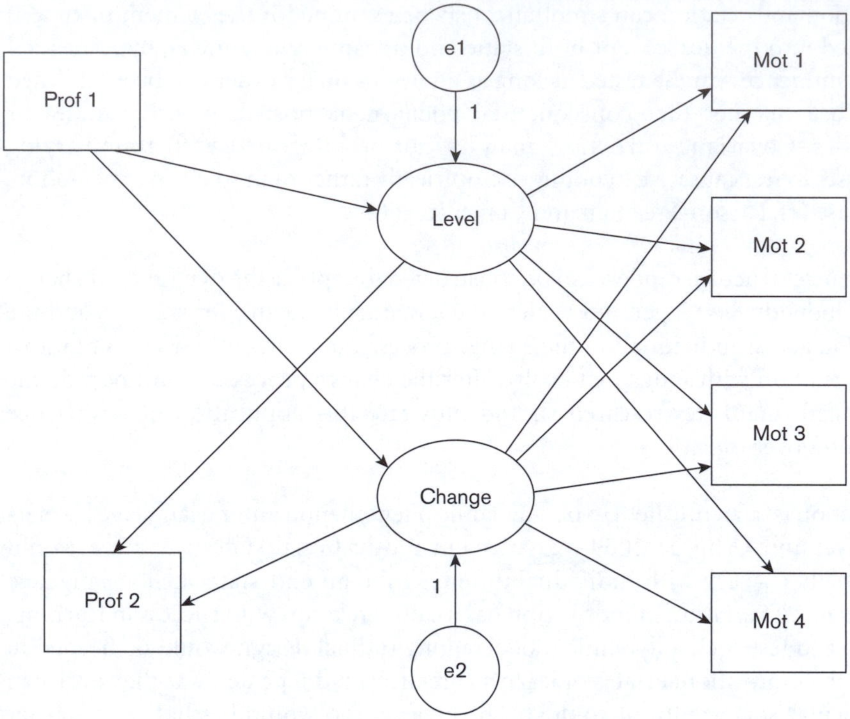

Figure 1.3 Latent growth model with predictor and outcome

and causal paths in the model. To the extent that the model fits a representative sample of language learners, the validity of the dynamic model and causal relations in it could be assessed.

Task C1.6

> Sketch out a growth or change process evolving over time like the one in Fig 1.3. Identify a possible consequence of the growth or change. What hypotheses would follow from such a design and what paths would serve to test them?

The quantitative approach to research can be used to describe, test hypotheses about relations among phenomena and test hypothesis about causes of group differences (Shadish, Cook and Campbell 2002). Causal factors in dynamic models can also be tested empirically (Singer and Willet 2003). Quantitative methods have utility for answering questions framed to describe what sample statistics are, test the magnitude of relations among variables of interest and test hypotheses why groups may differ from each as a consequence of differential experiences. The quantitative approach does not well address micro-level questions of *how* individuals interact with each other or *how* they go about their lives. Research questions about 'how things happen' are largely in complimentary distribution to the macro-level *what, that* and *why* focuses of the quantitative approach. The mixed-methods approach encourages a judicious use of quantitative and qualitative approaches to match the method to the research question, and to allow for deeper understanding of the phenomena of interest to researchers.

In the later chapters of this text, a number of quantitative studies are featured. In Chapter 2 Mackey (2006) cross-tabulates the frequency of episodes of noticing and the development of interrogatives in a classroom setting. In Chapter 4 Kitano (2001) uses multiple regression to examine the relative influence of affective and organizational variables on classroom anxiety. Lyster in Chapter 5 uses a repeated measures design to examine the impact of prompts and recasts in a four-group intervention design in a classroom setting. In Chapter 7 Ellis (2005) uses factor analysis to test the distinction between implicit and explicit knowledge on measures commonly used in second language acquisition research. The sampling of quantitative methods in the text is thus selective and is by no means comprehensive. The chapters featuring quantitative studies provide examples of some of the more commonly used data analysis methods in the field of applied linguistics.

C2 Introduction to qualitative research

In this section we examine the nature of qualitative research in more detail and introduce two traditions particularly associated with this approach to research: ethnographic research and conversation analysis. First, though, we briefly establish the more general context in which these are situated.

'Qualitative' isn't an accidental term because what researchers in this approach are interested in is the quality of social life, where 'quality' is understood in the sense of 'nature' or 'important characteristics'. The sort of question that interests both the ethnographer and the conversation analyst is 'How does X get done?' This involves us in trying to identify the social/interactional practices that provide an explanation of X and the way behaviour is designed (usually unconsciously) in order to achieve X. That's why qualitative researchers tend to be interested in the nature of our social/cultural/institutional worlds and our representations of them.

Task C2.1

➤ If we are interested in how things get done, why don't we simply ask the people who do them? What would that approach provide us with and what would be its limitations?

If I don't know how to play a forward defensive stroke in cricket, there are three approaches open to me: I can use trial and error until I reach a situation where I seem to be keeping out most of the balls bowled at me requiring this sort of stroke; I can watch expert cricketers and try to learn from their performance; or I can ask an expert to explain to me how to do it. In practice, I'd want to do all three, but there's no doubt that in terms of economy of time and effort the last option is most appealing. However, if I've chosen the right expert they will have spent a great deal of time studying, reflecting on and practising their technique, and their advice is likely to be largely technical in nature.

The problem when we try to apply this to people's social actions is that none of these conditions are likely to apply. We spend very little time reflecting on our social actions or consciously practising them, and although some people make good money by selling sure fire social and interactional 'techniques' designed to achieve desired ends, social encounters are highly complex phenomena not reducible to easily specifiable procedures. So if we ask social participants to explain what they were doing when they did *x*, we might learn a great deal about them, their beliefs and understandings, but we will not come very close to understanding how *x* got done. The reason for this is clear from Garfinkel's (1984: 9–10) description of how practical social accomplishments seem to the participants involved: 'for the member the organizational hows of these accomplishments are unproblematic, are known vaguely, and are known only in the doing which is done skillfully, reliably, uniformly, with enormous standardization and as an unaccountable matter.'

If we wish to understand the nature of the social world, then, we must find ways of examining it for ourselves. However, this is probably the limit of general agreement on what counts as qualitative research (for an excellent brief assessment of various attempts, see Silverman 1993: 20–29). Rather than offer a sample of the many descriptions available, we offer the following as a working characterisation on the understanding that its elements should be treated as representative rather than definitive:

Nature of data	Words and/or images (descriptions, accounts, interactions, etc.)
Sources of data	People, through their encounters, interactions, representations, etc.
Focus of analysis	Interest in meanings in context rather than specific features of behaviour
Nature of reasoning	Inductive, not hypothesis-driven

This, we believe, provides a useful guide though no more: data might include numbers; sources might include official analyses; specific features of behaviour may need to be singled out for close analysis; and reasoning may work from hypotheses and involve deductive elements. Taken together, though, the above description amounts to something that is distinctively qualitative. We now flesh out two complementary but distinct traditions within this general approach.

ETHNOGRAPHIC RESEARCH

Traditionally, and understandably, most research into language teaching and learning has focused on aspects of language and language acquisition, the effectiveness of particular methods and the nature of the language classroom. Inevitably, social aspects featured only peripherally, if at all, in such research and the individuals involved were viewed as participants rather than as subjects of interest in their own right. This is a perfectly legitimate way of approaching research, but it meant that for many years social and individual aspects of language learning tended to be ignored. More recently, though, the balance has shifted slightly and researchers have become increasingly interested in the social contexts in which learning and teaching take place and the nature of individuals' experiences, whether as teachers or learners. In order to understand these dimensions, it is necessary to spend time with those involved, using observation and/or interviews to understand the nature of their social worlds and experiences. These methods are normally described as 'ethnographic'.

The term 'ethnographic' tends to be used rather loosely in a way that allows the inclusion of interview studies, and because this book deals with observation (Chapter 3) and interviews (Chapter 4) separately, we use the term here to allow for a broader treatment of the latter than might be thought proper by many ethnographers (as Koro-Ljungberg and Greckhamer [2005] note, the wide use of the term 'ethnography' is often associated with issues of legitimacy). In fact, the terminological waters are fairly muddy because 'participant observation', 'ethnography' and 'fieldwork' all tend to be used interchangeably (Delamont 2006: 206) and it is hard to disagree with Harklau's conclusion (2005: 189): 'Given the varying approaches associated with ethnography, I believe it is undesirable or even impossible to develop absolute pronouncements for what ethnography is or should be in studies of second language teaching and learning.'

Our approach instead will be to accept a broad definition of ethnographic research as an attempt to understand aspects of the social world and, leaving matters of methodological detail to later chapters, to focus on the practical issue of what a researcher needs to bring to such research in terms of basic orientation.

The most fundamental fact about ethnographic research, and something that distinguishes it from the other approaches described in this chapter, is that *the researcher is the primary research instrument*. In other words, the researcher is implicated in the collection, construction and representation of the data and as a result cannot be abstracted from the analysis. Far from making life easy, the demands this makes in terms of empirical, analytical and representational rigour make ethnographic research an exhausting enterprise.

Another core characteristic of ethnography that makes it demanding is the requirement that researchers should immerse themselves in the relevant social world in order to develop a rich, situated understanding of it and of how it is constituted through its members. This means coming to understand their practices, their values, their beliefs and their understandings. In order to do this, the researcher must discover not only what is far from obvious to a casual observer, but what may be hidden from the members themselves.

This positioning is often described in terms of *emic* and *etic*, which are sometimes used to define an insider's perspective on events (emic) as opposed to an outsider's (etic). The terms are sometimes illegitimately used with evaluative force, implying that an insider's view is somehow 'better' than an outsider's, but this is a gross over-simplification that fails to capture the importance of maintaining a balance between the two so that the researcher can grasp things as a participant might grasp them while at the same time being able to stand back and see things that are hidden to participants.

This, of course, is less straightforward than it seems. One well-known challenge is what has become known as 'the observer's paradox', referring to the researcher's wish to observe behaviour that is normal or natural even though the presence of the observer undermines the very conditions under which this occurs. There are ethically sound ways of responding to this challenge, but Sarangi (2002, 2007) has pointed out that the challenge itself is rather more complex, embracing not only the observer's paradox but also the participant's paradox, which relates to the activity of participants who are in turn observing the observer, and the analyst's paradox, which refers to the researcher's need to draw on participants' insights but at the same time to represent them in the language of research. The lesson to take from this is not that ethnography is impossible but that it calls for very careful and constant reflection on the processes of data collection and analysis involved.

As so often, Geertz captures these complexities eloquently. Having discussed Ryle's discussion of the difference between an eye twitch and a wink and the implications of the latter, Geertz then provides an extract from his own field journal relating an incident in Morocco. He comments on this as follows (Geertz 1973: 9):

> Quoted raw, a note in a bottle, this passage conveys as any similar one similarly presented would do, a fair sense of how much goes into ethnographic description of even the most elemental sort – how extraordinarily 'thick' it is. In finished anthropological writings, including those collected here, this fact – that what we call our data are really our own constructions of other people's constructions of what they and their compatriots are up to – is obscured because most of what we need to comprehend a particular event, ritual, custom, idea, or whatever is insinuated as background information before the thing itself is directly examined. (Even to reveal that this little drama took place in the highlands of central Morocco in 1912 – and was recounted there in 1968 – is to determine much of our understanding of it.) There is nothing particularly wrong with this, and it is in any case inevitable. But is does lead to a view of anthropological research as rather more of an observational and rather less of an interpretive activity than it really is. Right down at the factual base, the hard rock, insofar as there is any, of the whole enterprise, we are already explicating: and worse, explicating explications. Winks upon winks upon winks.

Task C2.2

➤ How does the following extract from field notes on a teachers' staffroom illustrate something seen by the researcher but probably unnoticed by the observers?

> Paul enters: 'Well, they're beavering away, my group.' (To Harry, who has the other general group 23 hours a week.) Brief discussion about this group; Paul leaves.
>
> Jan enters: 'We didn't get into Unit 2.' (To Judith, who is sharing the 1–1 Turkish businessman with her.) Brief discussion of progress.
>
> What's interesting about these two exchanges is the absence of preliminaries: the staff room is obviously a place where the discussion of business is legitimate and can be introduced by any one at any stage. The above comments were not preceded by polite enquiries from the addressee or by any attempt to establish context on the part of the speaker.

We learn very quickly that we need to assess situations, which is why only children rush into rooms and begin speaking. But having learned what we need to do, we then do it without thinking – it becomes hidden to us. By the same token, if practices develop which suspend this basic rule, they are likely to arise 'naturally' and be hidden to participants. As an outsider and a careful observer of routines and everyday practices, the researcher has noticed something that is unusual in this staffroom, though it has not been remarked on by participants, who treat such behaviour as unproblematic. Repeated observation, combined with a sense of what it is like to return to a staffroom immediately after a lesson, allows the researcher to identify the topics as 'business' and eventually check that such immediate contributions are limited to this aspect of talk.

Ethnography is above all an empirical activity, depending for its success on extensive and detailed recording of the things happening in a setting (techniques for doing this are introduced in Chapter 3), but ethnographers also seek to establish different perspectives on the situation they are studying and will use different theories, methods, techniques, etc. in order to avoid a one-sided view. One of the best known techniques for doing this is *triangulation*, though this does not imply that only three sources can be used. The idea here is that something confirmed by, for example, interviews as well as observation, and two observers rather than just one, is more likely to be trustworthy than something identified by a single observer using just one method. Another useful method is *respondent validation*, where the researcher checks out his/her interpretation with participants in the field.

The way in which the researcher approaches data collection and interpretation is therefore a more pressing issue than disputes about definitions of ethnography. This makes Freebody's (2003: 40–41) characterization of qualitative research in education particularly valuable. He argues that the choices facing a researcher need to be made in the context of four considerations:

1. Foregrounding the propositions that participants used to organize the event under study;
2. Taking as relevant the relationship between the local contours of the sites in which educational activities are being conducted and the ways in which the activities themselves are structured;
3. Focusing on the jointly produced nature of educational events, not just on the activities of one category of participants;
4. Developing descriptions and explications of educational events before applying evaluations of those events.

These considerations apply once the ethnographer is in the field, but the question of what the researcher takes into the field is also important though often ignored, perhaps because of the emphasis that is placed on allowing themes to emerge from the data. Delamont (2006: 212) captures the essential point succinctly: 'The ethnography is only as good as the ideas the researcher deploys.'

Of course, ideas can and should be deployed at all stages in research, but Delamont also draws attention to the idea of *foreshadowed problems* that can be an invaluable point of orientation for the researcher. Such problems might emerge through reading, reflection or initial exposure to the field.

Task C2.3

➤ Hannah is just about to go into the field to study the work of teachers in an international school that draws staff from all over Europe and offers subjects in a number of languages. What sort of 'foreshadowed problems' might she have identified?

Hannah already knows that teachers come from many different countries and experience tells her that when people of different nationalities are brought together in a shared enterprise they bring different cultural values and expectations with them. It would be unusual, therefore, not to have problems involving adjustment to the new environment, the resolution of differences in beliefs about teaching, social conduct, etc. There may also be practical problems involved in moving to a new country and a new school. If Hannah has read research into school culture, she may also wonder whether national groupings might encourage a balkanized professional culture. All of these things, and many more, will provide some sense of shape that will help prevent the process of immersion from being too overwhelming.

The interplay of ideas, experience, contextual sensitivity, etc. will all be played out through writing, which may be the single defining activity of ethnography. Ethnography, it could be argued, is done *through* writing and the shape and substance of the project is realised through the act of writing. Atkinson (1992: 6) goes further: 'What may be generated as "data" ', he says, 'is affected by what the ethnographer can treat as "writable" and "readable".' This applies not only to field notes but also to the eventual representation of the research. Brannan *et al.* (2007: 400), for example, claim that making the 'lived reality of complex phenomena' accessible to those who have no experience in the field is one of the 'intractable dilemmas of ethnographic research'.

Perhaps unsurprisingly in the light of these demands, ethnographic research has not featured prominently in our field and has not had a glowing history – over 20 years ago Watson-Gegeo (1988) was warning about the dangers of not approaching it properly. This is perhaps surprising in view of the general acceptance of Hymes's dictum underlining the importance of rules of use to language learning, something that would seem to call particularly for research aimed at understanding a social world. It is reassuring, therefore, to see that at least some researchers have taken this on board to the extent of making the case for language learners as ethnographers (Roberts *et al.* 2001).

This brief review of the essential nature of ethnography has presented a mainstream view leaving no space for more unusual approaches such as autoethnography and performance ethnography (for a brief introduction to these and visual and arts-based ethnography, see Gwyther and Possamai-Inesedy 2009), though Chapter 6 introduces linguistic ethnography and visual ethnography. Anyone interested in exploring the literature further will find a valuable collection of resources in Gobo and Diotti (2008), while Hammersley (2006) raises interesting questions about the value of ethnography. The research papers discussed in this book have been chosen because they exemplify aspects of good practice in research using ethnographic methods but also, in some cases, because they include aspects which are open to challenge or which raise knotty questions of representation and interpretation.

One such 'knotty question' involves the place of recorded data and the approach to analyzing this. There are a number of approaches that might be adopted, but in this book we concentrate on one of these: conversation analysis. If this is to be used as part of an ethnographic study, the researcher will need to decide on how the relationship will play out; for example, will conversation analysis be used only for illuminating particular incidents or encounters, will the two approaches be integrated more fully or will ethnographic data be used to provide contextual detail to help frame a conversation analytic study (something many conversation analysts would reject out of hand)? These are questions that need to be considered at the design stage, and anyone seeking to understand more about the relationship between observation and the analysis of interaction should find Silverman (2006) helpful.

Task C2.4

➤ Read Hammersley (2006) and consider the following questions:

1. What does Hammersley regard as the drawbacks arising from the relatively short exposure to the field that is characteristic of contemporary educational ethnographies?
2. How far, if at all, do you think the author provides helpful ways forward in response to the problems of context which he identifies?
3. How do you feel about the prospects for 'virtual ethnography'? What advantages and disadvantages would you expect to be associated with it?
4. Note down any questions or queries you might have about interviews arising from the discussion of these in the paper and bring these into your reading of the treatment of interviews in Chapter 4.

INTRODUCTION TO CONVERSATION ANALYSIS[1]

There are a number of methodologies which may be used to study spoken interaction in relation to language teaching and learning. Other methodologies include discourse analysis (DA), critical discourse analysis (CDA), discursive psychology, sociocultural theory and systemic functional linguistics. This section introduces CA as a methodology for analyzing talk and then considers how it is useful in relation to researching language teaching and learning.

CA studies the organization and order of social action in interaction. This organization and order is one produced by the interactants by means of their talk and is oriented to by them. The analyst's task is to develop an 'emic' or participants' perspective, to uncover and describe this organization and order; the main interest is in uncovering the underlying *machinery* which enables interactants to achieve this organization and order. CA analysts aim to provide a 'holistic' portrayal of language use which reveals the reflexive relationships between form, function, sequence and social identity and social/institutional context. That is, the organization of the talk is seen to relate directly and reflexively to the social goals of the participants, whether institutional or otherwise. The following principles underlie CA:

- Talk in interaction is systematically organized, deeply ordered and methodic;
- The analysis of talk in interaction should be based on naturally occurring data;
- No order of detail can be dismissed, a priori, as disorderly, accidental or irrelevant;
- Analysis should not be constricted by prior theoretical assumptions;
- We cannot assume in advance that any contextual details are relevant. We can only invoke contextual factors if it is evident in the details of the talk that the participants themselves are orienting to contextual factors;
- Contributions to interaction are *context-shaped* and *context-renewing*. Contributions are context-shaped in that they cannot be adequately understood

> except by reference to the sequential environment in which they occur and in which the participants design them to occur. Contributions are context-renewing in that they inevitably form part of the sequential environment in which a next contribution will occur.

The essential question which we must ask at all stages of CA analysis of data is '**why that, in that way, right now?**' This encapsulates the perspective of interaction as action (why that) which is expressed by means of linguistic forms (in that way) in a developing sequence (right now). Talk is conceived of as social action, which is delivered in particular linguistic formatting, as part of an unfolding sequence.

A number of interactional organizations were uncovered by Sacks and associates by grappling with their data can now be employed in analysis by CA practitioners. First we should clarify that these organizations are *not* the same as 'units of analysis' in the linguistic sense. Rather, they should be understood as interactional organizations which interactants use normatively and reflexively both as an action template for the production of their social actions and as a point of reference for the interpretation of their actions. We as analysts should use them in the same way. The organizations are part of the context-free machinery which people make use of to orient themselves in indexical interaction i.e. people employ them in a context-sensitive way. Similarly, we are only able to interpret the context-sensitive social actions of others because there is a context-free machinery by reference to which we can make sense of them. It is because the participants (and we as analysts) are able to identify the gap between the context-free model and its context-sensitive implementation that they (and we as analysts) are able to understand the social significance of the context-sensitive implementation. This is the basis of the CA claim to be able to uncover the emic perspective.

ADJACENCY PAIRS

Adjacency pairs are paired utterances, for example question–answer, greeting–greeting, offer–acceptance. Schegloff and Sacks (1973) say that adjacency pairs are sequences of two utterances that are:

1. adjacent
2. produced by different speakers
3. ordered as a first part and a second part
4. typed, so that a particular first requires a particular second, e.g. offers require acceptance or rejection.

The norm is that, having produced a first of an adjacency pair, the current speaker must stop speaking, and the next speaker must produce a second to the same pair. In fact, strict adjacency is too strong a requirement: the two parts of the adjacency pair can be many turns apart in a dialogue. Sometimes first parts do not receive second parts. However, there is always the expectation that a second part will eventually be provided, or its absence accounted for, in the way that the absence of an A1 for Q1 is accounted for. So we can say that after the first of an adjacency pair, a second is immediately relevant and expectable: this is called conditional relevance. The adjacency pair concept does not claim that second parts are always provided for first parts. Rather, it is a *normative* frame of reference which provides a framework for understanding actions and providing social accountability. So if we ask a question to someone who does not then provide an answer, we may draw conclusions about that person.

Extract C2.1

A:	May I have a bottle of white wine?	(Q1)
B:	Are you eighteen?	(Q2)
A:	No.	(A2)
B:	No.	(A1)

(Levinson 1983: 304)

We can say that the second adjacency pair is embedded within the first one.

Task C2.5

➤ Look at the following dialogue and try to label the adjacency pairs:

Extract C2.2

A: Are you coming to dinner tonight?
B: Can I bring a guest?
A: Male or female?
B: What difference does that make?
A: An issue of balance.
B: Female.
A: Sure.
B: I'll be there.

TURN-TAKING

Sacks *et al.* (1974) provided the seminal account of the organization of **turn-taking** in ordinary conversation. There is a mechanism governing turn-taking which is termed a local management system: this means that decisions can be made by the participants, rather than having the turns allocated in advance, as is the case in a courtroom. There is a set of norms with options which the participants can select. Listeners project when a speaker is going to finish a turn, and the point at which speaker change may occur is known as the **transition relevance place** or **TRP.** At a

TRP the rules governing transition of speakers come into play: the speakers may change at that point, but they do not necessarily do so. The following norms apply at the first TRP of any turn:

a If current speaker selects the next speaker in the current turn, then the current speaker must stop speaking and the next speaker must speak;
b If the current speaker does not select a next speaker, then any other participant may select themselves as next speaker: the first person to speak at the TRP gains rights to the next turn;
c If the current speaker has not selected a next speaker, and if no other participant self-selects as per section b), then the current speaker may (but need not) continue.

The procedure then 'loops' or recycles until the end of the conversation, for which there are of course further rules. Overlap occurs for a number of reasons and in a number of ways. The system of turn-taking is normative, so speakers may choose to perform specific social actions 'by reference to one-party-at-a-time, even though they are realized through designedly simultaneous talk.' (Schegloff 2000: 48). Overlap, then, may be designedly used to intensify the affiliative or disaffiliative nature of particular social actions. In institutional settings the organization of turn-taking is constrained and related to the institutional goal, and this is the case in language classroom interaction (Markee 2000; Seedhouse 2004). The following examples (Levinson 1983: 299) illustrate that it is often possible to predict where overlap is likely to occur, and to distinguish between overlap and interruption.

Extract C2.3

J: Twelve pounds I think wasn't it.=
D: = [Can you bel*ie*ve it?
L: [Twelve pounds on the weight watchers' scale.

(Sacks *et al.* 1974: 707)

The transcription system shows that D and L have both tried to take a turn at exactly the same time and there is overlap: this is called a competing first start, as allowed under section b) above.

Extract C2.4

C: we:ll I wrote what I thought was a a–
rea:son[able explan<u>at</u>io:n
F: [I: think it was a <u>very</u> rude <u>le:</u>tter.

(Levinson 1983: 299)

F begins his/her turn in the middle of 'reasonable'. There is no way in which this could be considered a TRP, so it must be an interruption. This is confirmed by the aggressive content of F's turn. This extract illustrates that the norms of turn-taking can be broken: doing so has consequences for the progress of the interaction. How do you think the above conversation is likely to progress?

Task C2.6

Extract C2.5

D: he's got to talk to someone (very sor) supportive way
   towards you (.)
A: [Greg's (got wha-)]
G: [think you   sh-] think you should have one to: hold him

(Atkinson and Drew 1979: 44)

Why does G repeat 'think you'?

REPAIR

Repair comes into play whenever there are problems in the accomplishment of talk and may be defined as the treatment of trouble occurring in interactive language use. Of course conversationalists do not always understand each other, and in this case repair is undertaken. Trouble is anything which the participants judge is impeding their communication and a repairable item is one which constitutes trouble for the participants. Schegloff, Jefferson and Sacks (1977:363) point out that 'nothing is, in principle, excludable from the class "repairable"'. Repair is a vital mechanism for the maintenance of intersubjectivity. It is of particular importance for L2 learners and teachers to understand how breakdowns in communication and misunderstandings are repaired as repair in the L2 classroom tends to carry a heavier load than in other settings. It is important to distinguish self-initiated repair (I prompt repair of my mistake) from other-initiated repair (somebody else notices my mistake and initiates repair). Self-repair (I correct myself) must also be distinguished from other-repair (somebody corrects my mistake). There are therefore normally four repair trajectories:

Self-initiated self-repair

Extract C2.6

A: had to put new gaskets on the oil pan to strop-stop the
   leak

(Levinson 1983: 360)

Self-initiated other-repair

Extract C2.7

B: he had dis uh Mistuh W-m whatever k- I can't think of his first name, Watts on, the one that wrote [that piece
A: [Dan Watts

(Schegloff *et al.* 1977: 364)

Other-initiated self-repair

Extract C2.8

A: hey the first time they stopped me from selling cigarettes was this morning.
(1.0)
B: →from selling cigarettes?
A: →from buying cigarettes.

(Schegloff *et al.* 1977: 370)

Other-initiated other-repair

Extract C2.9

C: erm I'm just checking is that (.) right you know (0.5) I d- I don't know his flight number and [I'm not sure
A: [(whi-)
C: whether he's coming in to channel four eh:
(.)
A: →terminal four
C: yeah

(Hutchby and Wooffitt 1998: 63)

Task C2.7

➤ Identify the types of repair used in **all** the instances in the following extracts:

Extract C2.10

L: but y'know single beds'r awfully thin to sleep on.
S: what?
L: single beds. [they're-
E: [y'mean narrow?
L: they're awfully narrow yeah.

(Schegloff *et al.* 1977: 378)

Extract C2.11

A: . . . had to put new gaskets on the oil pan to strop-stop the
leak, an' then I put- and then-
R: that was a gas leak.
A: it was an oil leak buddy.
B: 't's a gas leak.
A: it's an oil leak.
((dispute continues for many turns))

(Levinson 1983: 360)

Having reviewed the basic components of interactional organization, we will now look at how these are used in the procedures of CA analysis. The first stage of CA analysis has been described as *unmotivated looking* or being open to discovering patterns or phenomena. Psathas (1995, pp. 24–25) describes the term unmotivated looking as a paradox 'since looking is motivated or there would be no looking being done in the first place'. So what is really meant is being open to discovering new phenomena rather than searching the data with preconceptions or hypotheses. Having identified a candidate phenomenon, the next phase is often an inductive search through a database to establish a collection of instances of the phenomenon. However, single case analysis can also be undertaken (Hutchby and Wooffitt 1998: 120–130).

After an inductive database search has been carried out, the next step is to establish regularities and patterns in relation to occurrences of the phenomenon and to show that these regularities are methodically produced and oriented to by the participants as normative organizations of action (Heritage 1988: 131). In order to explicate the emic logic or rational organization of the pattern uncovered, the next step is detailed analysis of single instances of the phenomenon. Finally a more generalized account is produced of how the phenomenon relates to interaction in that particular setting.

The following is an account of a single case analysis[2] focusing on a single data extract. We start the account after recording, transcription and unmotivated looking have taken place and after we have identified a single extract to focus on.

1. Locate an action sequence or sequences;
2. Characterize the actions in the sequence or sequences. An action sequence can be as short as an adjacency pair or last for hours. We are looking for a first speaker to initiate an action which is responded to in some way by a second speaker. This ends when the speakers move to perform a different action or series of actions. The idea of characterizing the actions in the sequence may be termed form–function matching. So we may, for example, identify a sequence in which an offer is made and then rejected or a complex sequence of embedded question and answer adjacency pairs (e.g. Levinson 1983: 305).
3. Examine the action sequence(s) in terms of the organization of turn-taking, focusing especially on any disturbances in the working of the system.

4. Examine the action sequence(s) in terms of sequence organization. Here we are looking at adjacency pairs but more widely at any action undertaken in response to other actions.
5. Examine the action sequence(s) in terms of the organization of repair.
6. Examine how the speakers package their actions in terms of the actual linguistic forms which they select from the alternatives available and consider the significance of these.
7. Uncover any roles, identities or relationships which emerge in the details of the interaction. CA normally tries to avoid making (premature) reference to background information such as institutional setting, personal details (age, gender, etc.) until after the initial analysis. This is so it can be established which aspects of context are demonstrably relevant to the actors in the interaction, i.e. that these aspects are manifest *in some way* in the details of the interaction.

CA has been introduced above in relation to spoken interaction in general and the discussion so far has not mentioned language teaching and learning. Why is CA a suitable methodology for language teaching and learning research? It provides a framework and methodology for describing and analyzing the micro-detail of interaction and relating this to the institutional business, i.e. language teaching and learning. From the 1980s, the importance of interaction as a vital element in the instructed second language learning process became clearer. Although time-consuming, CA seemed to promise a more useful perspective on interaction which was not only tightly focused on empirical detail, but also more holistic and multi-layered than had previously been possible. In order to understand the processes of instructed SLA, it is vital to analyze the fine detail of the relationship between pedagogy and interaction as it unfolds in classroom talk. CA is able to reveal the complex ways in which pedagogy and interaction are inextricably intertwined in a reflexive relationship. In recent years, CA studies have provided insights into language teaching and learning as a process, e.g. Brouwer and Wagner (2004), Markee (2008), Mondada and Pekarek Doehler (2004), Seedhouse, Walsh and Jenks (2010). Some of the studies reconceptualize language learning as a change in social participation patterns, whereas others show how a specific language item is learned via the process of interaction. CA has been employed to provide evidence of what actually happens during particular language learning activities, as opposed to what is supposed to happen, of how intended pedagogy gets converted to actual pedagogy. Instead of working from the static assumption that competence is something that one has a fixed degree of at a point in time, CA presents competence as variable and co-constructed by participants in interaction (e.g. Brown 2003).

Task C2.7

➤ The CA studies included in this volume are: Koshik (2002), Seedhouse and Almutairi (2009), Mori (2003) and Brown (2003). These illustrate the range of applications of CA to language teaching and learning research. Read the data analysis sections in each study and note how CA analysis of data may be undertaken.

➤ Then read the extract below. How is the interaction organized in terms of turn-taking, topic, sequence and repair? How is the organization of the interaction related to the process of language learning?

Extract C2.12

(The teacher has been asking learners to talk about their favourite movies)

1 L: Kung Fu.
2 T: Kung Fu? you like the movie Kung Fu?
3 L: yeah (.) fight.
4 T: that was about a great fighter? (.) a man who knows how to fight with his hands.
5 L: I fight (.) my hand.
6 T: you know how to fight with your hands?
7 L: I fight with my hand.
8 T: do you know karate?
9 L: I know karate.
10 T: watch out guys, Wang knows karate.

(Johnson 1995: 24)

For an analysis of the above data, see Seedhouse (2005).

For a more detailed introduction to CA in relation to language teaching and learning, see Markee (2000) and Seedhouse (2004). A number of websites now have resources available for training. Ethno/CA News at www2.fmg.uva.nl/emca has details of courses, conferences, publications, bibliographies, links to four email discussion lists and downloads for characters used in transcripts. It also has links to software for transcription of video data and to sample sound and video files and transcripts. Antaki's online CA tutorial is available at http://www-staff.lboro.ac.uk/~ssca1/ and Llewellyn's at http://sites.google.com/site/llewellynnick/tutorial. The Childes website at http://childes.psy.cmu.edu has extensive procedures and tools for CA analysis along with an enormous database. Schegloff's homepage at http://www.sscnet.ucla.edu/soc/faculty/schegloff/ has a transcription module, sound clips and access to his classic publications.

In Chapter 8 we return to methodological issues to compare issues such as validity, reliability, epistemology and context in relation to the three methodologies which have been reviewed.

NOTES

1 Some of the discussion in this section is based on Seedhouse (2004).
2 See Hutchby and Wooffitt (1998: 120–130).

CHAPTER 2
Interaction and pedagogy

Introduction

In this chapter we consider L2 classroom interaction, a phenomenon which involves the interplay of two fundamental concepts, namely spoken interaction and pedagogical action. Why should anyone be concerned with the interaction which takes place in second language classrooms? We know that the learning of first languages takes place through interaction: children who have been deprived of contact with other human beings have simply not learnt language like other children in the speech community. Second language learning can happen in many different ways, including learning through TV, pop music, reading grammar books, etc. – means which do not involve any interaction. It is also possible to learn a second language by living in the country but without taking any lessons. However, the research which has been done tentatively suggests that explicit instruction through classroom language learning is efficient (Norris and Ortega 2000) for adult learners. Until recent decades, interest in language teaching research was focused on consideration of teaching methods in isolation: what was the best teaching method? More recently, the focus has shifted towards classroom interaction as the most vital element in the instructed second language learning process.

Which kinds of interaction can best promote L2 learning? In recent years, there have been two fundamental approaches to this question, exemplified by the two articles in this chapter. The first approach tends to start with a theory or theories of language learning within a quantitative paradigm. In Mackey's study, these are the interaction hypothesis and the noticing hypothesis. An interactional phenomenon is then selected which relates to these theories – in this case, interactional feedback. An experimental design is then established in which an experimental group receives interactional feedback and a control group does not. A pre-test and post-test determine whether the treatment has led to learning of the targeted items or not. This approach tends to place primary emphasis on pedagogy/cognition and then to link this to interaction. The second approach, qualitative in nature, seeks to describe and analyze the organization of interaction in pedagogical settings, linking interaction to pedagogical action and to L2 learning processes. Koshik's article exemplifies this approach by examining in considerable detail a specific phenomenon which occurs during language teaching. The phenomenon of designedly incomplete utterances is a combination of a pedagogical and an interactional practice.

One problem in research into language learning is that there is a proliferation of terminology, and terms are often associated with particular approaches or methodologies. Hence, the same phenomenon may have a different name when examined using a different methodology. One example of this is in line 2 of the extract below:

1 L: No, little boy no drink.
2 → T: That's right, little boys don't drink.

(Johnson 1995: 23)

In line 2, there is positive evaluation of the propositional content of the learner utterance followed by an expansion of the learner utterance into a correct sequence of linguistic forms. The type of repair used is known in CA as *embedded correction* (Jefferson 1987: 95), that is, a correction done as a by-the-way occurrence in the context of a social action, which in this case is an action of agreement and confirmation. From a cognitive SLA perspective this would be known as a *recast:* 'Recasts are responses to non-targetlike utterances that provide a targetlike way of expressing the original meaning.' (Mackey 2006: 406). In a more sociocultural approach to SLA the phenomenon could be termed *scaffolding* (Johnson 1995: 75). Note that this phenomenon is a combination of an interactional move and a pedagogical move – in research in the L2 classroom, it is extremely difficult to disentangle the two levels. In the case of the teacher's embedded correction/recast/scaffolding move, a move of correction is made in the same turn as a social move of confirmation. Hence, we cannot be certain which of these moves a learner is paying attention to and responding to; indeed, the learner may be orienting to both.

A further problem is how to portray the homogeneity or heterogeneity of any turn at talk in the L2 classroom. When research prioritizes the interactional level, there is a tendency to analyze the particular instance in great detail and bring out its unique nature. When research prioritizes the pedagogical level, there is a tendency to consider the instance as one example of a particular pedagogical move and to evaluate its effectiveness compared with other pedagogical moves, which is generally what happens in research into recasts, for example. So there is always a tension between a description of an extract of L2 classroom interaction such as the one above as a unique occurence, locally produced by the participants, and between a description of it as something homogeneous or similar to other instances.

Seedhouse (2004) suggests there is a reflexive relationship between pedagogy and interaction in the L2 classroom, and that this relationship is the foundation of its context-free architecture. The omnipresent and unique feature of the L2 classroom is this interdependent relationship between pedagogy and interaction. So whoever is taking part in L2 classroom interaction and whatever the particular activity during which the interactants are speaking the L2, they are always displaying to one another their analyses of the current state of the evolving relationship between pedagogy and interaction and acting on the basis of these analyses. So interaction in the L2 classroom is organized around the relationship between pedagogy and interaction. When you read the two articles in this chapter, note whether the primary focus is on pedagogy or on interaction, and how the complex relationship between pedagogy and interaction is handled.

Section A
Introduction A1 Noticing

A basic premise in second language acquisition is that subliminal learning is not possible. Conscious attention is assumed to be a precondition to learning language, and thus precludes the possibility of acquisition while a learner is unconscious, asleep or even concurrently attending to some other cognitive activity. It is assumed that language acquirers must in some way be overtly cognitively aware of linguistic forms, words, morphemes, phonemes, etc. before they can associate linguistic forms to meaningful referents. Schmidt (1995, 2001) referred to this precondition for acquisition as the 'noticing hypothesis'.

In formal language learning contexts, it is also assumed that learners will have to contrast their own versions of the target language with models provided by teachers or other learners. For grammar to be acquirable, learners have to be able to notice and contrast their version of the target language form with a model proactively by an instructor, or vicariously when they notice another learner's usage being corrected. The focus of classroom interaction research has thus aimed to examine the processes by which learner errors can be made salient without disturbing the flow of interaction. A number of models have emerged as mechanisms for providing negative evidence to learners. Recasts (Mackey: 2003) are reformulations of learner utterances by the learners' interlocutors, which are then played back with embedded corrections so that the learner can notice the repaired version with the original.

Learner: . .and my brother work as cook.
Teacher: he works **<- recast**
Learner: he works as cook **<- modified output**

A basic research question in research on feedback, noticing and recasting, concerns the kinds of interactive tasks that can facilitate such noticing and subsequent uptake of repaired target language forms.

Task A.1.1

➤ Make a list of the kinds of errors that would be expected to occur in a language classroom. Speculate on the kinds of recasts that could be provided.

Introduction A2 Repair

A broad CA definition of *repair* is as the treatment of trouble occurring in interactive language use. *Trouble* is anything which the participants judge is impeding their communication and a repairable item is one which constitutes trouble for the participants. Any element of talk may in principle be the focus of repair, even an element which is well formed, propositionally correct and appropriate. In the L2 classroom, as elsewhere, repair does not necessarily imply that anyone has committed an error; if a train passes by and interactants are unable to hear each other, they will treat that as trouble and conduct repair. In the extract, below, for example, A has given the time using the 24-hour clock, with which C is not familiar; there is no error involved. This gap in knowledge is a trouble source, hence the need for repair.

Extract A2.1

```
1   C:  w-wu-what does that mean in
2       layme(h)n's te(h)rms [huhh
3   A:                       [oHh sorry um
4       that's fiftee-(H)hh fourteen forty five
5       is quarter to three
```

(Hutchby and Wooffitt 1998: 60)

As we saw in Chapter 1, it is important to understand the different *trajectories* of repair. Initiation and performance of correction can be undertaken by self or others, so a variety of trajectories are possible. We can distinguish self-initiated repair (I prompt repair of the trouble source) from other-initiated repair (somebody else notices the trouble and initiates repair). Self-repair (I carry out repair myself) must also be distinguished from other-repair (somebody else carries out repair on the trouble source). There are therefore normally four repair *trajectories*, which involve different combinations of the initiation and performance of repair:

- self-initiated self-repair;
- self-initiated other-repair;
- other-initiated self-repair;
- other-initiated other-repair.

In CA terms, correction is one kind of repair. A CA definition of *correction* is 'replacement of a trouble item by another item'. Remember that this does not necessarily involve anybody committing an error. Repair is the generic term and refers to the treatment of trouble. However, repair does not necessarily involve replacement. For example, if an external noise causes someone not to hear an utterance, they may initiate repetition, not replacement, i.e. repair but not correction. We will first see an example from conversation, and then an example from L2 classroom interaction.

Extract A2.2

1 *Ken*: 'E likes that waiter over there,
2 Al: → Wait-<u>er</u>?
3 *Ken*: Waitress, sorry,
4 Al: 'At's bedder,

(Schegloff *et al.* 1977: 377)

The trajectory here is other-initiated self-repair. Here the trouble source is located by Al in line 2 as being the incorrect gender inherent in the word 'waiter', and repair is initiated. Ken recognizes the trouble and self-corrects in line 3.

It is of particular importance for learners and teachers of foreign languages to understand how breakdowns in communication and misunderstandings are repaired. In the L2 classroom, the mechanism of repair becomes prominent, partly because learners produce relatively large numbers of errors in L2 and these may be corrected, as we see in Koshik's article. In L2 classrooms, the organization of repair and correction is more complex than in conversation, since the organization of interaction is reflexively related to the pedagogical focus, which is very variable (van Lier 1988, Seedhouse 2004). As noted above, turns operate on a pedagogical as well as an interactional level.

Extract A2.3

1 T: right, the cup is on top of the box. (T moves cup)
2 now, where is the cup?
3 L: in the box.
4 → T: the cup is (.) ?
5 L: in the box.
6 → T: the cup is in (.) ?
7 L: the cup is in the box.
8 T: right, very good, the cup is in the box.

(Johnson 1995: 10)

Even though the answers which L produces in lines 3 and 5 are linguistically correct and sequentially appropriate, T initiates correction in lines 4 and 6 until L self-corrects by producing exactly the targeted string of linguistic forms in line 7. Here, T treats as trouble in lines 3 and 5 the absence of the rest of the target string of linguistic forms; lines 3 and 5 are viewed as trouble items to be replaced by a complete string.

As suggested above, when analyzing L2 classroom interaction, it is vital to understand how the pedagogical focus is related to the organization of the interaction. In the extract above, a form and accuracy context is operating, in which the teacher's pedagogical focus aims at the production of a specific string of linguistic forms by the learners. Repair may be initiated by the teacher if the linguistic forms and patterns of interaction produced are not exactly identical to those intended by the teacher's pedagogical focus.

Since the focus in form and accuracy contexts is on the learners' production of specific strings of linguistic forms, it follows that when the learners produce utterances which are linguistically correct and appropriate, those utterances may still be subject to repair by the teacher, as in the extract above. Although we might view this as unnecessarily pedantic teacher behaviour, the point to be emphasized is that such repair is perfectly 'rational' within a form and accuracy context, where repair may be initiated by the teacher if the linguistic forms and patterns of interaction produced are *not exactly identical* to those targeted by the teacher's pedagogical focus.

So from a CA perspective, it is preferable to use the term 'correction' rather than 'error correction' in relation to L2 classroom interaction, since correction of trouble items is not necessarily related to linguistic errors. The organization of repair in the L2 classroom can best be understood in relation to the evolving and reflexive relationship between pedagogy and interaction. An error analysis or contrastive analysis approach, by contrast, cannot explicate why it is that L2 teachers sometimes correct learner utterances which are linguistically correct and at other times praise learner utterances which are riddled with linguistic errors. L2 teachers may characterize as trouble any learner utterance which does not align with the teacher's pedagogical focus at that point in the lesson, and may initiate correction of it.

CA methodology developed in relation to ordinary conversation and institutional interaction. So when CA started to be applied to L2 classroom interaction, a set terminology could be employed in relation to the interactional dimension. However, CA had no terminology to deal with the pedagogical dimension of L2 classroom interaction, and this has had to be slowly developed by researchers in this field. So, for example, Koshik's study coins the term 'designedly incomplete utterances' for a specific pedagogical sequence which occurs in L2 classrooms. CA research in L2 classrooms tends to be exploratory in nature and seeks to describe in some detail interactional phenomena related to language learning, possibly as a precursor to relating the phenomena to language learning processes, as with Koshik's study. Some assumptions in this type of research are that a) spoken interaction is a very complex phenomenon, whose organization can be revealed by painstaking analysis, b) the relationship between pedagogy and interaction is equally complex and reflexive, or two-way and c) it therefore cannot be assumed that intended pedagogical aims and ideas translate directly into actual classroom practice. This type of research is concerned with describing, analyzing and understanding what actually happens in classroom interaction, which may be different from what the teacher intends to happen. Analysis needs to portray the dual nature of L2 classroom interaction, namely that turns are functioning simultaneously on an interactional and a pedagogical level. So when analyzing repair in L2 classroom interaction, it is not only necessary to understand the trajectory and formatting of repair. It is also necessary to identify the trouble source and, if a linguistic error, to specify how the error is treated in pedagogical as well as interactional terms.

Task A2.1

➤ Examine the following extracts. Identify the trajectory that is being used, using the CA system outlined above. In particular, note who performs the correction. Identify the trouble in each extract. If the trouble is a linguistic error by the learner, specify what is wrong with it. Try to describe the way that correction is being conducted in each extract, giving a name to the correction technique if possible. Note the relationship between pedagogy and interaction in each example of correction. The first extract below is analyzed as an example.

Extract A2.4

L1: er and I: I am very good person, and [(laughs)] and give she another one.
LL: [(laugh)]
T: → give she?
L1: (.) give her another one.

(British Council 1985, vol. 2: 68)

The trajectory is other-intitiated self-repair, with T initiating and L1 conducting the repair. 'Give she' is the trouble item, being a grammatical error. The correction technique is to repeat the erroneous portion of the learner utterance with rising intonation. This technique locates the precise error but has sometimes been criticized for providing the learners with erroneous input. However, we can see in the above example that the learner is able to self-correct correctly. In this case, the sole business being conducted in T's turn is correction (this is called 'exposed correction' in CA), and the flow of interaction is interrupted to deal with the correction.

Extract A2.5

L: Because she can't
T: → Because she counted
L: Because she counted the wrong number of tourists.

(Tsui 1995: 48)

Extract A2.6

L: They runs they runs quickly.
T: → Once more.
L: They run quickly.
T: Yes, that's better.

(Tsui 1995: 42)

Extract A2.7

T: *Wohin ist Susan gefahren?*((tr: Where has Susan gone to?)) Michelle.
L: *Sie ist mit dem Zug nach Edinburg gefahren.* ((tr: She's gone to Edinburgh by train))
T: → *Ja. Gut. Könne wir genauer sein? Ich habe nur gefragt: Wohin? Nicht womit? Nur wohin?* ((tr: Yes. Good. Only can we be more precise? I only asked where? Not:how? Only where?))
L: *Sie ist nach Edinburg gefahren.* ((tr: She's gone to Edinburgh))
T: *Gut.* ((tr: Good))

(Westgate *et al.* 1985: 278)

Extract A2.8

T: where is the man?
L1: (2.5) <in the: se:cond floor>
→T: in the second floor? ((T's face shows disapproval))
L2: on the second [floor.
TLL: [on the second floor.
T: what's he wearing?

(Carr 2006, DVD 14)

Extract A2.9

T: er, Mr P, er what's the man doing (.) he's sitting, but what's he doing with his hand?
L1: she's pointing their hand.
T: → pardon?
L1: he is pointing his hand.
T: OK, he's pointing his hand and what
L1: and he is showing the seat in front of him.
T: OK, he's pointing his hand and what
L2: the menu (.) the menu (.)
T: the menu or (T gestures) look at the picture, look at the picture (.) he's pointing at this watch. Why is he pointing at his watch?

(Riley 1985: 54)

Extract A2.10

L1: *Erm, sie sind im Schirmgeschäft, weil, erm (.) sie (.) möchten eine (sic) Schirm kaufen.* ((tr: er, they're in the umbrella shop because, er, they want an umbrella to buy))
T: → *Was meinen die anderen? Ist das richtig, was Mary sagt?(.). Roger, Sie schütteln den Kopf. Verstehen Sie? Sie schütteln den Kopf.* ((tr: What do the others think?. Is what Mary says correct? Roger, you're shaking your head. Do you understand? You're shaking your head)) Shaking your head. *Wie sagen Sie es? Warum sind sie im Schirmgeschäft?* ((tr: How do you say it? Why are they in the umbrella shop?))

L2: *Erm, weil sie einen Schirm kaufen möchten.* ((tr: er, because they want to buy an umbrella))

(Ellis 1992: 115)

Extract A2.11

L: Why did the cook was arrested.
T: → Er, why did?
L: The cook was arrested. The French cook was arrested.

(Mackey 2006: 423)

Extract A2.12

1 T: what did I dream? Can you remember?
2 L1: you turned into a toothbrush
3 T: can I have a full sentence, Hugo?
4 L1: that you turned into a toothbrush
5 T: OK. you (.)?
6 L2: you turned into a toothbrush.
7 T: you (.)?
8 L2: you turned into a toothbrush.
9 L3: you dreamed.
10 T: you dreamt.
11 L3: you dreamt.
12 T: everyone
13 LL: dreamt
14 T: OK. I dreamt that I turned into a toothbrush.

(Ellis 1984: 105)

Task A2.2

➤ Now look at each extract again. This time, evaluate which types of repair might lead to effective student learning, and which might not. How are you reaching your conclusions as to the effectiveness of the type of repair? Think of a pedagogical rationale for each type of repair. Can you see any connections between the types of repair and theories of L2 learning with which you are familiar? Consider how you might research which types of correction are more or less effective in promoting L2 learning.

Section B
Extension B1

Mackey, A. (2006) 'Feedback, noticing and instructed language learning', *Applied Linguistics* 27, 405–430.

Mackey (2006) devised an experimental study in which English as a second language learners were randomly assigned to two classes. In an experimental intervention class, learners participated in role play sessions based on a quiz show simulation in which targeted linguistic forms (interrogatives, plurals and past tense) were primed for use in the role plays devised to elicit the target forms. When errors occurred during the quiz show role plays, teachers provided salient recasts to learners in the experimental group. In contrast, a control group was given equal input and output opportunities focused on the same targeted forms based on scenarios devised to be parallel to the quiz show content, but did not engage in interactions where feedback was available. Learners in both groups kept a learning journal as a way of monitoring their attention to feedback provided in their respective class environments. Audiotapes of both classes engaging in a total 150 minutes of instruction each were used to confirm that the feedback through interaction did not occur in the control group.

The focus of the study was on what the learners noticed. Four indicators of noticing were used. The learning journals, a questionnaire, focused questions and a follow-up questionnaire. A tally of noticing events pertinent to the feedback provided in class was used as an independent variable in the study design.

In order to confirm whether participants in the experimental group had noticed the recasts, 25 segments from the videotaped classes were used to create opportunities for stimulated recall. This step provided extra opportunities to notice the focus of the corrective interaction in the role plays.

Task B1.1

- Sketch the design noting the sequence of activities used for both the experimental and control groups. Discuss any differential time on task factors, and possible implications for group differences.

Evidence of language learning was based on a pre-test post-test design. Prior to the instruction, all learners were tested on their productive proficiency to orally describe a cartoon-based event in the past, to compare pictures with contrastive content devised to elicit plurals and a cartoon clip about which they were to form interrogatives. The same test was used as the post-test, though as the author notes, there was some attrition on the post-test version. After the post-test, all learners were given a questionnaire devised to elicit information about what learners had noticed in their language classes. Mackey dichotomized learners as either those with 'high' levels of noticing (two-thirds of possible contexts) or as those with 'low' levels of noticing. Learners in each condition could thus be classified as either high or low, depending on the cumulative picture provided by the four noticing instruments used: learning journals, two questionnaires and focused questions.

Evidence of learning was defined as differences in accuracy between the pre-test and post-test versions of the three tasks designed to measure tense, plural and interrogatives. Learners were categorized as either those who developed in their use of plurals, tense or interrogatives, or those who did not.

Task B1.2

➤ Given the outline of Mackey's study, describe what a likely hypothesis would be about 'noticing' and 'development'.

ANALYSIS

Mackey has opted for a non-parametric test because with just 28 participants, there are too few **degrees of freedom** to get stable means and **standard deviations** needed for a more powerful parametric test. Mackey aimed to employ three different chi-square tests of independence. Non-parametric tests have assumptions that must be met, one of which is cell sizes of at least five. Owing to attrition and the fact that the control group members might not have developed sufficiently, two of the three outcomes could not be tested statistically. For the one outcome meeting the statistical assumptions (interrogatives), Mackey employed the chi-square test of independence. The 2 × 2 contains the frequencies of group members who fall into each of the binary categories: high and low noticing, and plus or minus evidence of development in the accuracy of interrogatives. The four cells can be labelled the *a*, *b*, *c* and *d* cells. Since there is only one degree of freedom in a 2 × 2 cell, it must be corrected for continuity:

$$x^2 = \frac{N(|ad - bc| - N \div 2)^2}{(a + b)(c + d)(a + c)(b + d)}$$

The 2 × 2 matrix shows the cross tabulation of noticing and development as

	Less noticing	*More noticing*
No development	9(a)	2(b)
Development	2(c)	10(d)

When put in the 2 × 2, correction for continuity yields

$$\frac{23(|90-4|-23 \div 2)^2}{11 \times 12 \times 11 \times 12} = \frac{23(74.5^2)}{17424} = \frac{127655.7}{17424} = 7.326$$

With one degree of freedom, the critical value of chi-square is 3.84. To be statistically significant, or better than random variation, the observed chi-square must be larger than the critical chi-square. The observed is indeed larger than the critical value, so the inference is that learners who have noticed more of the feedback on interrogatives have developed more relative to those who did not notice how interrogatives are accurately formed.

Hatch and Lazaraton (1992) outline five assumptions of chi-square test of independence. These are:

1. the data are frequencies or tallies of an observable event (not percentages);
2. the categories created are unique, logical and non-overlapping;
3. non-occurrence of the phenomenon of interest is tallied and included in the design;
4. tallies are independent so that each event must go into only one cell. Multiple contributions from individuals are tallied;
5. sample sizes must be large enough to generate an expected cell size of at least five.

Task B1.3

➤ In light of the assumptions discuss why Mackey was wise to limit the test of independence to just the interrogatives.

Extension B2

Now read Koshik, I. (2002) 'Designedly incomplete utterances: A pedagogical practice for eliciting knowledge displays in error correction sequences', *Research on Language and Social Interaction* 35(3): 277–309.

Koshik's article seeks to describe and analyse the organization of interaction in pedagogical settings, linking interaction to pedagogical action and to L2 learning processes. She examines in considerable detail a specific phenomenon which occurs during language teaching, namely designedly incomplete utterances, which are a combination of a pedagogical and an interactional practices.

This article uses a conversation analytic framework to analyze a practice used by teachers in 1-on-1, second-language writing conferences when eliciting self-correction of students' written language errors. This type of turn, used to elicit a knowledge display from the student, is not a syntactic question or even a complete turn constructional unit. It is designed to be incomplete; hence the name designedly incomplete utterance (DIU). The teachers use DIUs made up of the students' own words to begin turns that they are prompting the students to complete. Several types of DIU are discussed, showing how their turn design is related to the action they are being used to do. DIUs are then compared to similar practices found in ordinary conversation (i.e. word searches and anticipatory completions), showing how DIUs are adaptations of these practices to accomplish specialized institutional tasks.

Error correction plays a central role in pedagogy, especially second-language pedagogy. This article uses a conversation analytic (CA) framework to analyze a practice used by teachers in one-on-one, second-language writing conferences when eliciting self-correction (Schegloff, Jefferson, & Sacks, 1977) by students, of their written language errors. The data are taken from a larger study of eight 20-min to 1-hr videotaped conferences, scheduled as part of a bridge course to freshman composition for English as a Second Language (ESL) students at a large U.S. university. I discuss several different varieties of this practice, showing how the turn design is related to the action these turns are being used to do, and how these turn designs are related to similar practices found in ordinary conversation. My aim is not to evaluate the pedagogy but to describe an institutional practice, showing how practices of ordinary conversation can be adapted for specialized institutional tasks.

One problem that writing teachers face, especially those teaching second-language writing, is how to deal with both language and content problems in writing conferences. When the focus of a sequence of talk is on something other than language error, dealing with language error interrupts the ongoing sequence and may derail it altogether, making it difficult to accomplish the pedagogical goals of that sequence. Perhaps partially because of this, the writing teachers in my study deal with written language errors in separate portions of the conference defined in some way as dealing with language problems. During these portions of the conference, the teachers in my data set tend to prompt students to self-correct *focal errors*, errors that are the focus of the sequence of talk, rather than correcting those errors themselves. Here is an example of the teacher (TJ) prompting (double arrow) for student (ST) self-correction (single arrow).

Extract 1

TJ: →> ((*reading*)) Joey Levick's life could have been saved.
→> i̲f. a̲ny of the bystanders that s̲aw him (3.0)
ST: → would have called the police?

One practice, demonstrated in Segment 1, that teachers use to elicit self-correction of written errors, is a type of turn that functions similar to a 'test' (Searle, 1969), 'known information' (Mehan, 1979), or 'display' (Long & Sato, 1983) question in that it is used to elicit a knowledge display from the student – knowledge that the teacher already has. However, this turn type is not a syntactic question or even a complete turn constructional unit (TCU). In fact, it is designed to be incomplete; hence the name designedly incomplete utterance (DIU). The DIU in Segment 1 is formed by reading a portion of student text, stopping before the 'trouble source', and leaving the remainder for the student to complete correctly.

The practice of using DIUs to initiate self-correction of spoken language errors is well known by teachers of second-language pedagogy. Omaggio Hadley (1993, p. 23), who called the practice 'pinpointing,' advocated using this technique to elicit student self-correction of errors during oral activities that focus on grammatical accuracy. In my data set, DIUs are by far the most common turn design used to elicit self-correction of focal written language errors. I first discuss DIUs used for this purpose, showing how they are constructed and how they work together with other practices to elicit self-correction. I then discuss DIUs that are used to elicit a repetition or an extension of a student's prior oral answer. Finally, I contrast these DIUs with DIUs that are used to elicit a continuation of the action in progress.

DIUs used contingently as hints

Segment 2, a portion of which was printed earlier as Segment 1, is part of a larger series of sequences in which the teacher (TJ) is modeling a strategy for the student (ST) to use to correct verb tenses on his own. This strategy involves first getting ST to name verb phrases in the first two sentences of his text. As ST names a verb phrase, TJ highlights it. This results in a series of highlighted 'candidate trouble sources'. After all verb phrases have been highlighted, TJ asks 'whaddya notice'. After a brief pause, ST says 'ah:↑dunno'. After several additional seconds of silence, during which ST displays an orientation to the text, he says 'this is wrong'. and corrects the first verb phrase highlighted. He then begins going through the remainder of candidate trouble sources; that is, highlighted verb phrases, checking them, one by one, either reading the verb phrase as is or correcting it.

Segment 2 is taken from this latter portion of the error correction sequence. After ST reads a portion of his text as is without correcting the highlighted verb phrase, TJ initiates a new strategy for self-correction. He covers ST's text and asks him to say what he had just read. When ST has trouble understanding what TJ wants him to do, TJ uses a DIU to target the verb tense error for correction by ST. This DIU is thus used contingently, when ST runs into problems correcting his text.

ST's paper is on bystander apathy. The relevant portion of ST's text is printed next. The following conventions will be used to show changes to the student text made up to this point in the conference: Boldface type represents highlighting, and italics and strike throughs show corrections made to the text. In the segments, except when otherwise noted, the double-headed arrows show the DIU, and the single-headed arrows show the student's self-correction.

Joey Levick's life **could have been save**_d_ if any of the bystanders that **saw** him **would have** the heart to called the police.

Extract 2

182 ST: saw?
183 (1.0) ((TJ *and* ST *continue eyegaze on text*))
184 TJ: saw him?
185 ST: saw him (.) would have: <the heart to call the> police?
186 TJ: ok.

187 (0.8) ((*sound of hand banging on table;* TJ *slams hand*
188 *palm down over portion of text* ST *has been reading and*
189 *turns body in chair to face* ST; *turns eyegaze to* ST;
190 *at bang,* ST *turns eyegaze to* TJ))
191 tell me what you just read.
192 (2.8) ((TJ *has eyegaze on* ST, *then turns text toward*
193 *himself, uncovers portion of text so he, but not* ST *has*
194 *access to text, and directs gaze toward text;* ST *gazes*
195 *toward text but is not in a position to read it*))
196 ST: °jus
197 (1.5) ((ST *throws back upper body and moves eyegaze*
198 *to* TJ; TJ *continues to gaze at text*))
199 ((*smile voice, surprise*)) *uh just say the first line?*
200 TJ: →> ((*reading*)) Joey Levick's life could have been saved.
201 →> if. any of the bystanders that saw him,
202 (1.0) ((TJ *turns upper body and gaze to* ST, *lifts*
203 *hand with pen in vertical motion as if conducting,*
204 *opens mouth on upward motion, closes on downward; then*
205 *does "conducting" gesture quickly three more times*))
206 (2.0) ((TJ *keeps eyegaze on* ST; ST *looks up at* TJ,
207 *then down*))
208 ST: → would have called the police?
209 TJ: [.h would have (1.0) ca:lled,
210 [(TJ *writes on text*))
211 (1.8) ((TJ *continues writing, then leans back in*
212 *chair, removing hand from text*))
213 [the police.
214 [(TJ *moves forward, places hand with pen over text*))
215 ST: °police.
216 (3.5) ((TJ *underlines in text several times*))
217 ST: o[k.

In this segment, ST reads the verb 'saw' as it was written (line 182), with upward intonation as if asking TJ to confirm that it is correct, and TJ repeats it (line 184): 'saw him?', adding the following word, 'him'. ST seems to see this repeat as a confirmation or a prompt to continue, or both.

He repeats 'saw him.' (line 185) and continues by reading the next verb with its complement, just as he has written it (except for the earlier correction of 'called' to 'call'): 'would have: <the heart to call the> police?' He finishes his reading with upward intonation as if seeking confirmation that the verb phrase is correct as it is. This verb phrase, however, is incorrect and should read 'would have' plus the past participle (i.e., 'would have had').

Rather than disconfirming the accuracy of the verb phrase ST reads, TJ begins to demonstrate a new strategy for self-correction of language errors. He covers the portion of text that ST has just read and says, 'tell me what you just read.' (line 191). TJ's new strategy may have its roots in ST's previously demonstrated ability to say correctly what he had written incorrectly. ST is an immigrant who has completed high school in the United States and has a quite good informal oral register, but he has problems with his written grammar. He has previously made two seemingly unconscious corrections while reading his text aloud. TJ seems to be trying to get him to make use of his more grammatically correct oral register to edit his written text by asking him to paraphrase the sentence rather than merely reading what he had written down. The new strategy involves reading a portion of the text, paraphrasing it without looking at it, and then comparing the paraphrase with the actual text.

After ST asks for clarification, 'uh just say the first line?' (line 199), TJ prompts ST by using a DIU to target a specific portion of text: the incorrect verb phrase. He reads the entire sentence from the beginning up to the part that needs correction: 'Joey Levick's life could have been saved. if. any of the bystanders that saw him,' (lines 200–201).

During the first part of the 3-sec pause following TJ's elicitation, TJ reinforces the invitation to complete his utterance with iconic gestures. After turning his upper body and eyegaze to ST, he brings his arm up vertically and then back down similar to a conductor signaling to a portion of the orchestra to come in at that point. He also opens his mouth wide as he brings up his arm, and closes it as the arm comes down, as if to signal a prompt for speaking. He then repeats the conducting gesture quickly, several more times.

After an additional 2-sec pause (line 206), ST completes TJ's utterance with the correct verb tense, making other changes also: 'would have called the police?' (line 208), again with upward intonation as if seeking confirmation. TJ then accepts the corrected version by repeating the first portion of it with continuing intonation, '.h would have (1.0) ca:lled,' as he simultaneously writes the correction on the text (lines 209 and 211). After a pause, during which he continues writing, TJ repeats the final portion of ST's correction, this time with final intonation, 'the police.' (line 213).

Summary

DIUs that operate on written text and are used to prompt correction of language errors in that text are *designed* as incomplete utterances: either grammatically incomplete sentences, phrases, or individual words to be continued, but not necessarily completed, by the student. These sentences, phrases, or words are taken from the student's written text. In Goffman's (1981) words, the teacher is 'animating' words 'authored' by the student. DIUs are recognizably complete actions, even though they are recognizably grammatically incomplete. In fact, their identity as recognizable actions (turns to be continued by the student) depends on them being recognizably grammatically incomplete. The DIUs can cue actual trouble sources by stopping just before a *candidate trouble source*, an instance of the type of language previously specified for repair in that sequence, usually with some prosodic marking such as a sound stretch in the last syllable, significant slowing at the end of the utterance, or continuing intonation, targeting that trouble source for correction. The prosodic marking, together with a pause and occasional gesture, as in Segment 2, can invite the student to continue the DIU. A previous framing of the activity as searching for errors, sometimes for a specific type of error such as a verb tense error, tells the student that the utterance must be continued by correcting the error. Because the DIU is eliciting self-correction of a language error and the text is often treated as a series of examples of candidate trouble sources by segmenting it intonationally into 'trouble source units', the DIU does not necessarily invite completion of a sentence or a grammatical unit – it invites completion of the task, the self-correction. Students rarely continue the sentence after the self-correction.

Before the DIU is uttered, students can be given various types of assistance to increase their chances of giving a correct answer, such as foregrounding candidate trouble sources by first highlighting them, providing a grammar explanation, or previously writing an editing symbol or a comment on the student's text. DIUs are therefore merely one in a series of practices that combine to assist the student in making the correction.

DIUs can be used to elicit correction in various sequential positions, targeting the location of the error. They can be used after a repair initiation as a hint to elicit self-correction of a student's prior verbal answer, as in Segment 2. In a sequence in which the student text is read aloud, segmenting it into candidate trouble sources DIUs can be used to target actual trouble sources, prompting correction of those errors. In sequences dealing with language errors in which the type of error is unspecified, DIUs can be used as hints to target the location of errors when the student is unable to find the error.

The design of the DIU, whether it is started from the beginning of the sentence, or is a phrase from the sentence, or a single word, depends in part on how much of the context is needed for the student to make an accurate correction, and on the type of sequence in which the DIU is used. If the teacher is doing a series of error corrections, reading the text sentence by sentence, breaking it up into candidate trouble sources, the DIUs are made up of phrases begun after the last candidate trouble source. If individual errors are being corrected, the design of the DIU varies according to the amount of context the student needs to make the correction.

Implications for research on second-language acquisition and pedagogy

I described in detail a set of practices that teachers in second-language writing conferences use to focus students on language form for self-correction. Although this study does not offer conclusions about second-language acquisition or pedagogy, it does have implications for research in these areas. I conclude with two brief implications. First, detailed descriptions of practices of second-language pedagogy are a necessary first step toward determining which practices are most effective. We cannot investigate pedagogical effectiveness if we do not know in some detail what the practices of teachers are and what functions they perform. Second, although conversational practices of talk are used in institutional settings, many of the practices of talk in institutional settings, such as DIUs, have been developed to meet institution-specific goals and are specific to the settings in which they are used. We have seen how even small variations in DIU design reflect the functions they are being used to perform. It is therefore especially important that researchers of pedagogical talk investigate individual practices for what they are being used to accomplish in a particular setting, and to avoid importing categories of analysis developed from other pedagogical settings or from ordinary conversation.

Task B2.1

➤ Define designedly incomplete utterances (DIU). What are the pedagogical functions of designedly incomplete utterances, i.e. why do teachers of writing employ them? What different kinds of DIUs are there? What kinds of non-verbal communication and prosodic features may accompany DIUs?

Task B2.2

➤ Evaluate the evidence in the article as to whether DIUs are effective or not. Are DIUs a pedagogical phenomenon, an interactional phenomenon or a combination of the two?

Task B2.3

➤ In Koshik's study, teacher utterances are treated as interactional phenomena. The study describes in detail how the specific feature (designedly incomplete utterance) is organized in interactional terms, how it is related to other features and what actions it performs. However, learning is absent from Koshik's study. What justification does Koshik give for not relating the feature to language learning processes? Do you think that designedly incomplete utterances can contribute to language learning? If so, how? Do you know of any theory of learning to which DIUs could be linked?

Task B2.3

➤ Koshik's study provides a very detailed description of how the interactional phenomenon (designedly incomplete utterance) is organized in interactional terms, how it is related to other features and what actions it performs. Now consider how you would evaluate the effectiveness of DIUs as a form of correction in L2 classrooms by comparison with other forms.

Section C
Exploration C 1

The analysis of frequencies like that in Mackey' study is a common non-parametric data analysis technique. Frequencies or tallies of phenomena are not reported as means or standard deviations, and are thus comparable to expected frequencies given the sample sizes of groups and categories. The construction of a tabulation of frequencies begins with categories of interest into which each case can be exclusively placed. In the Mackey (2006) study, two variables were of interest: whether the learners had evidenced development in their accurate use of interrogatives, and whether they had showed evidence of noticing the feedback provided to them. Open the Noticing.sav data table in SPSS and inspect the file structure. The construction of the data set can use categorical variables such as 'N' denoting non-development, contrasted with 'D', a learner who has been classified as having developed in the use of interrogatives. For the noticing variable, each learner was categorized as having demonstrated less noticing 'L' or more noticing 'M'. For all categorizations, a set of principles to justify the categories has to be applied to all cases, and needs to be verified by independent coders. As each case constitutes a unique entry, the count in the Mackey data is '1' for each of the 23 cases.

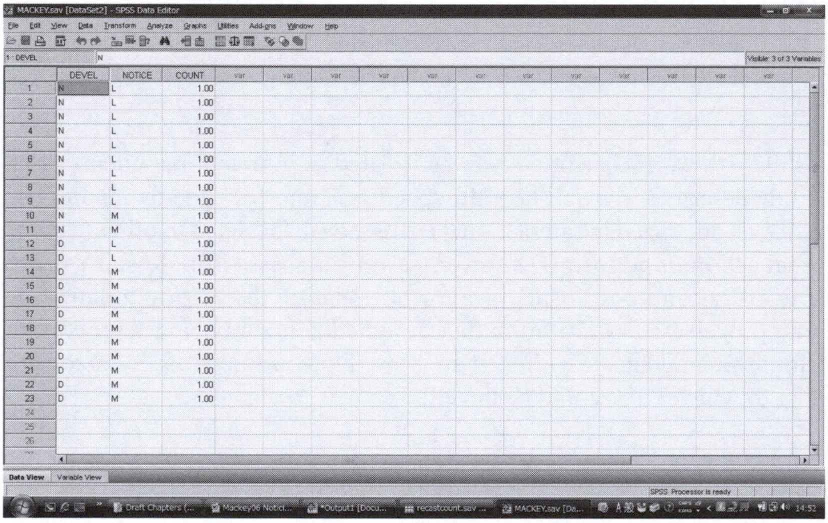

Figure 2.1 Data configuration for Noticing.sav

Reprint courtesy of International Business Machines Corporation. © SPSS Inc., an IBM company

Note: SPSS was acquired by IBM in October 2009

As there are 23 individuals and four cells in the noticing by development design, there are at least five cases that would be expected to fall into each cell if the two variables are actually independent of each other.

Task C1.1

➤ Identify the null and alternative hypotheses for the test of independence between 'noticing' and interrogative 'development'.

The test of independence can be performed through the Descriptive menu in SPSS. The Cross-tabulation option is used here because we have two variables in the design.

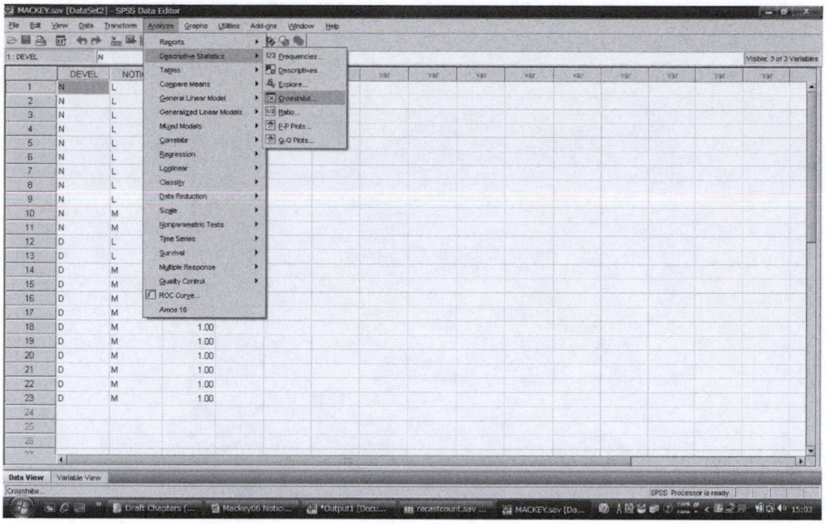

Figure 2.2 Descriptive analysis of Noticing.sav

Reprint courtesy of International Business Machines Corporation, © SPSS, Inc., an IBM company

Once the cross-tabulation has been invoked, insert the two variables into a row and column position, and insert the 'count' variable into the 'level' window.

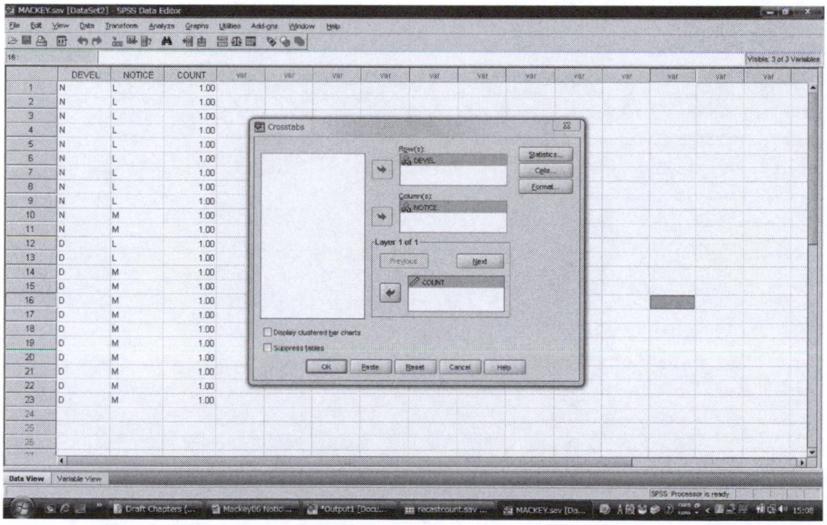

Figure 2.3 Cross-tabulation of Noticing.sav

Reprint courtesy of International Business Machines Corporation, © SPSS, Inc., an IBM company

Next, click on the STATISTICS option to specify the kind of analysis to be performed.

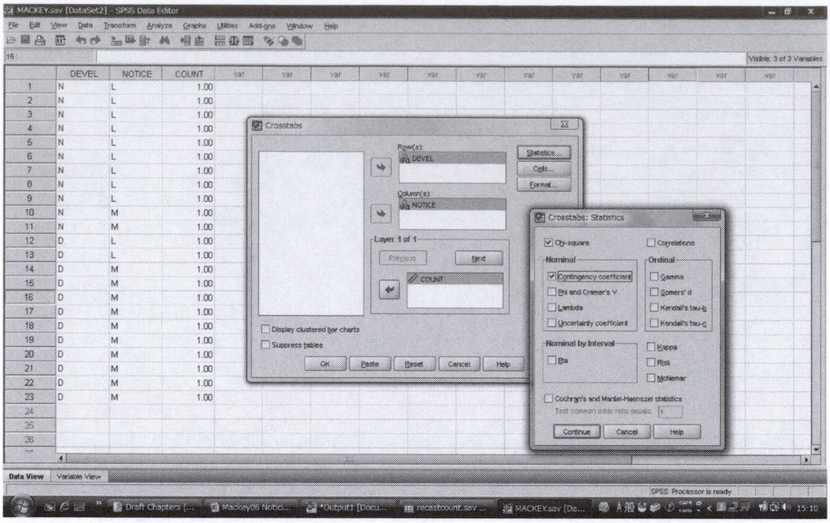

Figure 2.4 Analysis of Noticing.sav

Reprint courtesy of International Business Machines Corporation, © SPSS, Inc., an IBM company

Note that because this is a nominal 2 × 2 table (noticing/not noticing by development/no development), it has to be corrected with the contingency coefficient. For this type of test, a chi-square distribution will be appropriate. Once these have been specified, continue and click OK.

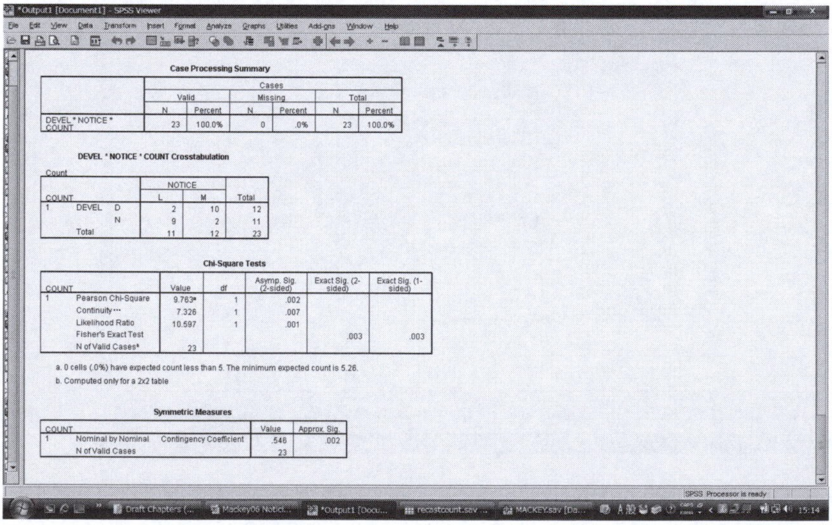
*Output1 [Document1] - SPSS Viewer

Case Processing Summary

	Valid N	Valid Percent	Missing N	Missing Percent	Total N	Total Percent
DEVEL * NOTICE * COUNT	23	100.0%	0	.0%	23	100.0%

DEVEL * NOTICE * COUNT Crosstabulation

Count

COUNT			NOTICE L	NOTICE M	Total
1	DEVEL	D	2	10	12
		N	9	2	11
	Total		11	12	23

Chi-Square Tests

COUNT		Value	df	Asymp. Sig. (2-sided)	Exact Sig. (2-sided)	Exact Sig. (1-sided)
1	Pearson Chi-Square	9.783a	1	.002		
	Continuity Correctionb	7.326	1	.007		
	Likelihood Ratio	10.597	1	.001		
	Fisher's Exact Test				.003	.003
	N of Valid Cases	23				

a. 0 cells (.0%) have expected count less than 5. The minimum expected count is 5.26.
b. Computed only for a 2x2 table

Symmetric Measures

COUNT			Value	Approx. Sig.
1	Nominal by Nominal	Contingency Coefficient	.546	.002
	N of Valid Cases		23	

Figure 2.5 Analysis results for Noticing.sav

Reprint courtesy of International Business Machines Corporation, © SPSS, Inc., an IBM company

The raw data is placed in the Notice by Development table with the cell counts in the cross-tabulation window. The chi-square test shows the continuity-corrected estimate of 7.326, which is significant at p=.007.

Task C1.2

➤ Interpret the probability of finding the distribution of the four cells in the table by random chance. Would the null hypothesis be accepted or rejected? Justify your interpretation.

Task C1.3

➤ Locate the data set Feedpref.sav. Consider this imaginary study: a survey of learner preferences for written (W) versus verbal (V) feedback from teachers is given to a group of 50 learners from Asia (A), Latin America (L), and Europe (E). Inspect the file structure. Formulate a hypothesis about preference for feedback.

Task C2.2

➤ Using SPSS Descriptive, perform a cross tabulation with a chi-square test. Note that there are three groups by two preferences, so no correction for continuity is required.

➤ Interpret the results in light of the hypothesis you formulated about expected frequencies in each cell.

Exploration C 2

Task C2.1

➤ Choose an interactional phenomenon in the L2 classroom (excluding recasts and designedly incomplete utterances). Design a research study which a) describes the phenomenon in interactional and pedagogical terms, as in Koshik's study b) investigates the effectiveness of this phenomenon in promoting language learning, connecting it to a theory of learning.

Task C2.2

➤ Examine the extent to which the two studies in this chapter are representative of different paradigms. Do you think it is possible to employ a mixed-methods approach to examine interactional phenomena relevant to language learning in a way which combines the advantages of both? If so, what would the design of such a project look like?

Task C2.3

➤ Design a project which investigates the outcomes of different classroom correction techniques using a mixed-methods approach which combines quantitative and qualitative data-gathering techniques. The aim is to answer the questions: which technique is the most effective in promoting L2 learning; which interactional and learning processes are engaged by each technique?

Task C2.4

➤ Consider the likely classroom interaction in Mackey's study on noticing. If transcripts were available, discuss the kinds of phenomena that would be amenable to a CA analysis of the interaction in the classroom.

CHAPTER 3
The classroom as a language learning environment

Section A
Introduction A1

In this chapter we explore two sides of what might be seen as the most fundamental distinction in approaches to research: that between observation and experiment, or descriptive and hypothetical-deductive research. Our purpose is not to argue the case for one or the other but to illustrate how they are approached and the thinking behind this, thus establishing a basis for understanding how they might be combined. We focus on the classroom not only because this is the setting for key learning encounters but because there are different ways of looking at it from this perspective.

Metaphorically, you might say that this chapter adopts a 'goldfish bowl' and a 'test tube' perspective, but this sort of reductionism is neither realistic nor illuminating. The classroom is many different things, and if we are to study what goes on there we need to consider it from the perspective of the purpose of our research. For example, we may have observed that certain sorts of task-based activities seem to be particularly effective in promoting the acquisition of particular forms in the target language. There may be many reasons for this, some of them peculiar to the classrooms with which we are familiar, so if we wish to make a more general claim about the effectiveness of this particular approach we will need to demonstrate that the outcomes we have observed are the result of that approach and are not influenced by other factors. In this case, we will need to establish appropriate experimental conditions and use a hypothetical-deductive design for our research.

Alternatively, we may already have completed a study using this approach and been encouraged by the outcome, but it may be clear that the changes to teaching practices that this would involve would be radical ones and that the introduction of it might be problematic. We might therefore decide that, in order to maximize the chances of successful implementation, we need to better understand the nature of the classroom communities that will be affected and the views of those who will be involved in putting the changes into practice. In this case we will need to turn to descriptive research, which will not allow us to make general claims about the advantages of one method over another but should generate the sorts of insights and understanding that will help us to make informed decisions about the process of implementation.

WORKING IN THE FIELD

Observation and interviewing involve working within a particular social/institutional environment, usually one with which the researcher is unfamiliar. This involves gaining access to the relevant setting and gaining permission to conduct research there.

Task A1.1

➤ How would you understand the term 'gatekeeper' as applied to a feature of the following description and what aspects the process of gaining access are evident here?

> [The owner of the Pen school agreed to my approaching the principal for the purposes of doing my fieldwork there.] My initial contact came via a telephone call to Jenny, the principal . . . My initial meeting with her lasted about an hour, and at the end of it she agreed to my coming to the Pen in the role of participant observer, subject to the approval of the teachers there . . . A Friday lunchtime meeting was arranged, during which I introduced myself and explained that I was interested in studying the way teachers work together and talk to one another. I emphasised that if they invited me to join them I would remain only as long as they were happy for me to be there. I explained that I would like to do some teaching in the school and to interview them about their lives and work, suggesting that eventually I might also ask if I could tape some of their staffroom talk, although I would fully understand if they felt that this would not be appropriate. We discussed the likely products of the research and I left them with some examples of my own work on teacher development to think over their response.
>
> (Richards 1996: 55–6)

The above description illustrates two key stages in the process of gaining access: negotiating with gatekeepers and representing the research. Gatekeepers are people who are in a position to refuse or allow access to the next stage in the process of gaining access. In this case the 'hierarchy of consent' (Dingwall 1980) began with the owner of the school, then involved the principal before concluding with the teachers at the Pen. The final stage also involved representing the research, a process that called for a general explanation of what the project was aiming to achieve, what data collection would involve and how it related to my other research. This is also the stage at which ethical issues (discussed in Chapter 1) can be addressed. If the process of negotiating entry is successful, the researcher can move into the field and begin data collection.

Task A1.2

➤ What does the following description suggest about the researcher's identity in the field? What are the implications of this for data collection?

> I described myself as a 'writer' who was interested in what school was like for them. Students failed to understand the term 'researcher'. Nevertheless, the students quickly gave me their own label and helped position me within the school . . . I was initially known as the 'follower', given that I followed certain students around; some even labelled me a 'leech' describing me as a person who latched onto people and sucked information from them, but as time passed I had progressed to 'Lisa'.
>
> (Russell 2005: 186)

There are various ways in which researchers might position themselves with respect to participants in the field, the most obvious distinction being between covert and overt observation, though the former would be very unusual in applied linguistics. As an overt observer, the researcher might be a participant observer (for example, by taking on teaching responsibilities) or simply an observer. Whatever the basic decision, however, this will not necessarily determine how the researcher is seen by participants, nor will his or her initial identity remain fixed – as the above extracts demonstrate.

This is not merely a matter of maintaining effective relations with participants; it also has an impact on the nature of the data collected. The researcher needs to remain sensitive to how he or she is seen by others because this may affect behaviour and will certainly influence the sorts of responses made. For example, if a researcher is seen as a teacher by a student, comments from the latter will be couched in terms 'suitable' to a teacher's ears, which is why being 'Lisa' may be very important to Russell in terms of the data she collects (these aspects are explored in more detail in her paper).

When researchers enter the field they see the world as an outsider, but as they become more familiar with it they begin to see things from the perspectives of those inside it (what is sometimes described as a shift from an *etic* to an *emic* perspective; see Sarangi and Candlin [2001] for a discussion of how these can be brought together). If they stay long enough they will lose the ability to stand outside events completely (a state sometimes referred to as 'going native'), so the decision about when to negotiate exit from the field is an important one. Of course, many researchers in applied linguistics will already have extensive experience as teachers and hence to some extent have insider status. However, contrary to some assumptions, this is not necessarily a disadvantage. As Dwyer says, '[a]s a qualitative researcher I do not think being an insider makes me a better or worse researcher; it just makes me a different type of researcher' (Dwyer and Buckle 2009: 56).

Although the insider–outsider relationship has rightly been seen as a central one in fieldwork, it is not the only relationship that is relevant to data collection. In their discussion of what they term 'the relational dimension', Sarangi and Candlin (2003: 278), drawing on Sarangi and Hall (1997), discuss different roles the researcher might adopt in applied/consultative research. Although they have the discourse analyst in mind, the aspects they highlight seem to us to be relevant to all forms of fieldwork. You might like to think of examples that might illustrate the categories they identify:

- Researcher as outsider/insider;
- Researcher as resource;
- Researcher as befriender;
- Researcher as target audience and assessor of performance;
- Researcher as expert/consultant and agent of change.

ETHNOGRAPHIC OBSERVATION

As we saw in Chapter 1, ethnography and fieldwork are inseparable, though what counts as fieldwork may vary according to circumstances. Writing five years ago, Delamont (2006: 206) noted that, anthropology excepted, the vast majority of qualitative studies over the previous 20 years had been based on interviews, and the situation has not changed. Ethnographic ('participant') observation, especially in our own field, has been sadly neglected. Even in a standard text such as Bryman's (2008) outstandingly rich introduction to social research methods, where practical advice is offered on structured observation, advice on participant observation is restricted to entry, field relations and note-taking. Yet good observation offers insights that cannot be generated by any other method of data collection.

In this section, we explore what is involved in observation, but in terms of developing practical skills, the 'classic position on fieldwork' is that 'you learn by getting your hands dirty' (Stenhouse 1984: 218.).

Task A1.3

➤ Choose a fairly busy setting with which you are familiar (a staff room would be ideal, but an office or even a café would do) and try to spend as much time as you can every day over a week or so to observe what happens there. Make notes on what you see, at the time or as soon as possible afterwards, then at the end of the period of observation reflect on the following questions:

- What did you find most difficult about the exercise? Did you find ways of overcoming initial challenges and if so what did you do?
- What aspects of the setting did you observe?
- What different sorts of cognitive processes on your part did the process involve?
- Did you notice any changes during the period of observation (e.g. in your approach to observing, the nature of your note-taking)?

One of the most obvious decisions the observer faces is what to observe, and one of the most widely known checklist of things to consider is provided by Spradley (1980), with space, actors, activities, objects, acts, events, time, goals and settings as key elements. Some writers (e.g. Corbetta 2003) follow this approach, while others (e.g. Runcie 1980, Merriam 1988) also draw attention to temporal features such as cycles, phases, frequency and duration.

All of these are important elements, but the novice observer has to begin somewhere and space offers an excellent point of departure, not least because it is something we take for granted. It is not only where action and interaction take place but also a reflection of how we choose to arrange our world. Space, as O'Toole and Were (2008: 617) observe, 'includes the interior and exterior spatial arrangements that make up our world'. There are, in fact, a number of initial questions about our social worlds that spatial arrangements might prompt:

- What space is available and how is it distributed? (*Distribution*)
- Are there distinct territories? Who inhabits them, who are the visitors and who is excluded? What are the rules relating to them? (*Territories*)
- Are particular activities related to particular spaces? Which spaces encourage particular activities and which spaces discourage them? How do people make use of the setting in their everyday activities? (*Activities*)
- Are there any spaces or rules relating to spaces that allow people to define themselves or their actions? (*Roles*)

This suggests possible steps in observation, although circumstances will dictate the best approach and strategies will develop over time:

1. Build up a description of the setting: objects and spaces.
3. Consider what these arrangements encourage/enforce.
4. Note how actors use the objects and spaces.
5. Describe the actors and their relationships.
6. Note down any relevant exchanges.
7. At all stages, review what has been learned about the setting and about observing it.

This offers a way of dealing with aspects of the setting, but it does not respond to the challenge of 'seeing' what is going on there. Extended exposure helps, but there are also strategies that can open up new perspectives. Whyte (1984: 86), for example, suggests sketching maps while Lofland and Lofland (2004) suggest that asking questions along the lines of 'What would happen if [X happened, Y changed, etc.]?' can be useful. Wolcott (1994: 161–164) recommends four general strategies that might be tried:

1. Observe and record everything.
2. Observe and look for nothing – that is, nothing in particular.
3. Look for paradoxes.
4. Identify the key problem confronting a group.

Another way of approaching this is to think in terms of the cognitive engagement between observer and setting, and Tjora's (2006: 437) 'modes of observing', based on an analysis of student field notes, provides a useful insight into what is required of the observer:

Naively describing	What did I see happen?
Generalizing	What is the interaction pattern?
Interpreting	Why are the actors doing this?
Wondering	What is in the actors' minds?
Explaining	Can this be the reason?
Quantifying	How many are there?
Dramatizing	Can my observation be interesting?
Experimenting	If I do this, what happens?
Reflecting and reacting	Being influenced by the field
Assessing	Evaluating people's behaviour

A final element in observation is making field notes. This involves more than merely 'capturing' observations because the process of writing itself prompts further recall, so field notes should be seen as part of observation rather than a separate activity. This means that whenever possible notes should be made in the field (lesson-planning or diary-keeping can provide a perfect cover in educational settings, while an obsession with texting is not likely to be remarked on in any setting) or at least as close to the experience as possible, which means that exposure to the setting may need to be limited or broken down into segments. It helps to train the memory, but even a few words jotted down at the time is better than nothing, and more detailed notes scribbled immediately after the experience will be of more use than an extensive description begun several hours later. Of course, it is important to make sure that field notes are not seen by those being observed and it is essential to ensure that no analytic notes or interpretations are brought into the setting.

This means that field notes will take various forms, from a single word scribbled in a margin to pages of typed script. It is useful to distinguish initial notes (usually handwritten) from lengthier and more detailed writing up on a computer. Styles of writing up will vary, but in may be helpful to separate description from interpretation, so that while the latter serves as a useful pointer in further observation and perhaps analysis, the former can serve as the text on which analysis is based. Section C contains an extract from field notes written up in this way and further advice can be found in Emerson *et al.* (1995) or Lofland and Lofland (2004), the latter providing an excellent introduction to fieldwork in general (anyone seeking a brief introduction to ethnography and fieldwork can do no better than Blommaert and Jie 2010).

ANALYSIS

An obvious reason for the relative neglect of observation is the length of time it requires in the field, but the challenge of analyzing field notes in the absence of any agreed and easily accessible system may also have something to do with this. As Attride-Stirling notes, while research design and data collection receive considerable attention, analysis 'suffers from gross under-reporting' (2001: 403), in part because of the lack of tools available for carrying it out. Two of the most common approaches to analysis are introduced in this section.

Task A1.4

➤ Comment on the following description as an example of how to approach the analysis of qualitative data:

> A researcher interested in teacher views of communicative language teaching spends a good deal of time breaking down this topic into various aspects informed by relevant activities and concepts such as task-based learning, fluency, information gap, etc. These then form the basis for the design of an interview guide which the researcher uses with a number of teachers involved in teaching a new curriculum. The researcher uses this guide as the basis for identifying relevant categories then selects extracts from the interviews to illustrate these.

Qualitative data analysis is neither straightforward nor easy; in fact, a sure sign of an inadequate analysis is that it is completed quickly and unproblematically. An 'analysis' of this sort will almost certainly be based on categories decided in advance by the researcher and populated by cherry-picked quotations and/or examples. Genuine analysis, however, is designed to ensure that categories and concepts emerge from the data (i.e. from the participants' own words and actions) rather than from the researcher's preconceptions.

With the exception of analytic induction, which is relatively uncommon and is based on developing hypotheses then searching for deviant cases or disconfirming evidence, all analysis involves a process of breaking down and building up the available data. Although approaches vary, the essential steps are fairly straightforward: immersion in the data and line-by-line coding; working with the codes (and data) to identify categories/themes/concepts and the relationships between them; identifying core themes and linking these to theory. While some approaches insist that all themes should emerge from the data, others view this as unrealistic and accept that researchers will normally approach analysis with some concepts in mind. The following interactions will be present throughout the process:

- Breaking down and building up;
- Writing and analysis;
- Description and interpretation.

Perhaps the most accessible and practically helpful treatment of analysis is provided by Craig and Cook (2007) in Chapter 8 ('Analysing field materials') of their introduction to ethnography, though more prescriptive advice is offered by the two dominant approaches to analysis: grounded theory and thematic analysis.

Grounded theory

The influence of this approach has been profound but also confusing because the two researchers who developed it, Glaser and Strauss (1967), came to disagree fundamentally about its nature. Leaving aside the differences resulting from this, there are also two aspects of the approach that have proved problematic. The first of these is the unrealistic expectation that all analysis will lead to the *generation* of theory. Second, as a number of researchers (e.g. Wacquant 2002, Wasserman *et al.* 2009) have observed, it is very unlikely that *all* concepts will emerge from the data – researchers inevitably carry some conceptual assumptions into the analysis.

Because there is no commonly agreed version of grounded theory (the best approach to using it is to follow the advice in a standard practical guide such as Charmaz 2006), what follows is a general representation of key features, designed to give a sense of how the process of analysis works. It involves a number of key processes: initial coding (identifying codes and concepts), constant comparison (everything compared with everything else), memo-making (a process of exploring emerging themes and connections between concepts so that codes become categories) and theoretical sampling (using emerging theory to inform further data collection).

Three types of coding are involved:

Open coding	Breaking down the data for the purpose of categorizing, conceptualizing and comparing (some researchers prefer the term 'initial coding').
Axial coding	Organizing the data, based on the 'axis' of a category. This involves relating categories to sub-categories and making connections between categories.
Selective coding	At this stage a central category (or explanatory concept) is identified, in terms of which other categories can be refined and integrated.

As will be immediately apparent, working with categories and concepts involves a process of moving backwards and forwards to the point of what Wasserman *et al.* (2009: 362) describe as a state of confidence: 'Just as postulated concepts have to enter into a dialogue with the raw observations until confidence emerges, so also do theoretical structures have to dialogue with both concepts and raw observations until confidence emerges.' Confidence, of course, is an individual matter, but grounded theory provides for three important validation checks: constant comparison, member validation and seeking negative evidence.

Grounded theory also proposes two terms that capture the process by which an explanatory picture emerges from the process of conceptual, analytical and theoretical refinement:

Constant comparison	The process by which connections between data and conceptualization are maintained, leading to the emergence of theoretical elaboration.
Theoretical saturation	The point that is eventually reached where any new data added to a particular category throw no new light on the relevant concepts.

The first of these is very clear, the second much less accessible. As a result, as Bowen points out in an excellent paper on saturation, 'explicit guidelines for determining saturation are almost nonexistent in the literature on qualitative methodologies' (2008: 138). He goes on to note that such guidelines may not actually be necessary but provides an example of his own criteria (noting that quantification is not essential):

> In my study, a data category was considered saturated if it was reflected in more than 70 percent of the interviews, confirmed by member checks (interviewee feedback on the analysed data), resonated with key informants, and made sense given prior research.
>
> (Bowen 2008: 148)

Thematic analysis

Thematic analysis is based on the identification of themes in a text at different levels, organizing them in order to reveal underlying patterns, then using this to identify global themes. There are different approaches to this, and the following description is based on the stages proposed by Attride-Stirling (2001: 390–394):

Stage A involves reducing or breaking down the text, which consists of three steps: first the material must be coded, which involves devising a coding framework and breaking the text down into segments using this. Then themes can be abstracted from these segments and refined. The final step involves constructing thematic networks, working from a preliminary arrangement of themes and the identification of *basic themes* which are then rearranged around *organizing themes*. These establish the basis for identifying *global themes*, which are then illustrated as networks, adjusted as the three sorts of themes are checked against the segments related to them.

Stage B is where the networks are described and explored in order to identify underlying patterns. This involves reading the text not in a linear manner but in terms of the three sorts of themes. The researcher then summarizes the thematic network in terms of themes and patterns.

Stage C requires the researcher to bring this summary to bear on the original research questions and relevant theory.

Attride-Stirling presents her approach in detailed steps, providing helpful network diagrams and an empirical example that takes the reader through the process, but Braun and Clarke (2006) offer in many ways a more accessible treatment that sets the approach in its broader context, offers useful practical advice and includes useful checklist of criteria for good thematic analysis (2006: 96). Their practical advice includes the following, which will apply to all qualitative analysis:

- Code for as many different themes as possible and include some of the surrounding data where these are relevant.
- Make use of visual representations when sorting the codes into themes.
- Do not to get carried away with endless re-coding but treat it like editing when writing – it's possible to tinker interminably, but you have a good sense of when the text works.
- By the time the themes are defined and named, the researcher should be able to name them in a couple of sentences.

Boyatzis (Chapter 4) provides a useful illustration of the process of developing codes and themes. Although this is based on managers' life stories and is comparative, it opens up the process of refinement and decision-making that is so important in this process.

Task A1.4

➤ Central to grounded theory and other forms of thematic analysis is the development of categories and the establishment of relationships between these (the stage known as axial coding). This is not simply a matter of identifying categories and finding examples to put in them; it is a constantly developing and shifting process that involves organization, re-organizaton, redefinition, etc. Visualization can play an important part in this, and the following task illustrates how a shift in representation not only reflected a shift in perception but also marked a change in understanding and heralded a new approach.

➤ Which of the following diagrams do you think reflects the change referred to above?

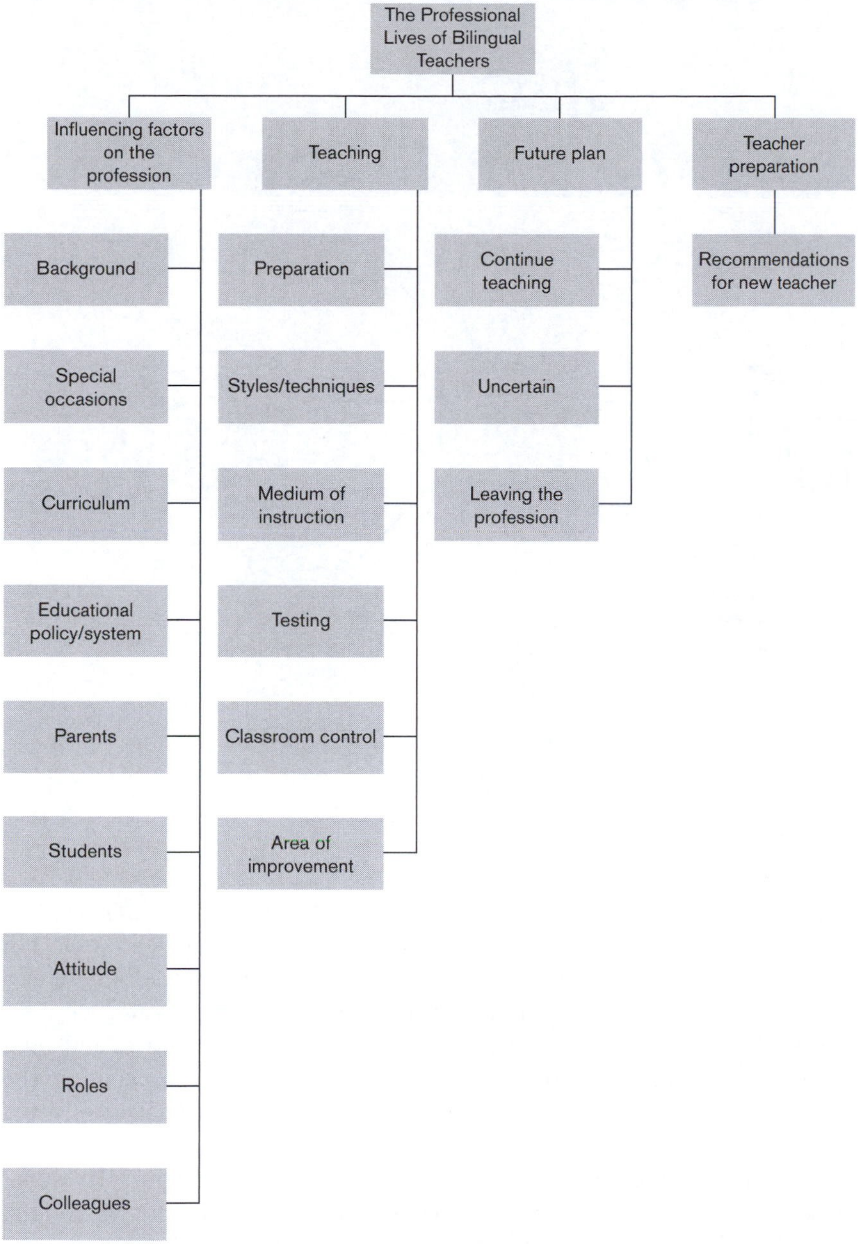

CODING DIAGRAM A

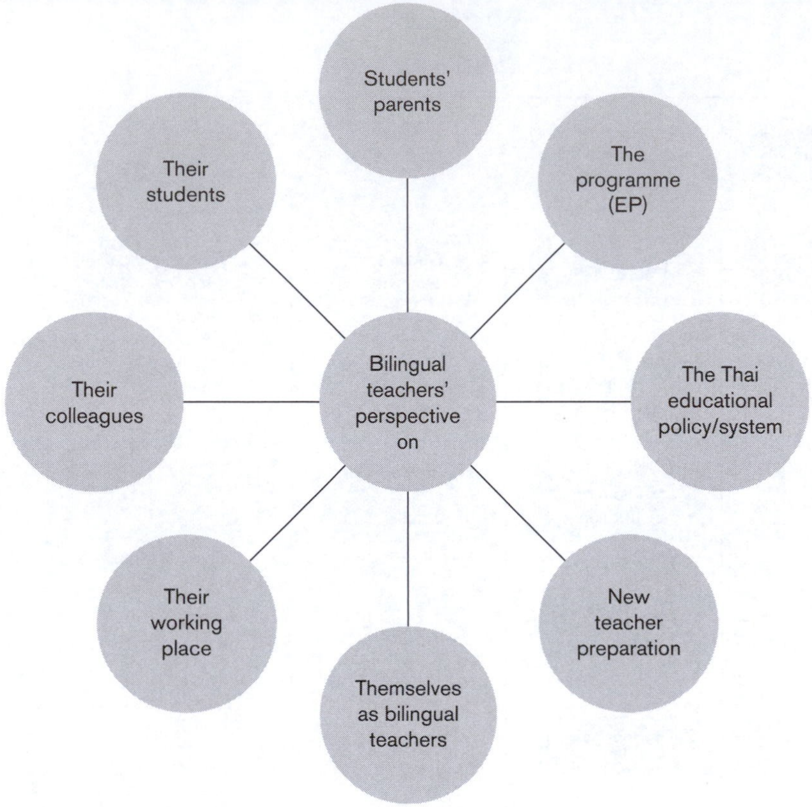

CODING DIAGRAM B

These diagrams represent a key point in the process of analysis in a Ph.D. research project using fieldwork (with observation, interviews as the main data sources) in two bilingual schools in Thailand (Tarnpichprasert 2009). Diagram A represents a fairly typical way of organizing findings, reflecting a hierarchy of categories. An arrangement like this allows the analyst to see links between categories and get a sense of how they relate, but in this case there seems to be a lack of balance in the way things have worked out. There is nothing wrong with this in itself, but the diagrammatic representation alerted the researcher to a potential problem in the way that she was thinking about the data. The perspective she had adopted was that of the researcher, who had used teachers' lives as a point of reference for her coding. However, she realized that this was creating a distortion not only in the way categories were emerging but in her perspective as an analyst. Instead, she decided, she needed to begin with the teacher's perspectives, and having spent some time revisiting the data (and experimenting with different representations of it), she produced Diagram B. This was not the end of the analytical process by any means – in fact it could almost be seen as the start – but it reflected an important shift which would ultimately help shape the thesis itself.

Introduction A2

In the mixed-method approach, both a hypothesis-testing and descriptive analysis can be deployed sequentially to establish initially whether there is any difference in an outcome of interest prior to a close up exploration of how or why the outcome turned out the way it did. In this way, descriptive analysis and a quantitative hypothesis testing apparatus complement one another in providing an optimally rich account of the research. The descriptive aspect of a mixed-method project can provide valuable information about how interventions were actually implemented. They can describe the processes by which the interventions were presented, how interaction transpired to make the intervention salient, how the interaction differed from that in the counter-factual group, and in some cases, provide the basis for an alternative interpretation of the assumed causal basis for inference. It is thus possible that the descriptive portion of a mixed-method study can illuminate how instructional processes in the intervention actually occurred in ways different from how the researchers had intended. The basis for accurate causal inference would be reinforced with such evidence.

Ethnographic accounts or micro-analysis of interaction can often provide the detail needed to understand why a null hypothesis in a hypothetical-deductive design is not rejected. The null hypothesis is in most cases assumed to be less likely than the alternative, which is a prediction about an expected outcome formulated as a test of a theory. When the null hypothesis is not rejected – for instance, when the means of two or more groups do not differ from each other – the researcher may be at a loss to explain why there was no difference. The null hypothesis may be true in the wider population, or it may be the consequence of some other process. In a mixed-method approach, a richer explanatory basis is made available, for a description of how the intervention actually differed from the counterfactual in its implementation can tell the story. It is thus possible to evaluate the quality of the study, which otherwise would not be interpreted to support the formulated hypothesis. Descriptive analysis may provide evidence the intervention never actually took place as planned, and the intended group difference was not observable because of problems in delivery of the intervention. In such cases, mistaken causal inference can be corrected with the use of descriptive and interpretive data analysis. The localized, close-up perspective thus can make hypothetical-deductive research more precise in differentiating well-articulated research from research that is ambiguous or possibly misleading.

Task A2.1

➤ Imagine a research design with both a hypothetical-deductive component and a descriptive component. Assume the focus of the research is teacher feedback on spoken errors in a classroom setting in which two teachers provide feedback, and for comparison purposes, two do not. Discuss the kind of descriptive evidence you would gather in order to confirm that the feedback was actually given in the intervention groups, and that feedback was not provided in the two counter-factual classes.

Task A2.2

➤ Review the description of Mackey's research on recasts outlined in Chapter 2. Discuss strategies that could be used to confirm that teachers actually provided substantially more recasts to the intervention group than to the counter-factual or control group. Discuss how such evidence could be gathered, and how it would be analyzed.

Section B
Development B1

Toohey, K. (1998) 'Breaking them up, taking them away': ESL students in Grade 1', *TESOL Quarterly* 32(1): 61–84.

In a discussion on evaluating research papers, Taber sums up the reader's position:

> The reader of research papers needs to be able to make judgments about the nature, quality and significance of the research reported. Making such judgments requires the report to include sufficient detail of how the focus was conceptualised, what data was collected, and how it was analysed, to be able to decide whether the researcher's findings seem justified.
>
> Taber (2007: 95)

We use Toohey's paper as an illustration of what making such judgements involves (in order to give you an idea of all the elements in the writing up of an ethnographic study, we include the full paper, divided into sections and including all notes and references, but omitting the diagram). Although it is based on a longitudinal study of a Grade 1 ESL classroom in a Canadian public (state) school and uses classroom observation and interviews to understand the nature of the classroom as a community of practice, the paper might stand for any other qualitative study in terms of how it is assessed, which is why it is reproduced in full. It focuses on three classroom practices and seeks to show how the process of differentiating participants from one another contributed to 'community stratification', resulting in the identification of some participants as 'deficient', thus effectively denying them access to practices which might have encouraged the development of linguistic competence.

If Toohey is able to make her case convincingly, then she will have exposed a hitherto unrecognized aspect of language classroom behaviour which could disadvantage those learners who have the greatest need for support. It will thereby draw attention to important issues of access and raise questions about the extent to which the problem identified by Toohey has been identified and might be addressed. Even though the evidence here is based on only one classroom, these questions are still pertinent, though of course the research can offer no evidence of how widespread these practices are.

This section will follow the organization of the paper, beginning with a couple of general questions. However, particular attention will be paid to the following aspects, covered in section A: setting up a study and researcher positioning, the visual dimension, presenting findings.

Task B1.1 Before you read

- In Chapter 1 you were introduced to different approaches to research. Which of these do you think might view L2 learning from a perspective of 'mentalism, behaviorism and individualism' (Davis 1995: 428) and what additional dimension might an alternative approach seek to explore?

- How might the concept of a community be relevant to a study of classroom behaviour and what sorts of behaviours might be relevant in research adopting this perspective?

[Introduction]

This article describes a longitudinal ethnographic research project in a Grade 1 classroom enrolling L2 learners and Anglophones. Using a community-of-practice perspective rarely applied in L2 research, the author examines three classroom practices that she argues contribute to the construction of L2 learners as individuals and as such reinforce traditional second language acquisition perspectives. More importantly, they serve to differentiate participants from one another and contribute to community stratification. In a stratified community in which the terms of stratification become increasingly visible to all, some students become defined as deficient and are thus systematically excluded from just those practices in which they might otherwise appropriate identities and practices of growing competence and expertise.

> I said: 'Some people do know more than others. That contributes to the impression that someone, somewhere, knows the whole thing.'
>
> 'Neapolitans know a lot,' said Gianni. 'But they know it collectively. Break them up, take them away, and they're hopeless, just as stupid as anyone else. It's the city, the phenomenon of Naples itself, that knows something.'
>
> (Hazzard, 1970, p. 38)

In a recent special-topic issue of TESOL *Quarterly* devoted to qualitative L2 education research, Davis (1995) argues that most second language acquisition (SLA) studies typically investigate L2 learning from the perspectives of 'mentalism, behaviorism, and individualism' (p. 428).[1] In such work, the concern is to investigate the processes by which individuals internalize aspects of the target language, and the notions of individual, internalization, and target language are taken to be unproblematic and uncontested.[2] Willett (1995) notes that this individualistically oriented SLA research has neither given conclusive results nor adequately accounted theoretically for the 'complex social context that interpenetrate individual functioning' (p. 474). Davis notes that there has been a 'dearth of socially situated SLA studies' that would view acquisition 'not only as a mental individualistic process, but one that is embedded in the sociocultural contexts in which it occurs' (p. 432).

Like Willett, Davis, and others, I am interested in how the learning of L2s can be conceptualized and investigated as situated cultural, institutional, and historical practices. My research, using a perspective based on sociocultural theories of children's development, investigates Canadian public school classrooms in which young children learn ESL over time. I wish to contribute to a discussion in which L2 learning and teaching are investigated in such a way as to include centrally the 'social, cultural and political dynamics of second language classrooms' (Pennycook, 1990, p. 16). Using a community-of-practice perspective (Lave & Wenger, 1991; Rogoff, Baker-Sennett, Lacasa, & Goldsmith, 1995) rarely applied in L2 learning research, I see the children in my study adopting community practices for using and interpreting oral and written English through participation in the social life of the classrooms in which they spend their time.

In this article I illustrate how three classroom practices I observed in a specific context constructed L2 learners as individuals and, as such, reinforced the traditional SLA perspective. I argue that the individualizing practices of this classroom, as they differentiated participants from one another, contributed to practices of community stratification. Finally, I argue that in a stratified community in which the terms of the stratification become increasingly visible to all, some students become defined as deficient and are thus systematically excluded from just those practices in which they might otherwise appropriate identities and practices of growing competence and expertise.

(Toohey 1998: 61–62)

LEGITIMATE PERIPHERAL PARTICIPATION IN COMMUNITIES OF PRACTICE

Task B1.2 Before reading

- In this section, the author questions Lave and Wenger's division of participants in communities of practice into either 'newcomers' or 'old-timers', suggesting that it may fail to represent adequately the experience of L2 learners in the classroom. She indicates that evidence of this will emerge from her study, but you might like to speculate on why such a division might be inadequate and what indications of this might emerge in this section.

Legitimate peripheral participation in communities of practice

Lave and Wenger's (1991) examination of learning and social practices begins with what they call *communities of practice*: the relations between groups of people engaged in specific, local, historically constructed, and changing practices. From their perspective, communities of practice include old-timers and newcomers, and learning is a process whereby newcomers to a community participate in attenuated ways with old-timers in the performance of community practices. The notion of 'legitimate peripheral participation' (p. 29) is suggested by Lave and Wenger to describe the engagement of participants who have varying degrees of familiarity with the practices of the community in those practices.

Recognizing that participants in any specific community might well have unequal access to particular identities, practices, and community resources, Lave and Wenger (1991) note that the 'social structure of the community of practice, its power relations, and its conditions for legitimacy define possibilities for learning (i.e. for legitimate peripheral participation)' (p. 98). Despite their recognition of the varieties of power relations (instantiated in community practices) that are possible in communities, their discussion of legitimate peripheral participation includes an analysis of only two sorts of participants: newcomers and old-timers, involved in 'learning trajectories' (p. 36), by which they move toward 'full participation' (p. 37) as they engage in community practices over time. Possible difficulties with this characterization, at least in the contexts with which I am familiar, are discussed later.

In the classrooms in which I observed, I examined participants (including myself) as members of communities of practice. From this perspective, L2 learners are seen as participants situated in one or more particular local communities and engaging in the practices of those communities. The practices of any particular local community might differ from those of other local communities. In a kindergarten community in which I observed, the identities, social practices, and resources available to two L2 learners appeared to be distributed such that their active verbal participation in the classroom was not essential and even could be seen as detrimental to their obtaining desired social ends there (Toohey, 1996).[3] Conceptualizing L2 learning as a process of moving from being an outsider to being an insider (marked either centrally or coincidentally by growing individual proficiency in the L2) was much too simple a way to describe at least these children's experiences in their classroom. These children were inside by virtue of their presence in the classroom (as legitimate peripheral participants), but inside was not a place wherein participants moved inexorably toward fuller and more powerful participation.

Mehan (1993) proposes a way of working from this perspective: 'In this line of work, people's everyday practices are examined for the way in which they exhibit, indeed, generate, the social structures of the relevant domain' (p. 243). Examining specific community practices in situations wherein some participants are a priori defined as L2 learners may allow one to see in more useful detail the social structures of these domains. In addition, L2 educators might examine these everyday practices to assess their social justice and to consider whether they might or should be accepted, resisted, or changed by particular participants over time.

(Toohey 1998: 62–64)

One of the things that might strike a reader as unusual about this paper is the absence of an extended discussion of relevant research. There are a few mentions in the opening section that position the research generally, but this section concentrates almost entirely on Lave and Wenger's work, with a reference to Mehan and a mention of another study by the author. One of the reasons for this is that, as the author says, this type of study is very unusual, but the main reason is that a core contribution of the paper is the light it throws on what it means to be a participant in a particular sort of community, so it is important to establish the relevant theoretical context at the outset.

The section introduces the concept of *communities of practice* and discusses participation in such communities in terms of being a 'newcomer' or 'old-timer', but it turns on the fulcrum of '[p]ossible difficulties with this characterization' at the end of the second paragraph. Drawing on the evidence of an earlier study she conducted, the author suggests that an insider/outsider division is too simplistic and suggests that being 'inside' a community does not necessarily lead to fuller participation. She therefore turns to the work of Mehan to situate her own study in the context of understanding how social structures are generated by participants, suggesting that situations in which some participants are defined in advance as L2 learners might be particularly relevant. By this point, the reader has a clear idea of how the research is oriented and what in general the researcher will be looking for, but no specific research questions are provided.

SCHOOL AND CLASSROOM COMMUNITY

As we saw in the first chapter, the issue of context is something that separates ethnographic research from conversation analysis, so the way this is represented in the former is particularly important. One of the reasons this paper has been chosen is because of the care it takes to describe the research setting and position the researcher within it.

Task B1.3 While reading

- What sort of information would you expect to have about the research setting and to what extent does this section provide it?
- How is research positioning integrated into the discussion and how is the presence of the researcher shown to be relevant in terms of interpretation?
- In what ways does the researcher share her thinking with the reader?

School and classroom community

The school in which this study was conducted was located on a busy four-lane suburban street near a large shopping mall in western Canada. The streets around the mall area were considered to be fairly dangerous because of youth violence at night, but during the day people considered the area simply busy because of the mall, other businesses, and a great deal of vehicular traffic leading to and from a nearby highway. The school catchment area residences were mixed: Low-rent, well-maintained townhouses lined the busy street with similarly well-kept single family dwellings located on the streets behind. The school itself was old and run-down; its demolition and the construction of a new school building had been delayed because of a government funding freeze. Most classrooms enrolled children from a wide range of L1 backgrounds: There were children who spoke Polish, Persian, Kurdish, Spanish, Japanese, Cantonese, Punjabi, Tagalog, Vietnamese, and other Southeast Asian languages as L1s. In almost every classroom in the school, about half of the enrollment consisted of children whose home/first languages were other than English.

I closely observed initially six and finally four children in this school from the beginning of their kindergarten year in October 1994 until the end of their Grade 2 year in June 1997. Selected as subjects in kindergarten were Harvey,[4] whose parents spoke Teochew as an L1; Amy, whose L1 was Cantonese; Julie and Adam, whose L1 was Polish; and Surjeet and Randy, whose L1 was Punjabi. In September 1995 these children were placed together in a Grade 1 classroom of 22 children, 11 of whom were designated as ESL students.[5] The bilingual students in the Grade 1 classroom at the beginning of the year spoke Polish (three students), Tagalog (one student), Cantonese (four students), Punjabi (two students), and Hindi (one student). The children's classroom teacher, Ms. Jones, was bilingual in English and French, was in her third year of teaching, and had had most of her previous public school teaching experience in teaching ESL pullout classes. Five of the bilingual students (Surjeet, Amy, Adam, and two others) were removed from the classroom for about 40 minutes two mornings a week for instruction by an ESL specialist. Another student, the Tagalog speaker, had not attended kindergarten in Canada and was deemed to have such severe English deficiencies that he was pulled out on his own. In an interview, the ESL teacher said that she had decided to work with her ESL charges outside of their classroom because 'there [were] such dramatic behaviour difficulties on the part of the other children, they [the ESL students] needed a break.' Ms. Jones' class had a reputation among some of the other teachers in the school as a particularly difficult group of children, and four of the students in the class saw the school counselor regularly.[6]

I visited this school for 3 school years, observing the same group of subjects in kindergarten, Grade 1, and Grade 2. I kept field notes of my observations and tape-recorded the children's conversations during my weekly, half-day visits. I very rarely interacted with the children and tried hard to be an unobtrusive observer. Tape recordings of the children's interactions with one another were selectively transcribed. Once a month, the class was videotaped by a professional technician. The children's classroom teacher was interviewed formally three times over the course of the year. The ESL teacher was interviewed formally once in December, and informal discussions with the classroom and ESL teachers took place throughout the year.

Like the children and the teacher, I was a legitimate peripheral participant in the classroom community. I became dramatically aware in this classroom of the importance of the observer's location or position, not only in terms of my identity as an adult and a researcher (and the freedom and power these entail) but also in terms of the positioning of my body vis-à-vis the positioning of the bodies of the children I was watching. The Grade 1 classroom was furnished with individual desks for all the students, unlike their kindergarten classroom, in which they had selected seating for themselves at round and rectangular tables. The boundaries of the desks were perceptually distinct, the spaces between desks were regulated, and joining a child at a desk felt much more intrusive to me than joining a group of children at a table, where the boundaries of each child's individual space were much less distinct. The desks were strung out in three rows across the room. As an adult and a researcher, I could legitimately move around the room with much more freedom than could any of the children. However, the aisles between the desks were very narrow, and it was difficult for an adult to move quickly or easily between them and to hear children who were at any distance. In addition, because of an injury that made it difficult for me to move easily, I became even more acutely aware that a classroom's spatial arrangements affect the movement and activity (and thus the knowledge) of participants who are not legitimately or physically able to move with ease and to choose freely their physical location with respect to others.

Classrooms are busy arenas, and even with limited participation such as mine, field work yielded very rich and extensive data. Observations about the children's physical arrangement, their borrowing and lending practices, and their oral and written copying are foci in this article, but there are, of course, many other ways of describing the data. Physical arrangements were an initial focus for me during the field work as I attempted to understand how activities in this Grade 1 classroom were the same as and different from what I thought I had seen in the children's kindergarten. My growing sense that the community had been broken up to some extent, as well as my own short-lived immobility, made me alert to patterns of placement and mobility. I kept detailed notes on the children's physical location throughout the field work. At the same time that I was developing the conviction that the children were isolated from one another, I began to see examples of actions that contradicted this interpretation: It became apparent to me that some children were actively using the act of borrowing to sustain frequent interactions with one another. I also made detailed notes on borrowing excursions (described below). As I observed the borrowing and lending of material goods, I began also to think about the borrowing and lending of intellectual property in the classroom, and this led me to document copying practices in the field observations.

Subsequently I examined field notes with regard to these matters, and I isolated, classified, and analyzed borrowing, lending, and copying episodes. In addition, the very high quality of the videotapes allowed repeated and systematic analysis of incidences of the practises of interest.[7] Both my research assistants and I examined the videotapes to see if the interaction on them corroborated or contradicted the patterns I believed evident in the field notes. In the descriptions of the practises below, I provide examples in which a particular practise was suspended or contradicted by other practises in the room. In addition, I solicited the teacher's opinions about the accuracy of the observations.

The researcher's view from the back and sides of the classroom, where one bears no responsibility for maintaining order or accomplishing legally binding educational objectives, can be, I believe, radically different from the teacher's view. In addition, a researcher's perspective is often constructed a good deal later in time than the teacher's, whose work with (different) children continues. Informal conversations throughout the field work allowed me to check impressions and matters of fact with the teacher as they came up, and I solicited Ms. Jones' overall impression of my perspective in response to a draft of this article.

Ms. Jones believed that my descriptions of the children's behaviour and the classroom practices were accurate. She felt that the specific practises of her classroom had been necessary because of its specific circumstances, which she interpreted somewhat differently than I did. She mentioned that she had been acutely aware that her classroom was located immediately adjacent to the school library and to an intermediate classroom, and she felt this placement meant she had to be extra vigilant in making sure her students were not noisy or disruptive. She also thought that the particular combination of children in her classroom presented extra challenges.

> 1. If you're teaching an ESL group of kids . . . you want them in groups where there's a lot of talking and dialogue going on. And as encouraging as much language use, even if it's like sharing, getting up out of your desk and running around the classroom. But for a regular Grade 1 classroom, when you have such a mix and behaviour problems, if you allow that kind of freedom, you know . . . it's chaos. So that's why I didn't allow it to happen. But ideally, if you have the right combination of kids and it's an ESL classroom, by all means, groups and talk, talk, talk. But when you have behaviour problems, ADHD [attention deficit hyperactivity disorder] kids who are disruptive, you're asking for trouble, because those kids need as much structure as possible.
>
> (IN, Gr1T, 1997)[8]

The teacher also felt that, because she was relatively new to the school and was to be evaluated internally that year, her practices needed to be congruent with those of the other teachers in the school. These constraints were not salient to me as I focused closely on the group of children in the room, and they underline the differences in our perspectives. Nevertheless, feeling more comfortable in her milieu, after that school year Ms. Jones was planning instruction for the next year's students that she felt would more closely reflect her own beliefs, and she expressed an interest in exploring alternative practices especially with regard to management of the physical and intellectual resources of the classroom.

(Toohey 1998: 64–68)

The section provides a detailed description of the urban context in which the school is set, implying that the pupils are drawn from this environment, though this is not made explicit. We are also provided with details of their linguistic backgrounds, including those of the six (later four) who were the focus of the study. However, we are not told why these six were chosen for special attention, and this represents a shortcoming. We also learn that the class is seen by other teachers as 'a particularly difficult group of children', though the author does not elaborate on this. In terms of the research, the teacher is represented in the same way as the researcher, as 'a legitimate peripheral participant in the classroom community', so this explains why we learn little about her beyond the fact that she is relatively new to the school. Her views of classroom organization and discipline, however, are represented.

This information is gleaned from an interview with the teacher, but the main form of data collection is observation, which took place on weekly half-day visits over three years. There are no rules about what constitutes 'adequate' exposure to the field in educational settings, but if we assume that the school year lasts 40 weeks this gives a figure of approximately 60 full days of attendance, which is very much in line with Hammersley's 62 days (1980: 305), the 60 days spent by Nias and her associates (1989: 5) and Richards' 57 days (1999: 146). This involved traditional fieldwork, featuring observation and field notes, supported by informal conversations and more formal interviews, but the researcher also recorded classroom interaction and video recordings were made once a month. From an ethnographic perspective, this looks like a very solid design, offering multiple perspectives but placing the researcher at the heart of data collection. We also get a sense of how triangulation was used, learning why teacher interviews were important and how field notes informed the analysis of video recordings. There is also an example of participant validation in the teacher's agreement with Toohey's reading of the children's behaviour.

It is a commonplace in ethnographic research that the researcher is the primary instrument of data collection and, as Ball notes, 'ethnographic fieldwork relies primarily on the engagement of the self' (1990: 158). One of the most interesting aspects of this section is the way researcher positioning is handled. It covers a number of different aspects, which might be summarized as follows:

Physical	The researcher is positioned at the back or side of the class, but this offers a very different perspective from that of the teacher, located at the front of the class. This both prompted and informed interviews with the teacher. The arrangement of desks meant that joining an individual child was much more intrusive than joining a group at a table.
Social	By virtue of their position, the teacher and the researcher had much more freedom to move around than the children. However, a temporary physical disability led the researcher to recognize constraints that might otherwise not have been apparent.
Analytical	As a result, the researcher became more aware of the constraints (physical and social) on movement imposed by the arrangement of the classroom. This awareness made her more conscious of issues of placement and mobility, which in turn led to a perception of isolation but also insights into how some children overcame this by borrowing. Reflection on borrowing practices in turn prompted the documentation of copying practices.

Temporal The retrospective construction of perspective by the researcher is different from the teacher's more immediate and continuing engagement, so this also informed interviews. We are also invited to consider how the researcher's understandings developed (see the previous point), in part as a result of her temporary incapacity.

A good ethnographer will take the reader into the field experience itself, and this is what Toohey does, allowing us to see the classroom from her perspective and taking us through some of the thought processes that informed her data collection. We are also invited to share the teacher's perspective on the classroom (which highlights the proximity of the library) and the children, described in her own words. The theme of movement is woven through the section in ways that allow us to see its relevance to the classroom community and the researcher.

PRACTICES IN GRADE 1

One of the challenges faced by any researcher who wishes to present the results of fieldwork is how to organize this and how to select relevant extracts from the data set. This demands a combination of general description and individual examples highlighting participants or events. This is achieved by embedding vignettes within more general descriptions or drawing on brief extracts from recorded exchanges or interviews. However, for it to be effective, the organization of the text must be very clear.

Task B1.4 While reading

- What does Toohey use as the basis for organizing her discussion, and what advantages does this have?
- Are there any differences in the general characteristics of each section in terms of representation?
- What sorts of claims does the author make and what is the status of these?

(Paragraphs in this extract are numbered for ease of reference.)

Practices in Grade 1

[1] I believe three practices of the classroom community in which I observed contributed to the *breaking up* of the children; that is, the reinforcement of the conviction that each child was an individual learner who, on his or her own, negotiated classroom life and internalized more or less efficiently the intellectual (and linguistic) resources provided by the classroom teacher. The practices examined here include (a) the

location of participants, (b) the management of the material, and (c) the source of the intellectual resources needed to complete school tasks. None of these practices is in any way unusual in the primary classrooms with which I am familiar, although they are somewhat different from the practices in the children's kindergarten classroom. I wish to explore my perceptions of how these practices in this particular locale affected the group of students I observed.

Sitting at your own desk

[2] The physical placement of participants in a classroom is one of those everyday practices 'which . . . exhibit, indeed, generate the social structures of the relevant domain' (Mehan, 1993, p. 243). Figure 1 shows the placement of furniture in the Grade 1 classroom and the seating arrangement of the children with regard to the L1s of the children and the placement of the students. Students who are referred to in this article are identified by name in the figure. Although the teacher had enacted several other arrangements, this one was the most long-lived, prevailing from the end of February to the end of the school year in June. The teacher's customary position is also noted, and it was her position and the direction in which the children faced that established the 'front' of the room. As an observer, I moved around the room at will, sitting or standing beside the children I was observing. In Grade 1, at the beginning of the year the teacher assigned the children to individual desks, and when the children were engaged in many classroom activities, the understanding was that they were to remain at those desks unless otherwise directed.[9]

[3] Commonly in classrooms, teachers assign seating to children on the basis of matters to do with management (e.g., they do not put two noisy friends beside one another, they put a noisy child beside a quiet one, they keep children who are unlikely to complete assignments or who might be suspected of daydreaming closer to the teacher's customary position). Ms. Jones remarked that such considerations guided her decision making in this Grade 1 classroom, and as she received new information about children, as new children joined or left the class, and as she devised new strategies for encouraging them to complete tasks, she announced and enacted new seating arrangements. The children collaborated with the teacher in enforcing the classroom practice with regard to staying at one's own desk.

2. *Luke*: Can we work at somebody else's desks?
   Ms. Jones: No, you work at your own desk. That's why you have one. (FN 2.1.96.11)

3. [Surjeet goes over to Amy's desk.]
   John: Surjeet, get in your desk! (FN 2.8.96.29)

[4] Figure 1 shows that many of the children learning ESL in this classroom were seated near the front of the room and that no children speaking the same L1s (other than English) were seated together.[10] Some of the Anglophone children were seated beside and among the bilingual children; these Anglophone children were perceived by the teacher not to be managing well the demands of the Grade 1 curriculum. With these children closer to the position she most commonly occupied at the central hexagonal table, the teacher felt she was more easily able to help them. It was evident that she was able to monitor the conversations and actions of those children closely. The Anglophone children whom the teacher perceived to be clearly in no danger of difficulties in school were seated on the right at the back of the room. They were observed

engaging in lengthy conversations with one another, conversations that mostly went uninterrupted by the teacher. Natalie, for example, frequently read and described to her neighbours the plots of the chapter books she was reading.

[5] Julie (L1 Polish) was seated in a back row; on either side of her were boys with whom she very seldom interacted. Julie was perceived by the teacher to have only minor problems because of her ESL learner status, and she was also perceived to be well behaved. Indeed, Julie was very quiet in the classroom that year, although, as in kindergarten, she continued to appear lively, socially active, and verbal on the playground.

[6] Adam (L1 Polish) was placed at the front corner of the room beside Ricardo, a student who had arrived in September from the Philippines and who was perceived to have the most serious English language deficiencies of all the students in the classroom. Adam was so placed because the teacher felt that she could monitor his completion of tasks more effectively if he were closer to her. It is my impression that Adam spoke very little after he was moved beside Ricardo, who had difficulty both understanding and responding to Adam's initiations.[11]

[7] Surjeet (L1 Punjabi) was seated beside an Anglophone girl who, although verbally active, seldom spoke with Surjeet. Surjeet interacted more with another Anglophone girl seated across the aisle from her to her left (Tiffany) and with another Anglophone girl seated in the same row on the far left (Mary). Surjeet's interactions with Tiffany were mostly friendly, but Mary frequently initiated unfriendly conversations with or about Surjeet.

4. *Mary* [to Tiffany]: Don't go to Surjeet's birthday. It would be Indian smell. [wrinkling nose]
   Tiffany: I won't.
   Mary: Will you come to my birthday? I'm Irish.
   Tiffany: OK.
   [Surjeet covers her ears and turns away.] (FN 2.8.96.28)

[8] Randy (L1 Punjabi) moved away in November, but before his move he was seated at the back of the classroom between two Anglophone boys with whom he had apparently enjoyable, sustained conversations. As mentioned earlier, Ms. Jones considered Randy to be one of her highest achieving students.

[9] Amy (L1 Cantonese) was seated at the front of the room beside an Anglophone girl who was frequently absent. Amy talked to this girl when she was present and to the Polish L1 boy in her row. Her borrowing excursions (described below) afforded her more opportunities to talk to children to whom she wished to talk.

[10] None of the children who were primary subjects of my study was seated beside children with whom they typically chose to play at playtime. None of them was placed beside children who spoke their L1. By placing Adam, Amy, and Surjeet close to her, the teacher could monitor and sometimes terminate conversations with the peers with whom the three did sit. Their seating facilitated conversations with the teacher, but I did not see her holding extended conversations more often with these children than with others.

[11] The children did not always sit at their desks. They also sat daily on the floor at the back of the room for the teacher's readings of stories, discussions, and sharing time. Although Adam, Randy, and Julie were relatively immobile during such times, maintaining what looked like close attention to the speaker, Amy and Surjeet were very mobile, with Surjeet often moving seven or eight times during a 10-minute reading. By the end of the year, both girls were observed to start on the floor but to move to their desks quite soon after the group had assembled itself on the floor, occupying themselves with tidying their desks, drawing, or watching other children.[12]

[12] During the previous year, in kindergarten, the Chinese- and Polish-speaking children I observed had sustained L1 subcommunities within the larger kindergarten community (Toohey, 1996). I wondered if the different physical arrangements of the Grade 1 classroom, as well as other factors, had contributed to the fact that, at least publicly within the classroom, the children very infrequently spoke their L1s except when they were so addressed by their parents when visiting the classroom at school opening or closing.

[13] One of the objectives and effects of placing the children in this way was apparently to restrict some children from conversing with some other children and for the teacher to watch some children more closely than others. On the other hand, as described in the next section, the ways in which the children managed their material resources appeared to provide them with opportunities to resist their physical separation from one another to some extent at least.

Using your own things

[14] The second practice of interest here has to do with the distribution and management of material resources in the classroom. The children in this classroom (unlike some other primary classrooms, in which resources are stored and utilized communally) were individually responsible for keeping their resources for task completion (crayons, scissors, rulers, glue sticks, notebooks, and the like) in box-shelves built under their individual desks. The teacher frequently reminded the children of the classroom rule to use their own materials, and some of the children, as well, reminded others.

5. *Surjeet*: Adam, use your own things, not other people's. (FN 11.15.95.4)

[15] The children in this classroom also engaged in a home reading program in which every day each child took home one of the collection of early literacy readers provided by the school. These books were taken home in addition to those the children selected at the school library once a week.

6. *Ms. Jones*: Boys and girls, it's silent reading. You each have to have your own book. (FN 2.1.96.14)

[16] The box-shelves in which materials were stored were short vertically, deep, dark, and placed so that the children had to huddle low in their chairs or get out of their chairs and squat on the floor to see inside. The children frequently lost or misplaced their individually owned materials in or outside their desks. In addition, when the children lost or used up some or any of their supplies, they were responsible for telling

their parents to replace them. Many children's supplies were incomplete fairly soon after school opening.

[17] Many of the children in this classroom solved their problems with keeping and managing their own inventory of materials by asking other children to lend them materials. Borrowing and lending led to social interaction, some conflict, and physical movement in the classroom. Whereas some children most frequently borrowed from the children sitting next to them, others would move to other children's locations to borrow. The teacher did not always tolerate this movement around the classroom, and the children knew she could terminate their movements.

[18] Julie's and Adam's lending and borrowing practices are somewhat simpler to describe than are those of the other two subject children. Julie and Adam borrowed relatively infrequently, and in no example in the data was Julie asked to lend her materials to others. Adam borrowed reciprocally with Ricardo and occasionally moved across the room to ask the L1 Polish boy sitting at the opposite corner to lend him felt crayons.

[19] Surjeet's and Amy's patterns of borrowing were more complex. Amy initially did not move much around the classroom to borrow, as for some months before the arrangement noted in Figure 1 she was seated by two boys who borrowed reciprocally with her. Later in the year, beginning in February according to the videos and my field notes, Amy began to range further afield to borrow. She would move around the classroom, lean on the desk of the potential lender, and engage him or her in short conversations. In kindergarten Amy had engaged in a great deal of friendly and affiliating behaviour with other children, and the girls in her kindergarten especially had treated her initiations positively (Toohey, 1996). Small, physically adept, and attractive, Amy had been a welcome peripheral participant in the activities of her kindergarten classmates. Her habits of soliciting connections with other children appeared to survive her physical separation from them, and she borrowed even when she had her own materials easily available. She seldom lent anything to others (and was seldom asked to lend anything); on those infrequent occasions when other children used her things, they went into her desk on their own, with her tacit permission, and retrieved the materials themselves.

[20] Surjeet, unlike Amy, was not always a welcome participant in the activities of other children, either in kindergarten or in her Grade 1 classroom. I have already described Mary's occasional hostile initiations with her. From the middle of February, Surjeet sat beside another Anglophone girl, Carla, who also was occasionally unfriendly toward her. Carla was observed rebuffing Surjeet's conversational advances and refusing to lend her materials. After a few refusals, Surjeet did not solicit the loan of materials from Carla. However, she often borrowed felt crayons from Mary (who was also occasionally hostile) as well as from Tiffany, seated closer beside her. Surjeet had to move a little away from her desk to borrow, especially from Mary, but I did not have the sense that the purpose of her solicitation was primarily to engage the lender in friendly conversation, as it appeared to be with Amy. Rather, Surjeet sometimes seemed fairly tense when borrowing from Mary, as if, I surmised, she was aware that her presence or her request might lead to a hostile remark. She was not apparently tense when exchanging materials with Tiffany; these interactions seemed friendly and easy. Surjeet was an enthusiastic lender and was alert to occasions on which the

children seated near her could use one of her resources. Despite Carla's unfriendliness, Surjeet continued to offer to lend her materials.

[21] The Anglophone children in this classroom also borrowed and lent materials. In particular, it was evident that several of the Anglophone boys roamed quite freely around the class on borrowing excursions. The Anglophone girls moved less, but their choices about whom to lend to and from whom to solicit loans, like the boys', was reflective of their changing social allegiances. Items that were particularly attractive were often solicited by many children. The Anglophone children who sat at the back of the room often appeared to have the most attractive materials in terms of other children's requests to borrow them.

[22] From the above description, it seems evident that borrowing and lending practices in this classroom were reflective of the social relations of the children therein. Two of the subject children lent and borrowed little; these particular children were also relatively quiet verbal participants in their classroom. One of the subject children borrowed a great deal from other children in what appeared to be attempts to solicit enjoyable affiliations with them. For the final subject child, borrowing and lending did not appear always to lead to enjoyable interactions with other children.

In this classroom borrowing and lending material resources were practices that intersected with the social relations of the community participants. These issues are also evident with regard to how some of the intellectual resources of the classroom were managed.

Using your own words and ideas

[23] In this Grade 1 classroom, as in many other classrooms, the teacher frequently enjoined the children to 'do their own work,' and the children quickly learned the 'rule' and enforced it themselves.

7. [Amy (L1 Chinese) is drawing a picture on a piece of paper on Adam's (L1 Polish) desk.]
Ms. Jones: Oh no, Amy, you're supposed to do that on your own. Everybody needs to do this sheet on their own. I need to know what everybody can do on their own. (FN 10.96. 13)
8. *Luke*: Ms. Jones, can I help Rita?
Ms. Jones: No.
[Luke goes to Rita's desk.]
John: [classmate sitting next to Rita, to Luke]: Ms. Jones said no.
[Luke sits on a bench near Rita.]
John: Luke, I'm keeping my eye on you. (FN 2. 8.96. 29)
9. [Linda comes up to teacher, who is talking to an aide.]
Linda: Ms. Jones, Surjeet was helping Tiffany.
Ms. Jones: Thank you Linda. Surjeet, do your own work. (FN 6.17.96.4)
10. *Natalie*: Ms. Jones, Terry and Amy are looking at our work!
Ms. Jones: Maybe you could move. (FN 3.6.96.70)

[24] Another example of the management of intellectual resources in the classroom was the customary response of the teacher and the children to oral 'copying.' Frequently

in this classroom, the children were asked individually to speculate on answers to mathematical estimations or were required to ask questions or make comments on one another's sharing-time contributions. Both the teacher (gently) and the children (often forcefully) made it known that repetitions were illegitimate contributions.

11. [Natalie (LI English) shows the class a book she has produced at home.]
    Natalie: Any questions or comments?
    Surjeet: You like it?
    Natalie: (Nods.)
    May [LI Cantonese]: How did you make that picture?
    Natalie: Like this.
    Amy: You like that book?
    Luke: We've already had that question, Amy. (FN 10.4.95.3)

12. [Children estimating how many pumpkin seeds are in the pumpkin. Ms. Jones writing the numbers on chart next to their names.]
    Adam: One zillion.
    Ms. Jones: I don't know how to write that.
    Adam: One and a lot of zeros.
    Ms. Jones: Pick a smaller number.
    Adam: One million.
    May: One thousand!
    Surjeet: One million.
    Ms. Jones: Somebody already guessed that. You can choose a number above or below.
    [Surjeet turns away]. (FN 10.12.96.31)

[25]At the beginning of the year, there were many instances when the bilingual students orally repeated like this, but there are no such instances in my field notes or in the videotaped data from after Christmas. It appeared that the children had learned effectively not to repeat in this way.

[26] In the kindergarten year, it was apparent to me that some children sometimes used oral and written (drawing) copying as an affiliative practice of flattery. The children would repeat the statements of their friends in language play; they would copy one another's drawings and make explicit statements about the similarity of their pictures as evidence of friendship. However, in Grade 1 the bilingual children who were the specific focus of the study appeared to learn quickly that oral repetitions were not welcome and that copying the written work of others was also seen as illegitimate.

[27] However, there were times in this classroom when a kind of copying or helping in this classroom was not illegitimate. On some occasions, helping was regarded positively. From time to time the teacher organized the children in small groups to complete a task. These small-group interaction tasks suspended the usual classroom practice of doing one's own work, and the children, unsurprisingly, appeared to require some negotiation time, especially at the beginning of such activities, to decide how to manage their contributions. Another task that required helping was associated with journal writing: Before the children wrote in their journals about their weekend activities, for example, they were encouraged to speak with an assigned classmate about what they were going to write. Most children refused this help.

[28] In summary, it was apparent that for children to help other children with their tasks was commonly a prohibited practice and that for children to 'help themselves' (by copying or repeating) was similarly negatively regarded. 'Helping' was not always so regarded, however, and some tasks were set up explicitly so that the children might help each other.

(Toohey 1998: 68–77)

This paper offers an excellent example of how to organize the presentation of field data. Toohey makes it clear at the very start of the section that she is interested in particular children, but the section is not organized on this basis. Instead, she takes three practices and uses these to explore her central concern with the nature of participation in a community of practice. This gives the reader a clear picture of the relevant elements and suggests a link between data and the theoretical context.

Because the practices are different, they call for slightly different forms of representation. The first is concerned with allocated positions, something that will form the basis for revealing in the following section how limitations associated with this are overcome. The author therefore takes great care to represent the arrangement of the classroom in detail, a diagram (not included here) providing a clear picture for the reader and a point of reference in the discussion of location that follows. This is based largely on field notes, but we are also provided with two recorded exchanges, one confirming the requirement that students work at their own desks and the other illustrating student relations. The description develops from details of where students were placed and the rationale for this in individual cases, which are then considered in terms of groupings. This final part of the section reveals that these students were not placed close to those with whom they would normally interact but that two of them 'were very mobile'.

The next 'practice' has already been hinted at in the reference to Amy's 'borrowing excursions'. Apart from a couple of brief quotations, the approach is entirely based on field notes (though video recordings might also have been used in the lessons that were recorded) and is rich in precise description designed to explain how movement was managed: 'The box-shelves in which materials were stored were short vertically, deep, dark, and placed so that the children had to huddle low in their chairs or get out their chairs and squat on the floor to see inside.' By this means, the writer develops a revealing picture of movements in the class, identifying differences between the movements of Julie and Adam and those of Surjeet and Amy, but also drawing attention to differences between the latter pair in terms of their relations with other students. Notice, as well, how just one observation, for example that Amy 'borrowed even when she had her own materials easily available', can provide key evidence supporting the researcher's interpretation.

The final section stands out in terms of representation, including a large proportion of recorded interaction to build up a picture of what 'using your own words' involved and how 'helping' featured.

This section could be labelled as 'organizing and presenting the evidence' in preparation for the interpretation that will be offered in the subsequent section, so the way in which the writer presents her claims is potentially very important. There are at least three sorts of claim in the text:

Personal impressions	Because the researcher is effectively the primary research 'instrument' in fieldwork, it would be misleading to detach the observer from the scene; rather, the aim should be to allow the reader to share the observer's impressions. So we find comments like 'I did not have the sense that' [(paragraph) 20] and 'it was apparent to me that . . .' [26] and at one point we are taken into the researcher's thinking ('I wondered if the different . . .' [12]).
Appeals to typicality	Claims such as this need to be carefully managed because typicality cannot be established on the basis of expressions. So the final qualification in a claim in the opening paragraph [1] is very important (emphasis mine): 'None of these practices is in any way unusual *in the primary classrooms with which I am familiar*'. Similarly, when in paragraph 3 Toohey claims that '[c]ommonly in classrooms, teachers assign seating to children on the basis of matters to do with management' we are also told that Ms Jones confirmed the details of this in terms of her placement of pupils. Nevertheless (perhaps inevitably) there are unqualified general claims in the text, such as 'with whom they typically chose to play' [10] and 'unlike some other primary classrooms' [14].
Interpretations	There is an interesting example of this in paragraph 22: 'From the above description, it seems evident that . . .' Notice, however, that the reader has access to the above description, so the basis for the claim is available for inspection.

COMMENTS

The outcomes of data analysis are not in themselves significant; they need to be interpreted and, if they are to have relevance beyond the setting being studied, positioned within a broader context of understanding. In order to do this, the researcher must make use of relevant concepts as part of a process of theoretical contextualization. The relationship between the terms *concept* and *theory* sometimes gives rise to confusion, but Bryman (2008: 143) offers a succinct specification of the relationship between the two: 'Concepts are the building blocks of theory and represent the points around which social research is conducted.' We can see this process in action in the Discussion section of the paper

Task B1.5 While reading

➤ This section includes a number of concepts. Which ones seem most important to you and how is the discussion of them developed?

Bryman (2008: 392) also claims that 'it is the quality of the theoretical inferences that are made out of qualitative data that is crucial to the assessment of generalization.' How does the author make use of such inferences to establish the wider relevance of her work?

Discussion

I have described three practices in a Grade 1 classroom, practices so commonplace in classrooms as to be almost invisible. I now examine how these practices contributed to the social structures of that site and what effects they may have had on the students who were the specific focus of my research.

Requiring the children to work at desks assigned by the teacher is a very common practice in primary classrooms. In the classroom I have described it is obvious that the effects of this practice were to control which children were in proximity with one another as well as to bring some children under close teacher surveillance and to disrupt verbal interactions for some but not all of the children. Those children defined as needing help because they spoke English as an L2, as well as Anglophone children perceived to be having some difficulty with school, were so placed as to make chatting between them more difficult than it was for other children. Children perceived to be coping well with the requirements of Grade 1 were seated together toward the back of the room, farther from the teacher, and were thus able to engage with one another in lengthy, obviously enjoyable conversations.

Postmodern philosophers have called attention to the purposes and effects of surveillance. Foucault (1979) writes about 18th-century innovations in French education, envisioned by Jean-Baptiste de la Salle, directed toward improving the efficiency of schooling.

> By assigning individual places it made possible the supervision of each individual and the simultaneous work of all. . . . It made the educational space function like a learning machine, but also as a machine for supervising, hierarchizing, rewarding. Jean-Baptiste de La Salle dreamt of a classroom in which the spatial distribution might provide a whole series of distinctions at once: according to the pupils' progress, worth, character, application, cleanliness and parents' fortune. . . . 'Pupils attending the highest lessons will be placed in the benches closest to the wall, followed by the others according to the order of the lessons moving toward the middle of the classroom. . . .' Things must be arranged so that 'those whose parents are neglectful and verminous must be separated from those

> who are careful and clean; that an unruly and frivolous pupil should be placed between two who are well-behaved and serious. . . .'
>
> (p. 147)

Foucault (1979) observes that classroom spatial arrangements that place individuals in separate locations facilitating supervision, hierarchy and rewards can be historically traced to about the time of the Industrial Revolution in Europe. Perpetual observation of individuals under this system provided for the establishment of norms and rank.

> In the eighteenth century, 'rank' begins to define the great form of distribution of individuals in the educational order: rows or ranks of pupils in the class, corridors, courtyards; rank attributed to each pupil at the end of each task and each examination; the rank he obtains from week to week, month to month, year to year.
>
> (pp. 146–147)

As Ryan (1989) notes with regard to the same time,

> Workers, prisoners, patients, students and citizens were compared, differentiated, and ranked according to where they stood in relation to the 'good' and the 'bad.' . . . Sanctions were universally employed to 'normalize' deviants who by their actions departed from accepted standards.
>
> (p. 400)

It may be that students who enter school speaking languages other than English are defined as something like *benignly deviant*, in Foucault's terms, in that their language departs from accepted standards, and that as a group these students constitute a rank that requires normalization. McDermott (1993) and Mehan (1993) point out the ways in which the rank of *learning disabled* has a reality in public schools independent of the individuals assigned to the rank. Thinking about ESL status as a similar rank, requiring normalization, could be helpful in disrupting taken-for-granted notions of what learning an L2 in schools might be.

The children whose desks were placed close to the teacher's customary position in the classroom were seen as appropriately interacting only or at least primarily with the teacher and then working on their own on the completion of teacher-assigned tasks. When they were removed from the class for ESL instruction, they came under the very close supervision of another teacher, as members of a much smaller group of children. In this way, relative to the children whom the teacher saw as capable students, the bilingual children I observed had relatively few unobstructed (or unsupervised) opportunities to speak to peers with whom they customarily chose to interact during unsupervised times at school. Therefore, the opportunities of the bilingual children who were seen as having difficulties to interact with more capable, English-speaking peers were curtailed. The legitimate verbal interaction for the children sitting at the front of the room was with the teacher. In one way, one might see this circumstance as facilitating their L2 learning by encouraging them to interact primarily with the most expert old-timer (in terms of English) in the room. Shuy (1981) points out a particular difficulty with this arrangement, however, in noting the sociolinguistic inappropriateness of students speaking like teachers.

Amy's and Surjeet's voluntary removal of themselves from large-group sessions, combined with their removal from the class for ESL, contributed to the impression of their increasing marginalization. Marginalization is the customary but, in this case, inapt metaphor. In truth, being on the margins, farther from the teacher's surveillance, could be seen in some ways as a more powerful position in that one's autonomy in choosing activities and verbal participation is greater than it is when one is more centrally located with regard to the teacher. Amy's and Surjeet's removal of themselves to their desks might be seen, therefore, as a practice of resistance to the centrally defined classroom activities.

A second practice in this classroom had to do with individual management of material resources. The children had desks in which they stored their individually purchased materials and were reminded frequently of the need to use their own materials, bring their own books, and so on. For a variety of reasons, many children did not always have available the resources they needed for task completion, so they borrowed from other students. Borrowing subverted in some ways the intent of the first classroom practice: keeping the children at their separate desks. Roaming for borrowing was risky because the teacher could and did stop the children from doing so and reprimand them for it, and other children could legitimately complain about it. The lessons reinforced in the performance of this borrowing practice were that some children had more resources than others, that some had 'better' resources than others, and that individual children had the power to decide whether or not they would share their resources. Lending was not stigmatized; borrowing was. In addition, of course, the children learned that whereas borrowing was not a teacher-legitimated practice, they could engage in it surreptitiously.

Finally, the practice of requiring that the children not copy one another's written or verbal productions was enforced by both the teacher and the children. Throughout the year, all the children became more physically vigilant about protecting their written productions from others (e.g., by leaning over their notebooks or covering their writing with their hands). The children learning ESL copied (repeated) other children's verbal productions more frequently than did Anglophone children at the beginning of the year. By the end of the year, I observed very little of this kind of verbal copying on the part of any of the students. Its unequivocally negative valuation might have been responsible for its disappearance from the data. Hull and Rose (1989) note that

> A fundamental social and psychological reality about discourse – oral or written – is that human beings continually appropriate each other's language to establish group membership, to grow and to define themselves. . . . [Our own] clearly documented writing may let us forget or even, camouflage how much more it is that we borrow from existing texts, how much we depend on membership in a community for our language, our voices, our very arguments.
>
> (pp. 151–152)

Learners of English in this classroom, as they were discouraged from explicit appropriation of others' words, were taught that words, like things, were individually owned and were not community resources.

Lave and Wenger (1991) write that 'learning is an integral and inseparable aspect of social practice' (p. 31). What do children learn in these three social practices? It seems to me that these practices of classrooms contribute to instantiating the notion that the individuality of the children must be established, reinforced, and protected.

Children sit at their own desks, use their own materials, do their own work, and use their own words. Knowing and staying in your place, having good materials in your own place, keeping track of and taking care of them, and having your own 'things' to write and draw and say establish each child as an individual who, on his or her own, negotiates classroom life. The community learns to see some children as more or less adept at these practices, more or less privileged with regard to their acquisitions, and more or less autonomous in deciding their activities and verbal participation.

In the same way that some children may have more or fewer crayons in their desks than others, these practices contribute to children's being seen by the whole community as having more or less English, literacy, mathematics, or whatever. One of the required tasks of a teacher is to ascertain how much any one individual has and report that to parents and authorities. In the classroom in which I observed, I noted the teacher's particularly frequent reminders to the children to work on their own just before she wrote and distributed report cards.

This individualizing of the children starts a process of community stratification that increasingly leads to the exclusion of some students from certain activities, practices, identities, and affiliations. Teachers 'break them apart, take them away.' L1 subcommunities do not survive; L2 learners become systematically excluded from just those conversations in which they legitimately might peripherally participate with child experts, English old-timers. They cannot speak like teachers, but teachers are the only experts with whom they are to interact legitimately.

Of course, many other practices of classrooms and their wider context reinforce the notion that individuals come to own knowledge. Certainly, the practices of researchers who have investigated L2 learning, as well as those of most educational psychologists (as discussed by Wertsch, 1991), also contribute to reinforcing this notion. I have identified here three locally observable practices that I believe contribute to the beginning of a process by which children who speak languages other than English at home begin to acquire school identities as persons whose inventory is smaller than the inventories of others. They begin to acquire identities that, in some very problematic and contradictory ways, require normalizing.

(Toohey 1998: 77–81)

The discussion begins with a description of how students are placed in the relevant classroom, distinguishing between those placed close to the teacher, where inter-pupil chat is difficult, and those at the back, who can talk with one another fairly freely. This then sets up a discussion of *surveillance* (concepts appearing in the paper are italicized) and its relation to *rank*, which has in turn been linked to the 'good' and the 'bad'. The writer then suggests that these ESL students may make up a rank that requires *normalization*, developing this position via a characterization of them as 'benignly deviant' (hence the need for normalization) and the idea that a rank may have a reality independent of the individuals assigned to it.

Having pointed out the inappropriateness in sociolinguistic terms of their interacting primarily with the teacher, Toohey then moves on to consider the students from the perspective of *marginalization*, concentrating on two of them. She questions the appropriateness of this concept because being at the margins in this setting represents 'a more powerful position' (p. 79). Instead, she sees movement from assigned positions as an act of *resistance*, facilitated by borrowing practices.

Nevertheless, Toohey argues, there is a deeper problem arising from a process of *individualizing*. Students learn to 'protect' their own productions from others, which not only undermines the sharing of each other's language that is so important to establishing group *membership*, but also conveys the idea that words are individual possessions rather than community resources. The concept of *ownership* allows Toohey to draw attention to a situation where some individuals are privileged in terms of their linguistic and material 'possessions', autonomy, etc. and others less so. Thus, she argues, the process of individualizing leads to *community stratification* which excludes some students from 'certain activities, practices, identities, and affiliations' (p. 80). This means that they are excluded from *peripheral participation* in conversations from which they would benefit and their legitimate participation is with the least suitable person in the class – the teacher.

CONCLUSION

Task B1.6 While reading

- All research projects must be able to demonstrate the value of its contribution. More bluntly put, it has to give a convincing response to the question, 'So what?' How does Toohey use the conclusion to demonstrate the relevance and importance of her research?

Conclusion

Lave and Wenger's (1991) discussion of learning as participation in communities of practice is offered as a way to 'extend . . . the study of learning beyond the context of pedagogical structuring, include the structure of the social world in the analysis, and take into account in a central way the conflictual nature of social practice' (p. 49). If one takes a community-of-participation perspective on this classroom, it is a community whose practices contribute to constructing children as individuals and their acquisitions as the salient points of analysis, a much different sort of analysis than if one begins by looking at individual children and examines how they negotiate a largely unexamined social milieu.

The children with whom I worked were 6 and 7 years old when I observed them in Grade 1. Any long-term effects of their positioning in their Grade 1 classroom are impossible, of course, to determine. Nevertheless, I find that a quote from a Toronto secondary student, a Japanese learner of ESL, portrays a disturbing and possible future for the children I observed.

> You go to [a non-ESL class] and sit with White people. You understand the content of the class, but when you have to find a partner and work on a group project, you can't get into a group. You feel too embarrassed to ask someone to

> be your partner. You feel like you're gonna be a burden on them. So you don't ask them; you wait until they ask you.
>
> (Kanno & Applebaum, 1995, p. 40)

Kanno and Applebaum also cite research by Brislin (1981), Furnham and Bochner (1986), and Klein, Alexander, and Tseng (1971) showing that 'many students from the Far East have difficulty developing a viable social network with North Americans' (p. 41). How does this happen? My research suggests that the everyday, almost invisible practices of classrooms beginning very early might contribute to these long-term effects.

To reverse these effects will not be a simple matter of putting the children back together again. As Kanno and Applebaum (1995) remark, 'Perhaps it is high time we discarded our romantic notion that if we put children of all ethnic/linguistic backgrounds in one place we will witness the development of true cross-cultural understanding' (p. 43). Mary's comments about birthday parties serve as a reminder that patterns of exclusion and domination persist. Paley (1992) describes her attempts to build resistance to 'the habit of rejection' by instituting the classroom rule for children 'You can't say you can't play' (p. 3). She observes in her classroom work that some children are positioned as outsiders and notes that

> The [traditional] approach has been to help the outsiders develop the characteristics that will make them more acceptable to the insiders. I am suggesting something different: The group must change its attitudes and expectations toward those who, for whatever reasons, are not yet part of the system.
>
> (p. 33)

Certainly the approach to the education of children who go to North American schools speaking languages other than the majority language has been to attempt to help them 'develop the characteristics [i.e., the language] which will make them more acceptable to insiders.' Paley asks how those groups can be made more inclusive; that is, how can the group change to allow those outsiders in? Freire (1970) sees the problem of outsider/insider somewhat differently.

> The truth is that the oppressed are not 'marginals,' are not people living 'outside' society. They have always been 'inside' – inside the structure that made them 'beings for others.' The solution is not to 'integrate' them into the structure of oppression, but to transform that structure so that they can become 'beings for themselves.'
>
> (p. 55)

This perspective, which sees educational structures (communities/practices) as particularly oppressive to some, is perhaps more critical than we as L2 educators are accustomed to seeing in L2 educational literature. Coming to understand how our research practices as well as our classroom practices collaborate in constructing ESL students as individuals who, on their own, acquire or do not acquire the capital of the classroom (the language) may go some way toward helping us find alternative practices that will permit those students to become and be seen as beings for themselves.

Packer (1993) cites Cazden's (1993) argument that coming 'to "participate" in a linguistic community is not a process without conflict: It involves the meeting and clash of divergent interests and the points of view to which these interests give rise' (as cited on p. 259). Although much SLA research is concerned with assessing how individual L2 learners move progressively (and more or less quickly) toward a more extensive acquisition of the L2 and, presumably, fuller participation in the activities of the L2 community, here the practices of a particular community appear in effect to prevent the increasing empowerment and active participation of some of those defined as L2 learners. Clearly, if educators are to understand how to transform the social structures in the milieus for which they have responsibility – classrooms – so as to prepare students effectively for the conflicts to which Cazden refers, investigation of the social practices in those situations must be ongoing, critical, and broad. Looking at furniture, crayons, and copying will be only the beginning.

(Toohey 1998: 81–83)

Task B1.7 After reading

➤ Below is a list of questions researchers might ask themselves about participation in a setting, taken from Craig and Cook (2007: 51) and based on Cloke *et al.* (2004: 201–204). How many of these has the researcher answered and what are the relevant details? If any answers are missing, can you account for this?

Where did you locate yourself in that setting that day?

Who introduced you to whom and how did they describe what you were doing?

How did you see, hear and get involved with what was going on?

What did you learn from talking and doing things with people there?

How could you describe this so readers can imagine being in your shoes?

NOTES

1 Wertsch (1991) similarly observes that much contemporary research in psychology 'examines human mental functioning as if it exists in a cultural, institutional, historical vacuum' (p. 2).
2 Here I will deal mainly with problems associated with a focus on individuals. Clearly, important future work will focus on problems with the notions of language and internalization that have heretofore informed such work. Lave and Wenger (1991) take up the matter of internalization, as does Packer (1993).
3 It is impossible to engage in this discussion in any detail here, but I believe it important to examine how students are assigned to ESL identities as well as to other stigmatized identities. In the classroom in which I observed, not all students who were designated as speakers of languages other than English were deemed to require special help. Randy, who spoke Punjabi as an L1, was considered one of the highest achieving of all students (including Anglophones) in the classroom I focus on here. In November, Randy moved

to another school, in which his teacher considered him one of the most 'dramatically affected ESL students' she had ever taught.

4 To protect the confidentiality of the subjects and teachers, all proper names used in this account are pseudonyms.

5 Harvey's parents asked for him to be removed as a subject in the study at the end of kindergarten. Randy moved in November of Grade 1.

6 One of the students, Harvey, decreased his verbal participation in the classroom over time, apparently learning that his presence in desirable social play events with peers was more likely to be tolerated if he talked less and took a less empowered position in these events. In the case of the other learner, Amy, it was evident that her silence and passivity were no impediment to her access to desirable social play episodes.

7 The video technician had videotaped the study children since their kindergarten year and had had a great deal of experience videotaping classrooms.

8 Interview transcripts are identified by IN, followed by a brief description of the individual interviewed and the date. Field notes are indicated by FN, followed by the date on which they were taken and the page number from which the excerpt is taken.

9 Early in the school year, one of the children in the classroom was diagnosed with head lice. The children's desks were moved farther away from one another for a couple of weeks, in the same arrangement, in an attempt to inhibit the spread of the mites. Later, the desks were moved closer together so that adjoining desks were touching one another (as illustrated in Figure 1).

10 In June, the teacher moved a Cantonese-speaking girl behind Amy, but she had not been placed there previously. Except for the movement of this girl, Figure 1 shows the placement of the children from the end of February to the end of June.

11 Typical of their sometimes difficult interactions was this one, recorded on audiotape in March:

Adam: Ricardo, where you got your ruler?
Ricardo: [pause] I got this from store. [shows an 'action' figure]
Adam: No! [angry] Ruler!
[Ricardo goes to the back of the room.] (TR 04.14.95.17)

12 Ms. Jones remarked, on reading a draft of this article, that she found this a common pattern for many of the ESL children she had taught and that she believed it reflected the children's lack of understanding of the stories.

(Toohey 1998: 83–84)

REFERENCES

Brislin, R. W. (1981) *Cross-Cultural Encounters: Face to Face Interaction.* New York: Pergamon Press.

Davis, K. A. (1995) 'Qualitative theory and methods in applied linguistics research', *TESOL Quarterly* 29: 427–454.

Foucault, M. (1979) *Discipline and Punish: The Birth of the Prison.* New York: Vintage.

Freire, P. (1970) *Pedagogy of the Oppressed.* New York: Seabury Press.

Furnham, A. and Bochner, S. (1986) *Culture Shock: Psychological Reactions to Unfamiliar Environments.* London: Routledge.

Hazzard, S. (1970) *The Bay of Noon.* New York: Penguin Books.

Hull, G. and Rose, M. (1989) 'Rethinking remediation: Towards a social-cognitive understanding of problematic reading and writing', *Written Communication* 6: 139–154.

Kanno, Y. and Applebaum, S. D. (1995) 'ESL students speak up: Their stories of how we are doing', *TESL Canada Journal 12*(2): 32–49.

Klein, M. H., Alexander, A. A. and Tseng, K.–H. (1971) 'The foreign students adaptation program: Social experience of Asian students', *International Educational and Cultural Exchange 6*(3): 77–90.

Lave, J. and Wenger, E. (1991) *Situated Learning: Legitimate Peripheral Participation.* Cambridge: Cambridge University Press.

McDermott, R. P. (1993) 'The acquisition of a child by a learning disability' in S. Chaiklin and J. Lave (eds) *Understanding Practice: Perspectives on Activity and Context*: 268–305. Cambridge: Cambridge University Press.

Mehan, H. (1993) 'Beneath the skin and between the ears: A case study in the politics of representation' in S. Chaiklin and J. Lave (eds) *Understanding Practice: Perspectives on Activity and Context*: 241–268. Cambridge: Cambridge University Press.

Packer, M. (1993) 'Away from internalization' in E. Forman, N. Minick and C. A. Stone (eds) *Contexts for Learning: Sociocultural Dynamics in Children's Development*: 254–265. New York: Oxford University Press.

Paley, V. G. (1992) *You Can't Say You Can't Play.* Cambridge, Mass. Harvard University Press.

Pennycook, A. (1990) 'Toward a critical applied linguistics for the 1990s', *Issues in Applied Linguistics.* 1: 8–28.

Rogoff, B., Baker-Sennett, J., Lacasa, P. and Goldsmith, D. (1995) 'Development through participation in sociocultural activities', in J. Goodnow, P. Miller and F. Kessel (eds) *Cultural Practices as Contexts for Development.* San Francisco: Jossey-Bass.

Ryan, W. (1989) 'Disciplining the Innut: Normalization, characterization and schooling', *Curriculum Inquiry* 19: 379–404.

Shuy, R. (1981) 'Learning to talk like teachers', *Language Arts* 58: 168–174.

Toohey, K. (1996) 'Learning ESL in kindergarten: A community of practice perspective', *Canadian Modern Language Review* 52: 549–576.

Wertsch, J. D. (1991) *Voices of the Mind.* Cambridge, Mass.: Harvard University Press.

Willett, J. (1995) 'Becoming first graders in an L2: An ethnographic study of language socialization', *TESOL Quarterly* 29: 473–504.

Extension B2

Toohey's ethnographic study of the Grade 1 ESL classroom involves considerable description based on direct observation of the classroom processes. The study focuses on patterns of participation by individuals over time and the evolution of a community of practice that may have long term consequences for the participants. The next study featured in this chapter is of shorter duration, and exemplies an intervention type of study. In contrast to Toohey's observational approach, DeRidder, Vangehuchten and Sesena Gomez design an elaborate task-based intervention they hypothesize to affect automaticity among learners of Spanish as a foreign language. The two studies illustrate the difference between an ethnographic study and a hypothetical-deductive study.

DeRidder, I., Vangehuchten, L. and Sesena Gomez, M. (2007) 'Enhancing automaticity through task-based language learning', *Applied Linguistics* 28/2: 309–315

In a randomized two-group interventional research design, DeRidder, Vangehuchten and Sesena Gomez investigated the differential impact of task-based practice on the development of automaticity among 68 intermediate learners of Spanish as a foreign language in Belgium. All the learners were business majors. The participants were randomized into two learning conditions. Both conditions feature three of the four instructional components: presentation, explanation and in-class exercises. The counterfactual (control) group was exposed to the year-long course of focus on form instruction followed by a fourth content-related communicative situation. Control group members were required to read 12 texts in Spanish about different companies. Individual learners had then to prepare a short presentation on each of the companies studied. The differential intervention for the experimental group was a fourth task-based component featuring communicative situations unrelated to the course content, but requiring use of the same lexical and grammatical content introduced in the three common components the control group was exposed to over the instructional term. The task-based fourth component for the experimental group was to create a Spanish-language TV advertisement for a novel product. The different fourth component conditions differed in one respect. The control group members expended 10 instructional hours out of a total of 40 instructional hours on individual reading and presentation preparation, while the experimental group members spent 10 instructional hours in preparing the advertisement through communicative practice sessions.

Assessments of speaking ability were collected separately for the two groups. For the control group, video recordings of the short presentations were the performances used to define the outcome variables. For the experimental group, a video of the produced advertisement provided the data for deriving a comparable outcome. For both types of performances, a set of sub-criteria were created to define the dependent variables: pronunciation, fluency, intonation, sociolinguistic adequacy, lexicon and grammar. Scoring was done by two independent raters using a 0 to 4 rating scale.

Task B2.1

➤ Based on the above description, what between-group differences would you hypothesize to emerge from the differential instruction procedures?

Trochim and Donnelly (2007) provide a shorthand system for describing and sketching out experimental and quasi-experimental designs. In their scheme, originally developed by Campbell and Stanley (1963), observations or measures of individuals or groups are represented with an O, while interventions are represented with an X. Group formation processes such as by complete randomization (R), assignment into groups through **matched pairs** of individuals (A) or forming **stratified groups** by cutting scores based on a pre-intervention measure (C), signify how between-group designs are constructed. Experimental designs always have an R component, while quasi-experimental designs do not. Instead, quasi-experimental designs have O measures that precede any differential intervention. The order of design components from left to right shows the chronology of data collection and the roles different components play as pre-tests, interventions, post-tests and how groups are formed (R, A or C). Rows indicate the number of groups in the research design. A row with a blank under an X represents the counterfactual or control condition. It is a group that does not get the intervention hypothesized to account for mean differences between the two groups.

Example:	X	O
		O

Such a design would be an intervention X prior to a measurement of a putative outcome. The second group does not have an intervention, but is also has a measurement of the outcome. This type of design would be problematic if the researcher's goal had been to a make a causal inference about O as a consequence of X. The reason is that there is no control over possible moderating variables which possibly account for differences between the two groups – the intervention versus the counterfactual group, independently of the intervention X. How the groups were formed is not known in such a design. Such a design would be subject to **selection bias**, which would undermine inferences about the efficacy of the intervention.

Task B2.2

➤ Examine the following design types and identity the function of each component of the design: O, X, R, A, or C. Identify each one as being experimental or quasi-experimental. Take note how many groups there are and which if any serve as experimental/intervention and which are counterfactual/control groups.

a)	O X O	b)	R X O R O	c)	O R X O O R O	d)	R Xa O R Xb O R O
e)	O C X O O C O	f)	O O O O X O O O O	g)	R X OOOOOO R OOOOOO	h)	O A X O O A O

Task B2.3

➤ Refer to the DeRidder *et al.* study and identify which kind of design they used.

The logic of randomization is that all sources of selection bias will be equally distributed equally to both the intervention and counterfactual (control) groups. Any between-group difference observed on measures (Os) after the intervention has been delivered is then hypothesized to be a consequence of the X or not X difference. This assumption rests on the adequacy of the randomization process and the sampling of each condition. In small scale studies, pre-existing group differences can still exist in spite of randomization. For this reason, design type c) offers the added benefit of providing a measure of group differences before the intervention. In this way, group differences can be checked prior to the main between-groups comparison on the post-test measure. In the event that there are still differences on the pre-test, between-group comparisons can proceed as a non-equivalent groups design (NEGD). Here the pre-test can serve as **covariate** to adjust for initial groups differences so that hypotheses can still be tested. Conventional research design wisdom stresses that randomized designs are preferable to non-equivalent group designs (see Shadish, Cook and Campbell 2002).

ANALYSIS

DeRidder, Vangehuchten and Sesena Gomez employ a series of independent group **t-tests** to test their hypotheses about the effects of the intervention. The t-test compares the mean and variance of the two contrastive groups (experimental and control) under the null hypothesis that the means and variances will be no different than that expected through random error. An alternative hypothesis would predict according to some expectation predicated on theory that there will directional mean differences attributable to the intervention relative to the control. It is important to note that the simple t-test assumes randomization has occurred, and that the randomization has left the two groups comparable in all other ways other than the intervention one of the groups receives.

The authors proceed to test their six hypotheses with individual t-tests. For example, the prediction was that the intervention group exposed to communicative practice would develop higher-rated pronunciation relative to the control group.

Figure B2.1

$$t = \frac{\bar{x}_e - \bar{x}_c}{\sqrt{\frac{s_e^2}{n_e} + \frac{s_c^2}{n_c}}} = \frac{58.58 - 74.76}{\sqrt{\frac{14.36^2}{33} + \frac{22.28^2}{35}}} = \frac{-16.18}{\sqrt{6.24 + 14.18}} = \frac{-16.18}{\sqrt{20.42}} = \frac{-16.18}{4.52} \approx -3.5$$

The t-test shown in Figure B2.1 shows the computation of the t-test for pronunciation. Setting the critical level of significance at $p<.05$, the level at which the authors infer there is a non-random between-group difference, the observed t-test result is significant, based on tabled value of t-ratios with n_e+n_c-2 degrees of freedom. The observed *t* is at deemed **significant** at $p=.001$, and so is very unlikely to be a matter of random variation. It is, however, in the opposite direction as that predicted by the authors. As it turned out, contrary to the prediction, the control group achieved higher ratings in pronunciation than the experimental group.

Task B2.4

➤ Examine the Results section of the DeRidder *et al.* paper (below) and note the size, direction and significance of the t-tests they computed. How many of their hypotheses were borne out in the analysis?

Table 1 describes the statistics for the six major criteria, expressed in percentages. The results were analysed with an independent samples t-test. All statistical tests were performed at .05 level. The results indicate that:(a) The control group outperformed the experimental group on pronunciation [t (66)._3.53, p (two tailed)..001_] and intonation [t (66)._2.73, p (two tailed)..008_]. This contradicts the hypothesis. (b) The experimental group outperformed the control group on grammar [t (66).6.06, p (two tailed)..000_], vocabulary [t (66).5.51, p (two tailed)..000_], and social adequacy [t (66).5.52, p (two tailed)..000_]. This was hypothesized. (c) No significant difference could be established on fluency. This also contradicts the hypothesis.

Table 1 Descriptive statistics of the results on the six major criteria in percentages

Criterion	*Condition*	*Mean*	*SD*	*Min.*	*Max.*	*N*
Pronunciation	Control	74.76	22.28	25.00	100.00	35
	Experimental	58.58	14.36	33.33	83.33	33
Intonation	Control	70.71	23.02	25.00	100.00	35
	Experimental	54.92	24.59	25.00	100.00	33
Grammar	Control	63.27	18.18	28.94	89.47	35
	Experimental	88.89	16.59	43.75	100.00	33
Vocabulary	Control	65.89	23.64	25.00	100.00	35
	Experimental	91.18	11.90	44.44	100.00	33
Social adequacy	Control	68.57	29.61	25.00	100.00	35
	Experimental	85.92	22.48	25.00	100.00	33
Fluency	Control	67.50	24.47	25.00	100.00	35
	Experimental	74.00	25.74	25.00	100.00	33

(DeRidder *et al.* 2007: 312–313)

Task B2.5

➤ Discuss how the DeRidder *et al.* study would benefit from an ethnographic component. What other kinds of interpretive data would be useful in order to arrive at a rich description of the intervention and the control condition?

Section C
Extension C3

Task C1.1

➤ In Chapter 1 we saw how in conversation analysis all features of talk are potentially relevant, and the same applies to observation. Study the following two extracts from Keith Richards' field notes, one describing the dress of five core members of a school's staff (Jenny is the principal) and the other how they are located in the main staffroom. Assuming that the teachers are dressed appropriately and you know that the school attracts two broad categories of adult learners, can you suggest what these might be and which pair of teachers is assigned to each? What does the arrangement in the staff room suggest about relations between teachers and the principal?

Staff room fieldnotes extract 1

Louise, like Jenny and Annette, is smartly dressed. Well made up, comfortable but serious blouse, short dark skirt and black tights. Attractive and friendly clothes, but definitely appropriate to business. Paul and Harry present a much more casual picture: crew neck jumpers, jeans (denims for Harry) and open-necked shirts. The contrast is clear but not stark.

Staff room fieldnotes extract 2

There are two staff rooms but this is the one everyone uses, probably because of the sink and kettle. The two foci are Harry's desk and Jenny's desk . . . with desk C for drifters. Jenny and Helen will tend to locate themselves at Jenny's desk, standing and leaning against it, facing the door. Harry sometimes adopts a similar position at his desk but is at least as likely to be sitting down, half turned to the floor. Annette and Louise tend to locate themselves in the desk C area but Paul is more of a drifter.

Task C1.2

➤ Study the arrangement of the following field notes (Richards') in terms of the comments made in Section B and comment on the contribution made by the notes in the right-hand column. Attempting to code isolated extracts in the absence of more extensive data is very difficult, but what sorts of topics might suggest themselves here?

Staff room fieldnotes extract 3

Two Polish students from David's class are in the staffroom. They're exchanging words with Bill and David and don't seem too happy. It transpires from David and Bill's discussion that the split between Poles and Japanese in the class is not working. The Japanese seem to have clammed up entirely and are not happy because they claim that the Poles are hogging all the talk in class, while the Poles are less than happy about their reception by the Japanese and their placement.

Bill: Do you think it's copable with?
David: It's all been a bit much, hasn't it? The whole bloody class is disintegrating.

There's some dissatisfaction (Bill and David mainly) about the way the local organisation has handled arrangements for this course, and the general feeling is that something should be said in order to prevent a recurrence.	The issue of placement seems to be particularly acute this term.
There's another, not unconnected, problem which is also bubbling to the surface. This concerns Keiko, a Japanese student who has been here since last summer and will stay until this summer. She feels, rightly, that she's not making much progress and is unhappy about this. One of the problems is that of level and another appears to be a personality clash between her and Tom, who is one of her teachers. [. . .] The conclusion they're moving towards is that Keiko will take 'time out' for one-to-one lessons and that after these she can probably be put in a class which Tom doesn't teach.	This is a problem which has obviously developed over time, and though I've seen hints of it, the issue is a delicate one and has probably been explored by Bill and Tom together. Bill has spent at least some of his time today working out the financial implications of one-to-one sessions for Keiko. She adds another dimension to the Japanese/Polish problem
The conversation between Bill and David on this subject settles on the topic of vocabulary and pre-reading. David: 'I'm not clear what they want. I mean, it's easy to see the group splitting into two. It was fine yesterday . . . I tried to address it going into the classroom – which was a mistake. . . . I don't know what she (Keiko) wants. I don't know whether she wants more grammar or less grammar.' He goes on to talk about the tendency of students just to leap into things.	David is always ready to explore in public issues which have arisen in his classes and it prepared to be very self-critical. This is a typical example of how he brings such things into the open.
[. . .]	
Bill: (to Jane C) Your Pole is alright, isn't she? *Jane*: Yes. Explains that she's paired with Ahmed. Brief exchange on this subject then the focus shifts to the two Polish students who were in the staffroom.	This seems to be more a 'kicking around' of information than an attempt to pin down and tackle a problem. It's a bit like an

David:	Those two have got status problems. Discussion of what this might mean.	addendum to the conversation which John and Steve have just had.
Jane:	Does she work for him?	
David:	Doesn't know.	
Emma:	Her card says she's a public relations officer.	
Jane:	What does the man do?	
David:	He's into import or export.	

BRIEF COMMENTS

With the exception of occasional specialist courses, the school involved offers broadly two types of course: business and general. Louise and Annette teach the former and Paul and Harry the latter. Arrangements in the staff room reflect the 'flat' organisational structure in the school, which was established by the teachers as a group. In fact, when the researcher confirmed the location of Jenny's desk with her, she made the following unprompted observation: 'Yes, we're very democratic here; I don't have my own office.'

The third extract is divided into two columns, the first descriptive and the second dedicated to comments involving an element of interpretation. Some of these place aspects of the description in a broader temporal ('particularly acute this term') or behavioural ('David is always ready to') context, while others assign a label ('a bit like an addendum') or a particular interpretation ('adds another dimension to the Japanese/Polish problem'). Such comments may contribute later to analytical notes, but they also help sensitize the observer to emerging aspects of a bigger picture.

The two most obvious topics of interest in the field notes (expressed in general terms) are relations between different national groups in the same class and relations between students and teachers, though throughout the extract we see teachers' responses to the challenges raised by these. In the process of analysis these features might appear in many different contexts. For example, they might be subsumed under 'student relations', 'teacher views of students', 'national stereotyping', 'dealing with classroom problems', etc. and each of these will produce different results in terms of organization. There are also options within each of these categories. For example, 'student relations' might be broken down into 'with teachers' and 'with students' or 'personal', 'pedagogic' and 'interactional'. Perhaps the only certain thing that emerges from Extract 3 is that from an analytical perspective even a short stretch of text is rich in possibilities.

Task C1.3

➤ Use the examples above as the basis for developing some notes of your own. Choose a setting that you know (a staffroom would be a natural choice) and see whether you can identify any groups within it in terms of their behaviour and/or presentation. For example, do heads of department dress differently from other colleagues, and if so where are the differences to be found? Is there anything distinctive about their behaviour that sets them apart from other colleagues? What about new and experienced colleagues?

If it is feasible (ethically and practically), you might try capturing a particular occurrence such as the one described in Task C1.2. Take detailed notes at the time or as soon as possible afterwards, then write these up as soon as you can using the left-hand column of a page divided as in the task. Concentrate on describing the event in as much detail as you can. Finally, in a place well away from the setting you have chosen, add comments in the right-hand section. If this is a familiar setting, ask yourself whether in doing this you have discovered something you had not noticed before.

Task C1.4

- Choose an activity in your classroom and observe it over time, building up a set of notes. An obvious focus here would be a particular group in task-based activities. Note how the group arranges itself; how materials are distributed and brought into play; how contributions are made and who makes them; how relationships are displayed and organized; how participation structures develop; identify unstated rules, procedures, etc.

When you have a good picture of one group and are confident about your approach to observation, the obvious next step is to compare one group with another, but another option would be to introduce a new member to the group (the choice of participant will be important here) in order to see what changes this produces.

At the end of the process, study your notes and identify what you have learned about the group and what this suggests about the class and about task-based work in your classes. You should also reflect on what you have learned about observation and making field notes.

Exploration C2

The independent t-test is one of the more straightforwardly used hypothesis testing techniques available in the domain of second-language studies. It is also one that has a number of assumptions, which, if ignored, will lead to faulty inferences about group differences. In addition to the design assumption that groups are formed through effective randomization, another assumption is that the variance (the standard deviation squared) is approximately equal between the groups. When different sizes of groups are involved, this assumption can be violated. It is also easily violated when learners are compared with native speakers of a language on performance tests or grammaticality judgements. Native speakers typically show near unanimity in their rejection of malformed grammar specimens, while learners will tend to vary considerably. Such a comparison can easily violate the assumption of equal variances.

Another assumption of the t-test is that it is a unique event. If this assumption is met, the setting of a critical significance level such as the conventional $p<.05$ will provide a basis for inference. When two groups are tested on multiple variables sequentially or simultaneously, the inferential error rate changes considerably. That is, it becomes progressively easier to find a 'significant' difference between groups the more tests of group differences there are. This error is referred to as a Type 1 error – that of finding a 'significant' difference by chance (Toothaker 1991). A common remedy for multiple t-tests is to reset the critical probability level to one that is based on the single test level divided by the number of intended tests. In the DeRidder *et al.* study, this would be $.05/6 = .008$. Any t-ratio that is larger than the $p=.008$ threshold would be considered as evidence in support of the null (or no difference) hypothesis.

Task C2.1

> Re-examine the t-tests reported by the authors and locate any results that would lead to the acceptance of the null hypothesis under the chance-corrected adjustment.

RESEARCH SCENARIO C2

Applied linguists want to examine the influence of incentives for vocabulary learning. In a single school setting, researchers randomly assign fifth-grade children into intervention and control conditions. The intervention is a program of incentives that induces children to locate and write down novel words in their neighbourhood environment. The control condition is conventional instruction featuring vocabulary learned through reading. At the end of one term, the students are tested for vocabulary knowledge.

Task C2.2

> Sketch the design of this study using the notation introduced in the Extension section of this chapter. Note the roles of the different variables you list. What would a plausible hypothesis be for this kind of study?

Task C2.3

> Locate the SPSS data file **'experiment.sav'**. In it are the data for the research scenario outlined in C2a. Open SPSS and follow the instructions below for running an independent samples t-test.

The samples are independent because the groups are randomly assigned to either the experimental or control condition.

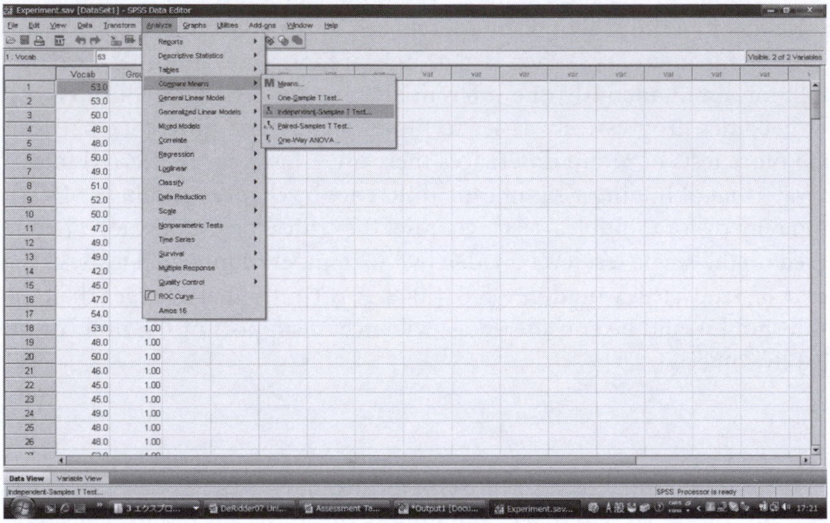

Figure 3.1 Independent means t-test for Experiment.sav

Reprint courtesy of International Business Machines Corporation, © SPSS, Inc., an IBM company

A window then appears for the variables in the data set to be assigned to different roles. In this case, the vocabulary is the dependent variable, and the group is the manipulated or independent variable.

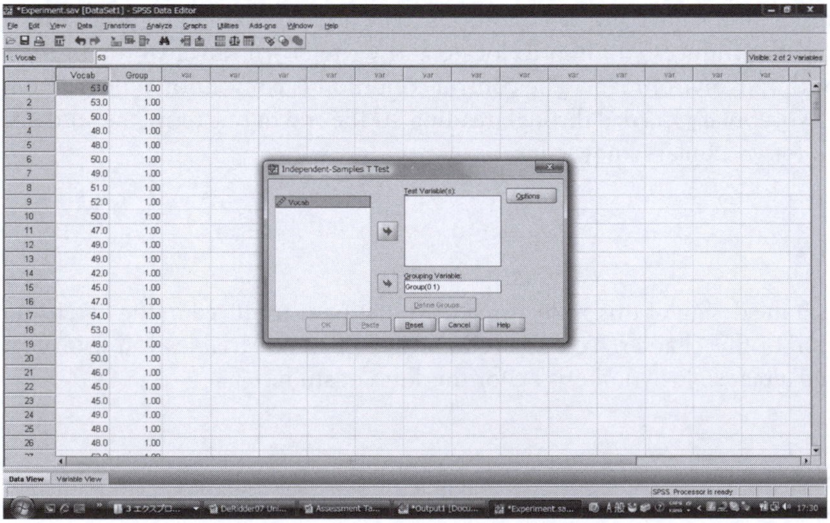

Figure 3.2 Variable selection for Experiment.sav

Reprint courtesy of International Business Machines Corporation, © SPSS, Inc., an IBM company

Note that the group variable has two levels. Level code 0 is the control or counterfactual condition. This group does not get the experimental intervention, but instead does the usual or conventional method of learning vocabulary. The intervention (experimental) group gets a code 1, which means that each case (row in the data matrix) is a member of the intervention group. Once both the vocabulary and group variables are moved into the analysis widow, the t-test can be performed by clicking OK.

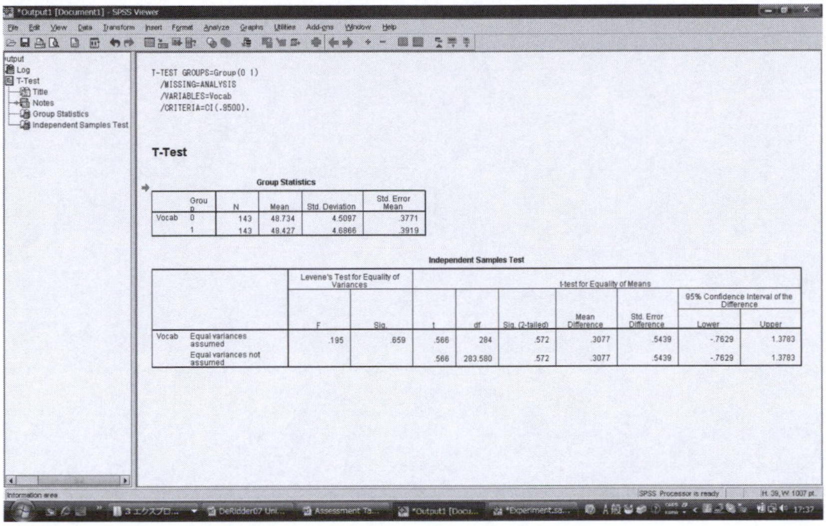

Figure 3.3 T-test results for Experiment.sav

Task C2.4

➢ Examine the output of the t-test. Compare the group means and standard deviations. Look for the t-test and significance level. Is your hypothesis supported?

The observed t of .566 with p=.572 would indicate that the two group means do not differ by anything more than chance variation.

Task C2.5

➢ Consider how an observational component would be useful in this kind of hypothetical-deductive study. Note that the 'intervention' in this case could happen outside the classroom context.

Task C2.6

- The results of the study did not reject the null hypothesis. What observational data would be needed to understand why there was no significant difference between the incentives-driven group and the in-class learners? Discuss how such observational data could be gathered.

CHAPTER 4
Affect and belief in language learning

Section A
Introduction A1

In the previous chapter we explored the classroom as a language-learning environment, revealing how both observational and experimental designs can help us to understand the nature and the outcomes of learning. In this chapter we turn our attention to the learner. From the researcher's perspective, this presents particular challenges because, unlike the classroom, the learner's head is not a public space. This means that we do not have direct access to the data and must rely on reports from the learner.

Two main approaches to understanding what is in the mind of the learner are typically used in applied research. One very common approach is to use learner self-report in the form of surveys. On such surveys, learners are asked to rate their own cognitive, attitude or affective states on an ordinal scale designed to lead to the inference that higher ratings mean more of the particular construct of interest. While the use of such scales is ubiquitous, there are risks associated with their use. One is that some respondents may not rate themselves in a consistent manner. For this reason, it is advisable to examine the coherence and internal consistency of surveys before attempts at interpretation. One approach is to use a Rasch analysis (Wright and Masters 1982), which examines the implicational order of items and persons. Inconsistent items or persons can be identified by their improbable rating patterns, and action can be taken to 'clean up' the data, or to pursue the reasons for the inconsistency. Another risk is that the questions may suggest to the respondents the goals of the researchers, and thus provoke socially desirable responses that do not accurately reflect the actual attitude the learner may have about the object of inquiry. Surveys about learner motivation and willingness to communicate are particularly susceptible to social desirability, and often need corroborating evidence before further analysis can be performed. Finally, because of the relative ease of survey construction and administration, there is a temptation to gather all information from learners through this method. The overuse of surveys invites a subtle bias that might not be evident to data analysts. If all information about learning, ability, strategy use, motivation, attitude and the like is collected through surveys, there may be a mono-method bias (Shadish *et al.* 2002) which will inflate the magnitude of the interrelations among the variables of interest. It is therefore wise to use different types of data gathering tools to avoid the overuse of the research survey.

One obvious way to do this is to use the research interview, but this carries with it the same risks as those identified above. Even if deliberate deception is set aside (as far as we know, this is very rare because of the effort required to pull it off, but there is no absolutely reliable way to detect it if it is suitably sophisticated), it is nevertheless the case that people will represent themselves in particular ways, see things from their own perspective, fit things into a narrative that may have been formed retrospectively in the light of the eventual outcome, etc. Similarly, there is the risk in all interviews that the interviewer's approach and responses to the respondent might influence how the latter represents things. In fact, because of the interactive nature of the interview, this danger is much greater than in the case of surveys, where the medium is more neutral by virtue of the distance between researcher and respondent. One obvious way of limiting the likelihood of misrepresentation in interviews is to use triangulation with other data (interviews with other people, observation, documentary records, etc.), but there are limitations to how far this can help. Researchers using interviews have therefore developed techniques for interpreting the interview as a situated event – something created *in situ* by the participants. By examining the way the interview is interactively constructed, the researcher is able to uncover not only where and how the interviewer's contributions might influence the respondent's talk but also the ways in which respondents represent themselves in the talk. Of course, this is not a substitute for proper training and practice in interview technique, which will always be fundamental to effective interviewing.

In what follows we introduce the considerations, techniques and procedures that contribute to effective interviewing and briefly discuss the relationship between surveys and interviews. Part B will then draw on two research papers in order to examine aspects of interview technique in more detail and explore key considerations in the quantitative analysis of survey results.

INTERVIEWS AND SURVEYS

Task A.1.1

➤ Suppose that you wish to find out about the following. In terms of data collection, which do you think would be most suitable for the use of interviews and which would be more likely to benefit from a survey approach?

- Angolan learners' beliefs about the value of extensive reading in English
- Brazilian learners' motivations for studying English

- Chinese learners' knowledge of cultural norms in the USA
- Dutch learners' experiences of English immersion classes

In broad terms, surveys provide specific information about a large population while interviews generate in-depth insights related to a small population, though of course this is a generalization and 'large' and 'small' are relative terms. Yin (2004: 33–46), for example, describes the *Yankee City* case study in the USA, which involved 17,000 interviews – hardly a 'small' research sample by any measure. More important are considerations of what the researcher expects the data to yield. So if we are interested in the nature of a learners' experiences of a particular situation, it will probably pay to use the interview as a means of collecting data because this will give us the flexibility to probe and explore aspects of experience in a way that will allow us, over time, to develop a rich picture of what that experience was like for the learners. On the other hand, if we want to find out about learners' knowledge, such probing will probably not be necessary and the picture we hope to develop will depend on the accumulation of very precise elements. In terms of the above list, therefore, the Dutch learners would probably be invited to participate in an interview study while the Chinese learners would be asked to complete a questionnaire.

A crude division between insight (interviews) and information (surveys) will take the researcher only so far, and most questions can be approached using either of these two data collection methods or both. For example, at first blush interviews might seem more appropriate for the Angolan study in the list above, while a survey would yield valuable information about the motivations of the Brazilian learners, but there are situations where we might wish to reverse this. If, for example, we had to decide whether or not to introduce a set of readers in Angola as part of a package including standard course books, we might want to use a survey in order to assess what the uptake of these would be, on the assumption that if the value of extensive reading is not widely recognized teachers will not recommend the purchase of reading sets. On the other hand, if we were planning to commission a set of readers to be used with our standard course books, we might wish to know more about what Angolan teachers value in such readers, in which case it would be a good idea to use interviews to explore this, perhaps as part of a mixed-methods study.

In what follows we deal with interviews and surveys separately, but at the end of the first section we will suggest how interviews can be used as part of questionnaire design and how surveys can provide a starting point for interview studies.

Task A1.2

➤ How might interviews be used to help design effective questionnaires and how might survey results be used to inform interview design?

INTERVIEW TYPES

Interviews are traditionally categorized in terms of their structure and whether they involve an individual or group (for useful brief introductions to focus group interviews, see Oates 2000 or Chapter 2 of Roulston 2010a, or, for a more extended practical account, Barbour 2007). In fact, it would be possible to extend this categorization to include other forms of interview including telephone interviews (for details of how to conduct these, see Genovese 2004; for a comparison with face-to-face interviews, see Sturges and Hanrahan 2004), email interviews (e.g. Gibson 2010) and even online focus groups (Kenny 2005), each with its own advantages and drawbacks (for a very brief comparison, see Opdenakker 2006). However, the success or failure of any interview depends on adequate preparation, interactional sensitivity and a developmental orientation. These are the aspects explored in what follows.

This approach will also involve setting aside the conventional division of interviews into structured, semi-structured and open (for a useful brief overview of the options here, including a helpful table of varieties of group interview, see Fontana and Frey 2000) in favour of an approach based on the assumption that all interviews are to some extent structured and that what matters is how that structuring is achieved. In fact, there are good grounds for questioning whether 'structured' and 'open' are helpful categories.

If an interview is completely structured in the sense that all the questions are determined in advance so that all the researcher has to do is read them out, it's probably more helpful to treat this as a spoken questionnaire. But even this is problematic, as Wooffitt and Widdicombe's (2006) revealing analysis of the interaction in such 'survey' or 'structure' demonstrates. They show that, far from representing a neutral option, such interviews breach normative expectations but ignore the interactional consequences of this in their representation of the data (see also Houtkoop-Steenstra 1997).

Similarly, there is no such thing as an 'open' interview in the sense that the interviewer goes in and simply encourages the respondent to start speaking, ready for anything that might emerge. For one thing, such non-directiveness is counter-productive: as Jones (1985: 47–48) has pointed out, respondents who don't have a clear idea of the researcher's interests are likely to expend a lot of energy trying to figure these out. More fundamentally, researchers who conduct this sort of interview are usually able to recognize and draw out emergent structures.

Task A1.3

- This does not mean that there are not different types of interview or different degrees of structuring. A and B are two different interview-based projects. Try to decide how the relevant interviews might differ in terms of structure and overall shape.

A The life history of a teacher in Sri Lanka
B Perceptions of communicative competence of EFL teachers in Iran.

➤ Now try to decide which of the extracts belongs to which project:

1. I don't go into the classroom with a very clear teaching plan because if you want students to learn in different ways so you need to kind of find a methodology which will be appropriate. I mean, yes we could pick and choose from books, from the literature, but I think it's a kind of contract or something that the teacher and the students should do together to find the best way. Like even with this group at [college] they're all aspiring young men and women . . . on day one what I did with them, with a new group, was I said can we look at the different ways that people of your age learn. So we had a discussion and then I said shall we try and use what you said for the next 10 lessons – and I'll be doing 10 lessons with them. So to me that sums [up], that's a methodology, a shared methodology.
2. I ask students to do silent reading so that they can concentrate on the reading passage individually. I also ask students some questions based on the reading passage, and they're also required to make questions based on the reading material. In this way, students cannot only **comprehend** the reading text but also <u>practise the language structures</u>.

As Talmy observes in his excellent discussion of the use of interviews in applied linguistics, there is an 'impressive diversity' of topics covered (2010: 132). His discussion of the interview as research instrument gathers these into three broad areas: ethnography and case study, narrative/life history, and 'qualitative', the last category something of a catch-all. Broadly speaking, approaches that are designed to elicit a narrative tend to be more open, with the researcher focusing on eliciting narrative trajectories as the interview progresses, though, as Wengraf's (2001) densely elaborated book shows, this does not dispense with the need for careful preparation. Other approaches are usually based around topics arising from external sources, which might include research questions, puzzles, insights or questions from the field, or the demands of a particular case study. An illustration of this will appear in the next section.

It should be clear at this point that the first of the examples above (A) relates to a narrative approach to interviewing, although interestingly the author (Hayes 2005) describes his approach as 'in-depth' (a fairly common term but slightly problematic because it carries the suggestion that other approaches are in some way superficial). Here one would expect extended responses from the interviewee and gentle prompts or probes from the researcher, allowing the narrative to unfold naturally. The extract that accompanies this is the first ('I don't go into the classroom . . .') and is introduced by the author as follows: 'Bandara's description of how he set about the search for appropriate methods with one of his Saturday classes' (Hayes 2005: 188). Notice how it begins with a description of the respondent's general approach, then eventually moves into a narrative of what the teacher did on 'day one'.

The second extract, which is part of the study of perceptions of communicative language teaching in Iran (Nazari 2007) is in response to the question, 'What kinds of activities do you ask your students to do in the classroom? Why?' (Nazari 2007: 206). Although the topic is almost identical to the first (what I do in my classroom), notice how differently it develops. The researcher has asked for a list of activities and the interviewee responds to this ('I ask . . . I also ask . . . and they're also required . . .'), concluding with a justification for the approach. This is what the question is designed to elicit and it forms part of a set of topics that the researcher has decided to explore in the interviews in order to establish what the perceptions of these teachers are.

These two interviews focused on approaches and beliefs, which are in many ways more accessible than affective factors, not least because people generally find it easier to talk about – and expand on – their experiences and beliefs than they do about their feelings. In fact, many people try to avoid talking about feelings and even those who are comfortable doing this are apt to find that the vocabulary at their disposal for doing so is relatively limited. This explains why direct questions about feeling are likely to elicit at best short responses. The above examples are also taken from teachers, who have the benefit of a relevant professional education and a job which involves a great deal of speaking. Learners rarely have these natural advantages and consequently may find it very difficult to talk at length about affective factors influencing their language learning (for an excellent example of how a combination of learner diaries and interviews can produce accounts in which the affective dimension emerges strongly, see Peirce 1995). The challenge to the interviewer is therefore all the greater and careful preparation is essential. It is to this that we now turn.

PREPARING FOR THE INTERVIEW

There are two elements involved in preparing for an interview: practical aspects and interview design. The first are often ignored, but the following discussion will highlight how these aspects can have an important impact on the nature and quality of the data collected. Interview design receives more attention, but approaches to this tend to be rather conventional, ignoring more creative options – which can be very valuable when dealing with the sort of sensitive issues that can arise in exploring the affective dimension.

Task A1.4

➤ What practical considerations (place, time, etc.) might influence how an interview develops? Jot down as many as you can think of and in each case add a note on what the effects might be. When you have finished, check your own list against the points that emerge from the following discussion.

The most immediate challenge for an interviewer is to find people willing to be interviewed (Noy 2009 provides an outstanding introduction to many of the practical issues here), so it is perhaps understandable that novice researchers take advantage of every opportunity that comes their way, often aiming to complete as many interviews as they can in the shortest possible time. The instinct to gather as much data as possible is a natural one, but a golden rule in all research is that quality takes precedence over quantity, so it is important to avoid the temptation to cram interviews together instead of allowing adequate time for each one.

There are no hard and fast rules here, but as an absolute minimum you should allow at least 15 (preferably 20) minutes either side of the anticipated time in order to allow for unexpected delays, necessary preliminaries, closing, etc. This means that if you expect to spend 45 minutes interviewing, you will need to allow at least an hour and a quarter (preferably an hour and a half) for the encounter. It is surprising how quickly time can disappear in an interview situation and a truncated encounter means that some avenues of exploration are left unexplored, responses are not adequately probed, illuminating examples are omitted, etc. For the same reason, you will need to leave a generous gap between one interview and the next: apart from the obvious need to allow time to reflect on a completed interview and think about the one to come, there is also the important but often neglected consideration that interviews can be very tiring and that this can affect the interviewer's performance.

There are other practical considerations that need to be borne in mind, especially when interviewing learners. Considerations of location are probably the most important of these. The obvious place to interview learners is in the institution where they are studying, but this can encourage 'institutional' responses, especially if the interviewer is a teacher and the respondents are young. It may be far better to locate the interviews outside the institution, perhaps in a nearby café, and if this is not possible the researcher should try to identify somewhere in the institution that is seen as neutral, such as a social space.

Part of the arrangements for any interview will include the gaining of informed consent as part of proper ethical preparation. A useful procedure here is to send the interviewee an information sheet and consent form prior to the interview (see Appendix G, website, for an example of this), giving the respondent sufficient time at the beginning of the interview meeting to ask any questions they may have before signing the consent form (Appendix F, website).

Timing also matters. Any interview conducted when the respondent or respondents have a pressing appointment or, worse, would rather be somewhere else is not likely to yield as much as an encounter at a time convenient to both participants. The interviewer should therefore try to determine the most convenient time for the respondents, and this may also involve considering what precedes the interview: students or teachers who have just finished an exhausting period in the classroom may not be in the best position to devote their energies to the interview and their views may be coloured by experiences immediately preceding the encounter. All arrangements are likely to be a matter of compromise, but a successful interviewer will try to make the best of the circumstances available.

This extends to practical arrangements such as ensuring that the interview is conducted in relative privacy in a place with minimum distractions (which is why some social spaces or cafés might not be ideal) and little if any likelihood of interruption. Ideally, water will be available in case it is needed (if nothing else, the provision of a bottle of water shows consideration on the part of the interviewer) and the interviewer will have checked the recording conditions. All this and a clear sense of how the introductory phase will be managed allow both participants to give full attention to what matters most: the interview itself. The success of the interview, though, will depend largely on how the interactional encounter is managed, which means that the interviewer should be thoroughly familiar with the topics to be explored in the interview.

Task A1.5

➤ It is commonly assumed that interviewing is a matter of asking the right questions at the right time, but not all responses need to be prompted by straightforward oral questions and not all enquiries need to be direct. Can you think of different ways in which responses might be stimulated and how delicate topics might be approached indirectly?

If the researcher has precise research questions in mind, it is reasonable to assume that interview questions will be generated from these, but that does not mean that preparing for an interview is simply a matter of drawing up a list of questions. In fact, the planned content of an interview is conventionally described as the interview schedule or interview guide, which captures very effectively the spirit with which this aspect of preparation should be approached. It is usually far better to think in terms of topics (or 'big questions') rather than a list of questions and it can help to divide preparation into three stages:

1. *Establish the aim of the interview*

This may seem an obvious thing to do, but if it is made explicit at the outset it will provide a point of orientation not only in the planning stage but also in the interview itself. In this case, let us assume that the aim is as follows: 'To elicit from learners examples in their learning experience where they have either felt positively motivated and energized to push ahead, or where they have felt demotivated with the result that carrying on has been very difficult, and to explore both the sources of this and nature of their feelings.'

2. *List core topics/questions*

Here the objective is to produce what might be described as the spine of the interview, something that will provide a solid core to which other questions can be attached. It should be something that can easily be remembered, so that the process of referring to it, although invisible to the respondent, is constantly available to the interviewer. Core questions for our hypothetical example could include the following: 'Are there any moments that really stand out in your experience of learning [language X]?' 'Have you ever felt like giving up completely?' 'Have there been any times where you felt that you had made a quantum leap in your learning?' These are obvious questions, but if they have not been covered by the time the interview ends then there will be something missing. Notice, though, that the answer to the first question may well prompt a response that opens up one or both of the other two questions.

3. *Identify lines of inquiry*

Once you have identified the main topics, it is helpful to give careful consideration to how these might be developed through subsidiary questions or prompts. The second and third of the above questions, for example, might be probed along the following lines: Was this something that emerged suddenly or out of a particular instance, or did it emerge gradually? If you had to list all the feelings you had at that time, what words would be at the top of that list? [Picking up on a particular feeling] How did that feeling show itself in your actions? How did you deal with it? Etc. This could be summed up as 'Emergence–dominant feelings–manifestations–response'.

Once the shape of the interview has been worked out, the interviewer needs to decide on an opening question that will lay the foundations for an exchange in which the respondent does most of the talking. Spradley's (1979) suggestion of a 'grand tour' question (e.g. 'Talk me through how you came to learn English in the first place') works well here.

However good the interview guide, sometimes the researcher needs to consider creative options in order to elicit the sort of detailed response that makes the difference between thin and rich data. If a topic is sensitive, for example, it may pay dividends to adopt an indirect approach in which the respondent can speak in the role of someone else. So, for example, if a student has indicated in their responses that during the course of their studies they have had to deal with severe examination nerves but clearly does not wish to discuss this, the researcher might return to the topic later and ask what advice the respondent would give to someone who suffered from severe examination nerves, thus positioning the respondent as 'expert' rather than 'victim'.

Interviewers have the opportunity to be even more creative when it comes to eliciting responses. (See Johnson and Weller 2002 for a general discussion of elicitation techniques.) For example, asking a learner to discuss which classroom arrangements seem to work best for them in which circumstances can prove a long and rather complex business, while the presentation of photographs showing different arrangements is likely to stimulate extended and detailed responses. (For a discussion of graphic elicitation involving stimuli such as self-portraits, relational maps, timelines, see Bagnoli 2009.) There is also no reason why the interview has to be conducted in a single place, when a walk taking in important locations might stimulate responses that might otherwise never emerge. (See De Leon and Cohen 2005 for a discussion of walking probes.) One researcher has even suggested that the video camera can be a powerful elicitation tool if used correctly. Here she describes its impact on the affective dimension (Pink 2004: 68): 'Some informants, in showing me an object on video described its meaning for them in terms of the emotional content of the feelings and relationships they associated it with.' The interview, then, is a creative space.

Finally, and most importantly, the interview must be piloted with respondents whose profile is as similar as possible to those who will feature in the study itself. This provides an invaluable opportunity not only to assess and if necessary revise the design of the interview, but also to examine carefully your interviewing technique. In order to do this, you will need to study the nature of the interaction in the interview, an aspect that is explored in the next section.

THE INTERVIEW AS SITUATED ACTION

Task A1.6

➤ What is your view of the following as guides to the stance an interviewer should take up? What are the implications of these positions for the nature of interview interaction?

> A general principle underlying the absence of stories and assessments is the need for interviewers to maintain *neutrality* during the interview. They must not, therefore, participate in language behaviour that reveals too much of their own personal circumstances and attitudes.
>
> (Delin 2000: 99, emphasis in original)

> [I]f interviews are taken as information-gathering techniques then they cannot, at the same time, be seen as collaborative interactions between the parties to the interview
>
> (Carlin 2009: 336)

The dangers of interviewer influence are clear enough, but there are those who advise pursuing a (probably unattainable) ideal of neutrality, ignorant of the attendant risks. Mallozzi (2009: 1046), for example, reports a colleague's advice that she should interview 'with no expression or reaction' in order 'not to influence' her respondent. Interviews, though, are human encounters, involving all the adjustments, alignments, positioning and performance associated with what Holstein and Gubrium (1995) call 'meaning making work'. This is why they need to be treated as not merely the product of *what* the participants talk about but also *how* they talk (e.g. Mishler 1986: viii).

Over 30 years ago Oakley (1981) challenged standard assumptions as to what count as 'proper' and 'improper' interviews, and Kvale's more recent discussion of confrontational interviews and leading questions (2007: 75–77/88–89) provides an excellent illustration of why standard prescriptions are unhelpful. It is also sobering to remember that assumptions we make about what an interview involves will not only influence the way we approach the encounter itself but may also have analytical implications. There is a very real danger, for example, that if we regard the interview as a way of neutrally extracting information, this will carry over into an approach to analysis that treats interviewee responses as unproblematic reports which can then be 'mined' for information (which is why it is advisable not to refer to the interviewee as an 'informant').

The title of this section therefore reflects Cicourel's (1964) representation of the interview as situated action and in what follows we adopt Baker's (1997) standpoint that interviews involve not data collection but data generation. This means that questions should not be seen as merely neutral invitations to speak and should be treated analytically as a key part of the data. In approaching the interview as a 'conversation with a purpose' (Burgess 1984: 102), we therefore focus on interactional sensitivity as the basis for developing appropriate interview technique and analytical awareness.

The primary implication of this for practice is that interviewers should approach the interview as an interactive encounter in which their part involves much more than merely asking questions and listening to the response. Instead, working within and around the sort of interview guide described in the last section, the aim should be to engage with the respondent in a way that stimulates productive talk, while recognizing that this will not always be a straightforward business (for a discussion of the reluctant respondent, see Adler and Adler 2003). In order to shift attention away from the interviewer-as-questioner, it is helpful to think of this process as 'active listenership'.

Active listenership positions the researcher as someone who is responsive not only to the interviewee but to the interactional shape of the evolving interview encounter, something that may be particularly important when researching a topic as potentially sensitive as affective aspects of language learning (for a discussion of interviews focusing on emotional experiences, see Ellis *et al.* 1997). It does not, however, involve a radical shift away from the range of question types available. At the most basic, these involve little more than *checking* understanding of a response or *reflecting* it back to the speaker, something which often stimulates an extension of the prior turn. More explicitly, the interviewer might use a *follow-up* question to invite expansion of a particular point, though it is with the *probe* that the interviewer is able to interrogate the account being developed. The nature of this may have an important bearing on how the interview develops, so probes need to be used sensitively. They may even produce challenges or objections from the respondent, although as Tanggaard (2007, 2008) has shown, this is not necessarily a negative development. Responses involving checking, reflecting, following-up and probing will all be based on the respondent's prior turn, but where the interviewer needs to move to a different topic and no obvious transition suggests itself, it may be necessary to use a *structuring* question.

These interviewer responses can be approached in terms of degrees of directiveness, which is what Whyte (1984: 99–110) proposes in the following list, beginning with the least directive:

1. 'Uh-huh,' nod of head etc.
2. Reflection
3. Probe the informant's last remark
4. Probe an idea in preceding turn
5. Probe an idea introduced earlier
6. Introduction of a new topic

However, as Mazeland and ten Have (1996: 101) note, even minimal responses 'seem mainly to serve local organizational purposes', so even these should not be taken for granted as irrelevant to the infolding interaction (see Richards 2011 for examples of this). It is therefore necessary to examine the interview, and the interviewer's contribution, in terms of its construction and in the light of the nature of the interview and its aims, something which cannot be reduced to a simple checklist. Nevertheless, interview performance in general invites reflection on certain aspects, some of which will have implications for analysis (for a more extensive treatment of developing as an interviewer, see Roulston 2010a):

1. Questions

   - How can I improve my questioning technique?

2. Distortions

   - Am I making any unwarranted assumptions?
   - Am I taking anything for granted?
   - Is there any evidence of bias?
   - Is there any evidence of my leading the interviewee?

3. Relationships

   - What signals am I sending out?
   - How are identities and relationships established and negotiated in the interview?
   - What are the implications of this for analysis?

4. The interviewee

- How does the interviewee present themself?
- What are the implications of this for analysis?

In view of the importance of questions in the development of interaction, these should receive particular attention (see Task C1.5) and should not be ignored in process of analysis (see Tasks B1.5 and B1.6). The nature of interaction means that interviewee turns will be designed to respond to prior turns and how these are constructed by interviewer, so the interview needs to be 'read' in this way. This in turn will have implications for how the interview is transcribed. As Rapley (2001) demonstrates very powerfully, transcription can have considerable interpretive significance (see also Task B1.8), and although delicate transcription is not the norm in interview research there may be instances where it is essential.

As Sarangi (2003: 79) points out, 'interview talk is not only a resource for social inquiry, but also an object of analysis in its own right' and there are various ways in which interview interaction might be analyzed. Roulston (2006), for example, reviews ethnomethodological and conversation analytic approaches, while Olsen 2006 explores sociolinguistic methods. Of course, the appropriate level of analytical sensitivity will vary according to the nature of the interview, but there is nevertheless a need for greater awareness of this dimension in interview research in our field (see the papers in Talmy and Richards 2011).

Close attention to the talk might reveal subtle shifts in interviewee or interviewer positioning and this can have important implications for interpretation. The process of construction involves both parties, each of whom might 'membership' themselves in different ways, so that the developing interaction 'serves to add to and elaborate on the categories and activities proposed in the initial description' (Baker 1997: 139). Interviews should therefore be read as accounts, not reports, and the basis of such accounts given due consideration (see Task B1.7). In a brief but illuminating case of the experiences of a learner shopping in London, for example, Block (2000) provides a telling account of the circumstances surrounding a particular interview and his relationship with the interviewee, which raised doubts in his mind about the nature of her responses.

The researcher's approach to transcription and analysis will, like the interview itself, depend partly on the nature of the research and the implications of this for how the interview is theorized. Talmy (2010) provides a helpful overview of different perspectives and Roulston (2010b) an extensive 'typology of conceptions of qualitative interviews'. Together these provide an excellent resource for the novice interviewer anxious about the relationship between the sort of thematic analysis introduced in Unit 3 of this book and the more delicate interactional analysis of the sort introduced in this unit. But whatever the outcome of the analysis, it is incumbent on the researcher to provide a sufficiently detailed account of the interview context, the nature of the interview and the procedures used for analysis (see Task B1.2), something which is often missing from papers in our own field.

The relationship between questionnaires and interviews provides a good example of how different interviews call for different approaches in terms of both design and analysis. When designing a questionnaire for a large-scale survey, for example, interviews might play a part at two stages. The first option would be to use interviews (perhaps individual interviews in this case) to help in the design of the questionnaire, exploring topics to be covered in order to understand them better and design more effective questions. Another useful step would be to conduct a group interview after piloting the questionnaire in order to identify problem questions, perhaps discuss timing issues, etc. In both these cases the interview would form part of the survey research project and the analysis would be very straightforward, providing points of information relevant to questionnaire design.

In mixed-methods research, however, the interview would be very different, reflecting its status in the project as a whole and its contribution to it. For example, a questionnaire-based survey might have identified certain factors as clear predictors of learner anxiety on pre-sessional language programmes, but in order to allow practical measures to be introduced designed to respond to this, the research plan also includes an interview element focused on understanding the part that these factors play in the learners' overall experience of such programmes. Here the interviews will probably be individual and the researcher will need to probe sensitively in order to draw out narratives that reveal significant experiences and underlying concerns. Analysis will be thematic, but close attention will also need to be paid to how the respondents construct their experiences, especially where these take the interview into sensitive territory.

In the next section we briefly review some of the research that has been done on the issue of anxiety in language learning as a preliminary to examining in Part B a survey-based investigation of Japanese learners' experience of this.

Introduction A2

Over the last 30 years of second language research, individual differences have been the focus of much research effort. Among ID factors, those related to learner affect have been prominent. Affective factors include motivation, attitudes toward the target language and its speakers, willingness to communicate and personality. Among the many personality traits examined in second language acquisition research, anxiety has proven to be among the most challenging. Scovel (1978) examined the role of anxiety as a factor in language-learning success. Scovel differentiated between trait anxiety – a person's propensity to be anxious in general – and state anxiety – anxiety emerging in reaction to stressful situations. Language learning in classroom contexts of 10 entails interaction with teachers and peers. Similar to the fear many people have about public speaking, speaking a foreign language when classmates are listening presents an anxiety-provoking state for many learners. Persons not normally anxious may feel nervous and tense in language classroom settings.

Research on the relation between state anxiety and language learning has produced mixed results. In some contexts, state anxiety has been found to short-circuit language learning, and thus has a negative correlation with success in formal learning situations (Horowitz 1986). In other situations, state anxiety is possibly dynamic. MacIntyre and Gardner (1994) found that anxiety levels change as learners get accustomed to anxiety-provoking stimuli, and may compensate for it with more focused effort. Ellis's (2008) summary of the research on anxiety in language learning suggests there is some degree of inconsistency in the overall pattern of outcomes. Specifically, it is not clear whether anxiety is a causal factor in unsuccessful learning, or whether anxiety is a consequence of learners' awareness of their relative lack of success.

Task A2.1

- Make a list of language-learning activities in a classroom context that could be anxiety-provoking.

The research on anxiety implies that language learners may be variably anxious in formal learning contexts, and their anxiety states may change with their level of proficiency. The way anxiety interacts with experience and level of proficiency is an area worthy of deeper empirical exploration. Given the complexity of interacting individual difference factors, it is apparent that simple correlations will not tell the whole story of how this affective factor influences language learning. Instead, multiple regression, which can isolate the effects of particular variables while controlling for others, provides an analysis method that can explore the relative importance of different variables in a set of models.

Section B
Extension B1

Gao, X. (2006), 'Strategies used by Chinese parents to support english language learning: Voices of "elite" university students', *RELC Journal* 37(3): 285–298

Using data from interviews with 20 students from the Chinese mainland, Gao (2006) investigates the ways in which (immediate and extended) family members are involved in students' learning and in particular how they provide support for this. Drawing on descriptions provided by the students, Gao reveals how family members are indirectly involved as advocates, facilitators and collaborators with teachers, and how they are more directly involved in their roles as advisers, coercers and nurturers. The research is designed to contribute to a relatively neglected area in our understanding of learning support and the findings are used as the basis for advocating better school–family–teacher–parent partnerships.

The research is designed to open a window on an aspect of support for learning that would repay further research, so Gao does not need to make claims about the extent to which what he discovers here is generally true of language learners, or even of Chinese language learners; but what he must do is convince the reader that the outcomes of his research provide adequate warrant for the claims he wishes to make and that they therefore represent at least a prima facie case for further investigation. In order to do this, his procedures for data collection and analysis must be sound. Nevertheless, the reader still has a right to ask whether the characteristics of the sample he has chosen make it in some way unusual. The remainder of this section is therefore devoted to a consideration of sampling, data collection, data analysis and the presentation of findings from the perspective of this paper as an example of interview-based research.

Task B1.1 Before you read

1. Given that you now know this is an interview-based project, jot down a brief list of the information you would expect to be given in the paper about the design of the research. What sort of details, for example, would you expect to find about the approach to data collection?
2. What would count as 'evidence' in a paper like this and how would you expect it to be presented?

When writing down your points, you may have considered the clues in the second part of the paper's title. It refers, for example, to 'voices', which suggests that the author will seek to represent those voices and you might have reflected on what this implies in terms of data presentation. The reference to 'elite' is also interesting because it gives us a clue to the nature of the sample.

Task B1.2 While reading

1. Read the extract below and jot down any questions you have about the approach. Identify any areas that might be problematic and places where you would have liked more information.

The Enquiry

Findings on parental involvement emerged from a larger interpretative enquiry into Chinese learners' English-learning experiences on the Chinese mainland and in Hong Kong. In the study, the concept of family is not restricted to their immediate family members including their parents but also applies to their extended family members, including grandparents, uncles and aunts and so on. Consequently, I define parental involvement *ad hoc* for this paper as parents' (as well as other senior family members') behaviours towards children's language learning (based on Gonzalez-DeHass *et al.* 2005: 101).

Participants

The enquiry involved twenty students (using pseudonyms) from the Chinese mainland who had just arrived in Hong Kong for their undergraduate studies in 2004. All participants came from well-off families in economically developed coastal provinces and major cities. They had all taken the National College Entrance Exam and achieved scores qualifying them for the top-level mainland institutions before being considered for admission by an English-as-medium-of-instruction tertiary institution in Hong Kong. In addition, they had to pass a written English test and interview before being accepted by the institution. Therefore, these students can be regarded as good English learners.

Procedures

I invited the students for interviews about their past English-learning experiences after their arrival in Hong Kong. The biographical method, where language learners' retrospective accounts of their experiences are collected and analyzed, has been gaining currency in language learning research. Many researchers (e.g. Johnson and Golombek 2002; Palfreyman 2003[b]; Benson 2005) have found this method helpful in capturing learners' voices and enhancing our understanding of what they really experience. The interview was semi-structured and normally started with questions like 'How did you learn English on the Chinese mainland?' or 'Can you tell me about your English-learning experiences on the Chinese mainland?' Then the participants would tell me about their past learning with occasional questions from me for clarification. All of the interviews, except one (done in English), were conducted in Putonghua, the language shared between the participants and myself. The interviews were recorded, transcribed verbatim, and checked by a peer for verification.

Analysis

I used methodological procedures from grounded theory to interpret the data (Strauss and Corbin 1998). However, I did not read through the transcripts with a blank mind. Instead, I took a 'paradigmatic cognition' approach and was assisted by a framework informed by sociocultural theory in the analysis as I looked for the specific social agents who had shaped the participants' English-learning (Smeyers and Verhesschen 2001; Erickson 2004). It quickly became apparent that the participants' family members, in particular parents, were highly visible in the participants' past English-learning experiences. Eighteen participants explicitly mentioned the family members' roles in their language learning and many went to great lengths to explain how their parents and other family members influenced their language learning. Struck by this phenomenon, I incorporated these references to the parental involvement into my coding and analysis. Through constant reading and comparisons (Strauss and Corbin 1998), these references can be broadly classified into two categories: in the first category, the participants described how their family members were involved in their English-learning and had an indirect impact on their development as language learners, confirming findings from numerous studies in educational research (Stevenson and Stigler 1992; Pang and Watkins 2000; Sung and Padilla 1998;, Hung and Marjoribanks 2005). In the second category, parental involvement was shown to have direct effects on language learning and strategy use, which points to a new direction by which language teachers could implement their learner development schemes.

(Gao 2006: 287–289)

2. Now return to the passage and consider any of the following questions which you have not already addressed:

   a If the writer were to describe these respondents as 'fairly typical' or representative, how far would you agree with him?
   b How much do we learn about the way the interview was designed and delivered?
   c What do we learn about the approach to analysis? What were the steps involved?

PARTICIPANTS

The author provides a good description of those participating in the study and it is clear from the outset that they represent a distinct group: they are from 'well-off families in economically developed coastal provinces and major cities' and they are high achievers. This immediately raises two (non-exclusive) possibilities: that families with this profile are more likely to provide active support for their children's study of a prestige language, and that they may have achieved their success at least in part because of the support they have received. Since we have no way of knowing, on the basis on a single interview study, which of these possibilities, if either, applies, we merely need to note that findings based on this sample may apply to quite a narrow range of possible participants.

As explained above, this does not matter in the case of a study designed merely to open up a new area – follow-up studies can follow the same line of inquiry with groups of students having very different profiles – but it does underline the need for an adequate description of the relevant sample in interview studies. While surveys of the sort described in the second part of this unit have very specific procedures for determining sample selection, selection in interview studies tends to be justified in terms of the particular case or cases selected. Provided that an adequate account is provided and that claims do not go further than is warranted by the sample, the greatest danger lies in an illegitimate appeal to typicality or representativeness. As part of a paper on the logic of case selection, Small provides an excellent critique of a hypothetical example involving an 'average' neighbourhood (2009: 15–18), demonstrating why no 'sample' of a single unit (such as a group of students from a single cohort in their first year at a tertiary institution in Hong Kong) can satisfy the criteria for an adequate representative sample.

PROCEDURES

Highly structured interviews aside (and these are best described as spoken questionnaires), it's very hard to pin down the structure and content of a research interview, so presenting anything more than the general structure or guiding questions is not really on the cards. However, we do need to understand how the interview was approached, how it was structured and what topics were covered. One way of representing the approach is to refer to a recognized tradition and this is what Gao does by setting his own study in the context of the 'biographical method'. He also provides some examples of researchers who have worked in this area and explains that it helps to capture learners' voices and enhance our understanding of 'what they really experience'. We learn that the interviews were 'semi-structured' and a couple of illustrative opening questions are provided. Finally, we are told about the language of the interviews and what arrangements were made to ensure accurate translation into English.

How much do we learn from this? The first thing to say is that the 'biographical method' actually embraces a whole range of approaches ranging from narrative approaches to those seeking to somehow 'get inside' particular experiences. It is perhaps not surprising then, to find a reference to '[t]he philosophy of my *biographical method*' (Finger 1988: 35, italics in original) in a paper looking to the hermeneutics of Dilthey and Habermas for inspiration. This sort of approach, which is represented crudely here in terms of 'getting inside experience', differs in many respects from narrative approaches and it seems clear from Gao's reference to Johnson and Golombek that it is the latter he has in mind. This is helpful, but the reference to 'what they [respondents] really experience' strikes a jarring note. One of the challenges in all interview research is how we are to treat the respondent's *representation* of their experiences, views, etc., and this is a particularly sensitive issue in narrative research.

All stories are told from a particular perspective and the logic of their development may well depend on how things eventually turned out or how the speaker positions themself within the story: a successful outcome might be seen retrospectively as in some way prefigured in events that lead up to it (though things might have looked very different at the time), some events might be excluded from the account because they are not seen as contributing to the outcome (and therefore don't move the 'plot' forward), and the speaker as the 'hero' of the story will be naturally inclined to construct events in a light that reinforces this image, perhaps omitting some less glorious episodes. This is why narrative researchers need to be very wary of thinking in term of 'real' or 'genuine' experience, as though this might be unproblematically accessible to them. Presenting a story *as* a story is one thing, but representing this as a reflection of a 'reality' outside the story is quite another. MacLure (1993) provides an excellent account of some of these problems and an interesting distinction between 'sacred' and 'mundane' biography.

In terms of the interview itself, the use of the term 'semi-structured' suggests that there are at least some topics that the researcher has planned in advance to cover, but we are not told what these are or what the general structure of the interview might have been. This is not necessarily a serious omission because the initial questions suggest that these interviews were in fact very open, but this could perhaps have been made more explicit.

ANALYSIS

The author provides us with a very clear picture of his approach to analysis, though space restrictions mean that he has to assume that we are familiar with the relevant procedures. The key references here are to *grounded theory* and *paradigmatic cognition*, though the source of the latter term is not acknowledged. We are told that attention to social agents who had 'shaped the participants' English-learning' revealed that family members were prominent. This was then incorporated into the coding of the data and that 'constant reading and comparisons' revealed two categories of influence: indirect, supporting previous research findings, and direct, which (given the lack of equivalent reference to previous research) seems to be a new and previously unrecognized category.

The use of grounded theory as a method of analysis was discussed in Chapter 3 and, using the standard terminology introduced there, it seems clear that 'family involvement' (or something along those lines) was introduced in the *axial coding* stage and that this category was eventually divided into two subcategories (although typically we are told nothing about *saturation*), one of which represents the main contribution of the paper. *Paradigmatic cognition* was not discussed in Unit 3, but the reference to it in a study using the 'biographical method' is important.

Bruner (1986) was the first person to draw a distinction between what he called *paradigmatic cognition* and *narrative cognition*, though the application of this distinction to narrative analysis by Polkinghorne (1995) is particularly relevant here (but note that in his paper Polkinghorne references Bruner 1986 as Bruner 1985). He draws on Bruner's challenge to the traditional assumption that 'logical' (cognitive) discourse is somehow legitimate while more expressive (emotional) representations are not only unreliable but potentially misleading. Bruner argued there are actually two modes of thought, each legitimate, and Polkinghorne (1995: 12) draws on this to distinguish two types of narrative inquiry: *analysis of narratives*, which employs paradigmatic reasoning, and *narrative analysis*, which uses narrative reasoning. Gao is therefore situating his research in the former category. This is consistent with his reference to grounded theory, since, as Polkinghorne (1995: 9) explains, '[t]he primary operation of paradigmatic cognition is classifying a particular instance as belonging to a category or concept.'

Task B1.3

➤ Categories also feature prominently in the quantitative analysis discussed in the second half of this Part. Jot down two things that you would expect to be similar about the nature of the categories used in survey and in interview research, and two things that you would expect to be different.

There are certain fundamental features that all categories (also called *codes*) should share. The most obvious is that they should have clear labels in order to avoid possible confusion and the most important is that their boundaries should be clear, so that one category does not 'leak' into the next and it is possible to specify clear criteria for assigning an item to a particular category, rather than a different category. However, in quantitative research the categories are predetermined and remain fixed throughout the process of data collection and analysis. This seems an obvious requirement, but in qualitative analysis this could be a dangerously restrictive imposition. Even where categorization is conceptually informed, so that the analyst is looking for manifestations of relevant concepts within the data, there must be openness to the possibility that categories will evolve, split, merge, etc. so that primacy is given to evidence that is *discovered in* the data rather than interpretations that are *imposed on* it. In analysis which is based on deriving concepts from the data, this idea of emergence is even more important.

The distinction between conceptually informed and emergent categorization applies to the second element in Bruner's distinction: narrative cognition. Polkinghorne describes this 'storied' approach as providing 'an explanatory knowledge of why a person acted as he or she did; it makes another's actions, as well as our own, understandable . . . the concern is not to identify the new episode as an instance of a general type but similar to a specific remembered episode' (1995: 11). This sort of analysis calls for a consideration of how the story is constructed. For example, its representation may involve some *narrative smoothing* (Spence 1986) as events which neither contradict the plot nor contribute to its development are left out of the storied narrative which represents the outcome of analysis.

Task B1.4

- In what ways do you think a grounded theory approach (or indeed thematic analysis generally) differs from an approach to analysis based on narrative cognition? Where might the differences in emphasis and focus lie?

- Compare your thoughts with those of Kontos (2005), available online. Since Gao is working within a paradigmatic cognition approach, these differences need not necessarily apply to his analysis, though the issue of 'tidying up' may still be relevant.

FINDINGS

Task B1.5 Before reading

- On the basis of what you have learnt about the distinction between the two different ways of knowing, how would you expect Gao to present his data? How would you expect extracts from the data to be used?

- You might also like to consider whether the presentation of the data here might be different from the approach that might be used by a researcher using narrative analysis.

Task B1.6 While reading

- Look at the quotations from the interviews in the extract which follows. Do you think they have been 'tidied up' and if so how? What things might be missing and why might these be important? Do you think it's acceptable just to present what the respondent says in the same way as you might quote from the text of a book or paper?

As Language Learning Facilitators

In at least seventeen participants' experiential narratives, parents were portrayed as active agents in providing learning conditions facilitating their language learning and uses of particular strategies. This observation seems to fit well the popular stereotypes of Chinese parents (Stevenson and Stigler 1992). They typically arranged good language learning environments for the participants, such as installing satellite TV to provide quality English TV programs, employing native speakers as home tutors, purchasing English movies or English magazines, and choosing the right schools. They would even create learning opportunities for the participants to practise uses of particular strategies. For example, Man Ning was encouraged by her English-speaking father, a scholar returned from overseas, to practise oral English at home:

> [. . .] At that time, my father just came back from US, he spoke English at home. Then sometimes he had his friends at home. At that time, I could speak English, too. I would even chat with my father's friends (Man Ning, Transcript No. 3, lines 111–13).

As Collaborators with Teachers

One of the most common ways for the participants' parents to get involved in their language learning was to finance private English tuition classes for the participants. Attending private English classes seemed to be a strategy for parents to give the participants extended language exposure, enhance interest and increase confidence in learning English:

> [. . .] a friend of my parents, she was an English teacher. She taught me ABC when I was nine (Jing, Transcript No. 17, page 4, lines 1–2).

> When I was very small, my mother took me to a private language class called 'Hong Kong English'. They used Hong Kong's text-books. There was a teacher from Hong Kong teaching us [. . .] I learnt a lot of vocabulary and became very much interested in learning English. The teacher also praised me. And I became very confident [. . .] (Zhuang, Transcript No.15, lines 147–51).

Private tutors helped these participants to reflect on their own ways of learning English. In other words, these parents used private English classes and recruited other social agents, English teachers, to positively affect the participants' development as language learners. Yao Jing told us of her experiences at a private English school in Beijing:

> I can remember a teacher from XXX school because he is so different from teachers I met in the high school. He knew a lot [. . .] I came to know that the English language is a vast ocean. He could tell you that some words are close to each other. Yet there could also be many differences in their meanings. It is a very special experience of learning English (Yao Jing, Transcript No. 3, lines 185–89).

As Language Learning Advisors

Six participants revealed that their parents were directly involved in their English-learning. It was not unusual for those parents who were English teachers themselves to start teaching their children the English language and how to learn English when they were young. However, those parents who did not necessarily have professional knowledge of language learning/teaching also gave suggestions to guide the participants' learning and strategy use. Jia Jia's mother, who presumably drew from her own past learning experiences, instructed Jia Jia to insist on listening to an audio cassette again and again until she had made progress in her listening comprehension:

> [. . .] at junior middle school, I was not good at listening comprehension. My mother told me to write down a sentence after listening to it. If I got it wrong, I needed to listen to it again and then write it again. I kept doing it for a month. My listening comprehension improved (Jia Jia, Transcript No. 12, lines 124–26).

Liu's father, who knew little English but tried his best to keep up to date about recent developments in English learning and teaching in China, provided critical guidance for Liu in how to learn English:

> Researcher: You look like that you have been learning English for a long time. When did you start it?
>
> Linda: Well, I have quite a lot of knowledge about it (how to learn English). I did spend a lot time on finding out how to learn it. Well, actually, I did not. It was my father. Although he was not good at English at all, he read widely in this area. I think that he was as good as a researcher on how to learn English [. . .] In fact, he knows little English. He did not even know how to figure out twenty-six letters (Liu, Transcript No. 11, lines 257–60).

As Language Learning Coercers

While these parents made various attempts to improve their children's language learning, two participants obviously had over-zealous parents who tried to force them to develop certain strategies out of their convictions about language learning. Yu, whose parents were convinced that she should start memorizing English vocabulary as soon as possible, was forced to memorize words at a young age. The experiences of memorizing difficult words by rote for Yu were not happy and made language learning a burden to her, although she later found that she always had good grades in English exams at secondary school:

> [. . .] he believed that I should start learning English at a very young age, but his method, I feel, is totally wrong! From the very start, he asked me to memorize and recite words. He asked me to memorize many many words. Because I finished all the words for the junior and senior school English, he asked me to memorize words for the second year college students when I WAS STILL IN PRIMARY SCHOOL. By memorization, I mean, if you ask, I should be able to tell you a particular word's meaning. Well, in fact, I do not think that I remember all of them (Yu, Transcript No. 6, lines 141–46).

As Language Learning Nurturers

Four participants were lucky to have parents who were tactful in fostering the use of certain strategies and learning beliefs among them. They had been closely involved themselves in the participants' learning by being with them and attended to the affective aspect of the participants' language learning and strategy use, which helped induce changes in the participants' strategy use and the adoption of certain language-learning beliefs. Miao Miao's acquired strategy of learning English by listening to English music might be a purposeful action or an accidental result from a shared hobby between the mother and the child learner: both of them liked to listen to English songs on radio:

> During my junior middle school days, I began to like to listen to radio (English by China Central Radio Station). Well, it was actually year 2 at my junior middle school. At that time, my mother started it. My mother liked English songs very much. Just because we wanted to listen to English songs so much, we began to listen (to the English radio) in Year 2 at my middle school [. . .] Later, I listened to it even at daytime [. . .] it often had five-minute news each hour. And I listened without turning it off. I did not understand it very well in the beginning. Later at senior middle school [. . .] I could understand quite much (Miao Miao, Transcript No. 9, lines 140–47).

In the case of Lin, her father casually played English recordings while she was working on something else so she could learn English at the same time. She did not question the utility of this, simply accepting her father's explanation:

> *Researcher*: How did you learn English then?
> *Lin*: At that time, my father played *English* 900 to me. I did not really understand it and just listened to it.

Researcher:	What a filial daughter!
Lin:	Well, he would let me do what I was doing, for example, he would let me continue doing my own things. He played the cassette aside and just told me to pay some attention to it. He said, it was like the child, who was born and learnt Chinese while listening to others. The child did not understand everything, but he listened and learnt to speak Chinese! (Lin, Transcript No. 16, lines 161–67).

In similar ways, Ying's father, who had returned from overseas, encouraged her in the belief that she should learn to speak English before learning to write it.

> My father, my father said that I should learn to speak first, then, well, just like kids. They all learn to speak first, then they learn to write (Ying, Transcript No. 13, lines 230–31).
>
> (Gao 2006: 289–294)

As you might expect, the findings are presented in terms of the categories identified by the researcher using grounded theory, and under each of the headings (categories) we are provided with a summary of the relevant behaviour as described by the students, followed by at least one illustrative extract from the data. The summary under 'Language Learning Facilitators', for example, includes examples of things that parents did to facilitate learning, such as installing satellite TV, buying English magazines and hiring tutors. The author then selects an example providing evidence that this facilitation sometimes worked even at the level of specific strategies.

The section on nurturers raises a couple of interesting issues. It begins with a fairly clear description of the category and the nature of the influence that these parents had on their children's learning, but the final example is slightly problematic. Ying's father encouraged her to learn to speak English before learning to write it, but it is not clear from either the author's statement or the accompanying extract why this counts as nurturing: there is certainly no evidence of the father 'being with' the learner or attending to 'the affective aspect' of her learning. In fact, this would seem to fit just as well, if not better, into the 'advisor' category. In terms of the researcher's general case this is relatively unimportant, but it does raise a question about the categorization.

More interesting is the way the data is represented. In Part A, the interview was described as something which is jointly constructed and where the contribution of the interviewer to how responses are framed cannot simply be ignored. It is therefore encouraging to see that in many cases Gao includes the interviewer's questions and responses. The extract from the interview with Lin provides a good example of the way respondents orient their contributions to the way the interviewer's prior turn is constructed.

Task B1.7

➤ Look at Lin's response to 'What a filial daughter!' in the penultimate interview extract above. How is it designed to respond to the interviewer's comment?

Lin has just said that she sat listening to *English 900* without understanding it and the interviewer calls her a 'filial daughter', which might suggest that she was someone who did as she was told even if this involved doing something that made no sense to her. As we saw in Part A, the way identity is constructed in interviews can be very important, and here Lin is quick to reject the suggestion that she is blindly obedient. She begins her response with 'Well', which is often a marker of disagreement, and then explains that she was allowed to continue what she was already doing, so that effectively the programme was in the background. She also explains that her father provided a clear rationale for her actions, so that by the end of her turn she has rejected the identity of blindly obedient and unthinking daughter and instead constructed a picture of someone who was able to understand the rationale behind her father's decision and 'pay some attention' to the relevant lesson while also pursuing her own activity. The researcher's comment has prompted not only more detail of the support but also some idea of how she wishes to be seen. Anyone interested in identity in interviews should find Baker (1997) an interesting read.

Although there is evidence of the researcher's contributions to the interaction, the text that we are given is clearly a 'tidied up' version. There is no evidence here of the sort of hesitations, false starts and pauses that characterize ordinary talk, and the transcription does not include features of delivery such as emphasis or sound-stretching. This is typical of much interview research and is therefore not a reason for criticizing the presentation in this paper, which is otherwise exemplary. However, the final task in this section illustrates what difference interviewer contributions can make and the part that aspects of delivery can play in this.

Task B1.8

➤ The extract below is part of an interview with a language teacher focusing on the feedback she and her colleagues give to students on their written texts. The teacher has just said that the language is important because it is a 'tool that is going to be transferred to other students and to other people, and to the outside world and that's what counts'. She then goes on to say the following.

➤ Study the two representations of her response below and decide whether or not there is any difference in terms of what we learn about her position. (Appendix E [website] has a list of the symbols used in Version B.)

Version A

So we take it for granted. If there are grammar mistakes, really serious ones, the student is penalised for the grammar mistakes more than for the content. We have to do that simply because it's more practical, simply because I'm looking for the general benefit of the public.

Version B

IE: So I- we take it for granted. IF=
IR: =Yeah=
IE: =there are grammar mistakes, really
serious ones,
(0.7)
IE: er the- the student is: penalised for
the grammar mistakes more than:
(5.0)
IE: for the
(4.0)
IE: content.
(2.0)
IR: ((Slightly doubtfully)) Ri::[ght
IE: [We have
to do tha:t [bec]ause=
IR: [Ye-]
IR: =Okay
IE: Simply (.) because it's more
practical.=e:r=
IR: =°y[eah°
IE: [simply because I:'m: looking (.)
for
(0.5)
IE: the:: general benefit
(0.6)
IE: of the public.=

(Richards 2011: 105)

It is immediately obvious that the second version would take a lot longer to transcribe than the first, and this may have implications for the amount of talk that can be transcribed in the time available, but our concern here is with the effect that the interviewer's turns, or lack of them, might have on the responses on which any analysis will be based. Although there are a number of different things that might be mentioned, what follows concentrates just two. The first is difficult to spot if you don't have the whole interview, but you may nevertheless have noticed that there are long silences in lines 8 and 10 (if you don't think five seconds is long, try saying something, pause for five seconds, then resume). It's clear that the speaker's turn isn't complete and it may be that this is just a case of thinking time, though that seems unlikely given the fairly standard contrast that is being drawn. However, this interviewer uses 'yeah' as a form of feedback fairly consistently (there are examples in lines 2 and 20), even when this might be interruptive. There is no such feedback here, and when it comes, in line 13, the tone of doubt in the voice is unmistakable, if relatively mild.

The interviewee's next turn is designed to respond to this. Notice, for example, the emphasis on 'have' in line 14 and the justification provided (it's more practical and it benefits the public). This is not part of the rationale behind the decision, as Version A might imply; it is a response to an implicit challenge. The analytical implications of this may be relatively trivial in this case, but there are also implications for what this interviewee might say in the remainder of the interview. Will they, for example, avoid making claims about the importance of grammar in order to avoid further implicit challenges? We cannot know, but it is nevertheless clear that the interviewer cannot be airbrushed out of the picture without sacrificing interpretive rigour. If you are interested in issues of transcription, you should read Rapley (2001), while a broader discussion of issues of representation is to be found in Potter and Hepburn (2005).

Such considerations are very important in research that seeks to understand the nature of participants' encounters with the world and their representations of this. Interviews, properly conducted and sensitively analysed, will yield deep and subtle insights into the nature of individual experience, but the complexity of this experience makes it dangerous to isolate particular aspects of it and treat them as representing a more general situation. However, there will be situations where researchers are interested in learning about specific aspects of experience as represented by broader populations. In such cases the interview is unlikely to serve as a useful data collection method; instead it is necessary to look to survey methodology. In the next section we take one aspect of the learning experience – anxiety – and examine how this was investigated in a specific study, this time drawing on responses from Japanese learners.

Extension B2

Kitano, K. (2001), 'Anxiety in the college Japanese language classroom', *The Modern Language Journal 85*, 549–566.

Kitano (2001) investigated two sources of anxiety among college level learners of Japanese. Using survey methodology, Kitano collected self-ratings from 211 learners of Japanese on their anxiety in Japanese language classes (JAX), their fear of negative evaluation (FNE), self-ratings of Japanese proficiency (CDS), confidence to study at the current level (CL) and the learners' expectation of how they would be perceived by Japanese speakers if they were to travel to Japan (EPJ). The surveys were designed to measure the two sources of anxiety (FNE and EPJ) and two indicators of the learners' perception of their current ability in the language (CDS and CL). The four variables allowed Kitano to examine the sources of anxiety while controlling for learners' proficiency.

Kitano summarized the relations among anxiety and the four possible predictors of it in a correlation matrix (from Kitano 2001, Appendix B):

JAX	1.0				
FNE	0.316	1.0			
CDS	–0.106	0.043	1.0		
CL	–0.509	–0.070	0.232	1.0	
EPJ	–0.389	0.041	0.485	0.657	1.0

When means and standard deviations are provided along with the correlation matrix, it is possible to replicate the original analysis using the SPSS syntax module. For such a reconstruction of the regression analysis, the SPSS Syntax Editor is used to open a new syntax page. The correlation matrix appearing in Appendix B of Kitano's paper can then be typed into the editor.

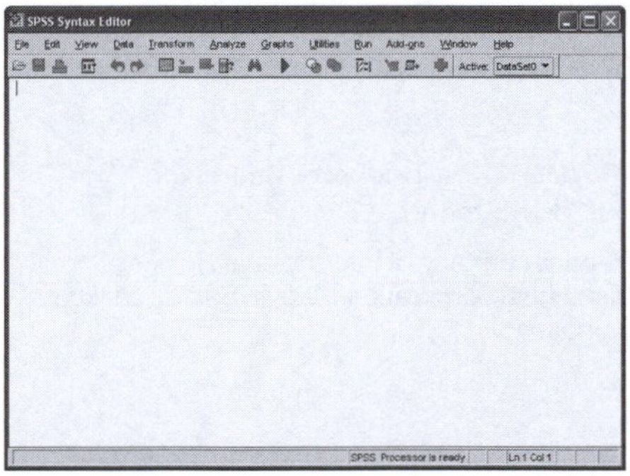

Figure 4.1 Syntax Editor for matrix input

Reprint courtesy of International Business Machines Corporation, © SPSS, Inc., an IBM company

The means, standard deviations, N sizes and correlation matrix from Kitano's Appendix B is typed directly into the syntax editor. Variables can be given the original or proxy names.

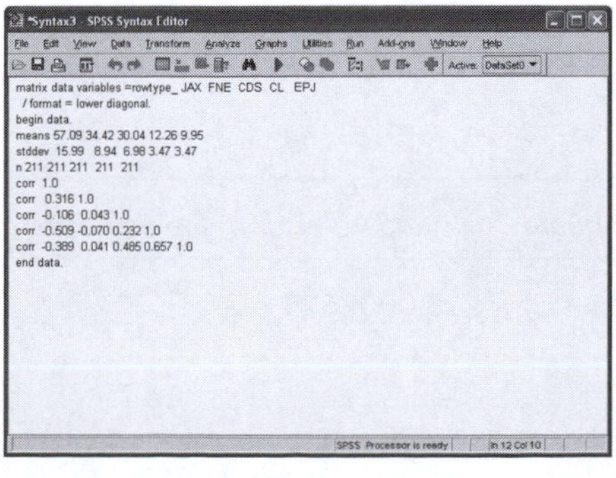

Figure 4.2 Syntax Editor with matrix data

Reprint courtesy of International Business Machines Corporation, © SPSS, Inc., an IBM company

In the original study, Kitano performed a series of **linear regression** analyses. In the first analysis, all four of the independent variables (predictors of anxiety) were forced into the model at the same time.

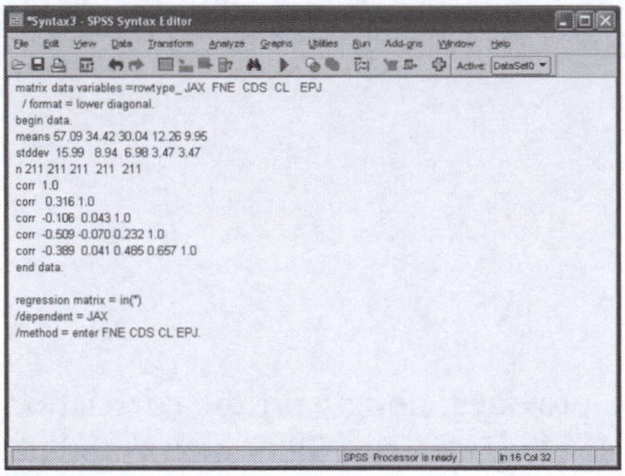

Figure 4.3 Hierarchical regression model commands

Reprint courtesy of International Business Machines Corporation, © SPSS, Inc., an IBM company

The last three command lines specify that the correlation matrix for regression analysis is already in the editor, and that the dependent variable is JAX (anxiety). The method line indicates all four predictors (FNE – EPJ) are entered at the same time. Once the model has been formulated, all lines in the syntax editor are run in sequence.

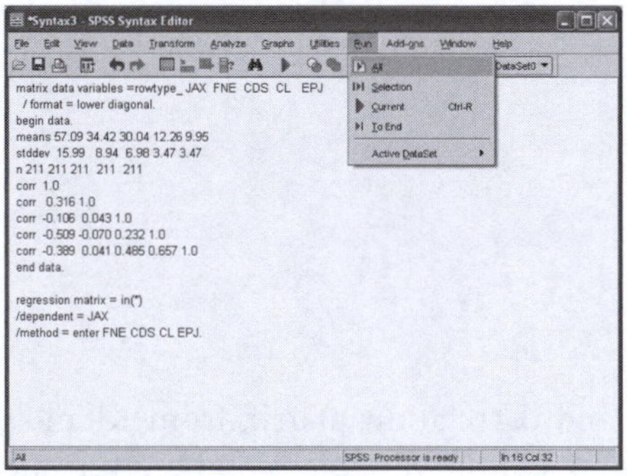

Figure 4.4 Model execution with pull-down menu

Reprint courtesy of International Business Machines Corporation, © SPSS, Inc., an IBM company

The results of the analysis show that the **adjusted R^2** is .339, which means that about 34 per cent of the individual differences in classroom anxiety are accounted for by the set of four independent variables

Table 4.1 Model summary

Model	*R*	*R Square*	*Adjusted R square*	*Standard error of the estimate*
1	.593[a]	.352	.339	13.0007526

a. Predictors: (Constant), EPJ, FNE, CDS, CL

A typical goal of regression analysis is to identify the most influential independent variable, controlling for the other variables in the equation. The question of which of the four variables is most influential can be deduced from the regression coefficients table (Appendix F in Kitano's study).

Table 4.2 Coefficients[a]

Model		*Unstandardized coefficients*		*Standardized coefficients*		
		B	*Standard error*	*Beta*	*t*	*Sig.*
1	(Constant)	65.041	5.914		10.998	.000
	FNE	.525	.101	.294	5.185	.000
	CDS	.127	.148	.055	.855	.394
	CL	−1.785	.349	−.387	−5.119	.000
	EPJ	−.799	.387	−.173	−2.066	.040

a. Dependent variable: JAX

The constant is the average level of anxiety expected when all four of the predictors are zero. On the anxiety scale used in the study, an average of about 65 would be expected even when all other variables are held at zero. For each self-rated point increase on the FNE scale, anxiety (JAX) would increase by .525, independently of the other three predictors. The change in anxiety attributable to fear of negative evaluation is statistically significant at $p<.001$. Self-assessed ability in Japanese does not influence anxiety more than random variation would ($p=.394$), and thus would be considered statistically insignificant. The higher the class level, the more the anxiety experienced. The negative coefficient reflects the valence of the JAX scale (higher ratings mean more anxiety). Similarly, for each rating scale increase in expected perception by Japanese, anxiety increases .80 of one anxiety scale point.

The **standardized coefficients** allow for a direct comparison of the four predictors of anxiety in relative terms. The largest standardized coefficient (Beta) is that for class level. About 38 per cent of a standard deviation in anxiety is increased for each step increase in the CL scale. Fear of negative evaluation (FNE) increases anxiety by about 29 per cent of a standard deviation.

Kitano modifies the regression analysis by removing each independent variable one at a time in order to gauge the effect of each IV's removal on the R^2 and the other predictors. The series of removal steps ('**backwards elimination**') can be replicated by adding a separate regression model to the Syntax editor. In total four models are specified in sequence. The order of removal can be motivated by the results of the initial 'forced entry' version with all four IVs entered. The second model removes CDS since it was not significant in the initial model. The third model drops EPJ out, and the fourth tests CL as the sole independent variable.

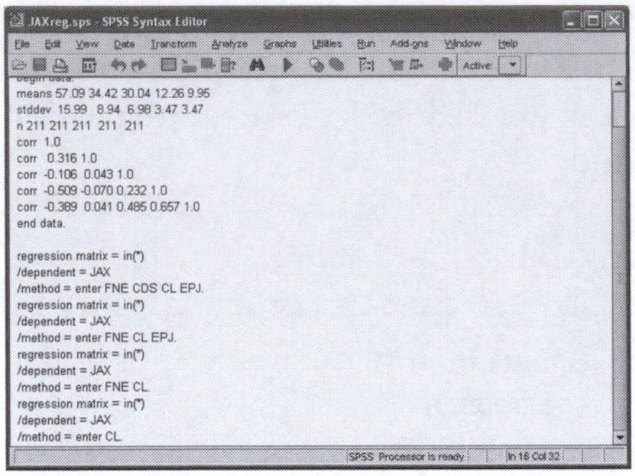

Figure 4.5 Hierarchical regression model using backward elimination

Reprint courtesy of International Business Machines Corporation, © SPSS, Inc., an IBM company

The penultimate model shows that FNE and CL are significant predictors of anxiety. After omitting CDS and EPJ, the R^2 decreased from .339 to .332 suggesting that virtually no explanatory power is lost with the omission of CDS and EPJ.

Table 4.3 Coefficients[a]

Model		*Unstandardized coefficients*		*Standardized coefficients*		
		B	*Standard error*	*Beta*	*t*	*Sig.*
1	(Constant)	67.386	4.969		13.560	.000
	FNE	.504	.101	.282	4.982	.000
	CL	−2.255	.261	−.489	−8.652	.000

a. Dependent variable: JAX

Kitano's study demonstrates the interrelatedness of factors influencing anxiety, and her regression analyses show that the magnitude of particular variables changes depending on the extent of inter-correlation among the set of predictors.

Task B2.1

- Given the issue of **mono-method bias**, how might the relations observed in Kitano's study differ if other data gathering methods had been used? What alternative methods of data collection would you use in a similar study of anxiety?

Section C
Exploration C1

This section will focus on a single interview and work through a series of tasks from planning through to analysis, before concluding with some suggestions for possible extensions.

As we saw in Part A, the degree and extent to which interviews are structured can vary, so no single example will provide fully adequate preparation for the different demands you are likely to face. Nevertheless, the narrative interview, explored in Part B, is an excellent candidate as a starting point for exploring the potential of the interview as a data collection method. There are various reasons for this, the most important of which is that it is deceptively simple: what looks at first sight like a very easy approach actually makes quite sophisticated demands on fundamental interviewing skills. As we saw in Part B, it also allows for two different approaches to analysis, so it has added value in terms of developing analytical skills, and it also happens to be something that appeals to most potential respondents, so finding someone willing to act as an interviewee is usually not difficult.

Task C1.1

- Decide on someone you would like to interview. This should be someone who you think will have an interesting story to tell, for example about their life, their career or their travels. Since this is your first interview, it is probably best to choose someone you know and someone who is likely to have a story they would like to share with you and perhaps with others.

- When you have decided on the person and the topic, prepare an information sheet and a consent form.

Task C1.2

- Jot down a list of topics you will need to cover on the information sheet, then compare your list with the one after Task C1.7.

- You will also need to prepare a consent form, using the one in Appendix F (website) as a guide.

Task C1.3

- Now think about the topics you would like to cover and decide on the sort of follow-up questions you might ask. Jot these down in two columns.

The trick here is not to include too many topics. You need to have a list that you can keep in your head and can cover in any order. Possible topics if you are interviewing someone about their career would be what made him or her decide to choose this career, what it was like on his/her first day/in his/her first year, whether there were times when (s)he contemplated a change of career, etc. The aim in drawing these up is not to produce a checklist but to sensitize you the interviewer to the sorts of things that might be covered and/or which you would like to cover. Similarly, follow-up questions should be merely indicative, so that you will have at least some ideas ready in case you need them. In fact, if the interview goes well, you will need very few of these indeed and they will probably emerge naturally.

Task C1.4

➤ Now set up and conduct the interview, using the advice offered in Part A. When you have completed this, transcribe it (or at least part of it). Now look closely at how the interview developed and assess your responses and questions critically (use the checklist on page 134 as a guide if you wish). Did they encourage the right sorts of responses or did they divert the talk away from potentially interesting topics? What sorts of prompts seemed to be the most effective? And so on.

However experienced the interviewer, it is rare to read a transcript of an interview and not have criticisms to make. You will probably have found that you were more directive than you need have been and that occasionally the responses might have been richer had you allowed them to develop more naturally. You may also find examples of the opposite outcome: potentially interesting lines of development that you failed to stimulate for want of an appropriate probe or prompt.

Task C1.5

➤ Now compare your own comments with those made by a novice interviewer. The extract opposite is taken from a pilot life history interview designed to elicit a narrative from an English language teacher working in Cyprus. The extract is taken from near the beginning of the interview and the teacher has been asked to explain how she decided to become an English teacher. Comment on the interviewer's questions in the context of the unfolding narrative and compare your analysis with the comments that follow the extract, developed in consultation with the researcher's supervisor. In the extract the interviewer's questions appear in italic.

Extract:

01 In the literature department we read many books, novels and the richness of
02 language and ideas changed my vision and I started to love English. I guess this is
03 one reason that helped me to enter this profession, the other is that even if I
04 wanted to stay at the literature department I had to teach in one way or another to
05 become an academic and related to this department I didn't have any other option
06 in Cyprus. I was not able to do anything else after studying literature but I also fell
07 in love with English and I wanted it to become and stay a part of my life. When I
08 travelled abroad it helped me to communicate with others and as a person I am
09 open-minded person and I want to improve myself all the time. I think these
10 affected my decisions to become an English language teacher and shaped my
11 career path.
12 *Do you think being a Turkish Cypriot had any influence in this decision?*
13 Actually, it has a big influence. This is something I discovered in my teaching that
14 we have a tendency or ability to learn English. In some way or another it is part of
15 our daily lives such as words that we use, relatives that we have in Britain, our
16 relations. They all influence us and get us closer to English. It becomes necessary
17 for us to use it because of the things I mentioned. And I actually like this.
18 OK. *What about being a non-native. What do you think about that?*
19 Being a non-native is a very difficult thing for an English language teacher at the
20 very beginning. When I started teaching ((long pause)) it hurt me a lot, not being in
21 an English speaking country. I now see it more clearly that I was an open minded
22 person who wanted to improve myself all the time. My accent was good compared
23 to my other friends. That is something that requires a special ability. Some people
24 are talented in music, I had a talent in learning languages. But it really hurt me not
25 being able to study and live abroad and I saw that as a drawback, a disadvantage,
26 something missing. But in 2002 I went to the USA for the first time to visit and that
27 was after I had been teaching for four years and it was the first time I was going
28 abroad. And when I went there I realised that I did not have anything negative and
29 it gave me more confidence. I started to build my confidence.

(Fatos Eren Bilgen)

The respondent begins by identifying two very different factors that led to her choosing teach English, then adds a third factor. First [(lines) 1–3] she comments on the impact of English literature and its 'richness of language and ideas' on her thinking, then she points to a more practical consideration: that in terms of employment prospects, the study of literature leads naturally to teaching [3–6]. She then goes on to add another consideration, the usefulness of English when travelling, linking this to her personality [7–9].

There are a number of things that might usefully be picked up here by the researcher, the most obvious of which is the teacher's description of herself as an open-minded person always looking to improve herself [8–9], which could even be linked to her comment on the effect that literature had on her thinking. However, the researcher's next question bears no relation to what has gone before. Although there was a mention of Cyprus, this was in the context of expectations in the educational system and the identity of the respondent as a Turkish Cypriot was not even alluded to. Yet this is what the researcher chooses to introduce as a possible additional factor in the respondent's decision.

The immediate response that follows [13] appears to support the introduction of this aspect of identity as a relevant factor, identifying it as 'a big influence', but as the turn develops it becomes clear that the respondent is not referring to her identity as a Turkish Cypriot but to the ability of those on the island (and as both respondents would know, this would apply equally to Greek Cypriots) to speak English well as a result of their use of the language in their daily lives and their contacts with English-speaking relatives [14–16]. In terms of how the question was framed, then, the interviewee has provided at best a tangential response which at least identifies the quality of being a good language learner as a potentially relevant feature. However, even this is problematic. Although it is not evident from this extract, just before this exchange the respondent had explained how her family was something of an exception because its members did *not* use English as part of their daily lives and did not have close relatives in England – so this factor does not apply in her case and therefore cannot help to account for her choice.

The design of the above turn is at least accommodative, but the interviewee's response to the researcher's next turn [18] fails completely to address the question, reinterpreting it as one about direct access to the 'native' language. In linking being 'non-native' to her experience as a language teacher [19], she ignores the fact that this question, building on the prior one, is addressed to her decision to *become* a teacher. The 'difficulty' for her as a teacher [19–22] arises from not having spent time in an English-speaking country. However, the interviewee once again highlights her open-mindedness and desire for self-improvement as key factors and points to her accent as an example of her natural ability to learn languages [22–24], something that became apparent on her visit to the USA.

There are two reasons why we should examine very carefully the questions we ask in research interviews: we can learn from them about our own technique, and we can also take note of how they might bear on any subsequent analysis. It was immediately clear to the researcher in this case that she had allowed her main research question to dominate her thinking, instead of listening to what the interviewee had to say. The research project for which this interview was a pilot involved a study of the professional identities of Turkish Cypriot teachers in northern Cyprus, so at some point in the interview aspects of this would need to be explored. However, introducing it so early and so abruptly in the interview threatens to distort the natural development of the teacher's own account, as well as planting the idea that this aspect is somehow important. The fact that the teacher does not respond to it directly means that if the aim of the interview is to be achieved this will need to be reintroduced. However, this will need careful management if the researcher is not to appear unduly concerned with this particular aspect.

From an analytical perspective, the responses to these two questions will need to be handled with care. It would be a mistake, for example, to include the claim that that 'it [being a Turkish Cypriot] has a big influence' on this respondent's decision to become a teacher because, although she says this explicitly, it is in response to an implicit suggestion from the researcher and is not borne out by the subsequent elaboration. That may seem like an easy mistake to avoid, but in the process of coding it would be all too easy to highlight the following: 'Being a non-native is a very difficult thing for an English language teacher at the very beginning.' It is an explicit claim and appears straightforward, but again the form is influenced by the researcher's question and does not reflect the way 'non-native' is constructed in the subsequent account. This is why it is essential not to airbrush the researcher's questions from the picture that develops through an interview.

You may have found some similarities between your own comments and those on the extract, but similarity is not really an issue; what matters is the development of sensitivity to your interaction as an interviewer. In fact, the above analysis is only part of a more extensive critique of her performance by the researcher involved, who then subjected the rest of the interview to an even more probing and detailed analysis. One interesting outcome of this – and something that you might wish to compare with your own insights – was that many of her observations reinforced comments made by one of the most successful interviewers of the twentieth century, Studs Terkel (Grimes 2008), about the secret of effective interviewing:

> If they think you're listening, they'll talk. It's more of a conversation than an interview.
>
> It isn't an inquisition; it's an exploration, usually an exploration into the past. So I think the gentlest question is the best one, and the gentlest is, 'And what happened then?'

Task C1.6

➢ If you would like to extend your analysis further, you could examine your interview from the perspective of its construction. How did your contributions influence the way the interviewee responded and how they constructed their story? And in terms of that story, what was their relationship to it? Did they construct particular identities to suit different episodes or when they were standing 'outside' events or evaluating them?

You may find it difficult to see any evidence that your participation in the interview has influenced the construction of the story in any particular way, and this may indeed be a fair reflection of what happened, but you will almost certainly find evidence of identity construction. You may need to look hard for this and go back to the text a number of times, but when you begin to see evidence of it and of how the speaker positions themselves with regard to events, this will probably prove to be the most exciting aspect of the whole experience.

Task C1.7

➢ Now move on to the next section and, as you become more confident in your understanding of the relevant procedures there, you might like to think about a two-stage project which would begin with interviews (probably not narrative interviews in this case) to open up a topic and provide valuable insights that could inform the design of a questionnaire to be used in a much wider survey.

Response to Task C1.2

➢ Your information sheet should have included details of the following:

- Description of the project
- Details of interview (e.g. approximate length, method of recording)
- Voluntary nature of participation and right to withdraw
- Storage of data, security, etc.
- Confidentiality and anonymity
- Uses to which data will be put (publication, conferences, materials, etc.)

Exploration C2

Linear regression with two variables is equivalent to a simple correlation. The degree of the correlation between the dependent (Y) and a single independent (X1) variable is represented as the percentage of variance in one accounted for by the other. The Venn diagram in Figure 1 shows how X1 accounts for about 10 per cent of the variance in Y.

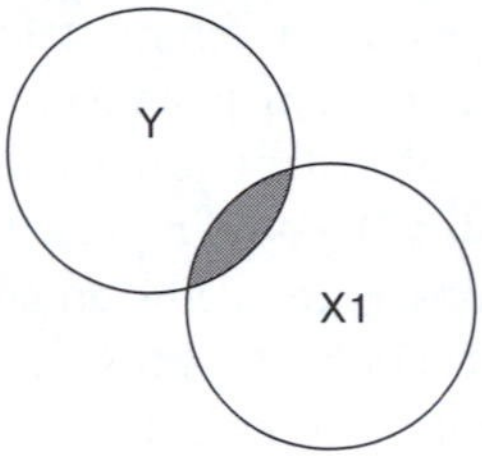

Figure 1

When a second independent variable is added to the model, the co-variation between two independent variables is taken into account. To the extent that a second independent variable (X2) correlates with the dependent variable (Y) independently of the other independent variable (X1), the multiple correlation of both X1 and X2 with Y grows larger. The Venn diagram in Figure 2 shows that about 30 per cent of the variance (R^2) in Y is accounted for by the combination of X1 and X2.

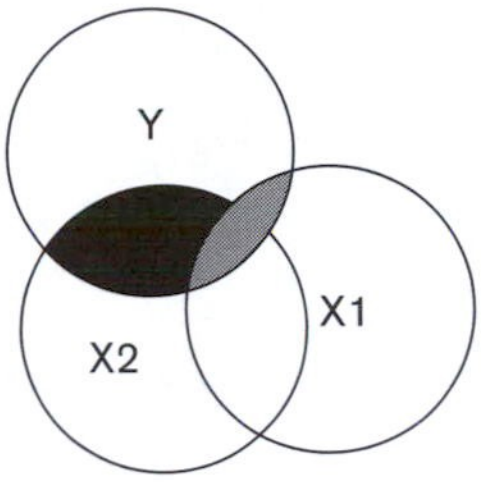

Figure 2

The influence of X2 relative to X1 on Y can be readily deduced. X1 by itself accounts for about 10 per cent of the variance in Y, while X2 accounts for about 20 per cent more variance, independently of X1. In this manner, the question of which independent variable is more influential on Y can be answered through a comparison of their relative contribution to the multiple correlation squared R^2.

Task C2.1

★

- Think of a language-learning outcome to be represented by the Y in Figure 2. Then think of individual difference variables such as aptitude, motivation, attitude, willingness to communicate, anxiety, etc. that could be represented as X1 and X2. Why would X1 and X2 account for different amounts of variance?

Linear regression analysis provides an absolute and relative comparison of each independent variable's influence on the dependent variable of interest. When the research question is to identify the change in the outcome occurring with each unit change in an independent variable, the unstandardized regression coefficient (B) is interpreted. Given that each independent variable may be on a different scale, the interpretation of each IV's influence is in the original scale. For instance, if the number of successful tasks is the outcome (Y) and hours of instruction is the first independent variable (X1), a regression such as $Y = B_0 + B(X1)$ would represent the model: tasks = constant+B(hours). Supposing that the observed coefficients were $B_0 = 3$ and $B(X1) = .10$, the interpretation would be for every hour of instruction, $\frac{1}{10}$ of a task is learned. If hours were at zero (the constant or 'intercept'), learners would on average be able to do three tasks anyway.

A primary purpose of multiple regression is to evaluate the influence of independent variables controlling for others already in a model. If the goal were, for instance, to evaluate the influence of a third independent variable entered after two other are in the model, the unique amount of variance in Y exclusively co-varying with X3 would be tested. Adding X3 to the model in Figure 2 could yield a Venn looking like Figure 3.

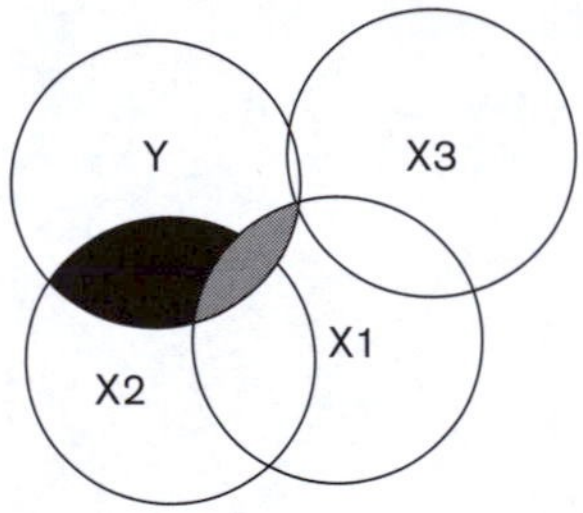

Figure 3

The amount of unique variance in Y attributable to X3, controlling for X1 and X2, appears to be about 2 per cent. Depending on the sample size, the addition of a small percentage of unique covariance with Y could be statistically insignificant. When independent variables are entered into a model in a hypothesis-driven order, they are entered hierarchically. The object of interest is to test the explanatory power of the last-entered IVs controlling for the other variables already in the model.

RESEARCH SCENARIO C2

Multiple regression can be used to test substantive hypotheses about the relative influence of independent variables on outcomes of interest. As an example of hypothesis testing, the data set Achprof.sav will be reused. In this scenario, proficiency developed after one year of intensive instruction is the dependent variable of interest. The research question would be 'Do individual differences in proficiency remain constant, or are proficiency differences the consequence of differential effort as observed in end of term achievement differences?' To explore this question, the dependent variable will be Prof2, the measure of proficiency after one year of foreign language study in university.

Entered into the model first will be the measure of proficiency taken prior to the start of instruction. If subsequent instruction does little to modify the ordering of individual learners, the original measure of proficiency can be expected to account for most of the variance in the post-tested measure of proficiency.

Opening the regression module under the Analysis menu, the Linear option is chosen.

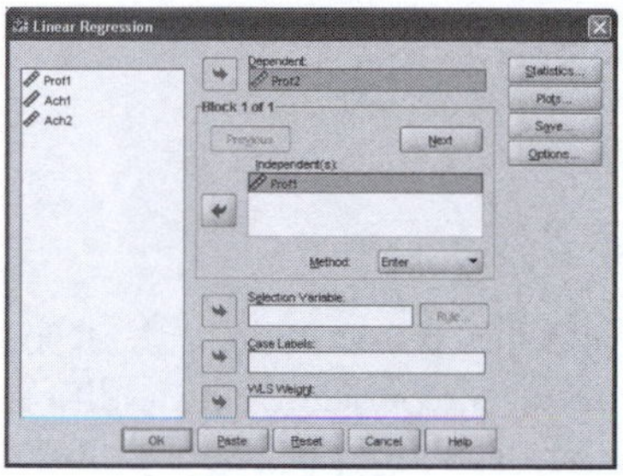

Figure 4.6 Hierarchical regression model for Achprof.sav

Reprint courtesy of International Business Machines Corporation, © SPSS, Inc., an IBM company

The post-tested Prof2 is entered as the dependent variable and the pre-instruction measure of proficiency is entered as the sole independent variable.

The resulting regression shows that about 53 per cent of the variance in the post-tested proficiency is explained by the pre-test (R^2=.529). This suggests that about 47 per cent of the variance in scores may be associated with some other process not yet modelled. Omission of possibly important explanatory variables is referred to as **specification error**. When potentially important variables are not part of a regression model, the error ($1–R^2$) possibly contains variance that would be attributable to a variable not yet included in the model. Researchers generally anticipate which variables are plausibly related to the dependent variable of interest, and strive to collect **reliable** data to represent them.

Table 4.4 Coefficients[a]

Model	*Unstandardized coefficients*		*Standardized coefficients*		
	B	*Standard error*	*Beta*	*t*	*Sig.*
1 (Constant)	117.930	15.464		7.626	.000
Prof1	.769	.036	.728	21.384	.000

a. Dependent variable: Prof2

The researchers might hypothesize that achievement motivation is ephemeral. If this is so, growth in proficiency (Prof2) would be related to the initial effort language learners make in class, which is reflected in their relative achievements. If such effort is short-lived, subsequent indicators of achievement would be expected to have less influence on post-tested proficiency than the initial achievement outcomes. To test this hypothesis, the first achievement measure (Ach1) would be entered into the revised regression model.

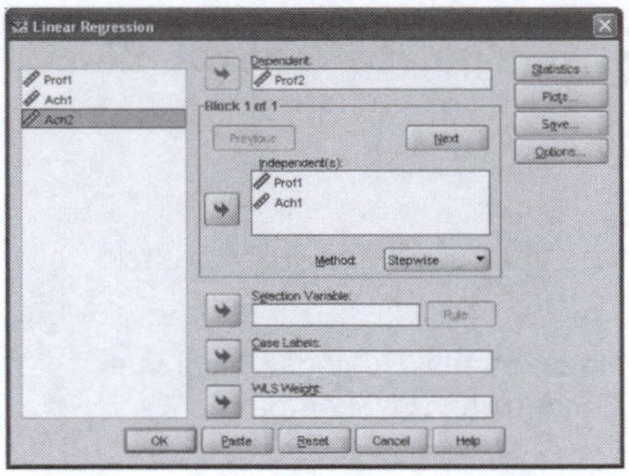

Figure 4.7 Hierarchical regression model with added predictors

Reprint courtesy of International Business Machines Corporation, © SPSS, Inc., an IBM company

The variance in Prof2 explained after the addition of Ach1 to the model is the R^2 of model 2 minus the R^2 of model 1, or .585 –.529 or about 5.6 per cent. The addition of Ach1 to the model accounts for more variance than starting proficiency alone. The size of the coefficient (1.58) is statistically significant at $p<.001$. This would imply that the observed change in the R^2 would happen less than 1 in 1000 occasions if purely randomly data were used.

Table 4.5 Coefficients[a]

Model		*Unstandardized coefficients*		*Standardized coefficients*		
		B	*Standard error*	*Beta*	*t*	*Sig.*
1	(Constant)	18.009	19.708		.914	.361
	Prof1	.714	.035	.675	20.589	.000
	Ach1	1.584	.211	.246	7.509	.000

a. Dependent variable: Prof2

For every grade point increase, proficiency increases by 1.58 points. In relative terms, the prior proficiency (Prof1) remains the more influential, though there is positive evidence that first term achievement adds to proficiency.

The last step of the hierarchical regression model adds Ach2 to the model.

The third model's R^2 grows to .591, indicating that by adding Ach2 less than 1 per cent of the variance in post-tested proficiency is accounted for. This tiny increment is still significant for this sample size.

Table 4.6 Coefficients[a]

Model		Unstandardized coefficients		Standardized coefficients		
		B	*Standard error*	*Beta*	*t*	*Sig.*
1	(Constant)	13.077	19.660		.665	.506
	Prof1	.703	.035	.665	20.272	.000
	Ach1	1.093	.282	.170	3.877	.000
	Ach2	.631	.243	.114	2.600	.010

a. Dependent variable: Prof2

The 'waning motivation' hypothesis is only weakly supported. The second term achievement is still significant, though in relative terms is less influential on the post-tested proficiency, explaining about 11 per cent of a standard deviation (Beta) in proficiency differences, controlling for pre-tested proficiency and the previous achievement outcomes.

Task C2.2

➤ In contrast to the hypothesized 'waning motivation' hypothesis, what other explanations for the relatively small influence of Ach2 can you think of? How would you test alternative hypotheses?

Exploration C3

Surveys are used in many fields to gauge respondents' attitudes, opinions and self-assessments about variables of interest to researchers. In contrast to the direct observation and participant observation commonly used in ethnomethological approaches, surveys are indirect in that they stimulate the respondents to think and reflect on their own cognition or behaviour. The interpretability of a survey depends on two factors. One is that the responses given on the survey, which may be open-ended responses, or responses on a rating scale with ordered categories, are internally consistent or reliable. Reliability is estimated directly or indirectly. The direct method is based on the assumption that the responses given on a survey are stable and ought not to change from one occasion to the next. This type of reliability, or stability, is predicated on the assumption that if the same persons were asked on two occasions, and no obvious intervening event had occurred to change their opinions, the relative ordering of the persons along the **construct** continuum measured on the survey would not change; persons with a strong opinion on one day should logically maintain the opinion on the next day unless there were some event to change that opinion. The assumption is not that they would give the exact responses, but rather that the responses would yield a stable rank order in the magnitude of the construct on the two occasions. For most research projects, administering the same survey twice is considered impractical.

The indirect way of estimating reliability is based on the **internal consistency** of the indicators designed to define the construct. Surveys are usually made up of a series of questions or items to which the respondents provide a rating. The items on the survey are typically organized into subsets that are designed to indicate a particular construct. To the extent that the items indicating a particular construct are interrelated, the better they cohere as indicators of the construct. If the items are incoherent, the summation of the items thought to indicate the construct will provide an unstable score for each person. Survey designers thus try to create items that are different ways of getting respondents to indicate their opinion about a particular construct. To the extent that the items representing a construct are intercorrelated, the score for each person will be measured with less error.

A number of ways of analyzing survey data are possible. One approach in common use is a probabilistic model which assumes that persons with a stronger opinion about a construct of interest are more likely to respond to survey questions more affirmatively than persons with a less strong opinion about the same construct. To test this assumption it is necessary to know how easy it is to agree with a particular item, and how each respondent is arranged on the continuum of opinion about the construct the collection of items represent. Once an estimate of the ease of agreement for each item and each respondent's agreeableness is made, the rating of each item by each person can be compared. For instance, if an item is easy to agree with, and a person has an overall strong opinion about the construct the item represents, the expectation is that the person will respond with a high rating on that item. Conversely, if another person has a moderate opinion about the construct the item represents, the expectation is that that person will respond with a lower rating than the person with the stronger opinion.

Learners are frequently surveyed about their motivation, attitudes, opinions or ability. A common object of interest is learner confidence to perform language learning tasks. Many times researchers are interested in comparing 'can do' surveys with actual performance analyses in order to validate proxy measurements of ability without the logistical problems of testing large numbers of candidates. In other projects, the goal may be to give learners the authority to self-assess their own achievement iteratively so that they become invested with more responsibility and control over their own learning. For both of these goals, the assumption the survey designers must make is that the learners are responding to the survey reliably, and that the collection of items cohere enough to define whatever construct the designers are trying to measure.

When self-assessments are designed, the items are typically ordered in terms of their assumed difficulty. The actual difficulty is however derived from the endorsement rate for each step of the survey item, which may be ordered on a **Likert** type scale implying more of the construct at the high end of the scale and less of the construct at the low end of the scale. A self-assessment 'can do' item for foreign language speaking ability might be worded as:

I can order food from a menu in a restaurant

Learners would use their own experience or prior learning to estimate their capacity to perform the food ordering task using a scale such as:

Cannot do at all					Can do wth ease		
1	2	3	4	5	6	7	8

The question survey designers need to answer has to do with the stability and coherence of the responses. The data, once collated, may look like a block of responses with the identification of the respondent at the left. In the example below, the first eight digits correspond to a name roster of learners who have self-assessed on 25 performance items like the specimen above. In all there are 70 respondents in the data set.

```
51110018555785134333333431542222
51110028678374136546443322322334
51110038688886128237877322232224
51110048588382128326522262222224
51110057667363333333333333333333
51110068688675335366556543322535
51110078668474145436444343333234
51110088578384115226322241332212
51110108288282124114112121221221
51110118588383336646766423443346
51110128788686337556566675655566
51110138688376335325443322433344
51110148588686547647675584655566
51110158668281115217341773533315
51110167436443125216253321323334
:       :       :       :       :       :
```

RASCH ANALYSIS

A convenient and powerful method of analyzing survey data is to perform a probabilistic analysis of the item responses. The **Rasch model** (Wright and Masters 1982, Bond and Fox 2002) can be deployed to estimate the stability and coherence of a set of responses like the can do self-assessment exemplified above. Essentially, the Rasch model tests the fit of the actual data to the probabilistic model outlined above. Items and respondents who show erratic patterns are flagged as misfitting the model. Such items and persons may need further investigation to determine the sources of the fit problem.

In addition to the matrix of raw data like the one above, a command file needs to be constructed using a text editor. The command file for performing Rasch analysis contains a few lines that are unique to the particular data at hand. Others are more or less fixed and need not be manipulated or changed from the basic template. The lines of the command file contain specific instructions to the software MINISTEPS.exe to execute the analyses. Many different and complex analyses are possible with even the Student Version of the Rasch Analysis software WINSTEPS. For the purpose of illustration, a simple rating scale analysis will be done on 25 'can do' self-assessment items completed by 70 language learners.

```
    &INST
    TITLE = Self-Assessment Rasch Analysis
    DATA = e:routcd10.dat
    NAME1 = 1 ; column of first character of person label
    NAMELEN = 8 ; length of person label
    ITEM1 = 9 ; column of response to first item in data record
    NI = 25 ; number of items
    XWIDE = 1 ; number of columns per item response
    CODES = 12345678 ; valid codes in data file
    CLFILE = *
1   Cannot do at all
2   Cannot do in most situations
3   Can only do in some situations with assistance
4   Can only do in some situations
5   Can sometimes do, but with difficulty
6   Can usually do alone
7   Can do in most situations
8   Can certainly do with ease
*
&END
```

The TITLE line contains the name of the data analysis; the DATA line specifies the location and name of the text file containing the matrix of data; NAME1= is the column in the data matrix where the first digit or letter of the person name or code number appears. In this data the NAMELEN = specifies that the string of numbers is eight digits long; Item1 = locates the column in the data matrix where the first item on the survey appears; NI = specifies the number of items to be analyzed; Xwide = is the width of each response; CODES are the letters or numbers that represent the ordered responses; the optional CLFILE = allows wording of the rating scale steps to be written out.

For a rating scale analysis, it is common that respondents may not all interpret the steps on the scale in the manner the designer has in mind. The rating scale analysis allows for a check on the measurement assumptions.

Task C3.1

➤ Google 'MINISTEP Rasch' to locate the WINSTEPS site. Download the MINISTEP trial version of the software and install it on your Windows system. Mac users may wish to use an emulator.

We will run a Rasch rating scale analysis on the sample 'can do' survey. To simulate the analysis MINISTEP needs to be installed. Once installed, it can be invoked by clicking on the 'W' icon. The opening menu will appear on the screen:

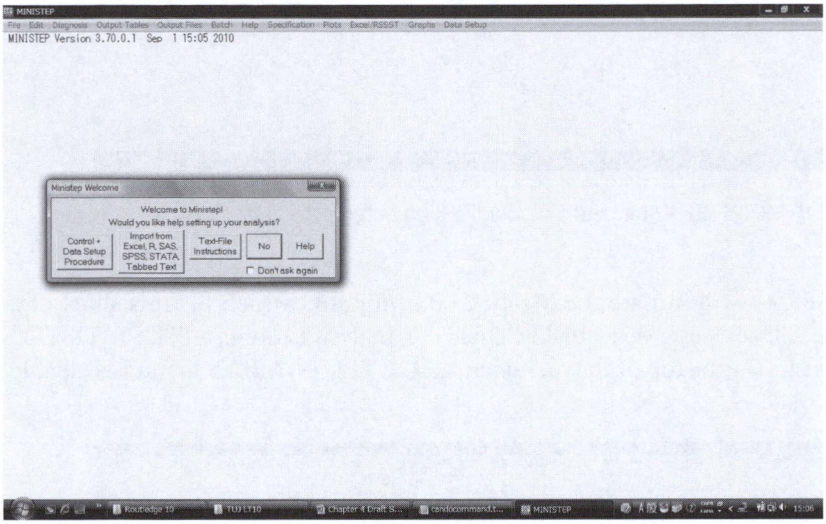

Figure 4.8 MINISTEP welcome screen

A handy semi-automated analysis set up is offered in MINISTEPS. We will, however, work with the command file, so NO is chosen from the menu.

Task C3.2

➤ From the Routledge site (http://www.routledge.com/cw/ross), locate the data set **candocommand. txt**. Copy it and the data set **routcd10.dat** to your own computer. Note the path, and if possible, save the files to an external drive or memory stick. From the FILE menu the command file candocommand.txt should be selected. It is automatically uploaded into the MINISTEP program. It is important to check that the path to the location of the data matrix is clearly specified. The command file will direct the program to the location of the data to be read in. Once the data file has been found, the program is poised for the start of the analysis.

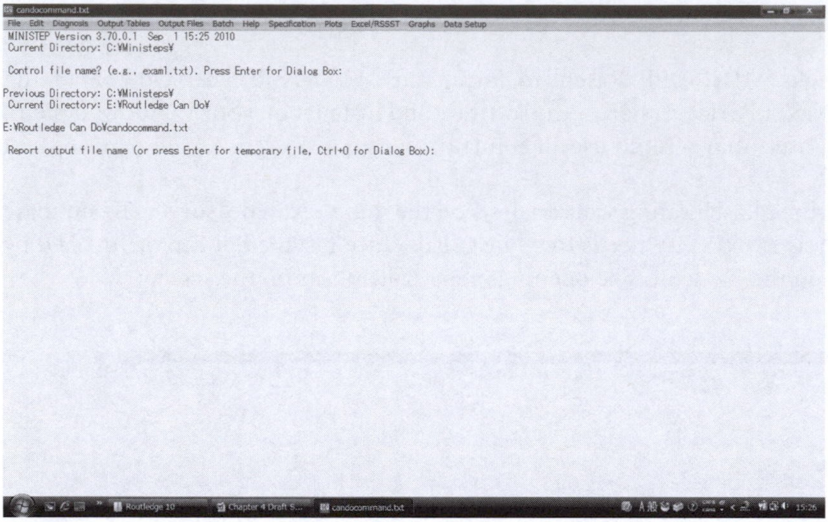

Figure 4.9 MINISTEP command file specification screen

An ENTER ← will initiate the MINISTEPS program, which for this short data example, will converge very quickly. Once the analysis is done, a FIT STATISTICS table appears. At the top of the menu bar, an OUTPUT TABLES menu is available.

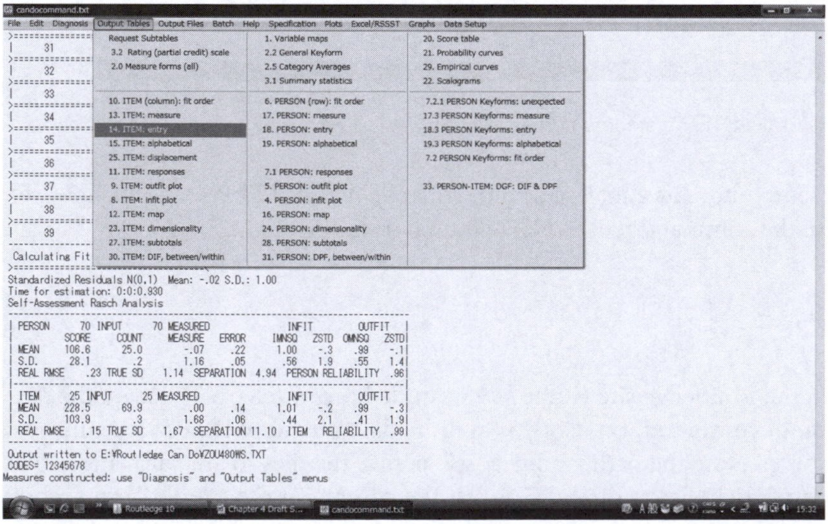

Figure 4.10 MINISTEP output table specification for item entry order

A quick examination of the 25 items gives a breakdown of their difficulty and fit to the model. Items that may be confusing or faulty will have an INFIT larger than about 1.5. The concept of 'fit' in the Rasch model reflects how responses to items are expected to conform to an implicational order. When actual responses accumulate deviations from the probabilistic expectations over the threshold of 1.5, the item or the persons generating the responses are flagged as potential cases of misfit. Items on a rating scale misfit because the steps between the categories are not clearly different in the minds of the respondent. Persons misfit because of inattention, responding indifferently or misunderstanding of the propositional content of the survey question. The fit diagnosis is very much like a localized index of reliability of the items or persons responding to them.

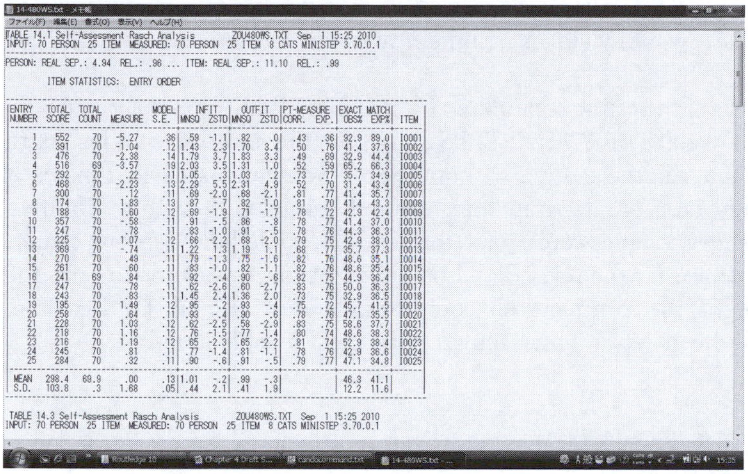

TABLE 14.1 Self-Assessment Rasch Analysis ZOU480WS.TXT Sep 1 15:25 2010
INPUT: 70 PERSON 25 ITEM MEASURED: 70 PERSON 25 ITEM 8 CATS MINISTEP 3.70.0.1

PERSON: REAL SEP.: 4.94 REL.: .96 ... ITEM: REAL SEP.: 11.10 REL.: .99

ITEM STATISTICS: ENTRY ORDER

ENTRY NUMBER	TOTAL SCORE	TOTAL COUNT	MEASURE	MODEL S.E.	INFIT MNSQ	INFIT ZSTD	OUTFIT MNSQ	OUTFIT ZSTD	PT-MEASURE CORR.	PT-MEASURE EXP.	EXACT MATCH OBS%	EXACT MATCH EXP%	ITEM
1	552	70	-5.27	.36	.59	-1.1	.82	.0	.43	.36	92.9	89.0	I0001
2	391	70	-1.04	.12	1.43	2.3	1.70	3.4	.50	.76	41.4	37.6	I0002
3	476	70	-2.38	.14	1.79	3.7	1.83	3.3	.49	.69	32.9	44.4	I0003
4	516	69	-3.57	.19	2.03	3.5	1.31	1.0	.52	.59	65.2	66.3	I0004
5	292	70	.22	.11	1.05	.3	1.03	.2	.73	.77	35.7	34.9	I0005
6	468	70	-2.23	.13	2.29	5.5	2.31	4.9	.52	.70	31.4	43.4	I0006
7	300	70	.12	.11	.69	-2.0	.68	-2.1	.81	.77	41.4	35.7	I0007
8	174	70	1.83	.13	.87	-.7	.82	-1.0	.81	.70	41.4	43.3	I0008
9	188	70	1.60	.12	.69	-1.9	.71	-1.7	.78	.72	42.9	42.4	I0009
10	357	70	-.58	.11	.91	-.5	.86	-.8	.78	.77	41.4	37.0	I0010
11	247	70	.78	.11	.83	-1.0	.91	-.5	.78	.76	44.3	36.3	I0011
12	225	70	1.07	.12	.66	-2.2	.68	-2.0	.79	.75	42.9	38.0	I0012
13	369	70	-.74	.11	1.22	1.3	1.19	1.1	.68	.77	35.7	37.3	I0013
14	270	70	.49	.11	.79	-1.3	.75	-1.6	.82	.76	48.6	35.1	I0014
15	261	70	.60	.11	.83	-1.0	.82	-1.1	.82	.76	48.6	35.4	I0015
16	241	69	.84	.11	.92	-.4	.90	-.6	.82	.75	44.9	36.4	I0016
17	247	70	.78	.11	.62	-2.6	.60	-2.7	.83	.76	50.0	36.3	I0017
18	243	70	.83	.11	1.45	2.4	1.36	2.0	.73	.75	32.9	36.5	I0018
19	195	70	1.49	.12	.95	-.2	.93	-.4	.75	.72	45.7	41.5	I0019
20	258	70	.64	.11	.93	-.4	.90	-.6	.78	.76	47.1	35.5	I0020
21	228	70	1.03	.12	.62	-2.5	.58	-2.9	.83	.75	58.6	37.7	I0021
22	218	70	1.16	.12	.76	-1.5	.77	-1.4	.80	.74	48.6	38.3	I0022
23	216	70	1.19	.12	.65	-2.3	.65	-2.2	.81	.74	52.9	38.4	I0023
24	245	70	.81	.11	.77	-1.4	.81	-1.1	.78	.76	42.9	36.6	I0024
25	284	70	.32	.11	.90	-.6	.91	-.5	.79	.77	47.1	34.8	I0025
MEAN	298.4	69.9	.00	.13	1.01	-.2	.99	-.3			46.3	41.1	
S.D.	103.8	.3	1.68	.05	.44	2.1	.41	1.9			12.2	11.6	

TABLE 14.3 Self-Assessment Rasch Analysis ZOU480WS.TXT Sep 1 15:25 2010
INPUT: 70 PERSON 25 ITEM MEASURED: 70 PERSON 25 ITEM 8 CATS MINISTEP 3.70.0.1

Figure 4.11 MINISTEP survey item measure and fit table

Items 3, 4 and 6 in Table 14.1 appear to misfit the model, and may require further examination. Scrolling down to Table 14.3 leads to a breakdown of the step endorsements for each of the items. The * marks items with rating scales steps that are out-of-order endorsements of the items on the rating scale.

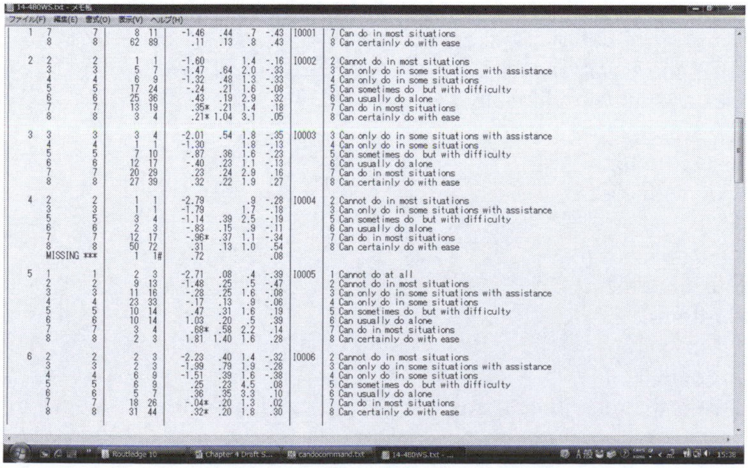

1	7	7	8	11	-1.46	.44	.7	-.43	I0001	7 Can do in most situations
	8	8	62	89	.11	.13	.8	.43		8 Can certainly do with ease
2	2	2	1	1	-1.60		1.4	-.16	I0002	2 Cannot do in most situations
	3	3	5	7	-1.47	.64	2.0	-.33		3 Can only do in some situations with assistance
	4	4	6	9	-1.32	.48	1.3	-.33		4 Can only do in some situations
	5	5	17	24	-.24	.21	1.6	-.08		5 Can sometimes do but with difficulty
	6	6	25	36	.43	.19	2.9	.32		6 Can usually do alone
	7	7	13	19	.35*	.21	1.4	.18		7 Can do in most situations
	8	8	3	4	.21*	1.04	3.1	.05		8 Can certainly do with ease
3	3	3	3	4	-2.01	.54	1.8	-.35	I0003	3 Can only do in some situations with assistance
	4	4	1	1	-1.30		1.8	-.13		4 Can only do in some situations
	5	5	7	10	-.87	.36	1.6	-.23		5 Can sometimes do but with difficulty
	6	6	12	17	-.40	.23	1.1	-.13		6 Can usually do alone
	7	7	20	29	.23	.24	2.9	.16		7 Can do in most situations
	8	8	27	39	.32	.22	1.9	.27		8 Can certainly do with ease
4	2	2	1	1	-2.79		.9	-.28	I0004	2 Cannot do in most situations
	3	3	1	1	-1.79		1.7	-.18		3 Can only do in some situations with assistance
	5	5	3	4	-1.14	.39	2.5	-.19		5 Can sometimes do but with difficulty
	6	6	2	3	-.83	.15	.9	-.11		6 Can usually do alone
	7	7	12	17	-.96*	.37	1.1	-.34		7 Can do in most situations
	8	8	50	72	.31	.13	1.0	.54		8 Can certainly do with ease
	MISSING ***		1	1#	.72			.08		
5	1	1	2	3	-2.71	.08	.4	-.39	I0005	1 Cannot do at all
	2	2	9	13	-1.48	.25	.5	-.47		2 Cannot do in most situations
	3	3	11	16	-.28	.25	1.6	-.08		3 Can only do in some situations with assistance
	4	4	23	33	-.17	.13	.9	-.06		4 Can only do in some situations
	5	5	10	14	.47	.31	1.6	.19		5 Can sometimes do but with difficulty
	6	6	10	14	1.03	.20	.5	.39		6 Can usually do alone
	7	7	3	4	.68*	.58	2.2	.14		7 Can do in most situations
	8	8	2	3	1.81	1.40	1.6	.28		8 Can certainly do with ease
6	2	2	2	3	-2.23	.40	1.4	-.32	I0006	2 Cannot do in most situations
	3	3	2	3	-1.99	.79	1.9	-.28		3 Can only do in some situations with assistance
	4	4	6	9	-1.51	.39	1.6	-.38		4 Can only do in some situations
	5	5	6	9	.25	.23	4.5	.08		5 Can sometimes do but with difficulty
	6	6	5	7	.36	.35	3.3	.10		6 Can usually do alone
	7	7	18	26	-.04*	.20	1.3	.02		7 Can do in most situations
	8	8	31	44	.32*	.20	1.8	.30		8 Can certainly do with ease

Figure 4.12 MINISTEP item measure and fit step structure

The fundamental assumption is that subgroups of learners with more overall confidence will endorse higher rating scale steps on each item than will learners with less confidence. For Item 6, the average confidence of the sub-group of learners endorsing step 6 on the rating scale is actually higher than the sub-group endorsing step 7 on the scale (.–04 being considerably less than .36). Moreover, the 44 per cent of the learners selecting step 8, actually have less overall confidence than the learners selecting steps 6 or 7 on the rating scale. The out-of-order use of the rating scale alerts us to the fact that using a raw score summation would be very misleading. For this item, rating category 8 does not mean more than 7 or 6, which if summed to construct a score, would yield an arithmetic anomaly.

The Rasch analysis of the rating scale allows for possible editing or reanalysis. A very useful feature of WINSTEPS/MINISTEPS allows for the addition of a few extra command lines to rerun the analysis without the offending items. The estimates of confidence would be more accurate and less ambiguous with such a modified analysis. If these survey items were a pilot, the designer would have a second chance to edit and re-administer the revised and possibly improved version. To omit the poorly fitting items, the command file could be amended with an IDFILE= line, which deletes all the items, and then reinserts the most reliable items.

```
     &INST
     TITLE = Self-Assessment Rasch Analysis
     DATA = e:routcd10.dat
     ITEM1 = 9 ; column of response to first item in data record
     NI = 25 ; number of items
     NAME1 = 1 ; column of first character of person label
     NAMELEN = 8 ; length of person label
     XWIDE = 1 ; number of columns per item response
     CODES = 12345678 ; valid codes in data file
     CLFILE = *
1    Cannot do at all
2    Cannot do in most situations
3    Can only do in some situations with assistance
4    Can only do in some situations
5    Can sometimes do, but with difficulty
6    Can usually do alone
7    Can do in most situations
8    Can certainly do with ease
*
     IDFILE=*
       1–25 ; delete all items
       +1 ; reinsert item 1
       +3 ; reinsert item 3
       +5 ; reinsert item 5
       +7–25 ; reinsert the remaining items
*
&END
```

It is a common occurrence that respondents lose interest in completing a survey, may get confused or just answer indifferently. Without knowing how the answers are generated, it is possible that the raw data will be contaminated with random or deceptive responses. It is thus useful to screen such data for respondents who do not fit the probabilistic model. The Rasch model as implemented through MINISTEPS facilitates the identification of misfitting persons in the output tables pertaining to person ability or opinion. In this way, the notion of reliability applies not only to the entire set items, it applies also to individual items and to the persons who respond to the survey questions.

Task C3.3

➤ Examine the Output Tables and find Table 18 (PERSON: entry) listing person confidence measures and fit to the model. Examine the Infit of the persons, and locate a few individuals with fit >1.5. Open the PERSON: responses table (Table 7.1) for the individuals you found to misfit. Discuss the rating pattern of these individuals and why they are rating themselves in unexpected ways.

CHAPTER 5
Language learning tasks

Task-based learning (TBLT) has assumed a central role in both pedagogy and research, particularly in Second Language Acquisition (SLA). There is now a considerable volume of research in TBLT and SLA, summarized in Skehan (2003), and book-length studies by Ellis (2003) and Nunan (2004) confirm the maturity of the field, linking together language learning and teaching theory and practice in a coherent perspective. Pica (1997) suggests that one of the best examples of compatibility in the relationship between pedagogy and research is the concept of 'task', while Ellis (2003: 320) proposes that 'there is a clear psycholinguistic rationale (and substantial empirical support) for choosing "task" as the basis for language pedagogy.'

TBLT prompts learners to achieve a goal or complete a task. Much like real-world tasks, such as asking for directions, TBLT seeks to develop students' language through providing a task and then using language to solve it. Some of the main features of TBLT are 1) meaning is primary (language use rather than form), 2) there is some communication problem to solve, 3) the classroom task relates directly to real-world activities and 4) the assessment is done in terms of outcomes. Tasks may be packaged together to form a curriculum and tasks form a link between curriculum design, materials design, classroom teaching and assessment. 'Task' is also a helpful concept when researching language learning, especially in classroom interaction or assessment. A description of a task specifies the type of input learners are expected to receive, if operating within an input–output model of learning. This means that it can be planned to include certain variables in the input but to exclude others. The table below summarizes the relationship between TBLT teaching, assessment and research:

	Pragmatic/pedagogic	Research
Teachers and teaching	• Task as a unit of work in a scheme of work • Interlinked activity sequences developing thematic unit • Methods of involving learners • Deliberate starting point for unknown direction or explorations	• Task as researchable unit • Neat, cross-sectional approach • Relatively brief time interventions • Focus on the isolation of variables • Search for 'effects' through manipulation
Learners and learning	• Learner orientation and autonomy • Task reinterpretability • Interactive development through collaboration of groups of learners • Authenticity of response	• Extent to which learning processes are catalysed • Identification of theorised methods of operationalising constructs and measuring dependent variables • Research designs to probe: – salient task variables – salient task conditions
Testing	• Formative evaluation • Provision of structured feedback on communication • Reactive, unstandardised and individual based	• Summative evaluation • Task as format • Comparability and standardisation • Issues in performance assessment

Figure 5.1 Two dimensions underlying the study of tasks (Bygate, Skehan and Swain 2001: 5)

However, 'task' has a complex personality when implemented in the classroom. There are different ways of conceptualizing a task as it evolves in time. In this chapter, we employ Breen's (1989) conception of the three phases of a task: task-as-workplan, task-in-process and task-as-outcomes. The task-as-workplan is the intended pedagogy, the plan made prior to classroom implementation of what the teachers and learners will do. The task-in-process is the actual pedagogy or what actually happens in the classroom. The task-as-outcomes is whatever is physically produced. This may be a piece of writing or a sheet marking the number of differences found in a spot-the-difference task.

It is important to track the relationship between these three phases as they unfold during the implementation of a task. The relationship may be a linear one, but this is not necessarily the case. That is, learners may implement the task in a different way to that intended. The difference between phases is particularly important when

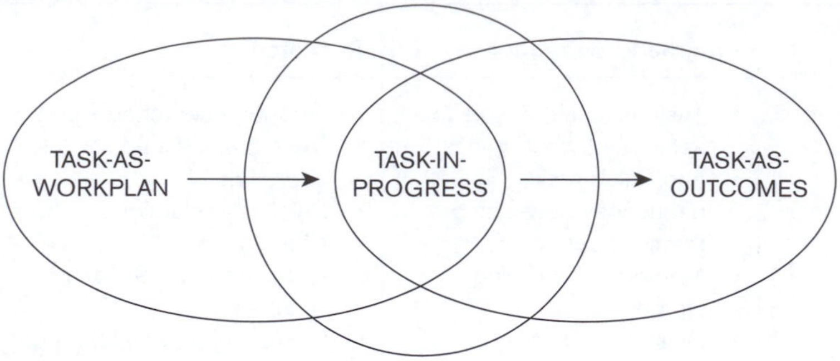

Figure 5.2 Three phases of a task (Breen 1989)

researching TBLT. If the study uses interactional data, then these derive from the task-in-process. However, research can also be based on tasks-as-outcomes, in terms of writing produced or test scores. There have been relatively few process studies of how TBLT is actually implemented in the classroom. Samuda (2001) notes that few TBL studies have been set in intact classes or examine the role of the teacher in the TBL process. Samuda's study, however, examines the teacher's pedagogical and interactional involvement in the task-in-process in an intact class. Moreover, her study traces the shifts in participant focus during the task-in-process; this alternates between a focus on form and on meaning. The following features of Samuda (2001) enable a focus on the task-in-process. The data are collected from an authentic classroom setting. There is a detailed contextual description of the setting, the participants, the teacher and the teacher's involvement. The task-as-workplan and teaching materials are described and there are a number of transcripts of the relevant interaction, so the task-in-process and the task-as-workplan can be compared.

It is important to determine whether tasks are being used to provide 'intervention' (pedagogical input), or as pre-tests and post-tests to determine the effectiveness of an intervention. In Lyster's study, tasks are employed in both ways. Alternatively, research may adopt a 'process' orientation and examine what happens when learners implement a task, as in Seedhouse and Almutairi's study. So in this chapter we examine two studies which employ tasks in rather different ways. Lyster's study uses tasks as two vital links in the research process, namely to provide specific pedagogical interventions and to conduct pre-tests and post-tests. Seedhouse and Almutairi's study is of the micro-interactional detail and processes generated by task implementation.

Section A
Introduction A1

Language acquisition requires systematic and extensive exposure to input from a speech community. For the vast majority of children, exposure to any human language is enough to trigger the language acquisition device and result in a well-formed grammatical system by the age of five. Child language acquirers are equipped to create a grammar from the positive evidence they are exposed to. For second-language learners exposed to the second language after puberty, both positive and negative evidence have been found useful in guiding the learner to the target grammar. The negative evidence made available to learners comes as some kind of feedback alerting the learner to a mismatch in a form used by the learner and its form in the target language.

The manner in which inter-language errors are dealt with by interlocutors has long been a focus of applied linguistics research. Classroom teachers have at their disposal a wide range of options for modifying input to learners in order to facilitate language learning. Lyster (2004) lists four main approaches to prompting accuracy from language learners:

Clarification requests:	indication that the learner's intended message has not been understood.
Repetition:	a replay of the learner's last utterance with a rising intonation
Metalinguistic clues:	questions or comments about the well-formedness of the learner's utterance.
Elicitation:	questions or pausing that allow the learner to reformulate an utterance which has been partially restructured by the interlocutor.

Task A1.1

➤ Examine the samples below and **classify** each as one of the four prompts from Lyster's list of prompt types:

a	*Learner:*	. . . and the man is platform
	Interlocutor:	huh?
	Learner:	the man is on the platform
b	*Interlocutor:*	Do you like playing golf?
	Learner:	Oh yes, I like
	Interlocutor:	You like what?
	Learner:	I like golf

c	*Interlocutor*	Where is the computer?
	Learner	It is in the table
	Interlocutor	It cannot be in it, can it?
	Learner	It is on the table
d	*Learner*	My families has five members
	Interlocutor	My families?
	Learner	My family

In addition to prompting by interlocutors, who in the main are language teachers, another way that negative evidence can be made available to learners is through the use of the 'recast' (Long 1996, Doughty 2001). Recasts are reformulations of learner utterances that make salient the difference between a learner's utterance and a reformulated version of the same utterance while preserving the meaning.

Learner: . . . and my brother work as a cook
Interlocutor: He works as a cook

Recasting is a way of providing implicit negative evidence to a learner that his utterance is not well formed. Reformulations or recasts can be noticed and repeated by a learner or can go unnoticed or ignored.

Introduction A2

In this section, we examine examples of interaction generated by tasks.

Task A2.1

➤ Look at the task-based interaction in the two extracts below. Can you work out what task they are working on? Can you understand what their talk means? If not, what other kind of information do you think you would require in order to understand it and analyze it? Examine line 20 of Extract 1. What do you think A means here?

Extract 1

C: °and looking at family photographs°
(1.0)
A: and not (0.7) oh that's full stop (0.6)
C: yeh (0.8)
A: no (0.6) ok (.) [photographs]
C: [what is this]
(2.8)
A: ok

19 (5.4)
20 → A: the story went
21 (1.3)
22 Y: the story went on yeh yeh yeh (.)
23 A: huh (.) do you [think]
24 C: [I think] so yeh why not
25 A: ok go ahead

(Seedhouse and Almutairi 2009)

Extract 2

1 S1: oo::: (1.7) you have to draw a big picture (4.3) ah (0.2) yes? (1.6) okay::: (1.2)
2 u::m (0.3) on the right (1.9) uh draw:: (.) a picture of a man.its similar to your:::
3 p[ictur]e
4 S2: [okay]
5 S1: (1.2) on the right yes, (1.0) a man is smiling yes (.) mm hm (1.4) yes (0.5)
6 and he has (0.8) a plate on top of his head (1.0) the picture is similar (0.4) the same
7 picture (0.3) hhh.hh
8 S2: uh the same picture?
9 S1: ye::s, (0.7)
10 S2: oh:::
11 S1: yes with [a a piece of cake]
12 S2: [then I can imagine]
13 S1: a piece of cake on top of the plate (0.3) yeah (0.4) and one fifth (0.6) is (.) taken
14 O- (.) taken out from the cake yes (0.8) yeah (1.1) mm hm (0.9)
15 S2: oh:::› I see (0.4)
16 S1: a::::nd (.) in the middle:::› (2.4) if you go to toilet (0.7) then you see this th.ing
17 (0.6) when you use toilet (1.0) I dont know how to call it> ((description continues))

(Jenks 2007)

In order to understand how tasks are implemented in the classroom, it is vital to consider the relationship between the nature of the task and the organization of the interaction. The example below (from Seedhouse 2004) shows that, in the case of an information-gap, 'convergent' task, there is a clear and reflexive relationship between the nature of the task and the turn-taking system. Warren (1985) describes the task-as-workplan as follows:

> The 'Maps' task below was based on the 'information gap' principle and was carried out by pairs of students separated from each other by a screen. Both students had a map of the same island but one of the maps had certain features missing from it. A key illustrating the missing features was given to each student so that they knew what these features were. In the case of the student with the completed map the key enabled him/her to know what was missing from the other map and in the case of the other participant it showed how the missing features were to be represented on his/her map. The student with the completed map had

> to tell the other student where missing features had to be drawn. Throughout the activity the teacher was present to ensure that the students did not abuse the presence of the screen. The idea behind having a screen to separate the participants was that they would then be forced to communicate verbally in order to complete the task.
>
> (Warren 1985: 56)

The following extract is typical of the interaction which resulted from this task.

Extract 3

L1: the road from the town to the Kampong Kelantan (pause) the coconut=
L2: =again, again.
L1: (.) the: the road, is from the town to Kampong Kelantan (6.5) the
town: is: (.) in the Jason Bay.
L2: (3.5) again. the town (.) where is the town?
L1: the town is: (.) on the Jason Bay.
L2: (1.0) the: road?
L1: the road is from the town to Kampong Kelantan (10.4) OK?
L2: OK
L1: (.) the mountain is: behind the beach, and the Jason Bay (8.1) the
river is: from the jungle, (.) to the Desaru (9.7) the mou- er the
volcano is above on the Kampong Kelantan (7.2) the coconut
tree is: (.) along the beach.

(Warren 1985: 271)

The progress of the interaction is jointly constructed here. Turn order, turn size and turn design are intimately related to the progress of the task. So, for example, in line 1, L1 provides one item of information to L2 and then proceeds with the second item of information without checking whether L2 has noted the first piece of information (the two learners cannot see each other). Because L2 has not finished noting the first piece of information, L2 initiates repetition. In line 2 we see that L2 is able to alter the course of the interaction through a repetition request which requires L1 to backtrack. In other words, because the task has not yet progressed sufficiently, L2 takes a turn to allocate both a turn and a turn type to L1 which will facilitate the progress of the task. In line 7, L2 asks where the road is. In line 8, L1 supplies the information, waits for 11 seconds and then makes a confirmation check ('OK?') to L2 to ascertain whether L2 has completed that subsection of the task. L1 appears to be orienting his utterances to L2's difficulty in completing the task in that L1 uses an identical sentence structure each time and in that L1 leaves pauses between different items of information. We can see these pauses in lines 3, 8, 10, 11 and 12, and they vary from 6.5 seconds to 10.4 seconds in length. Repetition requests are focused on information necessary for the task in lines 2, 5 and 7. In line 8 the confirmation check is focused on establishing whether a particular sub-section of the task has been accomplished or not.

We can see in the above extract that the nature of the task, in effect, tends to constrain the organization of turn-taking and sequence. In task-oriented interaction, the focus is on the accomplishment of the task. In order to accomplish this particular task, the learners must take turns in order to exchange information. The nature of the task here pushes L1 to make statements to which L2 will provide feedback, clarification or repetition requests or repair initiation. The speech-exchange system is thus constrained to some degree. However, the two learners are also to some extent actively developing a turn-taking system which is appropriate to the task and which excludes elements which are superfluous to the accomplishment of the task. So we should clarify that there is a reflexive relationship between the nature of the task as interpreted by the learners (the task-in-process) and the turn-taking system.

Section B
Extension B1

Lyster, R. (2004) 'Differential effects of prompts and recasts in form-focused instruction', *Studies in Second Language Acquisition* 26: 399–432.

In a quasi-experimental comparison of prompts and recasts, Lyster focuses on the morphology of grammatical gender in French taught to 179 fifth-grade immersion students in Montreal. Lyster's study examines Ellis's (1997) distinction between two types of language acquisition processes: internalization of newly noticed forms, and acquisition of control over forms that have not been fully acquired. The distinction implies that prompting of learner output will serve to increase grammatical accuracy, while recasting of partially acquired forms will not serve to increase accuracy, since the recasting will focus on input while the prompting forces the language learners to reformulate their own faulty output.

The research design allowed four teachers at three schools to self-select their own preferred interactional style favouring prompting, recasting, form-focused instruction or the conventional approach used at one of the schools. Each of the teachers taught two class sections leading to four different class types: form-focused instruction with prompting as feedback to learner errors, form-focused instruction with recasting of learner errors, form-focused instruction with no feedback on errors and the conventional class with no form-focused instruction. The three form-focused groups used the same pedagogical materials designed to feature noticing activities with typographically enhanced fonts, inductive tasks for rule-discovery and practice tasks for accuracy and fluency. The form-focused instruction on grammatical gender was spread over eight to ten hours during a five-week period.

Lyster's study involved three waves of tests focused on grammatical gender in French. The three test waves were given as pre-tests (before the intervention), as immediate post-tests and as delayed post-tests. The tests included two written tests: a binary-choice test of French articles and a gap-filling test, and two oral production tests: an object-identification test and a picture description test. Each test type employed a parallel form given in ABA or BAB order to random halves of each classroom.

Task B1.1

➤ Based on the description above, visualize the design of Lyster's study. Put the groups and the tests in the design box.

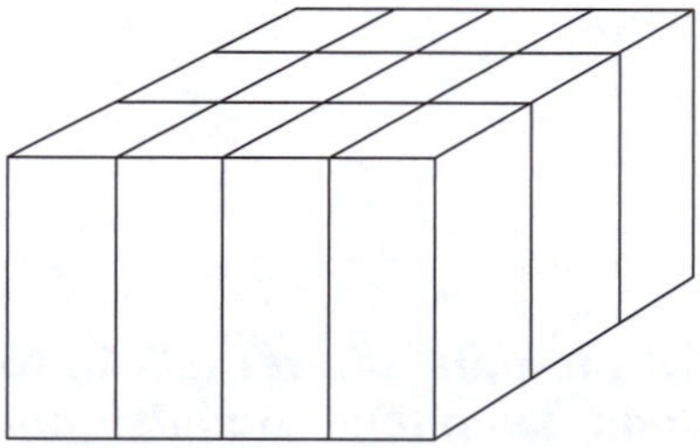

Figure 5.3 Factorial design box (Lyster 2004)

Design variables

The **dependent variables** in the design are those which depend on the differential effects of the form-focused instruction.

The **independent variables** are those manipulated by the researcher in order to test hypotheses.

Task B1.2

➤ Based on the summary of Lyster's study, identify the *independent* and *dependent* variables. Consider also potential *moderating* variables – those not included in the design but whose effect could possibly influence the outcomes.

Hypotheses

In quasi-experimental (non-randomized) and experimental (randomized) designs, it is conventional to formulate hypotheses motivating the analyses. The default *null hypothesis* is that there will no difference among the groups compared. An *alternative hypothesis* in contrast predicts that there will be systematic group differences. Alternative hypotheses are normally motivated by explanatory premises about *why* there ought to be group differences.

Task B1.3

➤ For each of Lyster's tests, decide if a null or alternative hypothesis would be used. If an alternative hypothesis is indicated, determine which groups would be predicted to have the highest means on the tests. On which test(s) would the null hypothesis be preferred?

ANALYSIS

When more than two groups are to be compared on tests resulting in normally distributed test scores, a common approach is to use the analysis of variance (ANOVA). The goal of the ANOVA is to detect systematic between-group differences on one or more dependent variables. If the dependent variable is measured serially, the sources of variation can be within the subjects over time as well as between the subjects nested in groups. Lyster's study employed a pre-test and two post-tests as outcomes and four groups – three types of form-focused intervention and a comparison group. The repeated measures ANOVA results can be shown descriptively as a graphic and inferentially as statistics with associated probabilities to test the null and alternative hypotheses.

A graphical representation of the results of Lyster's analysis of the object-identification speaking test shows the differences between the groups and the differences among the groups on the three tests.

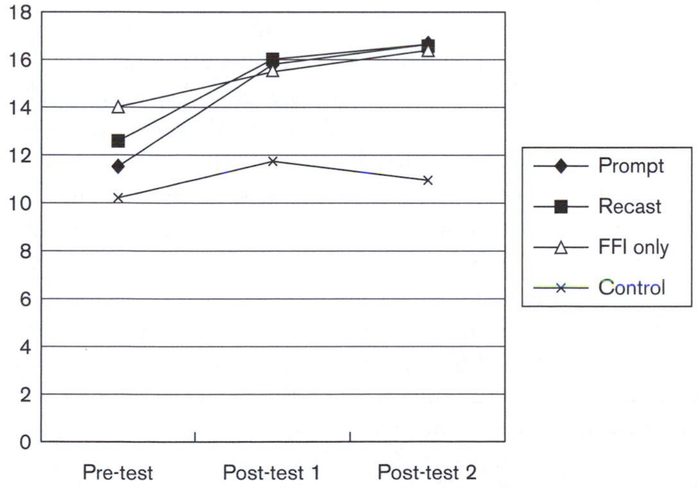

Figure 5.4 Object identification test results (adapted from Lyster 2004)

Task B1.4

➤ Examine Figure 2 and describe the mean outcomes for the four groups on the three tests used in Lyster's study. Relate these results to what you considered the null and alternative hypotheses to have been in Task B1.3.

INTERPRETING ANOVA RESULTS

Analysis of variance tests between-group differences. The simplest analysis of variance would have just one dependent variable and one independent variable (groups) with two or more 'levels' (number of groups).

Table 5.1 One-way analysis of variance in tabular form: **ANOVA**

Post	*Sum of squares*	*df*	*Mean square*	*F*	*Sig.*
Between groups	345.272	1	345.272	9.239	.003
Within groups	10240.061	274	37.372		
Total	10585.333	275			

The difference between the groups (here two) is shown in the F-ratio statistic. The larger the difference between the group means relative to the variation within the groups, the larger the F becomes. Conventionally, each test statistic has an associated inferential probability (its 'significance') which is an aid to interpreting whether the observed difference between the groups could have arisen by chance alone. Statistical reporting in journals is not always tabular. For instance, the result displayed in Table A1 could be reported in running text as $F(1,274)=9.24$, $p=.003$. This is read as 'the F-ratio based on two groups with 275 total participants showed a mean difference leading to an F of 9.24, which would occur three times in 1000 random events'. The usual benchmark for inferring that the observed differences expressed as an F-ratio are non-random is probability (p) less than .05 – or one chance in 20 that the differences observed could be the result of random variation. The F-ratio and associated probability depend on the number of groups and the number of subjects within each group. It is also important to realize that ANOVA assumes randomization and equal variances across the groups. The validity of ANOVA may be questionable when these assumptions are not met.

In more complex designs such as Lyster's repeated measures, ANOVA tests both the differences between the groups and the differences within the subjects across repeated measures of a dependent variable. In this case the effect for the differences within each group across the three measures would be the focus of interest, as well as any conditional effect particular to an interaction between the test event and the group. Such designs 'factorial repeated measures analysis of variance' are increasingly common in applied linguistics studies – often because follow-up tests are used to check on sustained learning.

Table 5.2 Tests of within-subjects contrasts (measure: repeated)

Source	*tests*	*Type III Sum of squares*	*df*	*Mean square*	*F*	*Sig.*
tests	Linear	153.394	1	153.394	7.597	.006
tests * group	Linear	76.698	1	76.698	3.798	.052
Error (tests)	Linear	5532.715	274	20.192		

Here we would again focus on the variation between the group's performance on the tests (we know there were two groups, because there is 2-1 'degrees of freedom' to vary). The F ratio is 7.6 with an associated probability of $p=.006$. We could infer then that the means of the two tests differ from each other from pre-test to post-test. The 'interaction' of the test and the group yields an F of 3.8 with a probability of $p=.052$. We could infer here that there is likely to be a differential pattern of change from pre- to post-test for each of the groups.

The repeated measures factorial analysis of variance reported in Lyster's analysis of the object-identification test shown graphically in Figure 2 were reported in the text of the journal article (p. 421) as 'between groups $F(3,56)=7.73$, $p<.01$, across time $F(2,55)=23.57$, $p<.01$ and a group × time interaction $F(6,110)=2.28$, $p<.05$.'

Task B1.5

- Re-examine the graphical display of the analysis of variance results in Figure 5.4 and identify which of the ANOVA results quoted in the paragraph above correspond to the line graphs in the figure. Identify where the 'interactions' occur leading to the significant group × time effect.

Extension B2

Now read the extracts from Seedhouse, P. and Almutairi, S. (2009), 'A holistic approach to task-based interaction', *International Journal of Applied Linguistics* 19, 3: 311–338.

This paper adopts a problem-solution approach. The problem is that interaction generated by tasks has previously been very difficult to analyse because of its highly indexical nature. Task-related actions and non-verbal communication could not be related easily to talk. A technological solution to this problem is presented, using a combination of task-tracking hardware and software, video recording and transcription.

This enables a holistic approach, i.e. one in which all elements of behaviour can be integrated in analysis.

It is difficult to relate the talk to the performance of the task. Transcripts of task-based interaction are sometimes difficult to read and analyse as they are highly indexical, with talk relating to physical movements undertaken when completing the tasks or reacting to data received from a computer. The extract below demonstrates the qualities of minimalisation and indexicality.

Extract 4

11	C:	°and looking at family photographs°
12		(1.0)
13	A:	and not (0.7) oh that's full stop (0.6)
14	C:	yeh (0.8)
15	A:	no (0.6) ok (.) [photographs]
16	C:	[what is this]
17		(2.8)
18	A:	ok
19		(5.4)
20	A:	the story went
21		(1.3)
22	Y:	the story went on yeh yeh yeh (.)
23	A:	huh (.) do you [think]
24	C:	[I think] so yeh why not
25	A:	ok go ahead
26	Y:	((*moves piece 5 to her left*))

The interaction is very hard to understand without knowing what exactly learners are physically doing during the task. In this case, access to non-verbal communication and details of the task being performed would render the interaction comprehensible and analysable, as we show below in relation to Extract 5. In order to develop a holistic perspective on task-based interaction, then, it is essential to be able to relate 1) non-verbal communication and 2) physical performance of the task to 3) the details of the talk. This paper presents a technological solution to the problems of portraying these three aspects simultaneously for analysis and study.

A technological solution

We used a combination of technologies to relate non-verbal communication and performance of the task to the details of the talk. We combined task-tracking hardware and software (digital tabletop), video/audio recording and transcription. Digital tabletops (figure 1) are multi-user, multi-touch interactive digital tables that combine face-to-face interaction with the full use of digital media. They also enable innovative task design.

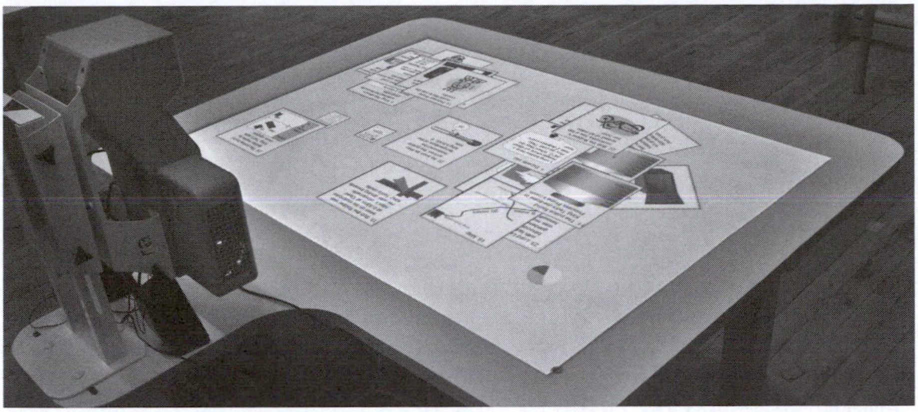

Figure 1 Digital tabletop

This type of horizontal tabletop display has great potential in educational settings. Its strength lies in the way it combines face-to-face interaction with the use of information resources. What makes this tool especially interesting is that it can adapt well to the study of task-based learning and teaching in terms of having groups of students working on a task using an electronically enhanced shared space. This space can be manipulated, monitored, tracked, or even connected to other sources of information. Text, audio, video and physical materials can be used on these tabletop displays and can be implemented in an interactive way.

Each digital display accepts input from three users simultaneously and provides a digital recording of how participants are actually completing a task.

It is true that not all classroom teaching and learning involves moving physical objects. However, different types of tasks can be designed for the table. A task can be making a story out of mini video clips on the table or can be trading off objects (digital/ physical) on the table with movement constraints and feedback (key vocabulary/price etc).

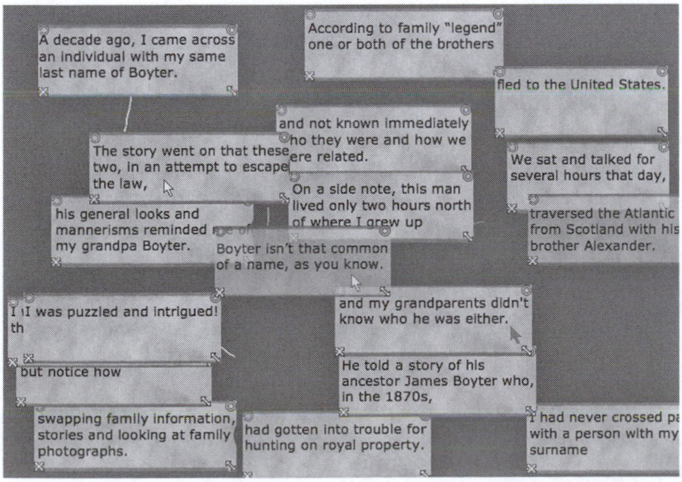

Figure 2 Screen capture of the jumbled text task used in this study

As figure 2 shows, the digital recording shows which of the participants has moved the text where. Three people use three stylus pens, with different colors, and the table can sense which pen does what at any given point in time. For our purposes, what made this even more interesting was that we were able to link this data to data from the video/audio equipment around the tabletop, as shown below in figure 3.

The Study

The study was conducted in a classroom in the Culture Lab at Newcastle University. A digital tabletop was put in the middle of the room and two video cameras were also used during the task to capture video and audio data. Screen capture (figure 2) was used to record the movement of the pieces of the story. The three learners had previously been introduced to the digital tabletop and the task using a dummy task.

The task in this study was a jumbled sentence text; a typical L2 classroom task which aimed to generate interaction between students. The story was taken from a textbook designed for advanced second language learners. The story was digitized and embedded in the table. The application mixes up the pieces randomly on the tabletop, where the learners can manipulate them. They can move, rotate, and maximize the pieces of text. The learners need to discuss among themselves how to rebuild the story and put the pieces in the correct order to rebuild the narrative.

In terms of the distinction between convergent and divergent tasks (Duff 1986), this activity represents a convergent task as the learners seek to come to an agreement with regard to the appropriate order of the pieces. They try to rebuild the story into its original order. So, the assumption here is that there is only one solution, although in reality and as the task unfolds as a task-as-process (Breen 1989), this single goal orientation might change as the interactants negotiate.

The setting in this study was not a normal classroom setting but more of a semi-experimental environment. However, the presence of the digital table and cameras did not seem to bring about any intrusive effect. The students felt comfortable and it was apparent that they were involved enthusiastically in the task.

The participants in this study were postgraduate international students at Newcastle University. Their English proficiency as shown by IELTS scores was quite advanced, the average IELTS score for the participants being 6.5. Data were collected from four groups of students (two triads and two pairs). Three groups represented Ph.D. students from a number of countries and one group included MA students in TESOL. Three groups shared the same first language (L1) while the fourth group included students with different L1s. Three groups were from the School of Education, Communication and Language Sciences and the fourth group was from Computer Science. All of the data shown in this article are from a single group.

Data sources:

The data sources in this study are shown in figure 3. Using Transana software to align the video and tabletop with the transcripts of the interaction on a single screen, we

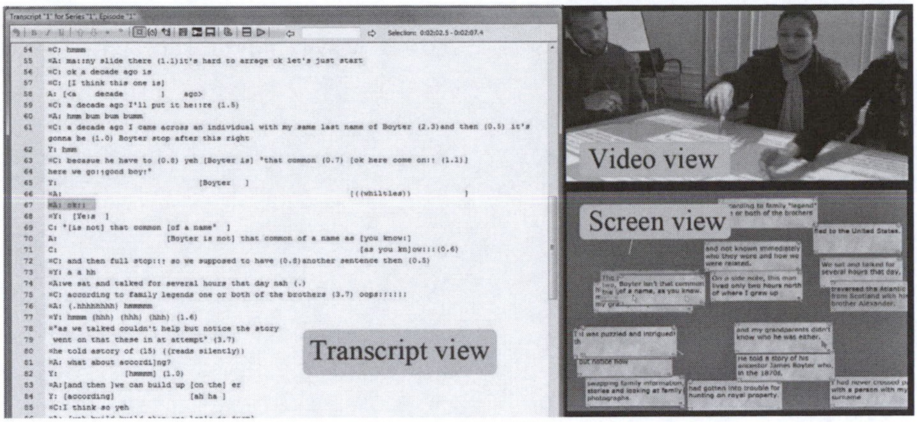

Figure 3 System layout: different modalities put together

are able to make three data sources available simultaneously for multimodal analysis. Of course, audio also plays simultaneously. The first source is the detailed transcript of the interaction (Transcript view). The audio recording was transcribed using CA conventions. The video view of the group around the table is another source of data (Video view). The third source was the screen capture, which shows movement related to task completion on the table (screen view). So, movement of the pieces of text can be viewed simultaneously on the video view and the screen view. Speech can be heard at the same time as the transcript is highlighted on the transcript view (figure 3). This presentation gives the analyst the convenience of examining all elements of task-based interaction as many times as needed. Moreover, the ability to review talk, non-verbal elements and task-completion actions simultaneously enables analysis of the interdependence of these three elements, as we demonstrate below. We propose that task-based talk can only be adequately analysed in conjunction with these two other elements.

Data Analysis

In this section of the article we examine episodes of task-based interaction. This has two aims: 1) to provide an example of how a holistic portrayal of interactional processes might be achieved, using the combination of task-tracking digital tabletop, video/audio recording and transcription. 2) to demonstrate the value added by such an approach. Task-relevant activities (digital tabletop) will be related to talk (transcript) and non-verbal communication (video).We seek to demonstrate that certain aspects of TBLT processes can only be revealed by such a detailed examination of the interaction. A segmental approach which focuses on discrete phenomena may present a rather different picture to a holistic one, as we suggest below.

Indexicality

We noted above that task-based interaction can be heavily indexical and minimalised, particularly when involving convergent tasks. It is therefore difficult or even impossible to read and analyse transcripts of talk without knowing what the learners are physically doing. The following transcript (Extract 5) shows a heavily indexical encounter.

Extract 5

C: °and looking at family photographs°
(1.0)
A: and not (0.7) oh that's full stop (0.6)
C: yeh (0.8)
A: no (0.6) ok (.) [photographs]
C: [what is this]
(2.8)
A: ok
(5.4)
A: the story went
(1.3)
Y: the story went on yeh yeh yeh (.)
A: huh (.) do you [think]
C: [I think] so yeh why not
A: ok go ahead
Y: ((*moves piece 5 to her left*))

If we only had the transcript one might think that A and Y were telling a story in lines 20 and 22 that would go on and some events would follow. This transcript becomes much more comprehensible when we show the video view and screen capture that accompany the transcript.

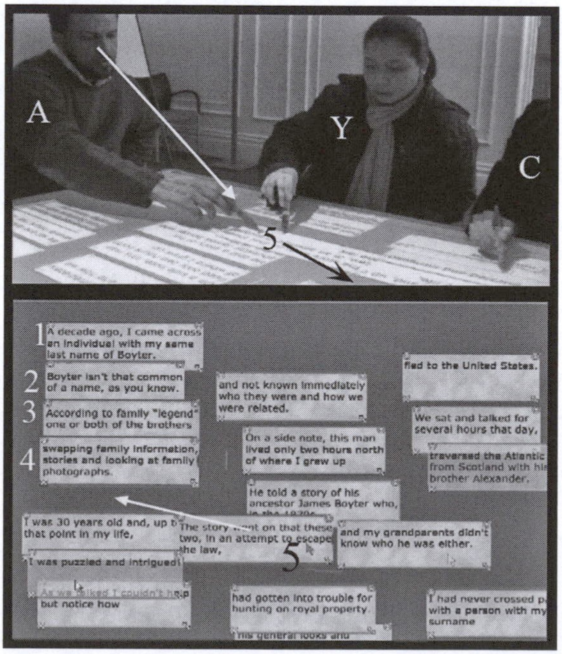

Figure 6 Juxtaposition of the visual elements (line 20)

The arrangement of the pieces in the screen capture shows the progress of the task. The four pieces (1–4) at the top left corner were picked as the first four pieces in the story. This frame was taken at line 20 from the extract above. Speaker A suggests that that piece (5) (that reads 'the story went . . .') is a potential candidate for the next move. He moves it slightly away from himself and finally at line 26, participant Y takes over the movement and puts it in place below pieces 1–4 on the top left. A's proposal is accepted by the other participants and jointly acted upon. So the multimodal data presentation helps us to analyse line 20. By placing his pen on piece 5, gazing at it and reading the first 3 words of the text out, A is proposing that piece 5 should be the next piece of text in the story. In line 22, Y agrees with this proposal. In line 23, A checks this proposal with C, who agrees, and in line 25, A asks Y to physically move piece 5 into position as he cannot reach over that far (see figure 6).

So an adequate analysis of this extract of task-based interaction is only possible with multimodal information. From a different angle, however, the analysis demonstrates that the three interactants have developed a multimodal speech exchange system appropriate to this task, in which verbal, non-verbal elements and task-completion actions are inextricably intertwined. Because of his gaze, pen position and because of the point they have reached in the task-completion sequence, all that is required for A to make a formal proposal that piece 5 should be the next piece of the story is for him to read out its first 3 words. Verbal indexicality and minimalisation are therefore built into the multimodal speech exchange system which participants have constructed for this task. As Goodwin (2000:1505) suggests, 'participants visibly attend to such graphic fields as crucial to the organization of the events and action that make up activity reflexively situated within a setting, and which contribute structure to that action.' The implication of this is that an emic perspective (i.e. an understanding of how participants organize their own talk) on task-based interaction is only possible if non-verbal communication and task-completion actions are available for analysis.

Self-repetitions, clarification requests, confirmation checks

In early TBLT studies based on the interaction hypothesis, features of interactional modifications were isolated for quantitative treatment, for example self-repetitions, clarification requests, confirmation checks.

Extract 6

36 A: yeh that's right what [I mean]
37 C: [the st]ory on that these two in an attempt to escape the law
38 (1.3)
39 C: to escape the law:↑ (0.9)
40 A: [the law:↑]
41 Y: [escape] the law:::(.)
42 A: the law:
43 (1.3)
44 C: and [not a se]nse here
45 A: [ok:] >what about<something there is hiding there
46 (1.1)

Lines 39–42 could in principle be coded as any of the above features. These lines show that all the participants are repeating the same thing. It is not clear from the transcript alone what the function of these repetitions is. They could be clarification requests or confirmation checks and C in line 39 may be doing self-repetition. However, when we look at the visual data together with the transcript, a radically different picture emerges.

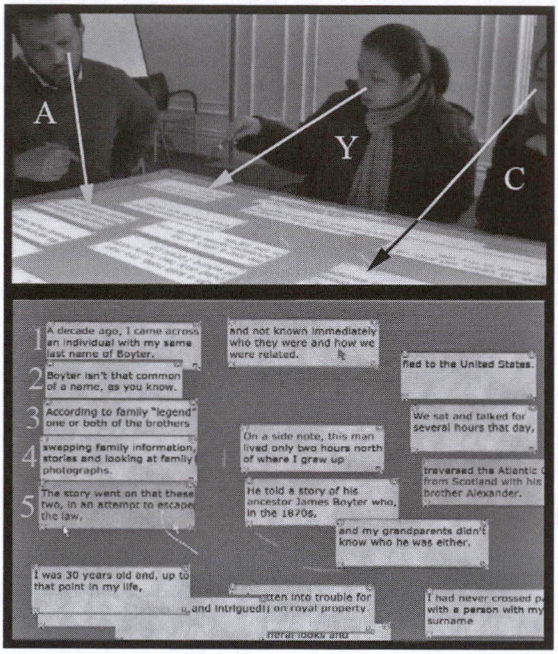

Figure 7 Eye gaze during repetitions

The meaning of the repetition of 'the law' in lines 39–42 can only be properly understood by reference to visual information on the video view and screen view. The three participants are scanning the board to find a piece 6 to put after piece 5 (the law). They are visually scanning different areas of the tabletop, as can be seen in figure 7. By repeating 'the law' they are displaying to each other their joint orientation that they are engaged in exactly the same part of the task at the same time. The repetition is a kind of cueing or anchoring system which shows that they are synchronizing their task focus, even though their gazes are diverging.

In early TBLT studies, self-repetitions, clarification requests, confirmation checks etc. were counted because they were thought to be evidence of negotiation of meaning, which was thought to be conducive to SLA. The multimodal analysis here, however, suggests that the repetitions in this extract are best understood as an integral part of the multimodal speech exchange system that the participants have developed for the completion of this specific task. It follows that it would be easy to mis-code or mis-analyse any verbal action in task-based interaction unless multi-modal information is integrated into the analysis.

Silent contributions

Throughout the extracts presented here, there are noticeable periods of silence. Often these are related to the nature of the task, as there is physical manipulation and spatial placement of the pieces taking place. This gives rise to lengthy pauses in the interaction as participants engage in activities which cannot be heard, but which can be understood by looking at video and tabletop data. Moments of silence, then, were often full of task-related action in which the learners were actually involved in the practicalities of the task.

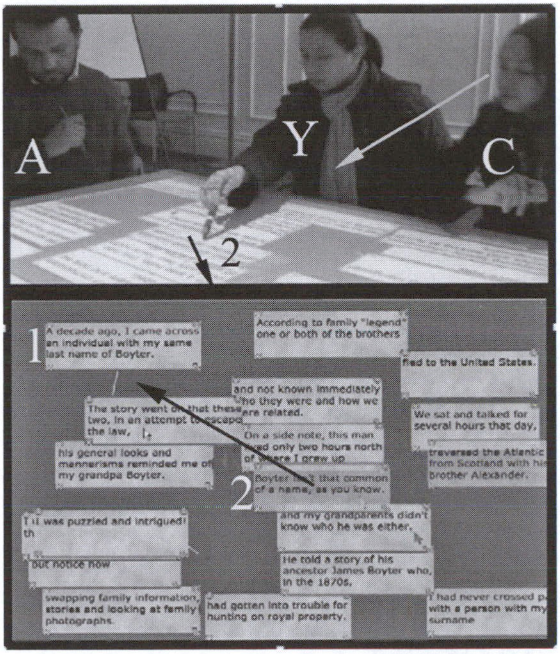

Figure 8 Silent contributions (line 5)

Extract 7

1 C: a decade ago I came across an individual with my same last name of Boyter
2 (2.3) and then↑ (0.5) it's gonna be (1.0) Boyter stop after this right↑°
3 Y: hmm
4 C: because he have to (0.8)
5 Y: ((moves one of the pieces))
6 C: yeh Boyer is (.) °that common (0.7) ok here come on:↑ (1.1) here we go:↑ good boy↑°

In figure 8 and extract 7 it is clear that Speaker Y is not saying anything. However, her manipulation of the pieces on the table did have consequences on the next move in the sequence of events. As speaker C finishes reading aloud piece number 1 and looks for the next piece (lines 1,2,4), speaker Y points to piece number 2 with her pen and moves it to her left without saying anything, as shown in figure 8. Moving the piece to the left is an indication that this piece should be the next. This grabs speaker C's attention and C agrees that this is a potential next piece as shown in extract 7 (line 5) and finally C moves it below piece number 1, where they arrange the pieces.

Without looking at Y's silent action in line 5, it would be hard to analyze fully the collaborative achievement of building the story. These physical manipulations have important consequences on the outcome of the task. Selecting piece number 2 and introducing it as the second piece in the puzzle took the story into a certain direction and imposed a certain narrative logic.

Our multimodal analysis can reveal that such instances of silent moves in fact demonstrate the mutual interplay between verbal and non-verbal elements and how they contribute to the organization of action. It also gives a different impression of speaker Y, who did not verbalize much during this task. From the transcripts alone, one might have gained the erroneous impression that she was not very engaged with the task. She uttered only 75 words (excluding reading text aloud) during a task which took 11 minutes to complete. However, her contribution in terms of task-related actions on the tabletop was equal to that of the other participants. Figure 8 and extract 7 also show that participants can creatively combine verbal and non-verbal aspects of task management. Here, Y is performing the physical movement and C is supplying the verbal accompaniment.

Task B2.1

➤ Having read the article, read again the extract below. This time, see whether you are able to understand the interaction and line 20 in particular.

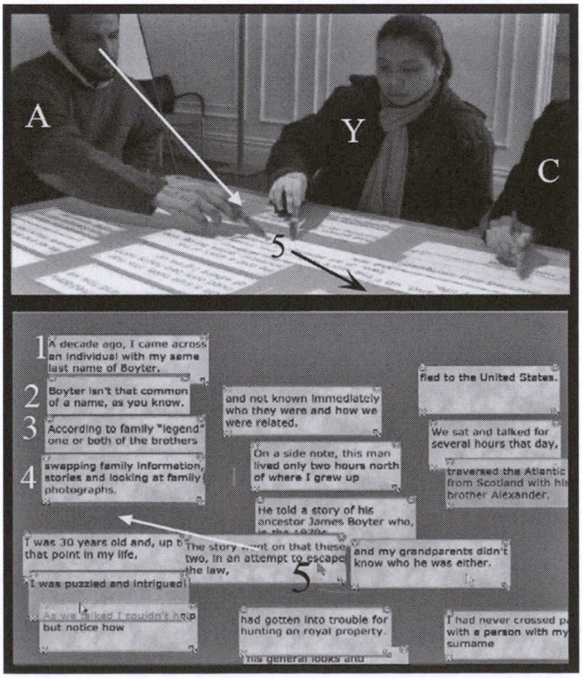

C: °and looking at family photographs°
(1.0)
A: and not (0.7) oh that's full stop (0.6)
C: yeh (0.8)
A: no (0.6) ok (.) [photographs]
C: [what is this]
(2.8)
A: ok
(5.4)
→ A: the story went
(1.3)
Y: the story went on yeh yeh yeh (.)
A: huh (.) do you [think]
C: [I think] so yeh why not
A: ok go ahead

(Seedhouse and Almutairi 2009)

Task B2.2

➤ Look at the transcript in task B2.1. Now look at the non-verbal aspects of the interaction present in the multimodal graphics in the same task. Can you see any way of adding these non-verbal aspects to the transcript?

Task B2.3

➤ Seedhouse and Almutairi claim that multimodality is vital to understanding task-based interaction. In the cases of self-repetitions and silent task contributions, they suggest that a multimodal analysis of task-based interaction provides a very different picture to that obtained by simply reading a transcript.

➤ From your knowledge and experience of interaction both inside and outside the classroom, list other features of interaction which might be revealed by multimodal analysis, but which would not be evident in a transcript.

Task 2.4

➤ Can you think of any aspect of interaction involving language learning which you would like to explore through multimodal analysis?

Task B2.5

➤ Visit the following websites, which explore the multimodal representation and analysis of interaction:

Charles Goodwin: http://www.sscnet.ucla.edu/clic/cgoodwin/

CORINTE: http://icar.univ-lyon2.fr/projets/corinte/index.htm

Emanuel Schegloff: http://www.sscnet.ucla.edu/soc/faculty/schegloff/

CHILDES: http://childes.psy.cmu.edu/

Task B2.6

- Seedhouse and Almutairi's article does not contain research questions. Rather, it might be said to have a problem–solution structure. Identify what the problem is and what the suggested solution is. In your view, is the problem a real one and is the proposed solution realistic? Clearly, this technological approach requires a great deal of time, money and effort. Do you think it is worth the trouble?

Section C
Exploration C1

RESEARCH SCENARIO C1

Program designers aim to test the effect of intensive versus extensive learning. Within a large institutional setting, foreign language courses are offered to learners in either **intensive** format 120 hours daily six hours per day for four weeks, or in **extensive** format with the 120 hours of instruction spread over two hours per day for 12 weeks. All participants are taught with the same materials within the institution and are tested with a proficiency measure (TOEIC Bridge) before instruction, after 60 hours and again after 120 hours. The object of the research is to measure the extent of the gain over time and to ascertain if extensive learning is more effective than intensive learning. Learners are allowed to self-select into either the extensive or intensive courses.

Task C1.1

- Using a 'design box' sketch the design of the study.

The researchers use **repeated measures** of learner proficiency over the 120 hours of instruction. There is also a **group** difference encoding the intensive and extensive course types. This design calls for a complex analysis of variance with variation within the subjects (changes on the three test scores) and variation between the two groups (the differential effects of the intensity of instruction variable).

The SPSS data file **rmgrowthshrt.sav** contains the formatted file ready for analysis.

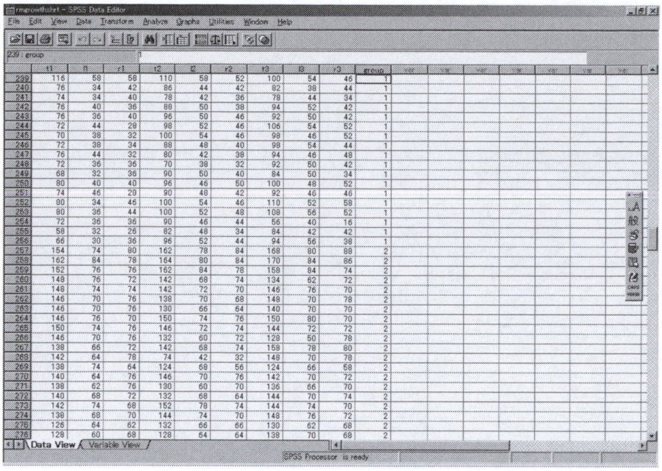

Figure 5.5 Data layout for Rm growthshrt.sav

Reprint courtesy of International Business Machines Corporation, © SPSS, Inc., an IBM company

The data are arrayed in a time series with the pre-instruction tests T1 – R1 on the left and the mid-term and post-instruction test results on the right. The group variable encodes membership in the intensive (1) and extensive (2) conditions.

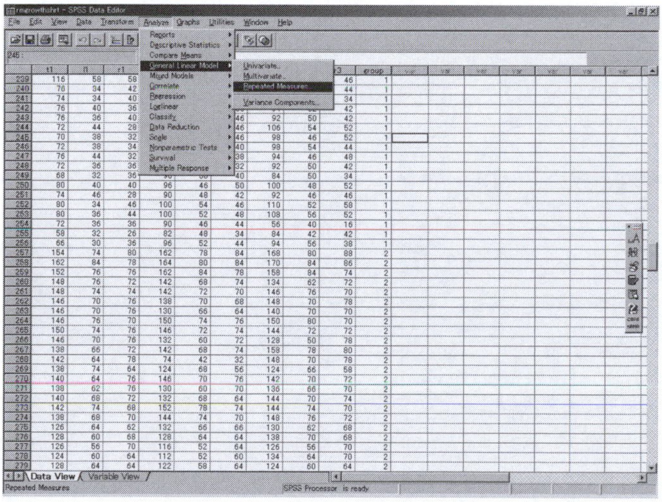

Figure 5.6 Specification of general linear model with repeated measures

Reprint courtesy of International Business Machines Corporation, © SPSS, Inc., an IBM company

Under the Analysis menu, select the General Linear Model and the Repeated Measures option. This leads to the design specifications. There are three repeated tests used.

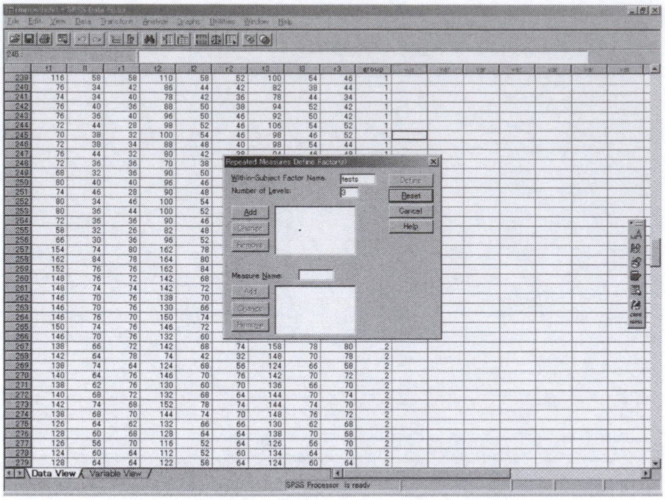

Figure 5.7 Specification of repeated measures

Reprint courtesy of International Business Machines Corporation, © SPSS, Inc., an IBM company

We start with testing the within-subject factor – the differences between the three tests. Once we specify that there are three measures for each person, we add the repeated measure factor to the analysis window. We then define the analysis variables.

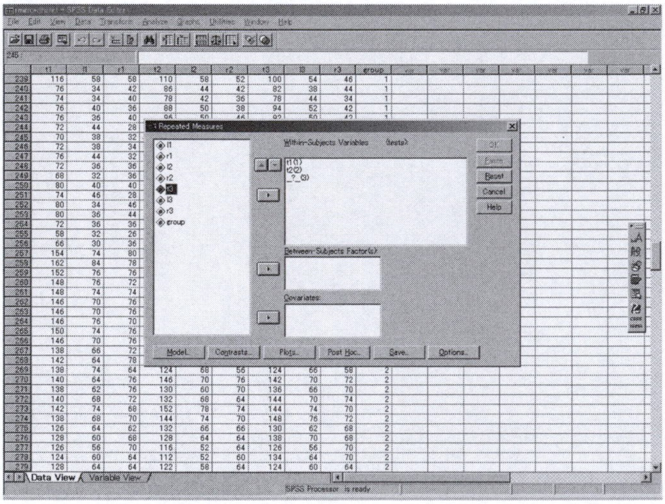

Figure 5.8 Specification of within-subjects measures

Reprint courtesy of International Business Machines Corporation, © SPSS, Inc., an IBM company

The first set of repeated measures is the series of TOEIC Bridge total scores T1–T3. Next, the between-subjects factor is added. In this case, it is the group (intensive or extensive) into which the individual learner self-selected.

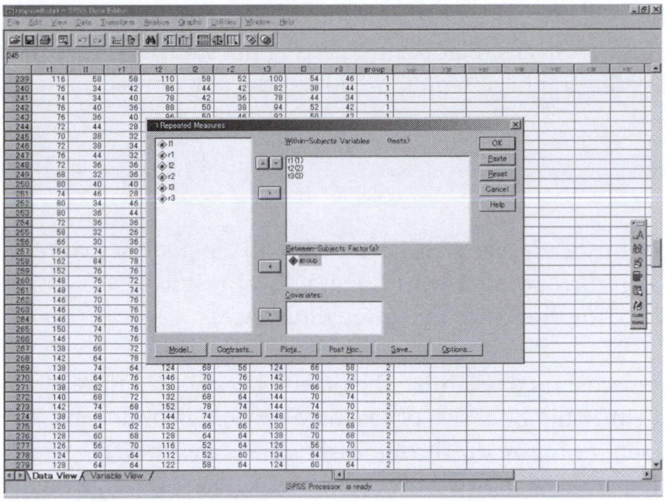

Figure 5.9 Specification of between-subjects measures

Reprint courtesy of International Business Machines Corporation, © SPSS, Inc., an IBM company

Task C1.2

➤ Based on the design specified so far, state what you consider the relevant hypotheses to be. Are there null or alternative hypotheses?

The analysis is now set up to test the equivalence of the repeated measures of proficiency, and to test the difference between the intensive and extensive courses. It will be useful to examine the graphical display of the results. We can call for the PLOT option to display the means for the proficiency measures and the groups.

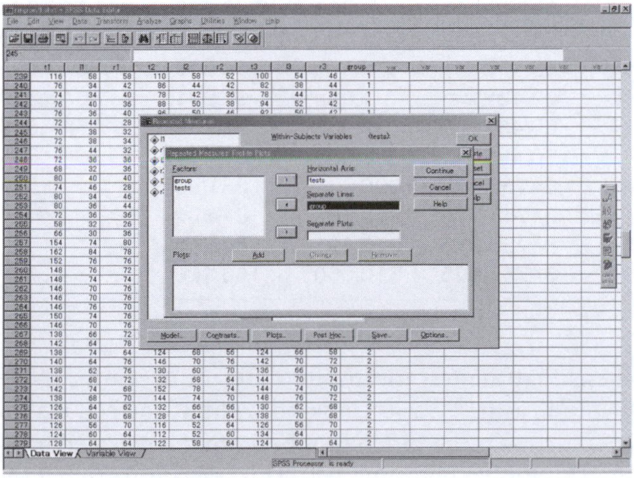

Figure 5.10 Plot specification for test * group interaction

Reprint courtesy of International Business Machines Corporation, © SPSS, Inc., an IBM company

After the tests and group variables are *added* to the plot specification, we are ready to see the test * group plot of means. Before interpreting the statistical tests, it is often useful to first check the graphical representation of the outcomes.

Task C1.3

- Interpret the plot of the test * group variables. Were the hypotheses you formulated in Task C1.2 corroborated with the graphical results? Discuss any ambiguities you notice for the test of the group differences.

The intention of the researchers is to examine the rate of growth over time by the two groups enrolled in either the intensive or extensive learning conditions. The graphical plot of the group means on the three measures indicates that the growth rates are approximately parallel. The two groups, however, are not equivalent. Test 1 was given prior to the program of instruction, yet we see that there is about a 10-point difference between the groups before the instruction even started. This difference will complicate the researcher's goal of comparing the groups.

STATISTICAL TESTS

Table 5.3 Tests of within-subjects effects (measure: repeated ANOVA)

Source		*Type III Sum of squares*	*df*	*Mean square*	*F*	*Sig.*
tests	Sphericity assumed	24797.021	2	12398.510	149.211	.000
	Greenhouse–Geisser	24797.021	1.893	13101.051	149.211	.000
	Huynh–Feldt	24797.021	1.903	13028.332	149.211	.000
	Lower-bound	24797.021	1.000	24797.021	149.211	.000
tests * group	Sphericity assumed	60.437	2	30.219	.364	.695
	Greenhouse–Geisser	60.437	1.893	31.931	.364	.683
	Huynh–Feldt	60.437	1.903	31.754	.364	.685
	Lower-bound	60.437	1.000	60.437	.364	.547
Error (tests)	Sphericity assumed	84755.875	1020	83.094		
	Greenhouse–Geisser	84755.875	965.303	87.802		
	Huynh–Feldt	84755.875	970.691	87.315		
	Lower-bound	84755.875	510.000	166.188		

We first check the hypothesis that the test means are different over time. Note that we have four versions of the same F-ratio with and without corrections for 'Sphericity' or equal variances across mean differences between the repeated measures. All tests show the same F-ratio $F=149.21$ $p<.000$. This test confirms that the means over time are *not* the same – and matches the plot indicating that there is growth over time. The second panel of the table test differential growth between the groups. Here, we see the F-ratio is very small F=.364 with a p=.695. We can infer that the two groups grow at the same rate – this too matches the pattern in the graphical display showing parallel growth.

Task C1.4

➤ Discuss which hypothesis is supported by the repeated measures factor in the above table.

The second part of the analysis tests the difference between the two groups – which is in fact the main focus of the research project.

Table 5.4 Tests of between-subjects effects: (measure: groups on repeated measures)

Source	*Type III Sum of squares*	*df*	*Mean square*	*F*	*Sig.*
Intercept	19999721.940	1	19999721.940	27361.404	.000
Group	31158.023	1	31158.023	42.627	.000
Error	372782.703	510	730.946		

The focus of attention is on the between-group difference. We can see that the F-ratio of 42.62 is highly 'significant' p=.000 which indicates that the mean differences observed are too large to have been a matter of chance.

Task C1.5

➤ Both the statistics and the graphics suggest that the learners in both groups make gains in proficiency over time. The group effect is, however, ambiguous. Identify the source of the ambiguity and discuss why it makes the group difference analysis problematic.

NON-EQUIVALENT GROUP DESIGN

The research designers decided to allow the learners to self-select into either the intensive or extensive groups. The graphical display of the means indicates clearly that the two groups were different even before the instruction began. The self-selection has unfortunately led to a form of selection bias – which makes group comparisons difficult. Randomized assignment to groups is the preferred antidote to selection bias – though for mainly logistical reasons it is often difficult to carry out.

Re-analysis of the repeated measures

We now know that the groups were different even before the courses began, so the intensive versus extensive instruction difference cannot unambiguously be a causal factor influencing the group differences. In such cases, we can modify our design to focus on the post-tests individually. We do this by removing the T1 measure from the set of repeated measures and instead using it as a covariate. A covariate can be used to as the measure of the *status quo ante*, and can be used to adjust the group means on the dependent variables. The ANCOVA approach is often a 'last resort' to designs affected by selection bias, but it is a much less robust alterative to a randomized design. In the present example, the General Linear Model can be modified so that a Univariate (single dependent variable) design is used.

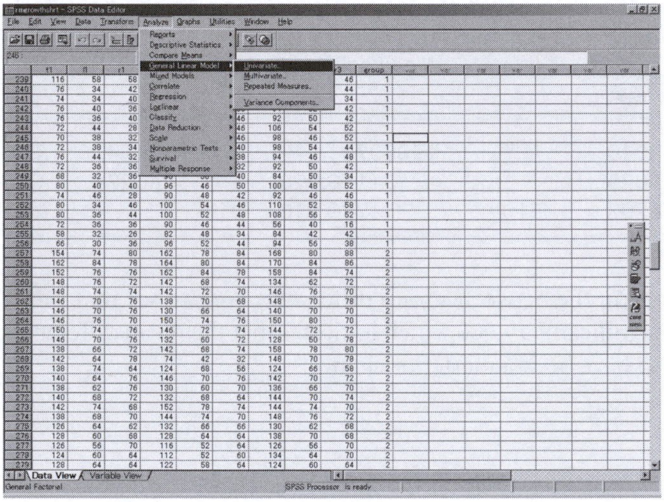

Figure 5.11 Model specification for analysis of covariance

The set up now differs from the repeated measures analysis in that only one dependent variable can be specified at a time. Here the focus of analysis will be the intermediate TOEIC Bridge test given after 60 hours of instruction.

The same variables are used, but they are now set in different relations to each other. The second TOEIC Bridge test result is the dependent variable, while the group variable encoding each subject's membership in either the intensive or extensive group is now a 'factor' to be tested. The pre-instruction measure of proficiency, T1, is now the measure of the group differences prior to the program of instruction, and thus plays the role of the covariate. In some designs, more than one covariate can be employed as 'filters' to isolate pre-existing group differences which would otherwise inject selection bias into a design.

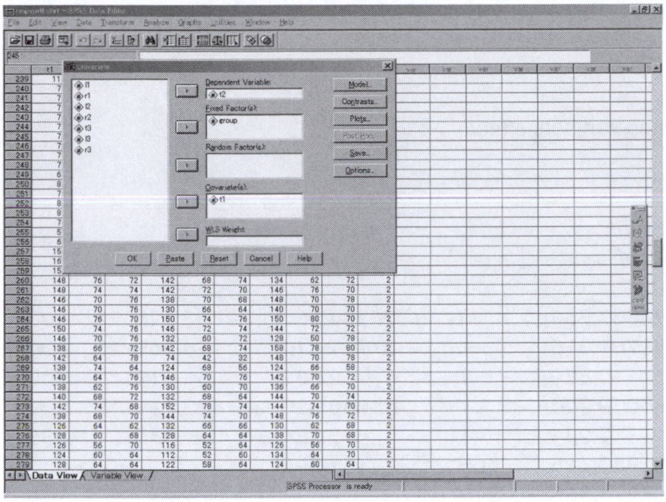

Figure 5.12 Variable selection for ANCOVA model

Reprint courtesy of International Business Machines Corporation, © SPSS, Inc., an IBM company

In the ANCOVA set up, the group variable (intensive versus extensive learning) is 'fixed' because there are only two kinds of groups contrasted in the study. A 'random' effect would be a selection from among all possible instruction types. Once the variables are inserted, the MODEL needs to be specified.

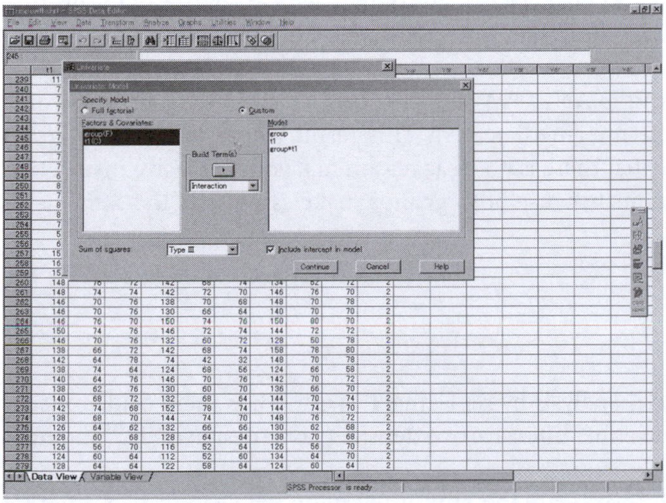

Figure 5.13 Group and covariate interaction model specification

Reprint courtesy of International Business Machines Corporation, © SPSS, Inc., an IBM company

The factor (group) is moved over to the 'customized' box. The T1 functioning as the covariate is likewise moved to the model window. Finally, both the group and T1 variables (shift key pressed with cursor covering both) are moved over to create a group * T1 interaction term. This will test whether the two groups improve at parallel rates of change.

Table 5.5 Tests of between-subjects effects

Dependent variable: t2

Source	*Type III Sum of squares*	*df*	*Mean square*	*F*	*Sig.*
Corrected model	74382.764(a)	3	24794.255	153.625	.000
Intercept	21781.616	1	21781.616	134.959	.000
Group	2.539	1	2.539	.016	.900
t1	65059.920	1	65059.920	403.111	.000
Group * t1	7.284	1	7.284	.045	.832
Error	81988.416	508	161.395		
Total	6644924.000	512			
Corrected Total	156371.180	511			

The analysis of covariance results indicates that the two groups do not differ from each other in their rate of change from T1 to T2: F=.016, p=.900. The group differences which existed before the intensive instruction program started remain constant. Nor is there an 'interaction' between the group and the pre-test: F=.045, p=.832. A significant interaction would suggest that subsets of group members make gains from T1 to T2 – and would imply that one of the instruction types, extensive or intensive, is differentially beneficial to some of the members of one of the groups. This phenomenon often indicates an 'aptitude-treatment interaction'.

The graphical display of the ANCOVA results shows a clear rate of improvement from the pre-test to the intermediate test. This result would lead the program researchers to conclude that there is no clear reason to favour intensive instruction over extensive instructions because both groups make essentially the same gains over time.

Task C1.6

- Modify the ANCOVA analysis by replacing T2 with T3. Is there evidence suggesting any benefit to either intensive or extensive course design in the 'long run'?
- Design a project to investigate the kind of learning involved in two different types of tasks: convergent tasks (e.g. information gap) and divergent tasks (e.g. debate).
- Design a study that involves different forms of feedback to learners on a specific grammatical or phonological feature. Test learners' accuracy on that feature in a pre–post intervention design.

Hauser, E. (2005), 'Coding 'corrective recasts': The maintenance of meaning and more fundamental problems' *Applied Linguistics* 26: 293–316

On what theoretical and empirical grounds does Hauser question the practice of coding corrective recasts?

Hauser's argument can be extended to the coding and counting of interactional phenomena more generally. Going back to your data analysis in Tasks B2.1 and B2.3, what problems do you encounter when you attempt to code and count the repairs and corrections? Can these problems be solved within a social constructionist framework? What conditions would have to be met in order for coding and counting to be compatible with a 'conversation-analytic mentality'?

NB towards the end of the volume we will discuss for what research goals and under what conditions quantification of interactional data can be meaningful and compatible with CA's project. We will draw in particular on Schegloff's quantification paper and Heritage's work using quantification of media discourse data.

C2 Exploration

In this section we explore how a research project might describe and analyze the processes involved in a TBLT lesson or lessons, relating the theory to an example of classroom practice. The stages involved are:

a Record and transcribe a lesson;
b Analyze the interaction using CA;
c Analyze the lesson plan, teaching materials and any learner products (e.g. writing);
d Compare the interaction, lesson plan and teaching materials to the theory of TBLT.

Although this example focuses on TBLT, the framework could in principle be employed in relation to any teaching approach for which theoretical literature is available.

a Record and transcribe a lesson.

Guidelines on recording lessons are available in Appendix D (website). Transcription tutorials are available on http://www-staff.lboro.ac.uk/~ssca1/ http://sites.google.com/site/llewellynnick/tutorial. http://www.sscnet.ucla.edu/soc/faculty/schegloff/

b Analyze the interaction using CA.

Chapter 1 contains an introduction to CA and the Seedhouse and Almutairi article in this chapter provides examples of analyses of task-based interaction.

c Analyze the lesson plan and teaching materials and any learner products (e.g. writing).

Willis (1996) contains very practical teaching materials and sample lesson plans for TBLT lessons; see also http://www.willis-elt.co.uk/

d Compare the interaction, lesson plan and teaching materials to the theory of TBLT.

A number of guides to the theory of TBLT are available, including Ellis (2004), Skehan (2003), Willis (1996), Willis and Willis (2007). There have been relatively few classroom studies of implementation of TBLT, but see Samuda (2001).

Task C2.1

➤ The following extended task uses transcripts and lesson plans from a TBLT lesson in a language school in London (Carr 2006). Lesson aims are (Carr 2006: 12, 10):

> By the end of the two sessions, the students will be better able to give a short talk recommending a tour of their country. This will be achieved by a) listening to a native speaker model b) focussing on and practising some useful phrases for this kind of talk c) allowing plenty of preparation time d) focussing on useful language emerging as a result of the task. Subsidiary aims are to give students the opportunity for extended speaking practice and to practise listening for general comprehension. Assumptions are that students have now had several task-based lessons and are accustomed to the idea of using the teacher as a resource in the preparation stage. Much lexis used in the initial listening has recently been covered.

There are seven stages to the lesson. For each stage, a quotation from the lesson plan precedes an extract from the interaction (all from Carr 2006: 12).

Lead-in: aim is to generate interest in the topic and task

Extract 4

T: OK have have you ever visited any places outside London
S7: me yesterday
T: [where've you been]
S7: in Portsmouth ee and Bournemouth
T: down
S7: [down south]
T: here
S7: yes

T: why::
S7: (0.4) my my girlfriend live here a:n um I like this a student place er all the peoples young a lot of (0.2) the go out in the evening an this very good
T: ri:ght anybody else?

Listening: aim is to give students a native-speaker model of the task they will be doing later and to give students a manageable task to focus their listening. The teacher talks through a five-day tour of England using map and guidebook pictures. The teacher gives simple listening questions beforehand. Students confer on the questions written on the flipchart, then answer.

Extract 5

T: the last day| (.) anyway the last day (.) is Oxford (.) which is he:re (0.4) a and I'm sure you now Oxford
SS: yes
T: Oxford's famous for its:
S4: university=
S6: =university yes
T: =yeah the university yes that's right (.) er this is the actually the Library (.) the Bodleian Library it's very famous it's a round library (.) and then you can go and look around all the colleges (.) the: er (0.2) Magdalen College is a very famous one and (.) New College where (.) there's a beautiful beautiful garden (.) °right° so you can wander around the colleges, (.) you can go shopping (.) and then my best recommendation is that you go punting
S6: punting
T: punting (.) do you know what that is
S: no
S: no
T: it's (0.2) what's that [name]?
S1: punting
T: punting
S1: ah punting is er (0.2) you go with a small boat on the river (.) you have a: a kind of a (.) a wood
T: mmhmm
S1: and you push the boat (.) like this
S: oh yes
S6: it's the same thing in Vienne yeah (0.2) like in Venice
T: [that's right]
S6: it's very romantic
S: Venice
T: have you done it?
S: no no no no (0.2) I like but it's
T: [hh hh hh hhh]
T: okay so you can go punting (.) all right and then when you're (.) really tired at the end of the day (.) you walk along the river (.) and there's a really good pub (0.2) called the Trout the Trout (.) it's a very famous
S6: [aah]
famous traditional pub (.) in Oxford

S7: yes
S6: we go to Oxford next week hh hh

Language Focus: aim is to introduce and give brief controlled practice of seven useful expressions for the task. This is intended to help the students improve the accuracy, fluency or complexity of how they speak.

Extract 6

T: the next one then (.) the next one [name]
S2: you should uh (.) definitely stop at Stonehenge
T: okay good (.) do I want you to stop at Stonehenge
(0.6)
S: you must
T: do I want you (.) to stop at Stonehenge
S6: yeah yeah
S2: [yes]
T: a little or a lot
S: a little
S6: no you recommend it
S2: [a lot]
T: I recommend it (.) stro:ngly (.) you should definitely stop at ho- Stonehenge (0.2) listen to me again you should definitely stop at Stonehenge together
SS: you should definitely stop at Stonehenge
T: again
SS: you should definitely stop at Stonehenge
T: right listen to me (.) should definitely (.) definitely
SS: should definitely
T: that's right say it again everybody you should definitely stop
SS: you should definitely stop at Stonehenge
SS: you should definitely stop at Stonehenge
SS: you should definitely stop at Stonehenge
T: that's good (0.2) okay right turn it over (.) try to remember it
S2: hh
(0.4)
S: °should definitely°
T: [name]
S1: you should definitely stop at Stonehenge
T: very good
S1: you should definitely stop at Stonehenge
T: right you can use other verbs for example you should definitely go to (.)

Task Preparation: Students prepare a talk on a five-day tour in their country, calling on the teacher for language help as required. The aim is to give students the opportunity and time to marshal their ideas and improve their ability to express them, using the teacher as a resource.

Extract 7

T: mm mm so you you decide .hh I'm going to give you a little bit of time now to: think about it (.) I'm going to give you a piece of paper
(1.5)
T: can you draw a quick picture of your country (.) or the region of your country that you'd like to choose .hhh we have some people from the same country here so (.) Italians hands up (.) Italians good I'd like you two to work together in a minute a:nd Brazilians (.) grea:t okay you're sitting together you can work together (.) hh hh hh hh
S: [(. . . . . . .)]
T: right the other people will work alone (.) right so here's a piece of paper
S4: (. . .) because I am from (. . .)
T: pass them round (0.3) so could uh
S6: [thank you]
(recording edited)
T: if you need any help from me please call me (0.2) if you need any vocabulary
(20 lines omitted)
S7: you should definitely go to Margarita Island (.) National Park it's one of the most beautiful cities around the
T: [mmhmm]
S7: world
T: uh not around
S7: cities
T: °do you remember the° (.) preposition (0.2) where's (0.4) where's the preposition here (0.4) here can you
see here
S7: yes
T: mm
S7: in the world?

Task Rehearsal: students practise their talk with a partner to build confidence before speaking in a larger group.

Extract 8

T: er later you're going to give your (.) tou:r to a big group but I want you to practise for a few minutes now in pai:rs (.) .hh so ah first of all one of you give the talk (.) and then I'll tell you to change and the other person
(0.2) if you need any help (.) on any expressions please call me all right
(students speak at the same time, so transcription is not possible)

Task Performance: students recommend their tour to a larger group. Aim is to practise speaking at some length and communicating ideas effectively. Listeners are encouraged to practise responding and clarifying. The public performance is intended to stretch students in a way that smaller, more informal pairwork may not.

Extract 9

S6: here is the Brabant (0.2) French here (0.2) and German here (0.2) I think it's here (0.2) only a little (0.2) there are a lot of um problem (0.2) linguistic problems
S2: mmhmm
S6: (0.2) you must abs- e:r absolutely you must ab- definitely go to Bruges (0.2) old (0.2) .hh old town a:nd very very:: they speak Flemish there (0.2) it is only (0.2) this problems hh hh hh hh
S2: they don't speak French
S6: er no:: yes::
S2: they speak but they don't like speak French
S6: be- I I speak French but i don't like speak Flemish and then (0.2) I
S2: the same (0.2) thing
S6: yes there you speak (.) Flemish all th- (.) and some of their speak F:rench
S4: [Flemish French]
S9: French but no everybody speak Flemish
S4: [Flemish mm]
S9: (0.2) af-ter i think it's better to go to Chimay you know the beer Chimay
S2: Chimay
S9: it's very well kn:owed beer (0.2) we make er beer (0.20 beer to drink
(recording edited)
T: that was rea:lly good (0.2) really really good .hh which country would you like to go to then [name] which one of yours would you like to go to

Follow-up/Feedback: focuses on useful language which was used by students or which was needed by them.

Extract 10

T: that's grea:t I'd like to look at some of the things you've said because you've said such good things here so uh this was an expression a lot of people have used (0.2) instead of fa:mous
S: it's well-known
S: [well-known]
S: [it's well-known]
T: yes so for example your country is=
S7: =it's well-known for its beautiful woman
T: ye: hh hh and Belgium
S6: it's well-known for the frites frish e::r fris?
T: what's that
S6: French frites
T: [↑fries oh French fries]
S6: French fries yes hh hh
T: [like chips]
S6: ye:s
T: ↑really
S6: [chips] yes very know oh yes
T: [fine okay]

Now analyze the interaction using a CA approach. Show how each extract is organized in terms of turn-taking, sequence, repair and topic. Relate the organization of the interaction in each extract to the shifting pedagogical focus in each episode.

Then relate the interaction and the lesson plan to the theory of TBLT, using some of the references provided above or the TBLT framework below, from Willis (1996: 155).

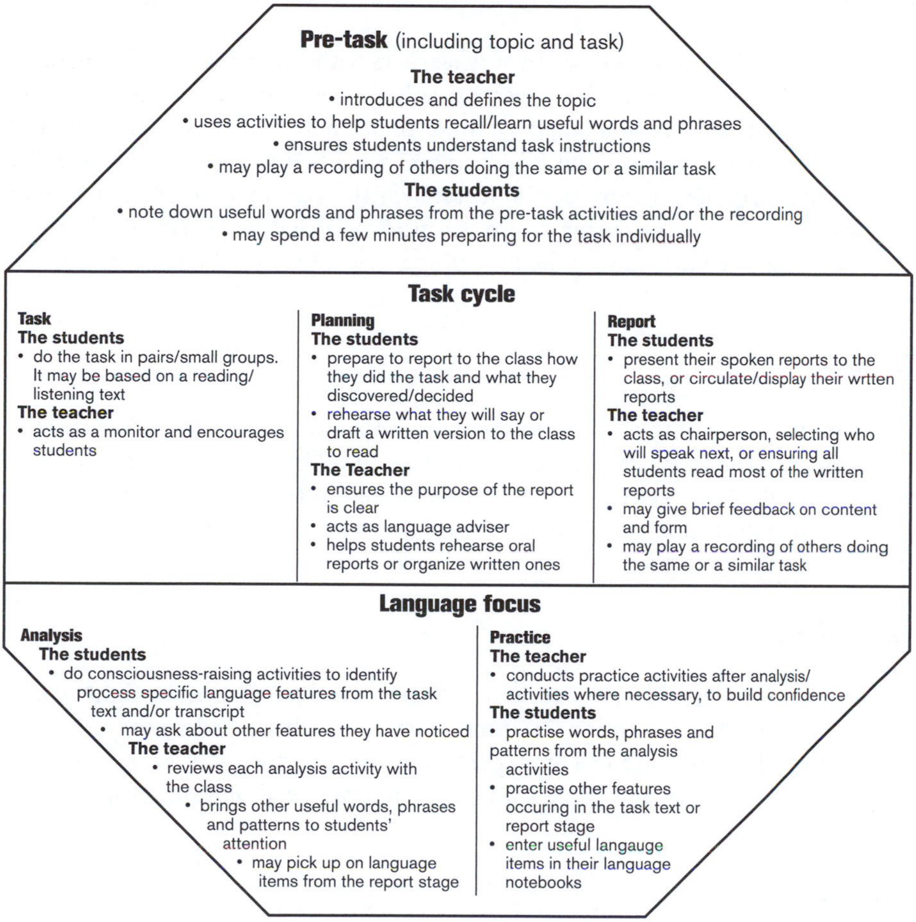

Figure 5.14 Overview of the TBL framework

Task C2.2

➤ Now plan a similar research project in relation to a different approach to language teaching, based in your local context. Describe and analyze the processes involved in a lesson or lessons, relating the theory to an example of classroom practice. The stages involved are:

a Recording and transcribing a lesson;
b Analyzing the interaction using CA;
c Analyzing the lesson plan, teaching materials and any learner products (e.g. writing);
d Comparing the interaction, lesson plan and teaching materials to the theory of the approach.

Task C2.3

➤ Lyster's study is designed to see how learners with English L1 can be made to learn a grammatical feature which exists in L2 (French) but not in L1. If you are a native speaker of a language other than English, choose a grammatical feature which exists in English but not in your L1. If you are a native speaker of English, choose a grammatical feature which exists in a target language but not in English. Then design a research study which determines whether this feature can be taught using the FFI approach employed in Lyster's article.

Task C2.4

➤ Compare and contrast the types of task used in these two articles. What is the basic purpose of the tasks in each research study? What are the differences in the way that the construct 'task' is approached in the two articles? Compare how the interaction generated by the tasks is treated in both articles.

Task C2.5

➤ Seedhouse's article does not contain research questions. Rather, it might be said to have a problem-solution structure. Identify another problem in the area of language learning and teaching, preferably one of which you have first-hand knowledge. Design a research study to try to provide a solution for it.

Task C2.6

➤ Consider the issue of generalizability in relation to each article. To what extent do Lyster's findings apply specifically to young learners in immersion classrooms learning this specific grammatical feature of French and to what extent is a universal point being made about FFI and feedback? To what extent do Seedhouse and Almutairi's points about task-based interaction apply to all task-based interaction and to what extent do they apply solely to the specific task being used by students in this specific setting?

Task C2.7

➤ Read the following three extracts from Algarawi (2010). Employing Lyster's research design, Algarawi recorded three parallel classes. One of these teachers did not employ any corrective feedback at all (no feedback group), one employed prompts as feedback (prompt group) and one teacher employed corrective recasts (recast group). The grammatical form being taught was the passive voice.

No-feedback group

Extract 10

1 T: Rawan.
2 L2: er the teacher er helped me er (3.5) I was been helped by the teacher.
3 T: next.
4 L3: er the teacher helped them. (.) we (.) we were (.) we were help (.) by the teacher.
5 T: next.

(Algarawi 2010: 108)

Prompt group

Extract 11

1 L3: the teacher helped them (.) they was helped by the teacher.
2→ T: they WAS or WERE? (.) we have to,
3 L3: was.
4→ T: no (.) you have er you should try (.) Anwar? ((goes to the board)) do you forget ?(.) =
5 = do you forget er that they↑ IS (.) plural (.) don't get confused please? (.) don't get =
6 = confused (.) you see? ((writes on the board)) THE (.) TEACHER (.) HELPED (.)=
7 =THEM (.) ok now↑ what is my subject here (.) Anwar?
8 L3: the teacher.
9→ T: the teacher is my subject, what is my verb here?
10 L3: helped.
11→ T: helped (.) ok (.) and this is (.) past tense (.) ok? this is help helped helped ok? and them =
12 = is my (.) ↑object here (.) so? THEM (.) when you change it from an object into a=
13 = subject (.) it will become (.) they (.) ok? the pronoun will become the::y (.) and then =
14 = they? (.) is ↑singular or plural?
15 L3: plural.
16→ T: plural (.) so people put (.) they were (.) and then?

17 L3: helped.
18→ T: helped (.) by whom? they were helped by the:?
19 L3: teacher.
20→ T: got it? Yes:: (.)↑ now say again (.) I want you to say it again.
21 L3: they were helped by the teacher.
22 T: they were helped by the teacher (.) do you understand?
23 L3: yes.

(Algarawi 2010: 130)

Recast group

Extract 12

1 T: ((pointing at L8)) number eight?
2 L8: when I arrived at the airport yes- (.) yesterday (.) I met by my cousin and a couple of her friends.
3 T: when I arrived at the airport yesterday? (.) I was met by my cousin and a couple of her Friends (.) number ni:ne.

(Algarawi 2010: 122)

Examine the interaction in the three different groups. Can you identify any differences in the L2 learning opportunities which are being experienced by the learners in the three different groups?

Can you see any way of developing a mixed methods approach by combining Lyster's design with video/audio recording, transcription and CA of the interaction which each of the parallel groups is engaged in?

DISCUSSION

The two studies in this chapter exemplify two different ways in which 'task' can be integrated into research processes.

Lyster's study employs task design as a) a means of delivering specific FFI input to a group of learners b) a means of assessing their learning of the target item. In Lyster's study, the construct 'task' is fully integrated into three stages of the quasi-experimental research design; the pre-treatment test, the treatment and the post-treatment test. In terms of the purposes of the tasks, they are to a) teach grammatical gender, to generate writing and speech in L2 and b) to evaluate whether grammatical gender has been learnt. 'Task' in this study therefore forms a number of different links in the chain of the research process. They are crucial links, since tasks provide both input for learning and evidence of learning. In terms of task phase, Lyster's study contains very detailed descriptions of the tasks-as-workplans (pp. 413–417), covering both the 'treatment' tasks and the assessment tasks. There is very little information on the tasks-in-process in terms of the type of interaction which resulted. However, the type of interaction generated is of little relevance to the stated goals of the research. The information on the tasks-as-outcomes phase of the assessment tasks is given in numerical form (pp. 418–425). Specifically, scores on the assessment tasks taken as pre-treatment tests are compared with scores on the same tasks taken post-treatment. The comparison then reveals the extent to which learning of the target items has taken place. Lyster's study aims to investigate whether FFI improves learning of grammatical gender and whether particular feedback types facilitate this. The study conceives of learning as a macro-level shift in cognitive state, and also presents learning as a process involving noticing and feedback.

In the empirical section of Seedhouse and Almutairi's study, the emphasis is firmly on task-in-process, although a holistic approach to task-based interaction is advocated at the end of the article which covers the whole process of TBLT. Their study portrays task implementation as a complex, multimodal process of interpretation and negotiation between participants. A major focus of the article is on multimodality and its contribution to the micro-level analysis of task-based interaction. Seedhouse and Almutairi seek to make the generalizable point that task-related actions and non-verbal elements are significant components of task-based learning. The article does not consider the learning outcomes of the interaction but provides a framework for analyzing task-based interaction.

Lyster's research design addresses the question of *why* the four groups featured in the study would differ from pre-test to post-test. The approach used in his study is hypothesis-driven, and seeks to test the differential impact of FFI interventions on group mean differences. By using a group mean comparison approach over time, Lyster provides a macro-level summary of differences among the groups, and by testing the group differences against a probability model (the F-ratio) arrives at an inference about the stability of the observed differences. The limits of generalizablity for the study are determined by the sampling strategy used, and how much they concur with other studies of the same phenomena. Researchers replicating this study would expect to find similar outcomes to those of Lyster. The extent to which Lyster's study would fit into a homogenous set of outcomes could be examined with the use of a research synthesis. Li (2010), in fact, subsumes Lyster's study into a meta-analysis of corrective feedback and thus situates the findings of Lyster's study into a cumulative summary. Research syntheses such as Li's allow for tests of the generalizability of many studies focused on the same putative causal phenomena. Such syntheses provide a descriptive picture of the average effect sizes of interventions and the degree to which they vary across studies.

This chapter has illustrated how tasks can be employed for different purposes at different stages of the research process. When using an input–output model for language learning research, tasks can provide the pedagogical input or the 'intervention' stage of the process. However, they can also be involved in the output stage of the process through being employed to assess learning. Typically, one aspect of the overall task process is selected for quantitative comparison, which in the case of Lyster's study is pre-test and post-test scores.

When a social-constructionist model of language learning research is employed, the emphasis tends to be on *how* a task is interpreted and implemented by learners in a social setting and on the interaction generated. The emphasis therefore tends to be very much on the task-in-process stage of the task cycle and on a holistic presentation of the interaction. Of course this approach is open to the criticism that it does not identify which specific aspects of the task process are most conducive to language acquisition, as Lyster's study attempts to do. One might therefore conclude that it would be fruitful to consider how both approaches to 'task' might be combined in a mixed-methods procedure.

Task C2.7

- Design a research project which employs tasks and which combines an input–output model and a social-constructionist model of language learning research.

CHAPTER 6
Interaction, context and identity

Introduction

In this unit we consider different qualitative approaches (CA and ethnography) to the issue of how context and identity can be described and analyzed in relation to spoken interaction. Identity has become a crucial construct in social sciences research in general. In the past it was often assumed that individuals had a fixed and static identity which could be specified in terms of social class, age, gender, etc. This is sometimes called an 'essentialist' approach. However, more recent approaches have revealed that individual identity may be much more fluid and variable, assuming different and/or multiple identities in relation to different people and contexts. Block (2006: 26), for example, suggests that 'identity is seen not as something fixed for life, but as fragmented and contested in nature'. He suggests a number of individual/collective identity types relevant to his study of multilingual identities in London: ethnic, racial, national, gendered, social class and language. Learner identity is becoming an increasingly important research issue, since it may be related to the following constructs: age, nationality, ethnicity, culture, gender, sexuality, native/non-native speaker, motivation, successful/unsuccessful learner, beginner/advanced, cross-cultural communication. These constructs may then be treated as variables in research. For example, if researching the effect of a specific type of language teaching on a large group of learners, one might relate increases in performance on tests to the above variables.

The basic problem, when trying to link talk and identity, is that there is an indefinite number of external aspects of cultural, social or personal identity which could be potentially relevant to any given instance of talk-in-interaction. So it might or might not be relevant, for example, that a speaker is a heterosexual male, that he has a beard, that he is a working-class socialist, has blond hair, is single, does karate, dislikes country music. Any of these characteristics might in principle be relevant to our analysis of the data. In this chapter we see how this problem is tackled by two methodologies. From a CA perspective, interactants themselves make relevant in the details of talk which aspects of identity they are currently orienting to. In CA analysis we need therefore to analyze how they are talking into being certain aspects of identity through their talk. Ethnographers are interested in the social construction of identity and will also seek to understand how participants construct aspects of their identity through their interaction with others and with their context. However, ethnographers also draw on local categories and broader constructs such as ethnicity or group membership in order to understand how aspects of identity are played out.

The same basic problem exists when trying to relate context to talk or human behaviour more generally. The number of aspects of context (external to the individual) which may be relevant is without limit and may change instantly. So it might or might not be relevant, for example, that the bright pink walls are giving people a headache, that the sound of a drill has just started up in an adjoining room or that a revolting smell has entered the room. As with identity, the CA position on context is to study how interactants orient to aspects of context in the details of their talk. As Schegloff puts it:

> In an interaction's moment-to-moment development, the parties, singly and together, select and display in their conduct which of the indefinitely many aspects of context they are making relevant, or are invoking, for the immediate moment.
>
> (Schegloff 1987: 219)

This precisely delineable 'immediate moment' is rarely available to ethnographers, who work instead over time, seeking to identify patterns of behaviour and social organization that will enable them to understand in broader terms the relationship between context and behaviour. The difference between the sort of evidence produced here and the recorded data available to conversation analysts is brought out by Le Compte and Goetz:

> Ethnographic research occurs in natural settings and often is undertaken to record processes of change. Because unique situations cannot be reconstructed precisely even the most exact replication of research methods may fail to produce identical results.
>
> (Le Compte and Goetz 1982: 35)

Section A
A1 Ethnography

A1.1 CONTEXT

At an abstract level, context would seem to present an almost insurmountable challenge to the ethnographer, who, unlike the conversation analyst, is unable to apply his/her attention to a particular data extract and insist that any context not made relevant within it must thereby be discounted as analytically inaccessible. Once these precise limits are removed, it would seem that the analyst is faced with a potentially infinite regress in which there is no limit to what might be invoked as an explanatory resource. However, for the ethnographer this does not represent a problem provided that careful attention is paid to the ways in which explanations of social phenomena are developed.

As we saw in Chapter 3, the ethnographer's data set is based on extended exposure to life in a particular setting and the analysis based on this is developed out of deep engagement with the full range of data collected. This means that it would be entirely illegitimate to abstract a segment (e.g. an event) from the data set and subject it to 'analysis' in terms of contextual factors selected as relevant by the researcher – a process that would immediately raise questions of legitimacy and limits. The researcher cannot presume to 'explain' an occurrence in terms of some arbitrary contextual factor (e.g. 'James shouted at the teacher because he was tired at the end of a long day') any more than they can presume to see inside a participant's head (e.g. 'James shouted at the teacher because he felt humiliated that she had asked him to return to his seat'). Instead, practices, events, incidents, exchanges, etc. are interpreted in terms of the patterns and themes which have emerged from analysis of the data, which means that they are descriptively and conceptually circumscribed.

The ethnographer is interested in social practices, in how people go about their business, and this can be understood only by noting patterns of behaviour, identifying routines, recognizing taken-for-granted rules or procedures etc. It is therefore not accidental that Geertz's term 'thick description' was quickly and widely adopted as a way of capturing the attempt to produce a richly detailed account of participants, practices and settings. While it is certainly true that participants make relevant aspects of context in their talk, they do so in all manner of other ways to which the ethnographer must be sensitive – even though they themselves may be entirely unaware of the nature of their behaviour.

This is why ethnographers need to immerse themselves in the social world they are studying, whether as participants or as observers. As we saw in Chapter 3, it was as a result of a temporary physical incapacity that Toohey (1998) became particularly conscious of the inhibiting effects of the physical arrangement of the classroom she was studying and this awareness was relevant to her understanding of what the borrowing practices of students in the class involved.

Task A1.1

- One of the things a researcher needs to develop is sensitivity to aspects of description and context that are analytically relevant. Consider the description of Amy as '[s]mall, physically adept, and attractive' in the following extract from Toohey (1998) and decide which, if any, of these characteristics might be relevant to the borrowing practices that the author is describing. (You may wish to re-acquaint yourself with the relevant section, which appears in full in Chapter 3.)

> Amy initially did not move much around the classroom to borrow, as for some months before the arrangement noted in Figure 1 she was seated by two boys who borrowed reciprocally with her. Later in the year, beginning in February according to the videos and my field notes, Amy began to range further afield to borrow. She would move around the classroom, lean on the desk of the potential lender, and engage him or her in short conversations. In kindergarten Amy had engaged in a great deal of friendly and affiliating behaviour with other children, and the girls in her kindergarten especially had treated her initiations positively (Toohey 1996). Small, physically adept, and attractive, Amy had been a welcome peripheral participant in the activities of her kindergarten classmates. Her habits of soliciting connections with other children appeared to survive her physical separation from them, and she borrowed even when she had her own materials easily available.
>
> (Toohey 1998: 73–74)

At first sight the description of Amy may seem superfluous to the practices the writer is describing, especially since the description applies to her previous (kindergarten) year. Reference is made to this because the writer is developing a description of borrowing practices that relates to interactional opportunity and legitimate peripheral participation, so evidence of successful interaction with other children in the kindergarten is relevant. The importance of the interaction itself for her is brought out in the final statement in the extract, which makes it clear that her borrowing visits are in fact unnecessary. The description of Amy is associated with her acceptance by classmates and its placement certainly implies that the researcher considers these qualities to be potentially relevant. However, the fact that she is small and physically adept is also relevant to the description of the classroom which the writer has presented earlier. The desks are close together and movement is difficult, so in an environment like this being small and physically adept facilitates relatively unobtrusive movement around the class.

Analytically, nothing hinges on the description of Amy, but the writer will go on to contrast her borrowing with that of another pupil as part of a bigger picture showing how some pupils are disadvantaged in terms of interactional (and thereby potentially developmental) opportunity. It is interesting to note, however, that interactional evidence plays very little part in this paper, and where it does so it is deployed as evidence in support of a single claim: that the practice of copying or repeating others' words in this class is discouraged. In fact, one of the criticisms leveled at ethnography is that its reliance on interviews or field notes leaves the process of situated production unexamined (ten Haven, 1990). While this is true, it may not be analytically relevant to the sort of work that ethnographers wish to do with extracts of talk captured either in field notes or recordings.

It is clear, for example, that context for the ethnographer is not the same thing as context for a discourse analyst. There is a sense in which the subject of ethnography is context itself, or at least context as it is constituted through the social practices of a particular group, but the essential point is that context is not something that can be separated out from the process of analysis. This is not necessarily the case where the analysis of discourse is concerned: in a situation where a teacher had insisted on the more intimate *tu* form of personal address in the classroom, the switch from *tu* to the more formal *vous* on stepping outside the classroom was contextually determined. Van Dijk has argued that people subjectively represent situations (e.g. a school lesson) and that these subjective, mental representations of the communicative event represent their 'context models' or simply 'contexts': 'we define contexts as the structure of all properties of the social situation that are systematically relevant for the production, comprehension, or functions of discourse and its structures' (Van Dijk 1999: 130). The pursuit of systematic relevance in this sense is not the business of the ethnographer.

Task A1.2

➤ We have suggested above that the ethnographer needs to approach interaction in the context of a broader analysis based on the data set within which such interaction is embedded. The following two extracts relate to classroom exchanges. Which of them seems to you to reflect this approach and, in the case of the other, can you see any potential dangers in the way in which contextual factors are brought into the description.

Extract A

The way that Hanif uses German just at a juncture where there's a problem of classroom management actually points to another general feature of adolescent Deutsch. Adolescent Deutsch was rather narrowly oriented to issues of classroom conduct and control, and in this regard, it was noticeably different from the ways in which, for example, these youngsters put on exaggerated 'posh' and 'Cockney' accents. Stylizations of 'posh' and 'Cockney' certainly did sometimes engage with issues of classroom order, but they also thematized sexuality, bodily demeanor, and issues of peer rapport.

(Rampton 2002: 506)

Extract B

When Ms. Melanie approached the group, the middle-class English speaker, Daniel, was holding the pen. A very strong student and known for his sometimes arrogant attitude during English class, Daniel had already had to ask the other two children, Maria and Oswaldo, both working-class Spanish-dominant students, for help to come up with the word for 'feathers' (*plumas*) in order to record his idea.

(Palmer 2009: 196)

It is, of course, unfair to extract short passages from what may be a very complex analysis developing over different dimensions, but nevertheless a comparison of these two extracts highlights some important considerations when drawing on contextual information. In Extract A, for example, we get a clear sense of the broader analytical context. The writer suggests that Hanif's use of 'adolescent Deutsch' at a point where classroom management is an issue may indicate that this particular form is 'narrowly oriented to issues of classroom conduct and control', providing support for this suggestion by contrasting it with the pupil's use of other accents. While he notes that the latter 'sometimes engage with classroom order', he is able to identify features of this use that distinguish it from adolescent Deutsch. We are not provided here with information that is designed to help us identify the 'meaning' of particular exchanges, but instead invited to consider, as part of a broader analysis, how particular linguistic forms are deployed in this environment. This provides an excellent illustration of Miller's description of the work of ethnographers in his comparison of ethnographic and conversation analytic approaches:

> Ethnographers' longer term and more varied experiences in social settings are more likely to acquaint them with the variety of ways in which setting participants orient to and use the interactional and interpretive conventions available to them.
>
> (Miller 1997: 157)

Extract B is part of a very interesting and well-theorized paper focusing on English/ Spanish bilingual immersion classes which highlights a situation where speakers from one linguistic group dominate and shows how the practices of one teacher increase the opportunities for linguistic access by the language-minority students in the class. The researcher makes it very clear from the beginning of the paper that she entered the field with questions about 'the role of status and power in language choice and participation patterns' and that the setting was, not untypically, 'divided fairly dramatically along race, class, and language lines' (Palmer 2009: 179).

In the extract, Daniel is characterized as middle-class, English and a very strong student but with an attitude that is seen as 'sometimes arrogant'. In terms of the argument of the paper, the fact that he is middle-class and English is relevant because of the linguistic dominance of this group (though some researchers might question the nature of the categorizations and the way they are deployed, that is part of a wider debate) and the fact that he is a strong student also relates to dominance, though it is hard to see how being perceived as arrogant is analytically relevant. However, the terms are not situated within that broader analysis, and by invoking them immediately prior to an exchange that will subsequently be analysed the researcher implies that they are in some way relevant to the analysis itself.

This is, in fact, what happens. In response to the teacher's question about what the items have in common, the group respond individually, beginning with Maria. After two wings (Maria), feathers, two eyes (Daniel) and two feet (Oswaldo), Daniel offers

'¿*Y que son vertebrados*? [And that they are vertebrates?]' which the writer describes as follows: 'Daniel proudly offered the word that he assumed was the centerpiece of the lesson, that these animals were vertebrates' (2009: 197). There is no evidence in the text that this was offered 'proudly' and the writer offers nothing else to support this interpretation. More seriously, the claim that follows this about Daniel's assumption illustrates perfectly the sort of psychological mind-reading that conversation analysts so emphatically reject.

It is also interesting to note that the writer claims that the teacher acknowledged all the responses 'equally and graciously', even though her misunderstanding of Daniel's proffered *plumas* ('No more? Just that? Oh feathers, you said!'), which seems deliberate given that they have been invited to identify avian characteristics. Taken together, then, the analysis seems to be motivated by the description of Daniel which precedes it. This is surprising given that the writer claims (2009: 188) that hers was 'a traditional ethnographic approach . . . and a microanalysis of discourse that followed methods used by conversation analysis'. It is perhaps this mixing of approaches that gives rise to the problem, and later in the chapter we introduce a relatively new approach that seeks to combine them in a systematic way (while recognizing that some researchers have for long insisted that the two make natural partners; see, for example, Auer 1995).

In questioning Palmer's approach to analysis here, we are not suggesting that characteristics such as arrogance and pride cannot account for Daniel's behaviour, or that being English and middle-class is irrelevant; the relevant analytical point is that we have no way of knowing whether and to what extent they contribute to this linguistic behaviour. The approaches of conversation analysis and ethnography adopt different evidential perspectives on this issue but they share the same insistence on the fundamental importance of linking evidence to claim.

A researcher who identified a student in terms of their linguistic or national identity and associated this with certain behavioural characteristics might be accused (unfairly in the case of Palmer, whose treatment is much more nuanced) of what Holliday has called 'culturism', a situation in which 'the members of a group to which an ethnic, national or international large cultural label has been attached are perceived as confined and *reduced* to pre-defined characteristics' (Holliday 1999: 245). The analytical unacceptability of this does not need to be spelt out, but it does point to an explanatory dimension that no researcher working within the social world can avoid: culture.

A1.2 CULTURE

We raise the issue of culture here not in order to address it as a topic in itself but to show how it raises important analytical considerations. In any case, as Spencer-Oatey notes, culture is 'notoriously difficult to define' (2000: 3), though she goes on to provide a characterization which is impressively undogmatic:

> Culture is a fuzzy set of attitudes, beliefs, behavioural conventions, and basic assumptions and values that are shared by a group of people, and that influence each member's behaviour and each member's interpretations of the 'meaning' of other people's behaviour.
>
> (Spencer-Oatey 2000: 4)

The strength of this characterization lies in its locus in the group and the group's shared construction of behaviour and meaning. It is a definition that would be acceptable to both an ethnographer and an ethnomethodologist, and it is therefore well suited to our purposes (for an excellent introduction to intercultural interaction, see Spencer-Oatey and Franklin 2009).

One of the reasons why culture makes such a useful candidate for consideration is that it is so often invoked casually for explanatory purposes. For example, the assumption that Asian students are 'passive' was once widely accepted and even well-known researchers were happy to subscribe to this assessment, sometimes justifying their assumptions by citing convenient philosophical traditions (e.g. Confucianism). However, a number of papers (e.g. Cheng 2000, Kumaravadivelu 2003, Clark and Gieve 2006) have exposed this sweeping generalization as dangerously misguided.

Errors of this sort do not undermine the value of investigating 'culture' in the broadest sense of that term and seeking to identify salient characteristics, but this is fraught with dangers and is definitely not the business of either ethnographers or conversation analysts. In fact, a leading figure in this approach and his associates have claimed that '[c]hoosing the appropriate level of analysis for the problem at hand is a major problem in a lot of social science research' (Hofstede *et al.* 1993: 484). What applies to a particular culture may not automatically apply to particular groups or individuals within that culture and the shift from the level of culture to that of individual is an example of what Hofstede (1980: 29) has called an ecological fallacy.

A culture, as Bond *et al.* note (2000: 53), is a social system, not a person. The issue, for ethnographers at least, is the nature of that social system and its relevance to their analysis. For this reason, they are unlikely to be interested in what Holliday refers to as 'large culture', something which would apply to the sort of categorization discussed above, where learning styles were assigned on the basis of perceived national or regional characteristics. Instead, Holliday proposes the concept of a 'small culture':

> Small culture is thus a dynamic, ongoing group process which operates in changing circumstances to enable group members to make sense of and operate meaningfully within those circumstances. When a researcher looks at an unfamiliar social grouping, it can be said to have a small culture when there is a discernible set of behaviours and understandings connected with group cohesion.
>
> (Holliday 1999: 248)

This distinction between 'large' and 'small' cultures provides a valuable point of orientation for those unfamiliar with ethnographic research, since it directs attention to the way a particular group constructs its practices and understandings in a particular situation. Although one would naturally expect small cultures to relate to small groups (rather than, for example, nations), Holliday is at pains to emphasize that small culture is not a matter of size but of 'paradigmatic difference.' His focus on group processes and cohesion within particular settings is important here. For example, while a school as an institution might be described as operating at a mezzo level, the classroom may be a 'small culture'.

Task A1.3

- In focusing on a small culture, the researcher does not thereby exclude any reference to broader cultural groupings. In the following extract, part of an investigation of playground behaviour, the researcher identifies two participants and describes how they construct a particular identity through their playground behaviour. Identify how she does this and how in delineating the characteristics of this group she makes connections with other cultural groups.

> Along with playing basketball, Mosa and Tim also play hip-hop music and use a kind of language, 'new Swedish', that often is described as typical for multi-cultural suburbs. This is a style of talking that goes together very closely with influences from a global youth culture like hip-hop music and American street culture, which basketball is a part of. Sernhede (2002) discusses young immigrant men in Swedish segregated neighbourhoods who in their identity work use attributes such as music and language in terms of a black macho style. In addition to being addressed this way by others, like when their classmates imitate the way they walk as a choreography of gangster rap, Mosa and Tim make identity claims themselves that go with being a young man from a multi-cultural suburb. In their identity work at the basketball court Tim and Mosa can be seen as performing as basketball players, as well as doing traditional categories such as gender, ethnicity and age, by constructing an *us* with the older (rowdy) boys playing basketball and also performing an *us* that differs from the other children in school. Even if many of the other children also have immigrant backgrounds they do not define themselves as belonging to a black ghetto culture like these boys.
>
> (Gustafson 2009: 12)

Although, like many other immigrant children in their school, Mosa and Tim are from a multicultural suburb, they have constructed a playground identity which defines themselves as belonging to 'a black ghetto culture' (the distinction between this and a 'multiculural suburb' does not need to be spelt out), which distinguishes them from other students. Gustafson provides behavioural (basketball), affective (a liking for hip hop music) and linguistic (the use of 'new Swedish') evidence which references a a global youth culture associated with the group with which they identify. Other practices such as walking in a particular way and associating with older, rowdy, boys provide further evidence of the way they seek to membership themselves. This is, of course, part of a bigger picture of the small culture of the playground, but it illustrates how local practices can be linked to broader categories without invoking 'large culture' as an explanatory resource.

One of the interesting features of Gustafson's paper is her use of photographs, one of which, for example, shows Mosa 'making an ordinary shot' in basketball, with a linked quotation from an interview with him in which he says how the basketball court is his 'favourite place' (2009: 12). The use of such visual evidence in ethnography is something that has not so far been adequately exploited in applied linguistics, or arguably in social science generally. In fact, as Becker (2004) notes with reference to photography, there is still no generally accepted methodological framework within which to work. Nevertheless, this is no bar to exploration, and it might be argued that it offers freedom that should be welcomed.

Language teachers work with words and in a world of words, but the process of teaching and learning is physically as well as socially situated. As O'Toole and Were (2008: 631) observe in their discussion of the place of material culture in qualitative research:

> Space and material culture is a pervading facet of human life. . . . To include space and material culture in our data collection and analysis is to include a rich source of insight that gives the researcher a deeper perception of the intangible and tacit through an examination of the corporeal and present.

As we saw from Toohey's paper in Chapter 3, a diagram of a setting can make a valuable contribution to developing an ethnographic account and the same applies to photographs, provided they are deployed within the context of a broader analysis. The teacher who claimed, for example, that 'I'm fairly *casual* in class and very cards on the table, "Let's work this out together" sort of thing. That really suits my personality' might have been photographed sitting on the side of a desk talking to a small group of students engaged in a task, and if this establishes a contrast between his style and the formal and very 'institutional' arrangement of the classroom, this might be analytically relevant to a more extended discussion of his place within the institution. Individuals represent themselves visually as well as linguistically and photographs might be very important in exploring aspects of identity. We saw in Task C3.1, for example, how the teachers in a particular school dressed in a way that reflected the focus of their teaching.

Although brief treatments of the use of pictorial analysis are available (e.g. Skåreus 2009), anyone interested in this aspect of analysis will find Rose's introduction very helpful. It is wide-ranging and covers the relevant conceptual issues as well as offering plenty of practical advice and examples of analysis.

A2 Conversation Analysis

To tackle some of the issues relating to a CA approach to identity and context, do the tasks below.

Task A2.1

➤ Read the extract below.

Extract 1

J: So who'r the boyfriends for the week.
(0.2)
M: 'k'hhhhh- Oh: go::d e-yih this one'n that one yihknow,
I jist, yihknow keep busy en go out when I wanna go
out John it's nothing 'hhh I don'have anybody
serious on the string,
J: So in other words you'd go out if I askedche out
One a' 'these times.
M: Yeah! Why not.

(Paul Drew's data [JGII:(b):8:14])

Who do you think these interactants might be? Can you guess any features of their identity, of the context in which they are talking? What are they talking about?

Extract 2

11 Dr F: Doctor Hollmann told me something like
12 you were running across the street not so
13 completely dressed or something like that,
14 Ms B: (h)yes: that's:- I am a child of God;=
15 I am his child;
16 (.)
17 Ms B: does a- does-=
18 =do you have children Doctor Fisch[er?
19 Dr F: [yes:
20 Ms B: yes what age,
21 Dr F: uh around s-seven eight [and eleven
22 Ms B: [yes and when they
23 were small these children,
24 Dr F: yes [:,
25 Ms B: [didn't they sometimes run around naked
26 [because they don't yet – because they
27 Dr F: [t(hh) u(h)

28 Ms B: don't (.) know that they must not do that. yes and in the same way:
29 you have to see that in my relationship to God

(Bergmann 1992: 149, translated from German)

Who do you think these interactants might be? Can you guess any features of their identity, of the context in which they are talking? What are they talking about?

What you should have become aware of from the above tasks is that there is a reflexive or two-way relationship between interaction and constructs such as identity and context. You only had details of the interaction, but tried to reconstruct information about the speakers' identities and context from those. In CA terms, interactants 'talk into being' their identities and the context through the details of their talk.

In this section, we will examine the relationship between interaction and context from a CA perspective. CA has a dynamic, complex, highly empirical perspective on context. The basic aim is to establish an emic perspective, i.e. to determine which elements of context are relevant to the interactants at any point in the interaction. The perspective is also an active one in which participants talk a context into being. The perspective is dynamic in that, as Heritage (1984: 242) puts it, 'The context of a next action is repeatedly renewed with every current action' and is transformable at any moment. A basic assumption of CA is that contributions to interaction are *context-shaped* and *context-renewing*. Contributions are context-shaped in that they cannot be adequately understood except by reference to the sequential environment in which they occur and in which the participants design them to occur. Contributions are context-renewing in that they create a sequential environment or template in which a next contribution will occur. Utterances document the participants' understanding of context. According to Schegloff (1987: 221), much CA work 'can be seen as an extended effort to elaborate just what a context is and what its explication or description might entail'. Evidence for the characterization of a context has to derive primarily from the orientations of the participants as documented in the details of the interactional data rather than from a description of the physical setting or the participants. The key to understanding why CA insists on being so tightly empirical is that the aim is to develop an 'emic' or participant perspective on how the participants display to each other their understanding of the context. Clearly this cannot be achieved by analysts deciding which aspects of context *they* think are relevant, particularly as there are an infinite number of potentially relevant contextual details which could be invoked. We can see an example of how features of context and identity can become relevant in the following extract from an L2 classroom.

Extract 3

407 L10: oh I see (.) I see the Chinese is uh (.) sanku
408 (0.6–0.9)
409 L11: unh?

410 L10: sanku
411 (.)
412 L9: what
413 L10: c [orals
414 L11: [corals
415 L9: corals oh okay

(Markee 2000: 27)

In this case L10's and L11's ethnic/linguistic identity as Chinese native speakers (L9 is from a different ethnic/linguistic background) becomes available and relevant to CA analysis since this is made relevant in the details of the interaction through L10 producing the Chinese translation of 'corals' and L10 and L11 then translating it back into English. From a CA perspective, then, an indefinite number of aspects if context and identity are always potentially relevant to any instance of talk. However, they only become relevant to the analysis when it is evident in the details of the interaction that the participants are orienting to them in the details of their talk – this is how CA develops an emic perspective. Let us see how this functions in relation to the extract which we have already seen above.

Extract 4

1 J: So who'r the boyfriends for the week.
2 (0.2)
3 M: 'k'hhhhh- Oh: go::d e-yih this one'n that one yihknow,
4 I jist, yihknow keep busy en go out when I wanna go
5 out John it's nothing 'hhh I don'have anybody
6 serious on the string,
7 J: So in other words you'd go out if I askedche out
8 One a' 'these times.
9 M: Yeah! Why not.

(Paul Drew's data [JGII:(b):8:14])

The essential question which we must ask at all stages of CA analysis of data is 'Why that, in that way, right now?' This encapsulates the perspective of interaction as action (why that) which is expressed by means of linguistic forms (in that way) in a developing sequence (right now). In order to understand the relationship between talk, identity and context, we must examine the reflexive relationship between them. In line 1 J asks 'So who'r the boyfriends for the week.' We should examine how the precise linguistic forms used talk identities and context into being. Of course J could have asked 'Do you have a serious boyfriend?' What J actually says, however, proposes a particular identity to M, namely that she is likely to have multiple boyfriends (plural) and that they are not likely to last long (for the week). It also talks into being an identity for J as being someone who is interested in whether M has a boyfriend or is available, and therefore also a context, namely of J and M negotiating the possibility of going out together, but in a light-hearted, jocular way. This is an example of CA analysts' interest in linguistic forms; the interest is not in the linguistic forms themselves, but rather in the way in which they are used to embody and express subtle differences in social actions. M's response in lines 3–6 to some extent accepts the proposed identity by saying 'this one'n that one yihknow, I jist, yihknow keep busy en go out when I wanna go out'. M does not actually answer J's question directly in that she does not name her current boyfriends. Her response displays her analysis of the context as being discussion of the possibility of going out together by saying 'it's nothing 'hhh I don'have anybody serious on the string', thus indicating her potential availability.

The identity components of gender and sexuality are relevant to the participants themselves in this extract. This is evident in the topic of the talk and in the social actions performed by the participants. The topic is sexual interest and availability, specifically whether M currently has a boyfriend and whether she is interested in going out with J if he were to ask her. The first move by J aims to determine potential availability of M and can be seen as a pre-invitation (Drew: 2004). M's response indicates that she has no serious boyfriend and is available and potentially not averse to an invitation. J follows up with an enquiry as to whether M would go out with him and M indicates that she would.

However, the point is that from a CA perspective we are only able to bring the constructs of gender and sexuality into the discussion because it is evident in the details of the interaction that the participants are orienting to these constructs. Essentially, there are no features of context or identity which are *always* relevant to a CA analysis. We need to determine which features of identity or context the participants are making relevant in their talk – if it is relevant to them, then it is relevant to us as analysts. It must be stressed that the CA claim is *not* that macro social structures such as culture or cultural frames do not exist except in the interaction. Talk is reflexively related to context, culture and macro social structures, and talk is certainly shaped by culture, context and identity. However, the methodological imperatives detailed by Schegloff (1987: 1992) dictate that we ground the analysis in the first instance in the details of the interaction. What needs to be shown in a CA analysis, however, is which of these innumerable, potentially relevant characteristics are *actually* procedurally relevant to those participants at that moment. The only feasible way to do this from a CA perspective is to start in the details of the interaction, rather than in the external details of context or identity. So from a CA perspective, any utterance is a display of the speaker's analysis of the prior utterance of another speaker, it performs a social action in response and it positions the speaker in a social system. It creates an identity for the speaker, may try to create an identity for the other speaker and creates a relationship between the speakers. It displays an understanding of the current sequential and social context and also renews it. Through their talk, interactants are constantly negotiating identity and context. To do this, they employ a wide range of resources, including choice of lexis, syntax, phonological and prosodic features, the interactional resources of turn-taking, sequence and repair, social action and non-verbal communication. These resources are combined and deployed with sophistication and precision to create intricate positioning in relation to context and identity, as we saw in Extract 4 above.

How do these points relate to language learning research, for example in classrooms? Let us consider two extracts.

Extract 5

1 T: ok ok I think we stop there. unless you have something else you want
2 to say >and you're not leaving yet< because I have a message for you
3 (22.0)
4 T: *eh* Oivind *ta og ti still naa for det en viktig beskjed som eg er noedt til aa gi*
((tr: Oivind keep quiet now because there is an important message I have to give))
(12 lines omitted)
17 T: *eg har diskutert med (name)* (1.0) *kor mye er klokka og tida? Men eg faar*
18 *ta det muntlig allikevel – odet er vanskeligt for oss aa sei at pga at der er tri*
19 *I klassen som- eller fire som er saa opptatt av ((unint* 2.0)) *eh kanskje kan vi*
20 *ikkje legge turen der, heller ta den seinere*
((tr: I have discussed with (name) (1.0) what time is it time? But I will do it verbally anyway – and it is hard for us to say that because there are three in the class that – or maybe four that are so concerned about ((unint 2.0)) eh can't we make the trip then, make it later instead))

(Seedhouse 2004: 201)

In Extract 5 above, T has been speaking L2 English for the whole of the English lesson but then switches back to L1 Norwegian in line 4 in order to give an administrative message. So the background context remains identical with the same participants in the same room. But in a CA analysis we take a major part of context to be created by participants in the details of their talk. By switching from L2 to L1 and by moving from a pedagogical focus to an administrative focus, T talks out of being the identity 'L2 teacher' and the institutional business 'L2 classroom interaction' and talks into being the identity 'teacher as administrator' and the institutional business 'local administration'.

In the extract below, we focus on shifts in learner identity. Markee demonstrates how learners recorded working on a pairwork task can switch instantly from on-task institutional talk to off-task social talk:

Extract 6

1 L9: this writer has a ra[ther- com- pli-] this is [co-] writer has a
2 L11: [I slept five ho-] [huh]
3 L9: complicated uh,
4 L11: yea:h [(h)] ((L11 looks left, lifts his left hand to his mouth
5 and looks down))
6 L9: [h] heh heh .hhh
7 L11: (what'd I say.)
8 (1.0) ((L9 scratches his forehead with his right hand.

9 Simultaneously, L11 drops his hand back to his lap.
10 As L11's hand reaches his lap, he begins his turn at line 11))
11 L11: I'm so tired I slept five hours ((L11 looks at his watch))
12 L11: that night ((L11 drops his hand back to his lap))
13 (0.6)
14 L9: a:::h. ((L9 uses a tone of mock sympathy))

(Markee 2005: 202)

In lines 1 and 3, L9 tries to continue the official on-task topic of discussion (the writer Günter Grass's position in the debate on German reunification). But as L9 harks back to this previous topic, L11 overlaps L9 at line 2 with the announcement that he only slept five hours and introduces off-task social talk. L11 later invites L9 to a party that night where free beer is available. The social chat is in L2 English as the two learners have different L1s. Markee demonstrates how the learners in the extract above carefully disguise their social talk from the teacher and are able to instantly switch back on-task when required. L11 talks the institutional context out of being precisely by moving away from the pedagogical focus in their talk towards a off-task social talk. By so doing, L11 talks the identity 'L2 learner' out of being and talks into being the identity 'party animal'.

As with context and identity, the CA position on culture is that it is relevant to analysis if the participants orient to it in the details of their talk. To talk of a cross-cultural encounter or interculture is only relevant when it is evident that the participants orient to such a construct in the details of their talk. This is Mori's position in the article below: although the participants are Japanese and American, interculturality is not always relevant to their talk. Mori shows how participants sometimes demonstrate the relevance of interculturality in the details of their talk, whilst at other times this is not relevant.

Section B
Extension B1

Creese, A. (2003) 'Language, ethnicity and the mediation of allegations of racism: Negotiating diversity and sameness in multilingual school discourses', *International Journal of Bilingual Education and Bilingualism* 6(3 and 4): 221–236.

Creese (2003) provides an excellent example of how a particular incident can provide a rich resource for understanding institutional practices. The incident in this case is a two-day student protest against a perceived racist incident in a London secondary school, but the focus of the paper is on the positioning of two bilingual English as an Additional Language (EAL) teachers who are at the centre of unfolding events. It shows how the school draws on the ethnicity and language resources of these teachers in order to '(re)produce a discourse of diversity' in order to level out difference, and the focus of the paper is on the ways in which these teachers 'mediate, negotiate and action identification positionings towards and away from the dominant discourse of institutional sameness. It finds that these bilingual teachers both collude with and challenge this discourse' (2003: 221).

At the heart of the paper are two student-produced texts, one accusing the school of racism and the other, written by a different group of students, challenging this interpretation. The analysis in the paper extends beyond these texts to the interactions occurring around them within the school community, but the first of the extracts included here focuses on the texts themselves.

Task B1.1

- Read the following two extracts and compare them, paying particular attention to what identities are made relevant in them. How do the writers position themselves and other relevant groups within the school, and to what extent does this positioning serve to advance the arguments of its producers? You might also wish to speculate on what aspects, if any, of a broader context might be drawn on by the researcher in discussing the two groups of writers involved.

Institutional Racism or Equal Opportunities?

On 12th October, 1994, at 8.45 am I entered Skonnington School as I had done for the previous five weeks to collect data for the ethnographic study I was conducting on the relationships, roles and talk of English as an Additional Language (EAL) teachers and the mainstream subject curriculum teachers with whom they worked. However, this day was immediately different. It started with a demonstration of 20–25 bilingual (Kurdish) Turkish/English-speaking girls from the school [newly arrived political refugees from south-east Turkey] who were outside the school gates with banners and a loud-hailer saying 'Black and White Unite Against Racism' and 'Beep your Horn if you are Against Racism'. The girls were also distributing the following text to passers-by and to teachers who had gone out to speak to them.

Text One (Spelling as in the original)

WE WANT TEACHERS NOT TO DIVIDE US BUT TO GIVE BETTER EDUCATION
On 11 October a group of students started arguing with the other groups of Turkish and Kurdish students.
They all forced them to get into a room and blackmailed, so that they don't tell the teachers about this. There wasn't a good reason for this. But only prejudice. That is not the first time its happened, it continues for years and years in our school. Also we are aware of that the students in schools of Borough X are facing the same problems. And attacks on the students is not the only problem in our school. Briefly the problems we are facing are;

1. When there is a complain about the foods we get, what staff tell is if the food is cleaner in your country then go back to your own country.
2. Some of our teachers e.g. the English teacher Miss X is insulting the students especially refugees.
3. The teachers in Skonnington school and other schools are treating to the students depending on their nationalities. While the other students get rid of everything, some students especially Turkish and Kurdish students are being blame.
4. By this they are trying to divide the students into aparts. We know that all the problems that we are facing can be solved. The teachers and the management of the school do not want to solve the problems deliberately. The students have nothing to attack each other. We only want to study and be educated in better methods. Students should be united against all other problems we are facing in our school. But the school management is avoiding this by dividing the students in spite of their nationalities. We don't want our teachers to divide us, we just want better education. We don't want racism in our schools, we want to unite with all black and white students. That is why we are having the boycout in our school and our demands are as follows.
   1. We don't want any racist teachers in our school, especially, Mrs X.
   2. We don't want teachers and managements to divide students by their nationalities.
   3. we want them to consider all the complaints that we have e.g. foods, bullying.
   4. Our only demand is to have friendly and egual education for all students

Later in the day, this was followed by a second text, written by a different group of girls, African Caribbean, who were contesting the writers of Text One's account. This text was distributed to students and teachers within the school community and also to the local BBC network, who had arrived at lunchtime.

Text Two (Spelling, bold [*sic*] and capitalisation as in the original)

STOP FOOLING AROUND
Due to recent letters that have been received by the students outside of Skonnington that are against your silly boycott we feel that you are making a mockery out of yourselves.
Nothing will be resolved if you carry on acting like immature little 5 year olds. This is only to make you see what fools you are. Some of us think that you are right to appeal against your rights but not in this manner. By holding up banners and posters saying that 'black and white unite' has no meaning because most of the people or students like each other and have no means for racism so we all think by what you are doing is wrong. You are making our school reputation go down and you are hurting alot of peoples feelings by what you are doing although you might have already noticed. Maybe what you are doing is right but you have no feelings and consideration of what other people think of you. Many turkish and kurdish people are not protesting because they feel that nothing will not be resolved and that they also think it is wrong.
We gather that some people are racist but a fact is that everybody in a way is racist and that includes all of the kurdish and turkish people. Fair enough we admit some of the students can be rascist but that does not allow you to bring any of the teachers into it and by doing that you have made things worse.
STUDENTS THAT CARE!!!

The most obvious differences between the two texts, as Creese notes, is in the way they construct teachers and the way they represent the student community. While the first text constructs students as innocent victims whose only desire is for a decent education and calls for student unity in the face of a racist an divisive staff (presumably dinner staff as well as teachers), the second challenges this as an immature and misrepresentative representation which is damaging to the school's reputation and hurtful to people's feelings. While in the first text staff are singled out as a source of division, here they are included in a wider category of 'people', including students, who may or may not be racist (there is also a suggestion that there is an element of racism in everybody).

Creese offers the following summaries (p. 227):

> Text One constructs the teachers as being racist and divisive. Teachers
>
> - insult refugees;
> - treat students differently depending on their national backgrounds;
> - single out Turkish and Kurdish pupils for blame;
> - divide students against one another;
> - let problems go unsolved and do not follow up complaints.
>
> On the other hand Text Two constructs the teachers as victims. They
>
> - have been hurt;
> - are having their reputation damaged;
> - are the same as anyone else.
>
> In Text One the writers present themselves as united with the rest of the student community. Students
>
> - should not attack one another;
> - are united in their need for better and fairer education.
>
> In Text Two, however, the writers present the student writers of Text One as different from the rest of the student community. They are
>
> - silly, immature, like 5 year olds, fools, wrong, hurtful;
> - not supported by other Turkish and Kurdish-speaking students;
> - have no feelings and show no consideration.

In her analysis of Text One, Creese draws attention to claims of ethnic difference and how different groups of students receive different treatment. She describes the text as a 'political manifesto' and highlights in particular the insistence on equal treatment for all nationalities, noting that as newly-arrived political refugees they may have had first-hand experience of fighting for their political and human rights. Creese also suggests that this meets a 'common educational discourse of equal opportunities' which they do not yet 'own'. She will go on to argue that the discourses they do own are 'rendered too difficult for the school to consider' (p. 227).

Since the girls themselves have made the issue of ethnicity relevant, this is analytically unproblematic in itself, but its deployment is a different matter. As Creese goes on to argue, what is at issue between the two groups is the positioning of the writers of the first letter. In that letter they identify themselves with a particular ethnic group that is the victim of discrimination, but the writers of the second letter challenge this positioning. Creese claims that they 'do own the equal opportunities discourse' and are able to deploy the notion of a school community to which a majority of teachers and students belong in order to exclude the writers of the first letter: 'The writers of Text Two are attempting to isolate these students not only from their ethnic group who they aspire to represent but also from the rest of the school community' (p. 228). In their letter, ethnicity is played down as are any differences within the school and the charge of racism is associated with a 'dissonant' group of students who represent neither the school nor the Turkish/Kurdish group within it.

Extension B2

The article below investigates how Japanese and American students initiate topical talk (in Japanese) as they get acquainted with each other during their initial encounter at a student-organized conversation table.

Task B2.1

- In which particular aspects of verbal and non-verbal behaviour would you expect cultural differences to emerge, in this specific setting?

- Now read the extracts from the article below.

Mori, J. (2003) 'Construction of interculturality: A study of initial encounters between Japanese and American students', *Research on Language and Social Interaction* 36(2): 143–184.

Whereas previous studies of intercultural communications tend to take interculturality for granted, this study investigates the observable and reportable ways in which the participants demonstrate the relevance, or the irrelevance, of interculturality in the development of the interaction. The participants in the data presented in this article recurrently produce a common set of questions that reflect on their categorizations of the coparticipants. This study closely examines vocal and nonvocal conduct associated with the delivery of these questions, the selection of respondents to these questions, and the treatment of problems emerging in the development of these question–answer sequences. In doing so, it explicates how the participants utilize their cultural differences as a resource for organizing their participation and, at the same time, recreates the salience of the interculturality of the interaction.

This article examines multiparty interactions among Japanese and American college students who met for the first time at a student-organized weekly conversation table. The examination uncovers how these students launch topical talk in their initial encounters and organize their participation through the nomination and development of common topics. Further, this article discusses how these conversational procedures often, but not always, exhibit the participants' orientation to the 'interculturality' of these interactions, and at the same time, how this interculturality is used as a resource for organizing the interaction.

When more than two participants are involved in a conversation, the distribution of opportunities to talk naturally goes beyond a pattern of simple alternation. The examination of techniques employed for next-speaker selection (Sacks, Schegloff, Jeffersons 1974) allows us to grasp the participants' orientation toward particular contextual and identity-related matters, including, but not limited to, interculturality. Second, whereas the previous studies primarily examine talk, this study accounts for not only vocal but also nonvocal conduct in detail. To examine the shifts of participation structures in face-to-face multiparty interactions, it is critical to pay attention to the participants' nonvocal conduct along with their talk. Third, the setting of the interactions examined in this study is quite different from a laboratory setting or a radio talk show. The interactions took place at a casual conversation table organized by students to practice their target language. There were no established guidelines for language use, topic of conversation, or formation of groups for interaction. The possible influence of this particular setting upon the development of talk, or conversely, the participants' orientation to the nature of the setting, will be also discussed as I examine the data.

The primary focus of this article is to describe how the construction of interculturality can be studied by examining the moment-by-moment shifts of participation structures in these question–answer sequences or the procedures for the next-speaker selection. However, as my analysis of the final excerpt illustrates, question–answer sequences, while demonstrating and reproducing interculturality, may also conversely lead to moments when interculturality, or the participants' cultural affiliations, are treated as irrelevant. In summary, the analytical challenge of searching for evidence to warrant the relevance of interculturality in interactions assumed to be intercultural renews our understanding of the sequential development of talk-in-interaction and the structure of participation. At the same time, the analysis of sequential development and participation structure enables us to explicate how the participants show that their cultural differences are salient for how they conduct themselves.

Categorization, discourse identities, and social identities

Before the examination of excerpts from the current data, several notions that will become critical to the current analysis should be clarified.

The first concept is the notion of categorization. Its application in and relevance to the development of talk-in-interaction was initially addressed by Sacks in the late 1960s (cf. Sacks, 1992), and was extensively discussed by scholars working within the theoretical framework of conversation analysis (CA). According to Sacks, a person can be correctly described as being a member of different categories. However, these categories are not equally relevant at a given point in time. From the set of applicable categories, a particular category may be selected as relevant by an individual or by his or her coparticipants in the course of a developing interaction. Thus, categorization, in this tradition, refers to the social processes through which the participants themselves make a certain social category visibly relevant in their talk; this view of categorization contrasts with the processes through which analysts invent or select categories a priori and apply them to the data.

Categorization may be accomplished by an explicit, direct reference to a particular category in talk, or by an inference drawn from a reference to a social relationship or activity bound to a particular category. The issue of categorization in the process of developing topical talk will be revisited in the next section when I examine the data.

Discourse identities (cf. Zimmerman, 1998) is another important notion that will be discussed in this study. Unlike common understandings of the term 'identity' in some other traditions, the term here does not mean an individual's internal, psychological sense of who he or she is. Rather, discourse identities refer to the classifications of the participants' immediate status in ongoing talk-in-interaction, which are ascribed through the sequential development of talk stand in relation to the others present at the site of interaction. For a simple example, when one delivers a question in a two-party conversation, the other participant is projected to be the respondent of the question. When one initiates a story, then the other is cast as the recipient of the story. Discourse identities refer to such relative participation statuses as questioner–respondent or teller–recipient, and these identities constantly shift as the participants take conversational turns to develop talk-in-interaction. In actual talk, a particular discourse identity cast by the current speaker's turn may not always be accepted by the next speaker. For instance, a participant cast as a respondent of a question at one moment of interaction may reject that discourse identity in the next moment by not answering the question, but by initiating a repair instead.

Further complexities in the ascription of discourse identities may be observed in multiparty conversation, where there is more than one recipient of the current speaker's talk. Goodwin (1987), for instance, explicates the current speaker's differentiated treatments of these multiple recipients that are exhibited through vocal and nonvocal conduct. Some recipients may be treated as 'knowing recipients' who are assumed to share the knowledge of the event being described in the current talk, whereas others may be treated as 'unknowing recipients,' who are assumed not to have any prior knowledge of the event. While the current speaker's talk is primarily addressed to unknowing recipients, any knowing recipient may join in the development of the current talk as a coteller. Or, they may participate in a word search whose necessity has been demonstrated in the midst of the current speaker's talk. More recently, Lerner (2003) discusses speaker selection techniques in multiparty interaction, building on the seminal work on the systematics of turn-taking by Sacks et al. (1974). In addition to techniques of explicit addressing such as the use of an address term or gaze direction, Lerner explains that the participant also counts on the 'thick particulars' available *in situ* at each interactional moment to determine which coparticipant is qualified to respond to the current speaker's sequence-initiating turn.

Discourse identities are closely linked to the sequential development of talk and to the social actions in progress, but they also reflect 'social identities' that go beyond the particular moment of talk. Social identities here refer to a social relationship between the participants such as a married couple or intimate friends, or a membership in a particular social category such as being a woman or being Japanese.

Task B2.2

➤ Next time you are involved in a multi-party conversation, note how the three aspects of identity introduced above were applied during the course of the conversation. Categorization: how were people assigned to categories during the conversation? Was it according to gender, profession, height, weight, hair colour, or something else? Discourse identity: which kinds of discourse identity did participants assume and did anyone reject any specific identity? Social identity: which social identities are referenced in the talk and does anyone reject identities imposed on them by others?

As stated in the introduction, this article is concerned with how the participants in the current data make visible the relevance or irrelevance of social identities such as being Japanese or American. Thus, this article examines the processes of categorization and the attribution and reattribution of discourse identities observed in the data, and discusses how these processes either do or do not reflect the social identities defined by the participants' affiliations with different cultures.

Namely, questions that indicate the participants' assumption of the others' status as students are recurrently observed, and their access to the setting, that is, a student-organized conversation table held at a coffee shop in a university town, reasonably warrants such an assumption. Thus, they recurrently ask questions concerning year in school, academic major, residence, and so on, or questions concerning activities bound to the categorizations. What is noticeable in this current data, however, is a subset of recurrently observed category-activity questions that seems to further specify the assumed categories of the participants. The subset includes questions concerning their visits to each other's country and their experiences with, or opinions toward, language, food, movies, or celebrities from each other's country, as exemplified in the following excerpts. Actual utterances appear in italics, and Japanese utterances are followed by word-by-word glosses . . . and the approximate English translation in the subsequent lines in boldface.

Excerpt 1: [Kanji]

Chris: *ja itsu::: (.) aa::: itsu amerika e:*
then when uhm when America to
°(*kimashita ka*)°?
came Q
'Then when:: (.) uhm when did you come to America?'
Hana: *etto::: (.) hachigatsu futsuka.*
uhm August second

'uh::m (.) August second.'

Chris: *(hatsuka) futsuka:*
twentieth second
'(Twentieth) second.'

Hana: *futsuka.*
second
'Second'

Chris: *ah huh hajimete?*
first-time
'ah huh first time?'

Hana: *etto nikaime de:::,*
uhm second-time and
'uhm second time an::d,'

Chris: *aa:::::[°(un)°*
oh uh-huh
'Oh:::uh huh'

Excerpt 2: [Tattoo]

Ken: *nihon no eega:: wa:: (0.4) su- shittemasu?*
Japan LK movie Top know
'Japanese movies (0.4) Do you know any of them?'
(0.3)

Ann: *un?*
'Un?'

Ken: *nihon no eega:: (0.5) nanika (0.5) shitttemasu?*
Japan LK movie something know
'Do you know some Japanese movies?'
(3.0)

Ann: *hai, aa::::: (2.5) shall we da:nce?*
yes uhm
'Yes, uh::::m (2.5) 'Shall We Da:nce?'

Ken: *a[a::: aa*
Oh oh
'Oh:::: oh'

These questions refer to activities that are associated with students of foreign languages and cultures. In other words, the questioners, by asking these questions, categorize the respondents not as natives but as novices to the language and culture. Categorization questions that would determine the nationality or culture of the interlocutors such as 'Are you Japanese?' or 'Are you from America?' are never asked. Rather, by selecting these sorts of category-activity questions, the participants indicate their assumption of the coparticipant's status as non-natives of the particular cultures. Such an assumption is understandable, considering that they participate in this event knowing that its purpose is to practice the target language, and that their appearance and proficiency in the language evidently indicate their native or non-native cultures.

However, the fact that the interaction is situated at a conversation table for practicing the languages they are studying does not automatically require the participants to talk about their learning of, or experience with, the language and culture. Indeed, there are occasions when the participants select different topics such as the weather, the coffee shop or the city where this meeting took place, or the recording equipment set up around them. At those moments when they are engaged in setting talk or talk about other categories or category-bound activities concerning their student status (year in school, local residence, course work, part-time job, etc.), then the participants are not treating interculturality as particularly relevant. In contrast, the nominations of topics concerning things Japanese or things American, and the allocations of turns that are evoked by these topics, make visible the participants' orientation to the interculturality of the interaction. These questions appear to be treated as part of the ritual of getting to know unacquainted coparticipants who are assumed to not belong to the same culture. By asking questions concerning each other's experience with, knowledge of, or perspective toward their own languages and cultures, the participants attempt to discover shared experience, or knowledge, across cultural boundaries, which may prompt them to effectively extend topical talk. In other words, the participants seem to treat language, food, travel, or popular culture as possible ingredients of the same society where they live as contemporaries, which may offer them an opportunity to develop a more intimate relationship through talk. This tendency seems particularly apparent in the interactions involving Japanese students who were participating in a short-term English as a Second Language (ESL) Program that lasted only three to four weeks. Compared to other Japanese students who are degree candidates at the university where these recordings were made, these short-term visitors have less shared knowledge or experience with their American coparticipants.

In the following sections, we will examine more closely how these question–answer sequences unfold in a multiparty conversation involving three Japanese students who were studying ESL for the three- to four-week session at the university and two American students.

Participation structures invoked by questions concerning cultural items

The previous section examined a subset of category-activity questions recurrently observed in the interaction at the conversation table that imply the questioners' assumption of their coparticipant's status as learners of a foreign language and culture. This section will consider how the delivery of these questions triggers a certain participation structure in multiparty interaction, that is, how the participants other than the questioner demonstrate their recognition of being selected, or not selected, as a possible respondent.

The interaction below involves two American students, Alan and David, and three Japanese students, Koji, Toru, and Yoshi. Alan and David have known each other through Japanese language courses, and Koji, Toru, and Yoshi have known each other through participating in the short-term ESL program at the same university. These Japanese and American students have just met for the first time and started a conversation. Such relationships among the participants and their cultural affiliations become visible through the ways in which they develop their talk-in-interaction. Let us first observe Excerpt 3, which starts with Toru's question, *ja nihon no eega wa::: mita koto arimasu ka*? (Have you seen any Japanese movies? or, more literally, Is there an experience of watching a Japanese movie?). This question, as well as the majority of questions produced in Japanese conversation (see other excerpts introduced in this article), does not include an address term nor a 'recipient proterm' comparable to the English *you*. In the absence of an explicit reference of a selected respondent, how do the participants of this multiparty interaction accomplish the allocation of next speaker?

The employment of nonvocal devices such as gaze direction can be considered a crucial resource. However, as pointed out by Lerner (2003), the employment of gaze direction as an addressing device may not be effective if the recipients are not attending to the current speaker's gaze. Further, Lerner (2003) points out that gaze direction may be redundant in some cases, in that tacit addressing shaped by the specifics of situatedness, identities, and particularities of content and context simultaneously operates for speaker selection. This seems precisely what is happening in the talk below. Toru's gaze in line 1 is directed toward the American students, although it is difficult to judge from the videotape exactly which one of them Toru is gazing at (see Figure 1). Upon completion of Toru's question, a short silence emerges in line 3, which may be due to the fact that there is no explicit addressing device used in Toru's question. After the short silence, however, the American students, David and Alan, in succession, display their recognition of being selected as a possible respondent. David does so by initiating a repair, *nan*? (what?) in line 4, while Alan does so by producing the vocalization *ee::::* (uhm) in line 5, which projects the onset of his talk.

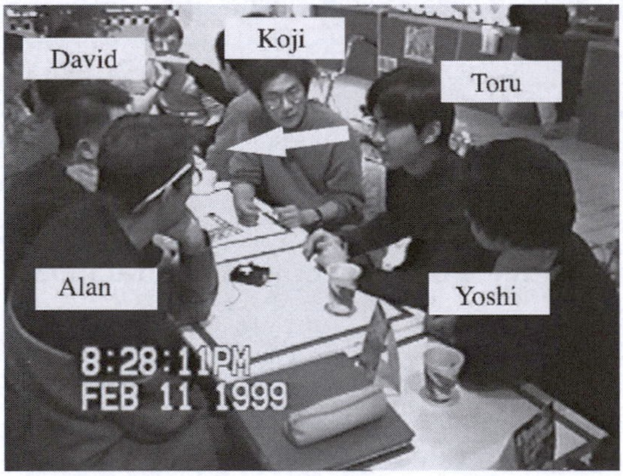

Figure 1

Excerpt 3: [Major League 8:28:10]

1	*Toru*:	ja [nihon no eega wa:: mita koto arimasu ka?
		then Japan LK movie Top saw experience exist Q
		'Then have you seen any Japanese movies?'
2	*Koji*:	[( )
3		(.)
4	*David*:	nan?
		what
		'What?'
5	*Alan*:	[ee::::
		uhm

'uh::m'

6 *Toru*: [nihon no eega wa mita koto [arimasu ka.
Japan LK movie Top saw experience exist **Q**
'Have you seen any Japanese movies?'
7 *David*: [ha::::::::
'ye::::::::'
8 a [HAI!
oh yes
'Oh Yes.'
9 *Alan*: [chotto °(arimasu.)°
a-little exist
'A little bit.'
10 (0.8)
11 *David*: [ee::::
uhm
'uh::m'
12 *Alan*: [ano:::: hotaru no haka: (.) mita [koto ga °(arimasu)°
uhm (movie-title) saw experience S exist
'Uh::m I've seen 'Hotaru no Haka'

In overlap with Alan's preanswering vocalization, Toru reacts to David's repair initiator and repeats the question in line 6. This time, David demonstrates his understanding of the question and answers the question with the affirmative token HAI! (yes) (lines 7 and 8). Alan also continues his answer in overlap with David (line 9). Receiving no uptake to their minimal answers (line 10), both David and Alan attempt to continue elaborating on their answer (lines 11 and 12). While only Alan continues his turn here and names the Japanese movie he has seen before, a few lines later (not included in the excerpt), after Alan has completed talking about the animated film he has seen and the Japanese recipients responded to the answer, David also refers to a Japanese movie he has seen.

Several observations can be made in regard to the accomplishment of speaker selection in this case. Toru does not explicitly refer to any particular coparticipant as the designated respondent of the question, although his gaze direction appears to select the American students as the possible respondents. In addition to the gaze direction, Toru's use of the so-called addressee honorific form of the verb *arimasu*, as opposed to its nonhonorific or plain form *aru*, indicates that the talk is addressed to the coparticipants who are not close friends of his. As will be seen in later excerpts, Toru uses nonhonorific forms when he is talking to his fellow Japanese interlocutors. Further, the participants' assumption of the specifics of their social identities also seems to play an important role in determining possible respondents. That is, the topic raised in this question, namely the experience of seeing a Japanese movie, seems to serve as a resource to identify the possible respondents. Namely, the participants seem to acknowledge implicitly that it would only be appropriate for the non-Japanese participants to voice whether they have seen a Japanese movie, not to mention that it would be taken for granted that the Japanese participants would have had such experiences. Thus, although the question does not directly categorize the participants in such a way as addressing them 'you, Americans' would, the specification of the country in the question about movies evokes the division between Japanese and non-Japanese.

Treating interculturality as irrelevant

The focus of the previous sections has been to demonstrate how interculturality is played out in interactions through the ways in which the participants nominate a particular set of topics, and the ways in which they organize their participation thereafter. However, discourse-specific identities created through the moment-by-moment development of this interaction are not always explicitly articulated with the social identities of Japanese or American. Thus, while the participants' membership in one culture or the other is often made relevant in this current data that has been examined so far, there are occasions when such a division based on cultural affiliation is treated as irrelevant. This section examines one of those incidents and discusses its implications for the overall sequential development observed in this current data.

This excerpt starts with Toru's question as to whether or not his coparticipants know a Japanese comedian called Ishibashi Takaaki who appears in an American movie, *Major League*. The identification of this actor becomes a problem that the participants need to work through, and the process, unlike the cases examined in the previous section, does not demonstrate a clear division of the teams based on the participants' cultural affiliation.

Excerpt 7: [Major League 8:27:22]

1	*Toru*:	nihon no::: (0.3) komedian no::: (0.5)
		Japan LK comedian LK
		'Japane::se (0.3) comedia:::n (0.5)'
2		ishibashi::: (.) takaaki.=
		family-name first-name
		'Ishibashi:::: (.) Takaaki.='
3		=Do you know Ishibashi Takaaki?
		'Do you know Ishibashi Takashi?'
4		(0.7)
5	*David*:	iie.
		no
		'No.'
6	*Toru*:	so:::
		'so:::'
7		(1.7)
8	*Toru*:	°un° Ishibashi Takaaki ga:::, (0.2) meijaa riigu ni
		family-name first-name S major league in
9		wa:::, deteimasu.
		Top appear
		'°un° Ishibashi Takaaki i::s (0.2) in Major Lea::gue, he appears.'
10		(0.2)
11	*David*:	°(moo ichido)°
		more once
		'°(once again) °'
12	*Toru*:	so: Japanese samurai UWAH::A!
		'so: Japanese samurai UWAH::A!'

13 *David*: aa:: aa:: [hai hai
oh oh yes yes
'oh:: oh:: yes yes.'
14 *Alan*: [aa::::::::
"oh::::::::"
15 (2.2)
16 *Alan*: aa:::n (.) is that [ma- major league
'aa:::n (.) **is that ma- major league'**
17 *Koji*: [wakarimasu ka?
understand Q
'Do you understand?'
18 *David*: hai. wakatta.
yes understood
'Yes. I understood.'
19 ?: °( )?°
'°( )?°'
20 *David*: ha?
'ha?'
21 (0.6)
22 *Alan*: major league what?
'major league what?'
23 (0.7)
24 *David*: un? ee:::
'uh?Uh::m'
25 *Koji*: [AA::::::::
'oh::::::::'
26 *Yoshi*: [°mejaa riigu° [tsu:: =
major league two
'°major league° two::'
27 *David*: [major league
'major league'
28 *Koji*: =two=
'two'
29 *Toru*: =[two::?=
'two::?'
30 *David*: [°two two°
'°two two°'
31 *Koji*: =three=
'three'
32 *Toru*: =two [ando three.
'two and three'
33 *Alan*: [GOT no:: ma:::rble. z that guy?
'GOT no::: ma:::rble. z that guy?'
34 *David*: i::i::e:
no
'no::::'
35 *Alan*: (wh [en)
'(when)'
36 *David*: [nihonjin.
Japanese

'Japanese'
37 (1.9)
38 *David*: >This is a< Japane:se in the movie.=
'This is a Japanese in the movie'
39 *Alan*: YEAH. He's the one that- (0.6)
'YEAH. He's the one that- (0.6)'
40 *Alan*: so [:: nihonjin:::.
so Japanese
'so:: Japane::se.'
41 *David*: [aa:: aa:: aa:: aa::
'oh:: oh:: oh:: oh::'
42 *Toru*: A!
'oh!'
43 *Alan*: nihonjin wa::, got no marble to:: °itteimashita.°
Japanese Top QT was-saying
'The Japanese was saying, "got no marbles"'

Once again, Toru's question in lines 1 through 3 does not include an address term. However, the use of English in line 3 and the fact that the question concerns a well-known Japanese comedian select David and Alan as respondents of this question. In response to the question, Alan produces horizontal head movements when David says *iie* (no) in line 5. As David and Alan indicate that they do not recognize the name of the comedian, Toru extends the description of this comedian by referring to an American movie in which this comedian appeared (line 8) and by mimicking an action that the comedian's character made in the movie (line 12). In fact, this segment occurs after the exchange of Alan's question regarding his coparticipant's favorite movie and Toru's answer, *Major League*. Thus, Toru's extension refers to the connection between this question and his previous answer. In lines 13 and 14, then, both David and Alan allude to their recognition of this comedian by producing the news-receipt token *aa*:::. After a pause, Alan attempts to confirm his understanding of the character by asking which *Major League* movie this comedian appeared in (lines 16 and 22).

Alan's confirmation question in English is not addressed to the Japanese participants but to David, who has just produced a stronger display of recognition *aa*::: *aa*:::: *hai hai* (line 13). Since Alan's initiation of the confirming question (line 16) is overlapped by Koji's confirmation of David's understanding (line 17), David responds first to Koji and again claims that he has identified this comedian (line 18). David then turns to Alan to initiate a repair (line 20), and Alan recompletes his confirmation question in English (line 22). At this point, the code-switching and the mutual gaze between Alan and David establish the appearance of in-group talk (Figure 6). The practice here is similar to the previous case concerning the identification of oatmeal in that an uncertain respondent turns to a certain respondent for clarification of the uncertainty.

Figure 6 Line 22 *major league what?*

However, the subsequent development of talk differs significantly from what we observed in the previous case. That is, while David does not immediately offer an answer to Alan's question (line 24), Koji, Yoshi, and Toru all respond to Alan's question, and each offers an answer both verbally and nonverbally (i.e., indicating the numbers by their fingers) in lines 25 though 32. Although Koji, Yoshi, and Toru delay their response and allow David, Alan's teammate, to respond to the question first. After recognizing the lack of immediate uptake they treat Alan's question as something they are warranted to answer, rather than something only David is obligated to answer. Though it was produced in English, Alan's question is accessible to all the participants and does not require an elaborate answer. The participation of Koji, Toru, and Yoshi in the clarification of uncertainty breaks the division initially proposed by Alan's question, which was initially directed to David. In the meantime, David, who has just claimed his understanding, has put himself in a position to demonstrate his understanding. As the Japanese participants start responding to Alan's question before him, David quickly joins into the answering turns and continues to situate his participation as that of a knowing participant (lines 27 and 30). This series of turns subsequently divides those who know or claim to have achieved the recognition of the actor and Alan, who is still not completely sure about the referent.

In his subsequent request for confirmation in line 33, Alan treats his interlocutors as two different types of recipients of his talk. While Alan recites a line of this character in the movie *Major League* mimicking this comedian in line 33, he faces Koji, Toru, and Yoshi. But, as Alan adds the English phrase *that guy*? at the end of the turn, he shifts his gaze to David, selecting David as a primary respondent (Figure 7A). However, in Japanese, David rejects Alan's identification of this character (lines 34 and 36) and thereby continues to assert his status as one who has already recognized the referent. After a rather long silence, David switches to English and re-responds to Alan's question (line 38). Then, Alan claims his understanding that the person being discussed is a Japanese character in the movie, and he again attempts to confirm his recognition in English. Nevertheless, he cuts off this English utterance in the middle and restarts in Japanese to restate his description of this character in an attempt to confirm his recognition. Alan's Japanese utterances in lines 40 and 43 are addressed to the Japanese participants (Figure 7B). This time, by clarifying that he is referring to the Japanese character's line in the movie, Alan successfully gains both David's and the Japanese students' recognition of his correct identification.

Figure 7A Line 33 *that guy?*

Figure 7B Line 43 *nihonjin wa::*

The examination of this last excerpt raises several points for consideration with regard to the formation of a team or the lack thereof based on cultural affiliation:

1. As we observed in the oatmeal example, this last excerpt also demonstrates how the mere fact that individuals know the item in question may be treated as irrelevant to the decision concerning from whom one may request assistance when trying to identify a cultural item. As demonstrated by Alan's behavior in this example, one's assumption as to who may be able to better understand the speaker, and who may be able to better design the requested response in a prompt manner appear to be crucial factors for the decision.
2. The formation of a team initiated by a participant's request for coparticipation in the clarification of uncertainty can be accomplished only when his or her coparticipants comply with their projected status. Those deemed as members of the same team are expected to respond to the call by demonstrating their alignment through gaze shift, use of a particular code, and prompt supply of the requested assistance. Further, those who are not deemed as members of the same party also demonstrate recognition of their position by refraining from participating in the process of clarifying the uncertainty. As shown in this last excerpt, once those who are not the addressed recipients of a call for assistance respond to the call, the appearance of a team is not fully achieved.
3. By rejecting the formation of a team through responding to a request for assistance originally addressed to a member of the same groups defined by the cultural affiliation, the participants can demonstrate that they treat the interculturality and the cultural affiliation irrelevant at the moment of interaction.

The nomination of a topic concerning the other participants' culture may trigger a participation structure which divides the participants into a questioner's side and a respondent's side; in other words, those who treat the cultural item as 'their own' and those who treat it as 'the others' property.' Further, the division of discourse identities of questioner versus respondent, as well as the assumption of the shared experiences and resources, may prompt the participants to form an alignment as a team in dealing with an uncertainty that has emerged in the question–answer sequences. However, once the cultural item introduced by those who 'own' it gets recognized by those who do not, the discovery of the experience and knowledge shared across the cultural boundary could serve to facilitate topical talk that deconstructs the formation of teams based on their cultural affiliation. This is what seems to have begun to happen in the last excerpt examined. The talk concerning a Japanese comedian who has appeared in an American movie offers the context in which all participants can engage in the talk as movie viewers. Similar shifts in the relevance of social identities – from those based on interculturality to those based on the shared activities and knowledge beyond the cultural boundary – are observed recurrently throughout the data.

Conclusion

This article examined the dynamics of multiparty conversations among Japanese and American students who met for the first time. Through this examination, this paper underscored the importance of demonstrating the relevance of social and cultural distinctions to actual interactions. To argue this point, the following procedures were closely observed:

1. A common set of categorization or category activity-questions produced in the data were examined. While the similar processes of initiating categorization questions or category activity questions to develop further talk were observed, the fact that the participants are from different cultural backgrounds is indeed reflected in their selection of a particular subset of category-activity questions.
2. The techniques and procedures employed for the selection of possible respondents for those category activity questions were investigated with reference to studies by Lerner (2003). In particular, the style or the code chosen for the delivery of the questions and the specification of a class of cultural items indicated in the questions serve as resources to select qualified respondents.
3. The ways in which the participants deal with uncertainties emerging in the question–answer sequences were described in detail with reference to the studies of word searches by Goodwin (1987). The ways in which the participants make an invitation to coparticipate in the clarification of uncertainty, and the ways in which they respond to such an invitation demonstrate their orientation to a particular feature of their social identities, or lack thereof, at particular moments of the interaction. In particular, the assumption of the language and experiences shared as a comember of a particular cultural community often plays a significant role in intercultural interactions such as those examined in this study. These processes create the appearance of a collective team.
4. A case in which the formation of a team described in number three of this list was not successfully accomplished was reported. As the participants develop their talk about cultural items, their discovery of shared experience across the cultural

boundary may create a moment when such a division based on the membership of cultural communities is treated as irrelevant.

The procedures summarized above provide the resources both for the participants to instantiate the relevance or the irrelevance of interculturality and other social matters, and for researchers to identify and demonstrate them.

It should be pointed out that this current data were recorded at a conversation table organized by and for students who are learning second or foreign languages. That is, although this may not be considered an 'official' site of learning and is considered closer to a 'real-life' interaction compared to classroom discourse, the makeup of the event assigned the participants 'situated identities' (Zimmerman 1998) as learners of each other's language. Furthermore, the participants often demonstrated their orientation to such characteristics of the event. In contrast, once these learners leave campus and attempt to blend into a community other than their own, different types of settings for initial encounters would be presumed to generate different types of assumptions toward the participants' identities, including those other than being native or non-native. Day (1998), for instance, documented the ways in which the ascription and resistance of an ethnic identity is achieved at multicultural workplaces in Europe. The relevance of interculturality or cultural identities made visible at these workplaces where interculturality is not necessarily foregrounded by the situational arrangements would have quite different implications for the organization of talk and the formation of the participants' relationships than what we observed at this conversation table. Thus, varying kinds of intercultural interaction should not be lumped together as intercultural just because they involve people with various backgrounds. Instead, its relevance or irrelevance should be discovered through the careful explication of the conversational procedures employed by the participants.

Task B.2.3

- Mori uses video still photographs in the article. What is gained by using these photos? Would the article have been less successful in making its points if the photos had not been used?

Task B.2.4

- Identify the ways in which the participants present interculturality as relevant or irrelevant through their behaviour (verbal and non-verbal).

Task B.2.5

- Now compare your answer to task B.2.4 to your answer to task B.2.1. Were the ways in which participants made interculturality relevant through their behaviour as you expected, or not?

Extension B3: Comparing the two studies

Task B3.1

➤ Ethnicity, cultural and linguistic identity are considered here as examples of a feature of identity or membership category. The two studies demonstrate different approaches to analysis of these membership categories. Compare how the construct of identity is approached in these two different qualitative methodologies.

Task B.3.2

➤ Read these two texts and compare and contrast them as cross-cultural encounters. Compare and contrast the relationship between language and culture and analyze how the concept of community is handled?

Task B.3.3

➤ Compare the type of data that both writers use. What do the two writers use as evidence to construct their arguments? Look at how claims are made by the researchers (e.g. Creese invokes membership of particular groups as an explanatory resource). This has important implications for interpretive positioning in the representation of research. What resources do researchers draw on in developing their analyses?

Task B.3.4

➤ Both CA and ethnography claim to represent the 'emic' or participants' perspective. Compare how this perspective is developed by the two authors.

Task B.3.5

➤ Study the field notes under 'Year 10 Geography' below from the perspective of how the main protagonists (Ayse and Jasmine, and Mr Hakan) are represented. How does the researcher use group membership in (a) her representation and (b) her analysis of the actions of these individuals. In examining this, consider the researcher's claims in terms of the nature of the evidence available to support them and the extent to which personal judgement features in them.

Year 10, Geography

During the first morning of the demonstration I attended, as usual, the Year 10 geography class. This class was in the unusual position of being supported by both the bilingual teacher, Mr Hakan, and another EAL teacher, Mr Noble, during different timetable periods. This was because of the high number of EAL/bilingual students in the class needing support. Some of the girls from this class were taking part in the demonstration. Below are my written-up fieldnotes from that morning.

Geography, year 10,12.10.1994–9.40 am

I go to the geography class but there are no teachers there and very few students. Mr Hakan is contacting parents of the demonstrating girls while the geography teacher, Mr Scott, has gone outside to talk to the girls and is trying to persuade them to come back in. I listen to one student speaking Turkish with Ayse, a newly arrived and early bilingual Cypriot Turkish speaking girl. This is the first time I have heard Ayse's interactant – Jasmine, speak Turkish. She is not known to the EAL staff as she is fully proficient in English and does not need their learning and language support. She usually sits at the front of the class away from the other EAL students. She and Ayse are talking about the demonstrators. In Turkish they ask each other if the girls outside had told them about the demonstration. It appears they were not told anything. They both say 'it has nothing to do with them' and 'they don't want anything to do with it'. The class is very much changed. The few students in there are not doing any work and there is a lot of discussion about what is going on outside. At 9.40 two of the girls who have been demonstrating outside return to class along with the two teachers, Mr Scott and Mr Hakan. The teachers get the class started on their work. Mr Hakan tries to settle the two returnees and help them with their work. However, they are angry with him and do not want his help. They respond much more warmly to me. He is seen as the enemy. However, they are slow to work and spend a lot of time arguing with the Ayse and Jasmin mentioned above. Their exchanges are angry. After class, I hear that the police were called in to frighten the demonstrators but he turned up on his bike and this didn't have the intended effect!

I wish to make three points from this vignette. The first is that the event itself brought out a speaker of Turkish in this class not known to the school. Moreover, it allowed this bilingual speaker of Turkish and English to use her Turkish in ways beyond the usual 'language support' for curriculum learning and all the deficit associations that often and unfairly go with this function. The second point to be made is that it appears that the Cypriot Turkish speaking girls were not involved in the organisation or implementation of the demonstration, which appeared to be under the ownership of one particular group of Turkish speaking Kurdish girls.

The third point to be made is that using Turkish with the Turkish speaking bilingual teacher for learning purposes in this class was rejected by the two girls who had returned to class from the demonstration. There are a number of possible reasons for this. Mr Hakan was clearly engaged in doing the work of the school in phoning their parents and therefore was acting against the demonstrators' objectives. Moreover, like the Cypriot girls they were arguing with, Mr Hakan was from the same background and did not have the same inheritance of Turkish that these girls had. This may have been particularly relevant as throughout the class Turkish was being used by different Turkish heritages to both endorse or reject the primary message put out by the girls demonstrating.

(Creese 2003: 229–230)

Notice how the researcher draws on contextual information to evaluate the force of Ayse and Jasmine's claim that the dispute 'has nothing to do with them' and 'they don't want anything to do with it'. Taken at face value, as it might appear in a recording of interaction between them, this might emerge analytically as a straightforward statement and as such the speakers would be placing themselves outside the 'Turkish' group which the writers of the first letter claim to represent. The issue, however, is whether or not they would count as members of this group in the first place. Here, the fact that Ayse is newly arrived and that Jasmine is not part of the EAL group ('She usually sits at the front of the class away from the other EAL students') suggest that they are students for whom the first group claim to speak. Here contextual information is essential if we are to interpret the significance, rather than merely the content, of their claim.

The representation of Mr Hakan in the field notes is interesting, both representationally and analytically. In terms of representation, the judgement of the observer features prominently and develops from description to evaluation. Having spent time with the two protesters outside the classroom, Mr Hakan returns with them and 'tries to settle the two returnees and help them with their work' (essentially descriptive), but 'they are angry with him and do not want his help' (there is an element of interpretation here, but anger and rejection of help, if sufficiently demonstrative, are not difficult to identify). In fact, they 'respond much more warmly' to the researcher (here an element of comparison is involved, carrying a much greater subjective load than the previous assessments) because Mr Hakan 'is seen as the enemy' (a highly subjective judgement that cannot be based on observation of this incident but draws on familiarity with the wider context and an evaluative assessment of what constitutes an 'enemy' within it). This is not meant as a criticism of Creese's interpretation here but as an illustration of how the availability of contextual information and the researcher's positioning *within* the relevant setting, produces different sorts of claims with different evidential foundations.

In her analysis of this event, Creese draws on membership of different groups to provide possible explanations for the protesters' rejection of Mr Hakan's intervention. At first sight, the fact that they share a common language would seem to unite them, but Creese argues that membership of this linguistic group is overridden by other considerations. First, in phoning parents, Mr Hakan memberships himself as part of the institution to which they are opposed and hence, in terms of the dispute, places himself outside their group. Furthermore, the use of Turkish as a language code does not thereby place the speaker within a specific group vis-à-vis the dispute because different Turkish heritage groups were aligned on opposite sides of the confrontation and the one to which he belongs is associated with rejection of the protesters' case. Notice here that the concept of community is central to this line of analysis: the rejection of Mr Hakan is explained in terms of his membership of the school community (as opposed to the protesters' community) and the Turkish-Cypriot community (as opposed to the Turkish-Kurdish community).

Section C
Exploration C1

In this section, we invite you to explore further how different aspects of identity, culture and context can be talked into being and ask you to consider the analytical implications of different forms of representing such talk. We also suggest projects that draw together ethnography and conversation analysis and introduce you to a relatively new approach which draws on the strengths of both. Readers who are interested in exploring this area further are recommended to read Young's (2008) excellent work on language and interaction.

Task C.1.1

➤ Read the following field notes and compare the way the talk is presented with the way Mori presents interaction in her paper. What methods does Creese use in order to represent the talk and its impact? When you have considered this, examine the interpretation provided by the author and identify any claims that seem to you to require further evidence to support them.

Staff meeting

During and following the demonstration, the head teacher held a series of *ad-hoc* and emergency staff meetings. One of these is reported in detail below.

Fieldnotes, 13th October.

The whole staff is assembled and school is to start late. The headteacher narrates the incident. A lot is made about the reputation of the school. She talks about the successes of the school; names some 'Turkish' girls who have been successful; and what a good reputation the school has for integrating all races. She explains there have been racist incidents in other schools in the borough but not in this school. She thanks the staff repeatedly for their support and says she does not want to see staff turn against one another. After she has finished speaking several teachers are selected to give their opinions. She starts with Mr Hakan and Miss Zengin. Both bilingual teachers support the Head's arguments that the group of girls were organised by outside groups; that there is a girl who has been trouble ever since she arrived, agitating the others. Both the bilingual teachers support the school's line that the girls, even if they have grievances should have gone through the regular channels. The majority of teachers who speak, say that girls should be disciplined, that they were lying if they say they did not know about the anti racist policy. The teachers react angrily to the girls' accusation that the teachers treat the Afro Caribbean girls differently from the Turkish girls because, they the teachers, are afraid of confrontation. The physical education teacher is really angry and says, 'that's a load of rubbish.' In the main it is only those who are taking the same line as the headteacher's who speak out. Only one teacher offers an alternative view when he says that 'we' the teachers should admire the girls for demonstrating because we have all done this in our lives, 'After all they wouldn't be able to do this in Turkey.' While he is speaking, the teacher accused of racism gets up and walks out. He continues saying that we must look into the comment that the girls don't know about the anti racist statement. He is the only teacher to take a different line. Following his comment there is uncomfortable silence. The meeting is near the end and the head teacher tells her teachers she will keep them fully informed.

This vignette makes salient some of the interpretations made by the head and her teaching staff towards the accusations made in Text One. The headteacher develops three arguments against the girls' behaviour. One theme that the students of Text One had raised was the lack of follow-up by staff of their grievances when racist incidents occurred. The headteacher does not address this directly, but she (and her teachers) are adamant that the students themselves have not followed the correct procedures. This was central to the head as it allowed her to show the school as having equal measures for all when dealing with racism. There seems to be little awareness that the students might not have followed normal procedure because of their frustrations in the past or that the school had not been successful in making its procedures known.

Related to the discussion of procedures is the second theme the head develops which is the description of the girls as rude and heavily influenced by outsiders. This interpretation of the girls' behaviour is similar to that made by the students in Text Two. The demonstrators are presented as foolish and easily influenced by others. They are stripped of their intentions to make claims and demands. The girls are presented as outside of the school community because of their rudeness and lack of willingness to play by the school's rules.

A third theme apparent in the fieldnotes is the reaction to accusations of racism and the argument that teachers treat different ethnic groups differently in the school. Teachers are outraged by this suggestion and a discussion about the feasibility of this cannot even be developed in the staff meeting – such is the anger it creates. The general consensus is that all groups are treated equally and in the same way within the school.

The interpretations the head and the majority of teachers choose to take up around the event are parallel to those developed by the student writers of Text Two. Both the staff meeting and Text Two develop a position of shared and equal agendas. Diversity is celebrated in the same way, with each 'multi' culture treated as if it were equal and the same. Only those teachers who are seen to be central in supporting this discourse are recruited to help in its endorsement. Some teachers are silenced either because their views are considered to be too dangerous or not seen to be relevant. The two bilingual teachers were seen as central to supporting the school's central message and were actively recruited during the staff meeting to lend their voices to the headteacher's.

(Creese 2003: 230–231)

The process of writing field notes, as anyone who has worked done fieldwork knows, is a very demanding activity and one fraught with all sorts of challenges, not least that of finding a time and place to get something down on paper. Inevitably, then, there are representational compromises and long stretches of talk have to be represented briefly. To compensate for this, many observers look for the telling detail that will indicate the impact of particular actions or utterances. For example, the selection of Mr Hakan and Miss Zengin to speak first adds weight to the argument that the school had co-opted them to support its position, while the response to a single dissenting voice underlines the claim that this is not representative.

Here are some examples of these features in the representation:

- Brief summaries of long stretches of talk: 'She thanks the staff repeatedly for their support and says she does not want to see staff turn against one another.'
- Representations of actions, sometimes in very general terms (e.g. with no indication of what selection involves) and sometimes with specific detail (e.g. who was 'selected' first): 'After she has finished speaking several teachers are selected to give their opinions. She starts with Mr Hakan and Miss Zengin.'
- Assessment of numbers of speakers involved: 'The majority of teachers who speak, say that girls should be disciplined'; 'He is the only teacher to take a different line.'
- Interpretation of affective aspects of delivery or receipt: 'The physical education teacher is really angry and says, "that's a load of rubbish."'; 'Following his comment there is uncomfortable silence.'
- Selection of interpretively 'significant' actions: 'While he is speaking, the teacher accused of racism gets up and walks out.'

Because the analysis is approached from the broader context of the researcher's full set of field notes and her experience of the incident and its impact, the ethnographer is likely to make claims (perhaps 'suggestions' would be more accurate) that would be completely inappropriate in conversation analysis. Drawing a line between what seems analytically appropriate and what is mere speculation can be very difficult, as the following three claims illustrate:

1. 'There seems to be little awareness that the students might not have followed normal procedure because of their frustrations in the past or that the school had not been successful in making its procedures known.' This is not something that appears in the meeting exchanges, but the researcher legitimately points out that in pursuing one line of interpretation the meeting ignores an alternative one. Sometimes, drawing attention to something that is absent can be as

important as describing what is present. Notice, though, that the 'absence' here has a very different status from the sort of 'absences' that feature in CA (e.g. the absence of a second pair part following a first pair part).

2. 'They are stripped of their intentions to make claims and demands.' This summarizes a position taken up by the school but not one that can be captured in a particular exchange. In representing the protesters as easily influenced, the school effectively denies them even the 'intention' to make claims and demands and implicitly positions them as mouthpieces for others. While there is some evidence for this in Text Two, the claim is a strong one and might have benefited from more direct evidence drawn from exchanges in the meeting or in other encounters. However, the nature of fieldnotes means that such evidence might be difficult to obtain.
3. 'Some teachers are silenced either because their views are considered to be too dangerous or not seen to be relevant.' The researcher produces no evidence in the meeting description of such 'silencing' or of the motivation proposed, and in the absence of such evidence this claim must be regarded as speculative.

The analysis in Creese depends on the identification of different communities and membership of these is used as an interpretive resource in a way that would not feature in a conversation analytic approach. Although 'situated responses' and shifts in positioning and orientation are important in the paper, the microinteractional processes through which these are achieved are not the focus of analysis. However, the advantages of combining ethnography with the micro-analysis of interaction (e.g. using CA) are obvious and this provides the foundation for the relatively new approach known as *linguistic ethnography.*

The conceptual heart of linguistic ethnography is its assumption of a reflexive relationship between language and the social world in which each influences and shapes the other in ways that allow an approach to analysis bringing together ethnography and linguistics. Rampton *et al.* (2004: 4) in terms of 'tying ethnography down' and 'opening linguistics up'. Clearly, 'linguistics' is much broader than 'conversation', but nevertheless much of the linguistic analysis that is involved in this research involves the sort of micro-analysis that is characteristic of CA. For those interested in exploring this approach further, an excellent website (with useful downloadable papers) is available: http://www.ling-ethnog.org.uk/. There is also a very good collection of papers in Tusting and Maybin (2007), though most of these engage with theoretical rather than practical issues.

In this book we have concentrated on conversation analysis because this provides probably the best – and certainly the 'purest' – introduction to the task of analyzing the fine detail of talk. However, this by no means the only option available to the researcher. For example, any researcher adopting a critical ethnographic approach would almost certainly wish to draw on critical discourse analysis. For an outstanding example of how discourse analysis and ethnography can be combined to excellent effect, see Maybin (2006), who works in a tradition very different from that of CA.

Task C.2.1

- Take some time to reflect on a situation with which you are familiar and try to think of what aspects of identity seem particularly relevant to that situation. For example, in a staff room this might be 'experienced teacher' and 'new teacher'; in a classroom it might be a matter of being a 'serious student' or 'a troublemaker'; in other social contexts it might be a matter of social or ethnic allegiance. Design a project in which you find out how people talk this aspect of identity in and out of being in their interaction and/or how this aspect of identity is treated in the media.

- If you have the time to pursue this further, identify a situation where this aspect of identity is likely to feature and design some small-scale data collection (making sure that you follow appropriate ethical procedures). This might involve observing, recording and interviewing. If you are able to use these different data sources, compare the different contributions they make to your understanding of the relevant aspect of identity and its social and interactional construction.

Task C.2.2

- Particular identities can be invoked for a range of purposes, some serious some entertaining. Here are two examples involving Ed, both from the same staff room setting, the first taken from field notes and the second from a recording. Try to identify the different identities involved.

In the first extract (from field notes), Ed is preparing a lesson:

Ed goes over to bookcase 1 in search of material. He takes down a book and begins to examine a section.

Paul:	'Don't bother doing that with my group.'
Ed:	Responds with a problem (to do with names?).
Paul:	'They were asking that all day yesterday.'
Ed:	Expression on his face and his shrug, makes it clear that he hasn't found what he's after.
Harry:	'A fruitless quest.'
Ed:	(In detective voice) 'That sometimes happens in my line of investigation.'

Returns to his desk.

(Richards)

In the second extract, Ed has just flicked an elastic band:

01 *Paul*: Ed being mischievous was he?
02 *Annette*: he observation ⌈wasn't in a (xxxxxxxx)⌉
03 *Harry*: ⌊It wasn't a- it wasn't⌋=
04 =really in a (.) ⌈sort of lesson as such.

05 *Paul*: ⌊*Just like schoolboys.*
06 *Annette*: Yeah.
07 *Paul*: ((In a deep, schoolmaster's voice, with an
08 authoritarian tone.)) 'Put it awa:y, Ed.'
09 ((Laughter and from Keith and Paul.
10 interspersed with odd, half-formed mutterings
11 in the same tone.))
12 *Harry*: (xxxxxxx) he's er (.) described it.
13 *Ed*: 'Yes you boy. Let's all see what you're doi-'
14 *Susan*: Yeah.
16 (1.0)
17 *Harry*: (xxxxxxxxxxxxxxx)
18 *Paul??*: Yeah.
19 *Keith*: 'Let's all have a look at it.'
20 *Harry*: Heheh hehehehehehehh
21 *Keith*: Heheh

(Richards)

In the first extract, Ed begins by doing something that teachers regularly do when they are preparing lessons: look for materials. His first exchange with Paul is also typical of teachers in the staff room in terms of its focus on teaching and students. However, when Harry comments on his failure to find materials he responds not as a teacher but as a detective, making light of his failure to track down a suitable text.

The second extract is in some ways more interesting because when Paul refers to schoolboys in line 5 he has Ed in mind, as is clear from his instruction to Ed in line 8, using a well-worn expression used especially by teachers of children and teenagers. Ed has therefore been positioned as a troublesome schoolboy (consistent with his behaviour as a flicker of rubber bands), but he does not reply as a schoolboy. Instead, in line 13 he responds as an authoritarian teacher addressing an invisible student with another clichéd expression (for a fuller picture of aspects of Ed's identity, see Richards [forthcoming]).

Choose an individual in a setting to which you have regular access and note – in fact, note down if possible – evidence of identity shifts of this sort. What do they seem to be designed to achieve, and what do they reveal about the individual and the activities in which he or she is involved?

Task C2.3

➤ Not all identity shifts are so light-hearted, and it may be important sometimes for individuals to find ways of escaping from the pressures imposed by particular identities. Spencer-Oatey and Franklin refer to the concept of 'space' as representing something into which one can escape the pressures of place (that which is fixed and familiar). They write (2009: 163):

> People's identities are continually developing and changing, and 'space' provides them with the opportunity to do so. People's self-narratives emerge as they move from an original place into a space, and then use that space to lead themselves to a new place. In exploiting spaces, people may be grappling with a range of challenges; for example, they may be striving to bring coherence to their sense of identity, and addressing questions such as 'How can I be both a Jew and a Christian?' Or 'How can I be both a competent professional and a dedicated mother or father?' When people perceive they have multiple identities that are seemingly incompatible, this can be very unsettling.

If you are aware of someone in this situation (it might be a student struggling to adjust to a new class or culture, or a colleague juggling two different identities) and feel that it would be useful to both them and you to understand their situation better, you could use the interview techniques introduced in Chapter 4 to explore this with them. Such an interview could be very helpful in the process of adjustment, but there are also risks involved, so you should consider these very carefully. This can be a very sensitive area and you should not pursue this simply for research purposes

Task C.2.4

➤ Look at the extracts of L2 classroom interaction below. Show how interactants talk into being different aspects of identity, culture and context.

Extract 7

(An ESOL class in a British university)

T: could you tell me something about marriage in Algeria?
who is married here?
L1: Azo, only Azo.
T: alright, your opinion about that.
L2: he will marry.
T: oh, he is engaged, engaged. tell me something about the
institution of marriage in Algeria. tell me something
about it.
L3: there are several institutions.
T: you don't have marriage in Algeria. what do you have
then?
L4: only women and men.
T: yes, that's what marriage is.
L1: the marriage in Algeria isn't like the marriage in
England.
T: what do you mean?
L2: for get marriage you must pay two thousand.
L5: yes more expensive than here.

T: why do you have to pay money?
L6: no. It's our religion.
L7: not religion but our tradition.
L8: no, religion, religion. in religion we must pay women,
but not high price, but tradition.
L5: between women, women does not like to married to a low
money because it is not, it is (.)
T: oh, dowry, oh dear.

(Hasan 1988: 258–259)

Extract 8

(An English lesson in a Norwegian school)

L2: e:r inter intermarriage is looked upon as the key to Americanization. (3 sec)
L2: intermarriage is that=
L1: =I think it is true=
L2: =yeah that's true.
LL: (laugh)
L2: so what is intermarriage
L1: ((unintelligible 1 sec))=
L2: =is that one foreign=
L1: =maybe two ethnic groups.
L2: yeah
L3: hm?
L1: maybe two people from two ethnic groups.
L2: and I guess it's especially one white and one=
L3: =one black or
L2: yeah one
L1: I don't know,
L2: yeah well it could be
L1: it cause a lot of problems I think.
L2: yeah e:r . . ., . . ., when you look at in the . . ., *ekteskap* ((tr: marriage))
LL: marriage
L2: marriage yeah you just look at marriage and you think it will cause problems for the two for the two people living together?=
L1: =no for the children.
L2: the children? . . ., yeah . . ., I think it could be a problem for the marriage itself too e:r because I I read e:r a survey=
L1: =((unintelligible 2 sec))
L2: yeah, yeah and I just e:r how to how you behave and how which which what kind of moral you have, I read a survey from Norway e:r which said that most divorces was caused with the marriages between a Norwegian and a foreigner=
L3: mhm.
L2: =so that e:r – the marriages are more unstable . . ., . . ., and yeah it might be that it would cause problems for the childrens
L3: ((unintelligible 2 sec))
L2: yeah yeah, what kind of religion they should get, I think that's quite important that the US e:r they are more concerned about the religion,

L1: ((unintelligible 6 sec))
L2: yeah, yes that's probably true.
L1: ((unintelligible 6 sec))
L2: yeah I think it it's a it's it is it is a key to Americanization . . ., don't you think?=
L1: =hm,
L2: because=
L3: =I don't know because if you=
L1: =some people just marry each other for one who hasn't got American citizenship can=
L2: yeah
L1: =can=
L2: =yes that's true but if they if they love each other and if they are living in a steady relationship it will it's a:r the foreigner will adapt more to the . . ., Americanization process than if just two Pakistan – two people from Pakistan just move to the States and live their life e:r more separate from the society=
L1: =but I think if one from Pakistan and one from America are to be married, the one from Pakistan will bring much of his culture in, cause I don't think he want let go of his religion and that . . ., . . ., I don't know
L2: no, I guess not . . ., but there will be e:m just like:e the Americans will learn from the others=
L1: yes
L2: =so it would be
L1: in a way=
L2: =I suppose it could be (5 sec)
LL: (laugh)

(Seedhouse 1996)

Task C.2.5

➤ Observe a classroom or watch a video of a lesson and analyze how participants talk in and out of being the relevance of aspects of identity. Employ the three aspects of identity introduced in Mori's article: categorization, discourse identity and social identity.

CHAPTER 7
Assessing language and accessing constructs

In this unit we examine how research processes relate to the constructs typically researched in language learning. Research in applied linguistics employs many different constructs. Some of these have been used for many decades and are familiar in the world outside applied linguistics, e.g. motivation, fluency, bilingualism. Some constructs are newer, more restricted in use, and are still being developed, e.g. mediation, translanguaging, teachability.

We use the term 'construct' to stress the point that all of these concepts or ideas have been created by researchers. This means that a construct's ontology or existence does not have the same status as that of a wooden table or a car. In general, constructs in applied linguistics have been formulated to explain, categorize or analyze phenomena which have been noticed in language use. These constructs may be rather different in terms of their ontology. Let us consider individual differences in students, which may be considered to be related to language learning, for example, age and motivation. The age of a learner can normally be determined without difficulty, remains stable (although we all age!) and uni-dimensional, and is thus closer to a 'natural' construct. There is a large body of research which relates age to language learning. The construct of motivation is more abstract, and refers to 'the effort which learners put into learning an L2 as a result of their need or desire to learn it' (Ellis 1994: 715). Motivation is dynamic rather than stable in that we can become more or less motivated by our experiences of language learning. It cannot be determined in the same way as age. Much motivation research involves using questionnaires or interviews with learners, which is an indirect way of accessing the construct in that learners may not always give accurate or truthful accounts of their motivation, for a variety of reasons. Some people do of course lie about their age, again for a variety of reasons. Research on motivation (e.g. Dörnyei 2001) demonstrates that motivation is a multi-dimensional construct. So although both age and motivation are factors which vary among individuals and which affect language learning, they are rather different constructs and need to be researched in different ways.

Students who are at a preliminary stage in researching language learning often start with very 'linear' assumptions. These are that a straight line can be drawn without difficulty from the research questions through the data gathered by research instruments to the research object or construct. So if the research question is 'Which learning strategies are used by a group of learners?', this can be answered directly by asking the learners to complete questionnaires which ask them which strategies they use when learning particular aspects of the language. The assumption, then, is that the data permit the researcher direct access to the construct. However, more experienced researchers tend to perceive a more complex, reflexive relationship between the components of the research process. In the case of the example above, the problem is that questionnaires ask participants what they do/would do, rather than providing evidence of what they actually do in practice. There is now substantial evidence throughout the social sciences of a frequent mismatch between what people say they do and what they actually do. This issue is explored by Golato (2003). So, if we go back to the example given above, the research question which is *actually* being answered by means of the data is 'Which learning strategies do a group of learners say that they use?' In other words, there is a slight misalignment between the construct being researched and the processes used to research it. So we constantly need to be checking, at all stages of the research process, what the relationship is between the components of the research process and whether they are all moving in the same direction or not. This need for confirming that an indicator of a construct such as strategy use is actually related to a phenomenon such as language learning success is referred to as construct validation. This does not mean that there is anything inherently wrong in asking people what they do/would do by employing questionnaires and interviews. Rather, the implications are that a) we should show awareness of the limitations of the design and b) we should be looking for evidence of what people actually do to compared with what they say they do, possibly as part of a mixed-methods approach; see Chapter 8.

In this chapter we examine how two researchers go about researching key constructs in language learning. These are 'implicit knowledge and explicit knowledge of language' (Ellis 2005) and 'proficiency' (Brown 2003). In a sense, proficiency is a key underlying construct in the majority of language learning research studies, in that it is bound in as a crucial outcome component in very many research studies. These often examine the effects of particular interventions on the learning process and seek to show that these interventions or variables will improve learner proficiency to a greater extent than others. Improvements in learner proficiency are measured by tests of some kind. So a stable construct like 'proficiency' is an underlying assumption in much research and improvements in task performances or test scores are taken to indicate improvements in the proficiency construct.

Constructs, also referred to as latent variables, are not directly observable, and are hypothesized to be indicated by measures or other overt observations. A single observation or measure is insufficient to adequately define a stable construct. Modern test theory is based on the idea that a construct must be first represented by a score, which itself is derived from the sum of many repeated measures of the construct through items crafted to resample the construct. Even summations of a set of items may, however, not sufficiently define a construct. The summation score is an intermediate step in defining the latent construct. Researchers aiming to measure a construct through tests or surveys frequently use a third, and more abstract criterion that integrates the items to the scores to the construct. The third method uses the logic of a nomological network (Chapter 1), which examines evidence that the summation scores are interrelated in clusters of correlations. These clusters are taken to indicate the latent factors representing the constructs. The following section and Section B2 featuring research by R. Ellis introduces a common method used to explore the relationship among summation scores on measurements hypothesized to be indicators of different constructs. The validity of hypothesized distinguishability between putative constructs is tested with factor analysis tools.

Section A
Introduction A1 (Ellis 2005)

The distinction between implicit knowledge and explicit knowledge has been expressed in numerous ways over the last 30 years of second language acquisition research. Krashen (1981) early on differentiated between learning and acquisition to account for conscious awareness of linguistic rules that often did not seem to govern learners' capacity to generate well-formed instantiations of the very same grammatical rules. The two types of language knowledge were evident from the contrast between spontaneously generated language use for which a speaker has no retrievable rule explanation other than an intuition that the generated utterance 'sounded right', and the ability to provide explanations why particular forms are 'correct'. The distinction between the two forms of language knowledge, Krashen insisted, were on the one hand products of spontaneous acquisition processes resulting from *in situ* inductive associations between forms and meanings, and formal rule learning on the other.

In accounting for similar phenomena, Anderson (1984) concluded that linguistic knowledge splits into that which is declarative and consciously available to some form of metalinguistic description, and that which is procedural, considered to be beyond access to conscious description. A key element in the distinction between declarative and procedural types of knowledge is the time pressure under which language is comprehended or generated. Bialystok (1982) identified task dependencies as possible correlates of access to declarative knowledge. If tasks are relatively untimed, learners could have access to learned or deduced rules and could apply them to off line analysis of language form–function relationships. If tasks are performed under time constraints, the same learners would have much less access to declarative analytical rules they may have learned.

Early researchers in SLA worked with the notion that declarative and procedural types of language knowledge were distinct and evolved through separate cognitive mechanisms. More recent research on the declarative versus procedural distinction has claimed that declarative forms of knowledge can eventually be made automatic through repeated opportunities for practice (DeKeyser 2003; 2007). The opposite pathway, conscious access to procedural memory as an antecedent to declarations about what such procedures entail, is deemed to be a neurolinguistic impossibility. There is, however, a possibility that deductive rules can be sped up through repeated practice to make rule application appear more automatic (Paradis 2009).

The varying descriptions of explicit and implicit language knowledge have often been confounded by the instruments devised to measure the two constructs. Ellis (2005) identified seven ways that implicit and explicit knowledge can be distinguished, and argued that different approaches to measurement yield distinct descriptions of the explicit and implicit knowledge constructs. Ellis argued that language tests can be designed to tap into the two different constructs if they are manipulated to promote or constrain the learners' degree of awareness, planning time, attention focus and access to metalinguistic knowledge.

Task A1.1

➤ Consider the following language assessment tasks and classify them as indicators of implicit or explicit language knowledge.

1. Locate the error in the following sentence. Provide a correction if you can.

   She waited at the station until 2pm, but her friend never come.

2. In three minutes or less, sketch a simple four-frame story, and then narrate your story.

3. Give the grammatical term for the underlined portion of the sentence

   Having already eaten a late breakfast, John declined the invitation to lunch.

4. Listen and repeat:

   'Susan's boyfriend, whose name escapes me, won the lottery'

Task A1.2

➤ Use a + or – dichotomous classification for each of the following elicitation procedures.

	Imitation	Narrative	Error correction	Describe rule
Awareness				
Time				
Attention				
Metalinguistic				

Make your own exemplars of each type of task.

A2 Introduction (Brown 2003)

As mentioned above, the construct 'proficiency' underlies the majority of applied linguistics research. Assessing language proficiency is the subject of another book in this series (Fulcher and Davidson 2007). The emphasis in this section is on the research processes involved in accessing the construct 'proficiency'. At one end of the scale, a language teacher may devise a one-off proficiency test for his/her class of 10 students. At the other end of the scale there are large-scale proficiency tests such as IELTS and TOEFL. In the case of the IELTS test (the subject of Brown's 2003 study), over 2,000 certified examiners administer over a million tests annually in over 100 countries around the world. Whatever the scale, a crucial element in the test design process is reliability. Fulcher and Davidson (2007: 375) define this as 'consistency of measurement, usually over time, rater or content'. This means that all of the candidates taking the test have an equal opportunity to display their proficiency, whoever they are interacting with in the assessment process, which in turn means that the test score will align accurately with their actual level of proficiency. In theory, any aspect of test design could function as a variable which might cause some candidates to achieve a higher score than other candidates. It is now common for large-scale proficiency tests such as IELTS to assess the four skills separately. One might imagine that in assessing writing, there would be few issues in relation to ensuring that all of the candidates taking the test have an equal opportunity to display their proficiency; after all, they all have the same essay title, for example. However, we will see in task A2.1 that the matter is not so straightforward.

Task A2.1

➤ Imagine that, in an English writing proficiency test for students around the world, the following essay titles are given. Identify which categories of candidate (according to gender, nationality, race, age, religion) might potentially be advantaged or disadvantaged by particular tasks:

a Write about the advantages and disadvantages of using free internet music download sites.
b 'Christmas is the best time of year' – discuss.
c Which country should host the 2018 World Cup competition?

➤ Now think of an essay title which would not advantage or disadvantage any category of candidate anywhere in the world.

In the case of speaking tests, the situation can be much more complex, in that the tests generally (but not always) involve an examiner speaking to a candidate, which typically involves asking questions.

Task A2.2

➤ Make a list of the variables which might influence how well a candidate performs in a speaking test with an examiner.

Task A2.3

➤ Think back to language tests you have taken in the past and identify any times when you got a much lower or much higher score than you or your teacher had expected. What were the factors which you think caused this unexpectedly high or low score?

Task A2.4

➤ Read the following extract. Do you think the examiner's response in line 3 might influence the candidate's performance? If so, how?

Extract 1

I: Where is your mother? What does your mother do?
S: She's dead.
→ I: A:h – she's dead. Very good.

(Van Lier 1989: 499)

After completing the above tasks, you should be clear that there are many variables which can potentially influence a candidate's performance in a speaking test. The task of the assessment designer is to minimize the influence of these variables in order to maximize reliability and to ensure that all candidates have an equal opportunity to display their proficiency. This is a particular problem in a speaking test as this generally involves face-to-face interaction, which in turn involves a social relationship between examiner and candidate which often involves an element of unpredictability. Even if an examiner asks scripted questions, there are many aspects to examiner verbal and non-verbal behaviour which might influence a candidate's performance in a test. Conversation analysis studies have examined examiner behaviour in the micro-detail of interaction in test situations and suggested some ways in which this may influence candidate performance.

Task A2.5

➤ Examine the two extracts below, which feature two different sets of examiners (E) and candidates (C). Are the examiners following the same or different policies when the candidate asks for a question to be repeated. Which policy do you think is more likely to provide an advantage or disadvantage to a student?

Extract 2

E: what qualifications or certificates do you hope to get? (0.4)
→ C: sorry? (0.4)
E: what qualifications or (.) certificates (0.3) do you hope to get (2.2)
C: could you ask me in another way (.) I'm not quite sure (.) quite sure about this (1.3)
E: it's alright (0.3) thank you (0.5) uh:: can we talk about your childhood? (0.7)

Extract 3

E: okay (0.3) uh:m what d'you think is the most important (0.6) household task? (1.4)
C: household task? (0.4)
E: mm=
C: =uh:m sorry I [can't]

E: → [most importa]nt job (.) in the house (0.8)
C: → in the house (1.5) uh:m (0.7) I think (0.4) the: most important job is (.)
cleaning hh (0.5) because my house is quite big (0.3)

(Both extracts from Seedhouse and Egbert 2006)

Section B

Extension B1

Ellis, R. (2005) 'Measuring implicit and explicit knowledge of a second language,' *Studies in Second Language Acquisition* 27: 141–172.

R. Ellis devised a battery of language processing tasks to test whether the tasks create clusters of measures that can differentiate between implicit and explicit types of second language knowledge. Ellis administered the test battery to 111 participants made up of native speakers and learners of English. The aim of the study was to test the hypothesis that measurements that required extemporaneous comprehension or production of language with little planning time would correlate among each other. Ellis also hypothesized that tasks assessing language knowledge which allowed for attention resources to be focused on formal features of language with sufficient time for analysis would correlate among themselves, but would not correlate with the timed extemporaneous tasks. The clusters of correlations were hypothesized to indicate latent constructs.

Ellis constructed five types of measures for the study. He created an imitation task for which participants had to repeat a spoken utterance and while doing so, correct any error heard during the imitation task. The second task Ellis used was a story-retelling task. The story was read twice, and contained a number of target structures in it. The participants had to retell the story from memory. Their versions of the story were recorded for analysis. Ellis's third task was a computer-delivered timed grammaticality judgement test with 68 items. Participants had to decide if each sentence presented to them was well formed or contained an error. Responses were timed and recorded as correct or incorrect. The fourth task was an untimed version of the third, though in the untimed version, participants provided a degree of certainty rating for their decision about the grammaticality of each item, as well as a self-report about whether they used a rule or an intuitive feel during their judgement. The fifth task was the most complex. Participants had to select from among four rule descriptions that accounted for the ungrammaticality of seventeen sentences. Thereafter, participants read a text and had to find 21 grammatical features that corresponded to a set of parts of speech descriptors. Ellis hypothesized that the first three tasks would measure participants' implicit grammatical knowledge, while the latter two would tap into their explicit grammar knowledge.

Task B1.1

➤ Based on the preceding paragraphs, identify the constructs and their indicators.

Ellis expected specific patterns and magnitudes of correlations among the different measures in the study. A correlation measures the extent to which two variables co-vary in such a manner that as the value of one variable increases, the other increases or decreases correspondingly. The correlation can be expressed as a coefficient, or plotted for a visual representation.

Task B1.2

➤ Think of language learning phenomena that correlate with each other positively. Consider also two phenomena that ought not to have any correlation with each other. Finally, consider phenomena that you would expect to have a negative correlation with each other.

Task B1.3

➤ Consider Ellis's set of measures of implicit and explicit knowledge. Which of these measures would you think should correlate with each other? Which should have a relatively lower correlation? Would you expect any of them to have a zero or negative correlation with the other measures?

Ellis provided a table (reproduced below) of correlations among the five measures of the variables measured in his study. Note in the table below that '1' refers to the expected correlation between a variable and itself.

	Imitation	Narrative	Timed GJT	Untimed GJT	MetaLing
Imitation	1				
Narrative	.48	1			
Timed GJT	.58	.36	1		
Untimed GJT	.59	.36	.57	1	
MetaLing	.28	.27	.24	.60	1

Task B1.4

➤ Examine the pattern of correlations from Ellis (2005). Note any correlations that are higher or lower than what you had anticipated in Task B1.3.

Ellis's main goal was to explore the notion that different kinds of measures can be constructed to indicate latent constructs or factors. The matrix of correlations observed in Ellis's study was tested for its factor structure. The core hypothesis Ellis entertained was that there are two different kinds of linguistic knowledge: implicit knowledge, which is tapped when learners do not have time to access declarative knowledge when they interpret or generate a second language, and explicit knowledge, which manifests itself when there is time for learners to monitor and plan their production. Ellis tested this hypothesis by conducting a factor analysis on the correlation matrix. A factor analysis is a statistical method which examines clusters of correlations in a matrix of correlations derived from a battery of measurements. The clusters of correlations are taken as evidence of a latent construct – the underlying reason why sets of variables are intercorrelated. Patterns can be predicted beforehand, or can be explored post hoc.

ANALYSIS

SPSS can be used to conduct a factor analysis with published data, as long as a correlation matrix is made available by the authors in the body or appendix of their published paper. We will replicate Ellis's results by reproducing it in an SPSS Syntax file and adding a few FACTOR command lines under the reproduced correlation matrix.

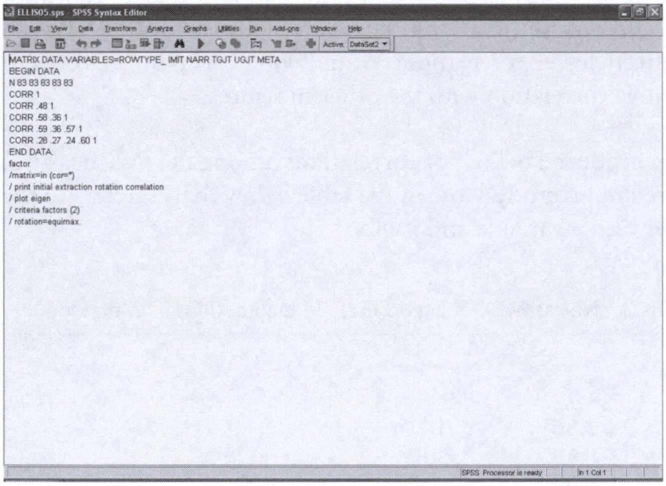

Figure 7.1 Syntax Editor matrix input for factor analysis

Ellis (2005) justified extracting two factors based on his hypothesis, and the fact that a second factor identified in a preliminary analysis accounted for a substantive amount of covariance among the scores. He was exploring the constructs of implicit versus explicit knowledge, and thus hypothesized a priorical there would be two latent constructs in the pattern of correlations. We can replicate this step of Ellis's research by 'forcing' the extraction of two factors (/criteria factors (2)). After the syntax is entered into the window, we can simply submit the command file under the RUN menu option.

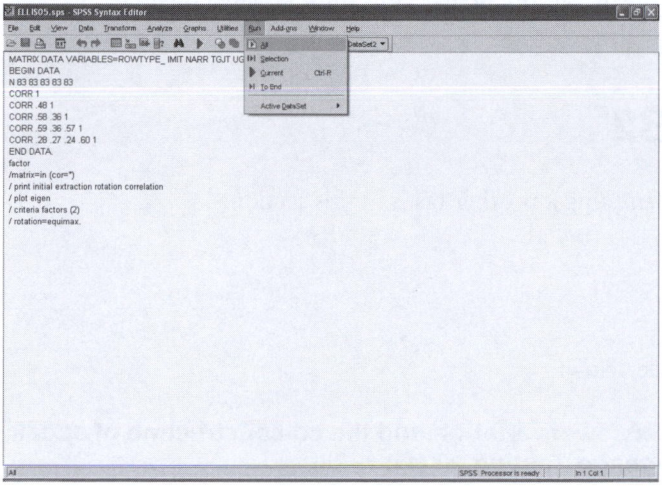

Figure 7.2 Model execution for exploratory factor analysis

Reprint courtesy of International Business Machines Corporation, © SPSS, Inc., an IBM company

The results of the replication yield results very similar to those reported by Ellis. Of primary interest to Ellis was the rotated component matrix. The evidence to support Ellis's hypothesis that implicit and explicit forms of second language knowledge can be measured is found in the rotated component loadings. The loadings are correlations between each measured variable and a latent construct implied by the patterns of correlations among the measures. Imitation, the oral narrative and the timed grammaticality judgement task all correlate with Component 1. The rotation moves them to their extremes and fixes each component relative to its dominant member (IMIT for Component 1 and META for Component 2).

Rotated matrix[a]	*Component*	
	Component 1	2
IMIT	.838	.217
NARR	.708	.116
TGJT	.793	.193
UGJT	.545	.714
META	.086	.953

The untimed grammaticality judgment task and the metalinguistic task both correlated with Component 2.

Task B1.5

➤ Given the pattern of loadings in the Component Loading Matrix, what are possible labels for the two components? How did Ellis label them?

Extension B2

Do task B2.1 before attempting any other tasks in this section.

Task B2.1

➤ Now read the article below:

Brown, A. (2003) 'Interviewer variation and the co-construction of speaking proficiency', *Language Testing* 20 (1): 1–25.

It should be pointed out that this article does not deal with the current IELTS Speaking Test, but with that in use prior to 2001.

In the present study, two of the IELTS Speaking Module interviews which formed the basis of the study reported in Brown and Hill (1998) are analysed. These involved two interviewers who differed significantly in terms of their difficulty, and a single candidate. The analysis aims to show how the different strategies used by each of the interviewers resulted in qualitatively different performances in (and hence ratings for) the two interviews. In order to confirm the supposed link between interviewer behaviour and score outcomes (for this is all it can be at the level of the analysis of discourse), reference is made to comments produced by raters in retrospective verbal reports, where they discussed their reactions to the candidates' performance and the reasons for the scores they awarded.

The study

The two interviews were conducted on the same day and involved the same candidate, Esther, with each of two interviewers, Pam and Ian. Of the 6 interviewers in Brown and Hill's study, Pam had been ranked the easiest (with a difficulty measure of –0.86 logits) and Ian the most difficult (with a measure of 0.75 logits). The difference in the difficulty measures corresponded to a difference in difficulty of 0.6 of a band on the IELTS speaking test scale. This fractional difference is attributable to the method of analysis, which derived interviewer difficulty from an averaging of all the ratings awarded to all the interviews by each interviewer. However, the fact that the difference is greater than 0.5 of a band indicates that candidates are more likely to be awarded different ratings with the two interviewers than they are the same ratings.

In order to produce stable estimates of candidate ability, a total of 8 ratings had been elicited for the two interviews.[1] Because Rasch analysis was used to analyse the data, it was possible to ensure that raters did not encounter both interviews by the same candidate, avoiding the possibility of one rating influencing another. Table 1 shows that Esther received a mean score of 5.8 (over the 8 raters) for her interview with Pam, and a mean score of 5 for her interviews with Ian. In general, then, she appears to be perceived by the raters as being more proficient when being interviewed by Pam than when she is being interviewed by Ian.

Table 1 Interview ratings

Candidate	*Interviewer*	*Scores*								*Mean*	*Median*
Esther	Pam	5	5	5	6	6	6	6	7	5.8	6.0
Esther	Ian	4	5	5	5	5	5	5	6	5.0	5.0

The IELTS *interview*

The IELTS Speaking Module consists of 5 phases of which the first and last – the opening and closing – are very short. Other than in the middle phase – which consists of a role play – the speaking module is basically a conversational interview in which candidates are invited to talk on a range of topics covering a range of functional and discoursal skills (such as description, argument, narration and speculation). For the purposes of this study the role play was excluded in order to focus more specifically on the conversational part of the interview.

Phases 2 and 4 of the IELTS interview, the 'conversational' phases, are structured around a series of topics on which the interviewer attempts to engage the candidate in conversation. Interviewers are provided with a list of suggested topics from which to select in order to elicit a range of functional uses of language (description, comparison and narration in Phase 2 and speculation and opinion and hypothesizing in Phase 4). Ingram and Wylie (1996: 3–4) comment that the main phases of the interview were designed to 'give candidates the initiative from the start, to encourage them to become active participants in the conversational exchange rather than just provide minimal responses to a series of questions'. Interviewers are told they must be ready to respond to what the candidate says in order to develop the interview. They are told to take advantage of topics that arise during the interview (British Council *et al.* 1997: A16), and they are also told that if the candidate wants to expand on a certain topic or if they feel that a topic could benefit from supplementary questions, then they should pursue it.

The emphasis of the test is on 'measuring candidates' communication skills in the language in everyday situations rather than formal knowledge of grammar, vocabulary or other elements of the language' (British Council *et al.* 1996: 3). This orientation is captured within the IELTS band descriptors through the term 'communicative effectiveness', which refers to test-takers' ability to 'talk at length on a range of topics displaying a range of functional and discoursal skills' (description, argument, narration and speculation, for example). This is in addition to the more traditional linguistic criteria of grammatical accuracy, syntactic complexity and vocabulary.

Methodology of the discourse analysis

Given the focus of the assessment on candidates' communicative effectiveness, the perspective taken within the analysis is also on communication, on the interplay between interviewer and candidate. As an analysis of interviewer moves alone would reveal little about their impact on candidate performance, the analysis consists not simply of a count of prespecified interviewer behaviours, but of a sequential analysis of the talk as a whole. This will allow us to ascertain not only the ways in which interviewer behaviour differs but also how these differences affect the quality of the candidate's talk and construct different pictures of her proficiency.

An approach to the analysis of spoken interaction which takes this perspective – the turn-by-turn construction of interaction – is conversation analysis (CA). Whilst CA is most closely associated with the analysis of 'natural' (i.e., nontest) conversational interaction (Sacks *et al.* 1974), it is now widely used in the analysis of institutional interaction, providing useful perspectives on the ways in which participants understand and carry out their roles within specific contexts (see, in particular, Drew and Heritage 1992). In the context of the oral interview, CA can help us to describe and understand the nature of the interaction between interviewers and candidates.

The analysis itself followed the convention of CA studies in that the transcription stage was an important part of the analysis, not a preliminary step. The analysis took topical sequences as the structural units within the interviews, and focused on the ways in which the two interviewers implemented their topical choices in order to elicit a performance from the candidate. Repeated close listening to the interviews allowed the researcher to build up a clear picture of each interviewer's style of topic development and conversational management, as well as its impact on the candidate's speech. It emerged that the interviewers differed along a number of dimensions, and that they did indeed exhibit stable styles. For the sake of brevity, the ways in which the two interviewers manage the interviews and elicit talk from the candidate are described here through a detailed analysis of a single sequence drawn from each interview. These sequences, it should be noted, were selected for detailed analysis here not because they stood out, but because they contained behaviours which were representative of the interviewers.

Analysis

The analysis starts with Pam, the 'easier' of the two interviewers. Sequence 1 is taken from Phase 2 of her interview:

Sequence 1 Tape 44 Interviewer: Pam Candidate: Esther

I . . . do you live in a fla:t?
C er no hostel
I in a hostel.
C Carlton College.
I is it? [(.)] tell me about the hostel; (.) I haven't seen that one.
C [°mm°]
(1.6)
C oh um: it's aum: international college, =

I = mm,
(0.8)
C er >I mean a hostel, < er: (1.0) and I knew- (.) I- (1.0) knew:
that (.) hostel: by: (0.9) a counselling centre, (1.2) and: (1.9)
and it's: (0.5) er: quite good for: (0.8) u:m: (.) >suitable for
me;< [to live] there.
I [is it?]
I what do you like about it Esther?
C um: (3.0) er >the food_< (0.8) yeah is: >quite good< er: but it's
(.) everyday f- western food.
I is it? [(.) what] do they give you: to eat.
C [yeah]
C er (.) potatoes,
I oh yes.
C yeah (.) everday potatoes, er: a:nd (0.6) sometimes got er:(.)
beef_ (0.8) lamb chops_ (.) and: (.) others (.) like noodles, =
I = mhm =
C = °°mm°°
I .hh (.) do you sometimes go and buy food?
(1.8)
C mm buy food for:_
I d'you d'you go to: (.) maybe McDona:lds or K F C?
C oh I seldom go:
I a:h y [es]
C [>be]cause< they: offer: tree meals (.) a day.
I so (.) yeah that's plenty for you [is it?] yes: yeah .hh =
C [yeah.]
I =^what else do you like about (.) living in the hostel.
C mm:: (1.0) my friends are all there_
I ah good, [(.) yeah]
C [yeah all] came from (0.6) my: same school.
I did they¿ (.) ye:s, yeah, .hh. . . . . .

The sequence begins with a closed question 'Do you live in a flat?', which introduces the topic 'living arrangements'. Esther responds, relevantly, with 'No', but elaborates then with the fact that she lives in a hostel and its name. Pam responds to this information with a newsmarker 'Is it?', which she immediately follows with a question that topicalizes the new information (the hostel) and explicitly elicits an extended response: 'Tell me about . . .'. The statement 'I haven't seen that one' also indicates a level of interest in Esther's response as it implies that she is familiar with other hostels and is therefore interested in learning how this one compares. After some hesitation (line 7) Esther begins an extended response to this prompt (lines 8–14).

This approach to topic establishment is typical of Pam. Extract 1 shows a further such example taken from later in the same interview. Here, the new line of questioning is introduced by the closed question 'Do you have a room on your own?', and the follow-up question 'Can you describe . . .?' elicits an extended piece of description.

Extract 1: Tape 44 Pam/Esther

I . . . .hh so- (.) do you have a room, on your own?
C no I'm sharing with my friend.=
I → = mhm can you describe your room to me?
C er it's quite big [mm,] erm: (2.0) mm: (0.8) I'm sharing with my friend, (.) er Celia, (0.5) and: (1.3) we have (0.9) we have (.) two table for (0.5) >each of us,< [mm,] (0.7) an:d, (2.0) we have a double decker bed,

Lazaraton (1996) comments on this behaviour in relation to a different test, the Cambridge Assessment of Spoken English (CASE). She regards 'topic-priming' (as she terms it) as supportive, scaffolding behaviour, an attempt by the interviewer to make the upcoming 'interview' question understandable. However, as the strategy was found to be used by some interviewers more than others. Lazaraton argues that such variation will lead to unfairness in assessment as those candidates who are provided with this sort of scaffolding are likely to produce a better performance than those who are not given 'the benefit of assistance'.

Returning to Sequence 1, once the topic has been introduced and Esther has completed her response to the first extended-response question ('Tell me about . . .'), Pam develops it further by (again) topicalizing information provided in Esther's previous response. This happens twice in Sequence 1. In line 16 (Extract 2) Pam responds to Esther's response ('It's quite good for, suitable for me') with a newsmarker and a question that topicalizes the word 'suitable' ('Is it? What do you like about it Esther?'). This elicits a descriptive response. In line 19 again she incorporates the newly-introduced idea of 'food' ('The food is quite good but it's everyday western food') into her next question in the same way: 'Is it? What do they give you to eat?' Again, this approach to topic development is typical of Pam.

Extract 2: Tape 44 Pam/Esther

C . . . and it's: (0.5) er: quite good for: (0.8) u:m: (.) >suitable for
me;< [to live] there.
I [is it?]
I → what do you like about it Esther?
C um: (3.0) er >the food_< (0.8) yeah is: >quite good< er: but it's
(.) everyday f- western food.
I → is it? [(.) what] do they give you: to eat.
C [yeah]
C er (.) potatoes,
I oh yes.

After the three open-ended prompts in Sequence 1, Pam introduces a new line of questioning, 'eating out' (Extract 3), a topic that is conceptually related to the previous one (i.e., 'food'). As before, she first produces a closed question, in which she seeks to ascertain whether Esther eats out at all (line 27). This potential new topic direction proves to be relatively fruitless, however: Esther responds that she rarely eats out. In response, Pam produces a formulation ('So yeah that's plenty for you is it?'), a typical topic-closing move that summarizes the gist of the previous talk; in this case Esther's response that she seldom eats out because the hostel provides three meals a day.

Extract 3: Tape 44 Pam/Esther

I .hh (.) do you sometimes go and buy food?
(1.8)
C mm buy food for:_
I d'you d'you go to: (.) maybe McDona:lds or K F C?
C oh I seldom go:
I a:h y [es]
C [>be]cause< they: offer: tree meals (.) a day.
I so (.) yeah that's plenty for you [is it?] yes: yeah .hh =
C [yeah.]
I = –what else do you like about (.) living in the hostel.

Following the failed topic probe and its closure, Pam returns to the earlier topic of life in the hostel. She maintains topic continuity through a recycling of her earlier prompt, asking '*What else* do you like about living in the hostel?' and eliciting further detail in response to the earlier question. This technique for extending topics is again typical of Pam's interviewing technique.

In addition to her consistent approach to topic introduction, development and maintenance, Pam also closes topics consistently and in a way that foreshadows topic shift for the candidate. Just as she produced a formulation to close off the failed topic direction described above, she tends to close all topics with formulations or assessments. Formulations, as we have seen, are summaries of 'gist'; assessments consist of evaluations of the content of what was said (e.g., 'That's great'). In an oral interview context, moves such as these can also be considered supportive behaviours, because they indicate to the candidate that his or her talk has been understood.

Turning now to Ian's interview we find that like Pam, he starts off with a closed question, in this case an *or*-question (Sequence 2[2] below). Esther provides a minimal response, selecting one of the alternatives provided: 'More Malay'. However, rather than following this with an extended-response question as Pam does, Ian produces an echo-and-tag question ('More Malay, is it?'). Esther appears to interpret this echo as a confirmation request, as she responds with agreement, 'mm'.

Sequence 2 Tape 50 Interviewer: Ian Candidate: Esther

I >in Kelang is it- is it many Malay or there a lot of Chinese or
(.) or what is it (.) in Kelang(.) [the populations.<]
C [yeah more] Malay.
I >more Malay is it.<
C °°mm°°
I °right.° (1.2) erm (.) >what about the< foods there.
(1.2)
C er: they are Indian food (.) Chinese food (.) a:nd Malay food
[(.) th]ey are a:ll (0.8) mix.

I [mhm]
(1.0)
I they're mixed are they.
C yea:h (0.4) all mix (0.6) e:verything () hhnhhn
Iyeah? (.) >is it good that way is it.<
C yeah hhh.
(1.2)
I ah- which is the spiciest food.
C um:: (0.7) Indian.
I °°Indian°°
C °°mm°°
(0.7)
I so- (.) you're from the Chinese community yourself is that [right?]
C [yes.]
I >so do- Chinese people eat a lot of Indian food< or is it mainly
(.)Chinese food.
C oh mainly Chinese food.
(0.6)
I >but sometimes you eat Indian¿<
C e::r yeah sometimes
(0.9)
I sometimes Malay.
C mmm::
(0.9)
C yeah [hnhnhn] .hh hh. (.) not very often.
I [not often though]
I (°I see. °) (1.0) erm now tell me your plans are w-when. . .

Ian's 'acceptance' of this minimal response is followed by a long pause, which indicates that he is either waiting for Esther to add to her response or has not yet formulated a next question. Whatever the case, the pause is an indication that Esther's response was not as full as was expected. When Esther also does not take up the turn – presumably having responded to her own satisfaction, if not Ian's – Ian eventually comes out with a next question.

With this question – 'What about the foods there?' – Ian shifts topic, introducing a new referent, 'food', to replace 'people'. Given the apparent inexplicitness of the question 'What about . . .?' Esther infers, appropriately, that she is being asked about ethnic styles of food, just as the previous question asked about the ethnic mix of people. She responds accordingly, naming the foods by ethnicity. Ian responds to this naming by producing a continuer ('*mhm*') followed by a 1-second pause, which indicates that he is expecting more than the minimal response Esther has provided. When no continuation is forthcoming Ian produces yet another echo-plus-tag ('They're mixed, are they?'), despite the earlier failure of this turn-type to elicit the expected response. Yet again the echo elicits only a confirmation from Esther, this time with an upgrading of force through the added repetition of her earlier response, 'Yeah, all mix, everything'. Ian follows this response with another closed question which again – given the long pause in line 16 following Esther's response – seems to be intended to elicit an elaborated response. A further closed question also elicits a minimal response and after a pause Ian shifts the focus of the talk to a related but new area, the eating habits of ethnic groups.

Here again, Ian produces a string of closed questions and, ultimately statements, in lines 22, 24, 28 and 31, each of which appears to be intended to elicit extended responses, as can be inferred from the pauses following Esther's responses, in lines 27, 30 and 33. Again, the topic tails off without Esther having produced anything more than a repetition of input or a series of agreement tokens. In fact, at Esther's level of pragmatic interpretation, her responses are fully appropriate: she responds to the first (*or-*) question with a selected response, and to the subsequent yes–no question (line 25) and statement (line 31) with confirmation tokens. It is noteworthy that after the final long pause (line 34) she appears to understand that more is expected. She produces an elaboration on her previous response ('not very often'). This overlaps with Ian's own elaboration, 'Not often though', which precedes a shift of topic.

In Sequence 2, although Ian is obviously attempting to elicit extended responses he is less explicit in his questioning than Pam. Whereas Pam's prompts consist either of open-ended questions or requests for the candidate to produce an extended piece of talk ('Tell me about . . ., etc.), Ian's tend to be framed as closed questions or statements, or consist of ambiguous moves such as echoes and tag questions. When Esther misinterprets the pragmatic force of Ian's moves, problems tend to arise in the smoothness of the interaction and the development of the topic. The interaction is studded with long pauses that follow minimal responses by the candidate. This failure to elicit extended speech from the candidate is compounded as Ian struggles to maintain the interaction and keep the topic alive, repeatedly producing closed questions (yes–no and *or-*questions) to elicit extended descriptive responses despite their failure to do so. Again, the examples of inexplicit or ambiguous prompts and closed questions seen here are not isolated incidents; Ian uses them regularly.

As we have seen, the problems that tend to develop in Ian's interviews occur because he is inexplicit about the type of response required. Esther often misinterprets the pragmatic force of the prompts, and her typically brief responses are often followed by a long pause while Ian waits for a response or formulates his next question, and these pauses give the discourse a sense of disfluency. Despite the obvious problems that Esther has with interpreting the pragmatic force of Ian's moves, Ian does not appear to have the strategies to reformulate when she misinterprets and produces an inadequate or insufficient response.

In Pam's interviews such misinterpretations are rare, not because Esther is more 'proficient' but simply because Pam's questions tend to be more explicit than Ian's. In addition, on the rare occasion that Esther does misinterpret the pragmatics of a prompt (occurrences that indicate quite clearly that Esther herself is consistent across the two interviews), Pam has strategies that she uses to resolve the problem.

Extract 6: Tape 44 Pam/Esther

Talking about living arrangements . . .

I . . . is it very different? from: the way you lived in (.) Malaysia?
C er yeah.
I yeah. can you tell me some of the <u>di</u>fferences?

In Extract 6 Esther responds to the question 'Is it very different . . .?' literally, with 'yeah'; that is, she treats it as a closed question. Pam acknowledges Esther's response, also with 'yeah', and then represents the same prompt, but this time more explicitly eliciting an extended descriptive response ('Can you tell me . . .'). In another instance (Extract 7), after Esther responds literally twice ('Can you tell me. . . – 'yeah' and 'Can you think of . . .' – name), Pam breaks the prompt down into three separate questions, each explicitly eliciting a description: 'What does your family do?' When this also fails to elicit much, she re-presents it as 'Do you have anything special that you must do?' Despite a fairly lengthy response to this question, following a digression in which the quality of television programmes is discussed, Pam persists with eliciting a rich description of Chinese New Year activities; she continues with two more description-eliciting questions: 'What do children do?' and 'What do parents do?' Together these final prompts elicit the response sought by the original prompt ('Can you tell me about any special festivals that you have in Malaysia'). So, by breaking down unsuccessful prompts into one or more explicitly focused questions, Pam skilfully elicits an extended piece of descriptive talk from Esther. And, unlike Ian's interviews – which tend to be somewhat dis-fluent because of the frequent pauses – Pam's tend to flow relatively smoothly without long lapses.

Extract 7: Tape 44 Pam/Esther

I . . . can you: (0.5) er:(.) tell me about any special festivals that you
have; in Malaysia.
(1.4)
C oh, yeah:. =
I = any celebrations that (.) everybody ha:s at sometime during the year,
C yeah =
I = can you think of one special one?
(0.8)
C er: special one.(0.8) Chi(h)nese New Ye(h)ar,
I it is. yeah? mhm, and what does your family do:.(.) at Chinese New Year.
(0.6)
C er we will visit our relatives, =
I = mm,
C a:nd (0.7) stay at home (.) fo:r (1.5) er: waiting for:(.) er: others
people to visit us, [mhm] a:nd—(1.4) we wi:ll s:>tay at home to<:
(0.5) er watch all the er: (0.6) vide- er: >tv< programs, (0.8) they
have some very interesting tv programs; every Chinese New Year.
I → yeah? .hh (.) do you have anything special that you must do at Chinese New
Year?
C erm:
(1.6)
I → what do the- the children do in the family.
(0.8)
C mm// (0.8) we don't have to do: (.) special things. (1.5) er waiting
(.) to get (.) red pack(h)ets he he =
I → -> = you wait to get the red packets; what do the ^parents do then
at Chinese New Year.

Ian also does not demonstrate the same skill as Pam in developing topics by integrating information provided in Esther's responses into the conversation. Because his questions tend to be closed, they do not elicit new content that can be topicalized, unlike Pam's open question. His attempts to elicit more on the topic tend to consist of tokens such as echo-plus-tag in (Sequence 1, lines 4 and 12: 'More Malay, is it?', 'They're mixed, are they?'), echo in line 19 ('Indian'), and other tokens such as 'yeah?' and 'mhm'. However, just as the use of closed questions failed to elicit extended responses, these also fail in the same way. Esther appears to interpret them as either providing feedback, which she acknowledges, or as seeking confirmation, which she also gives. In other words, she responds to them minimally rather than as a request to continue.

In fact, Esther is being consistent in her interpretation of such tokens across the two interviews; she does exactly the same in the interview with Pam, providing agreement or confirmation after the tokens 'do you?', 'yeah' and 'mm' (Sequence 1, lines 6, 20, 35). The difference is simply that Pam typically provides tokens such as these as feedback and not as turn-eliciting moves. In her interviews they are almost always immediately followed by further interviewer talk, which overlaps the candidate's minimal responses and which propels the interaction forward, whereas Ian uses them as prompts, which fail to elicit elaboration and are followed by a lapse in the talk, thus slowing down the rate of the interaction. So, in his interview, these tokens and their responses do not add substantial content to the previous talk, and the talk does not progress so fluidly. Esther, as candidate, is not able to capitalize on (or does not see) the opportunity to produce substantial content; she appears reactive rather than proactive.

Ian is also both less consistent and less explicit than Pam in providing markers of structural movement from one topic to another. Whereas Pam tends to close sequences with formulations or assessments that indicate both understanding and closure, in Ian's sequence there are few such explicit structural markers. His topic shifts tend to be preceded only by receipt tokens such as 'right' or 'I see' (Extracts 8–10), which – because of their abruptness and failure to acknowledge prior talk (unlike Pam's formulations) – are not indicative of a successful elicitation of talk from the candidate.

Extract 8: Tape 50 Ian/Esther

C . . . °yeah.° so: (0.7) I: come here_
(1.4)
I → now if you study commerce here; (0.8) I imagine . . .

Extract 9: Tape 50 Ian/Esther

C . . . yeah [hnhnhn] .hh hh. (.) not very often.
I [not often though]
I → (°I see.°) (1.0) erm now tell me your plans are w-when . . .

Extract 10: Tape 50 Ian/Esther

C . . . is (1.2) is er Ma<u>lay</u> language.
(1.0)
I → right.>in K—is it . . .

Summary of interviewer techniques

Table 2 Interview management techniques

Pam	*Ian*
Structuring of topical sequences	
■ Closed question establishes topic; open question elicits extended response	■ No specific topic establishment strategy
■ Topic recycling	■ Little structural marking
■ Integration of candidate's content into next question	■ Frequent topic shift
■ Reformulation of failed prompts	■ Little integration of candidate's content
■ Explicit closure: formulations, assessments	■ Failure to reformulate failed prompts
Questioning technique	
■ Open and closed prompts explicit	■ Closed questions used to elicit extended responses (misinterpreted)
■ Tokens typically used as feedback, not prompt	■ Tokens frequently used as prompt (misinterpreted)
	■ Continuer (misinterpreted)
■ Response extension typically elicited through explicit 'next'	■ Response extension typically elicited through ✓tokens (misinterpreted)
Feedback and rapport	
■ Frequent positive feedback (newsmarkers, continuers)	■ Infrequent positive feedback
■ Demonstrations of understanding (formulations, assessments)	■ Little explicit statement of interest
■ Explicit statements of interest	

Table 2 summarizes the main differences in Pam and Ian's approaches to interview management. Pam structures topics in a way that maintains and develops them. She typically establishes the topic through closed questions, which elicit background information, following these with prompts, which explicitly elicit extended responses. She extends topics by recycling and by topicalizing information provided by the candidate, and she has strategies for repairing breakdowns that result from the candidate misinterpreting the pragmatic force of the prompt. She indicates understanding by structurally marking topic closure with formulations and assessments.

Pam is explicit in her questioning technique and regularly provides feedback as well as assessments and formulations that indicate understanding and, often, interest. She also integrates information provided by the candidate into her prompts. Ian, on the other hand, has little or no apparent topic development plan. He does not use closed and open questions systematically to introduce and maintain the topic. His moves tend to consist of closed questions, or at least questions that are interpreted as closed, and continuers that are interpreted as seeking confirmation. The pragmatic force of his questions is often inexplicit, as is the pragmatic force of tokens such as echoes and newsmarkers, which are often turn-constitutive. He also has no strategies for reformulating when prompts fail and tends frequently to react by producing further ambiguous utterances or by shifting topic.

Ian does not signal topic closure in ways other than with a single brief topic shift marker and, in addition, rarely integrates the candidate's responses into his subsequent questions, and he provides little positive feedback or other indications of interest.

Pam's style can be characterized, in general, as teacherly. She scaffolds Esther's contribution in a way that makes the communication flow and allows Esther to appear reasonably effective as a communicator. She provides explicit direction to Esther about what is expected, smoothes over problems and develops and extends topics skilfully, facilitating an effective-appearing piece of communication. Ian's style of interviewing is in some ways more 'casual' in that he uses conversational strategies to elicit talk rather than explicit questions. In this respect it reflects more closely nontest conversational interaction; however, in terms of interview management this behaviour does not support the candidate in the way that Pam's behaviour does. His questions appear to confuse Esther whereas hers draw talk out; Esther gives a substantially different performance with each of the two interviewers.

The rater protocols

Finally, in order to show how profoundly dependent the raters' views of Esther's proficiency are on the interviewers' behaviour, we turn to the raters' commentaries on their ratings. As mentioned earlier, the interviews were rated using the IELTS band descriptors for the speaking test. As raters had been told in the rater training, the overall focus is on effectiveness of communication rather than on discrete linguistic features. However, as tends to be the case in holistic scales used for the assessment of speaking – where it is important not to require the interviewer to read too much whilst interviewing – the focus is vague: 'effective', 'communicator'. The differences between the two levels are couched in unspecific and relative terms.

Retrospective verbal reports were collected from 4 of the raters for each of the interviews analysed here. Immediately after rating each interview the raters were asked to summarize their reasons for awarding that rating. A review of these verbal reports indicated that whilst raters did focus on linguistic features (such as aspects of vocabulary and grammar, or sophistication of syntax), the presence or otherwise of extended discourse was also a major concern. The raters were, in general, more positive about Esther's performance when she was interviewed by Pam than when she was interviewed by Ian. In Pam's interview Esther was characterized as being a willing and responsive interlocutor with something to say:

Extract 11: Raters' comments, interview with Pam

- 'She communicates readily and fairly precisely . . . She's quite fluent, she's got native-speaker-like features.'
- 'She had quite a high level of fluency, and, again, reasonably natural . . . She was willing to talk.'
- 'What little she said she said well . . . it was short and sharp and reasonably correct . . . and she could talk about things that are relevant to her okay.'
- 'The candidate understands every word that's coming out of the examiner's mouth . . . The candidate comes back quickly with her answers . . . I think there's a really sharp mind there, and she understands the questions immediately.'
- 'She's expressing what she wants to say quite reasonably.'

In the interview with Ian, on the other hand, there was a perception that Esther was unforthcoming or uncooperative, in that she provided only minimal responses and tended not to elaborate:

Extract 12: Raters' comments, interview with Ian

- 'Such a sort of beginners' style.'
- 'She didn't show any initiative in her answers, in taking control.'
- 'This is just the first example of many minimal chunks which I find frustrating, she just gives little, minimal answers.'
- 'For it to have been effective communication it could have been fuller.'
- 'She was very hesitant most of the time when she spoke, so you know it tended to be long pauses.'
- 'She's not being helpful, you know . . . there's no sort of purpose to what she's talking about.'

The difference between the raters' perceptions of Esther's communicative effectiveness in the two interviews is quite marked. However, given what we have seen of the different techniques used by Pam and Ian to developing and maintaining their interactions, it is hardly surprising. In the interaction with Pam, topics developed smoothly and readily because Pam was explicit in her requests for information as well as using strategies such as recycling and the topicalization of candidate input to develop topics and to elicit descriptive speech from Esther; Ether responded 'readily', as one of the raters commented. With Ian, however, responses tended to be brief and there were frequent breakdowns where Esther, it seems, misinterpreted the pragmatic intent of his moves. Whilst it could be argued that the interview with Ian provides evidence of the limitations of Esther's pragmatic competence, the issue here is fairness: these limitations are made evident in one interview but not the other. Whether or not this pragmatic competence should be tested is another question. One could argue that the ability to interpret pragmatic intent is crucial to real-world interaction; certainly in the context of these IELTS interviews it was considered important enough by the raters that it affected their judgements of communicative effectiveness.

NOTES

[1]Operational ratings are single and awarded by the interviewer himself or herself. As this is an experimental study of the effect of the interviewer on candidate performance, it was not appropriate to use the operational rating only as this would confound interviewer difficulty (in terms of challenge presented to candidate) and rater severity. For this reason, multiple ratings were elicited in order to produce stable measures of candidate proficiency.

[2]Like Sequence 1, Sequence 2 was selected because it contained features of interviewer talk that were typical of that interviewer.

Task B2.2

➤ In this study, the different interactional styles of two examiners are suggested to have resulted in different scores for the same candidate. Which features of examiner interactional style have been selected for comparison? In which ways are the interactional styles of the two examiners different?

Task B2.3

➤ The following phenomena feature in this study: validity; reliability; standardization; fairness; proficiency; communicative competence; examiner interactional style. Explain the relationship between these variables as portrayed in this study.

Task B2.4

➤ In any kind of research, it can be very difficult to prove beyond doubt to a sceptical readership that a single variable is responsible for a specific consequence: this is the issue of proving causation. Even the most rigorous research only generates plausible causal inference. For example, medical research in a number of countries had to battle for decades in the courts to prove beyond doubt that smoking causes lung cancer (and other diseases). The reason that causation is difficult to prove conclusively is that there are always other variables which could conceivably create the same consequences. In the case of smoking and lung cancer, cigarette manufacturers argued that other variables (such as air pollution) might be to blame, and that the simultaneous surges in incidence of smoking and lung cancer cases were coincidental, not causal.

Brown's study seeks to make the generalizable point that the interactional style of the interviewer in such interviews is a variable which can affect candidate scores. Although Brown makes no explicit claims of causation, the paper is designed so that a single variable (the interactional style of the interviewer) is seen to be responsible for a significantly different rating of the proficiency of the same candidate.

Are you convinced that causation has been proven in this study, i.e. that the different interactional styles of the interviewers is responsible for a significantly different rating of the proficiency of the same candidate? If so, which aspects of the study have persuaded you of this? If not, can you think of other possible explanations for the same candidate having received two significantly different ratings in the two tests? That is, are there other variables which could have produced the same effect?

Task B2.5

- This study employed triangulation of two different data types. Why was it necessary to use rater reports in addition to the CA analyses of spoken data? Do the rater reports add anything to our understanding which was not evident in the interactional data?

Task B2.6

- What are the implications of Brown's study in terms of test design and examiner training?

Section C
Exploration C1

Correlation evidence can be very simple, such as the relation between two variables (bivariate), or more complex, as patterns of correlations among a number of variables hypothesized to be interrelated, as in Ellis's study. An example should illustrate the simple bivariate case.

Consider two language learning assessment outcomes (course grades) that are collected at the end of each of two semesters. If the expectation is that the relative standing of learners on the two achievement indicators is stable, we would expect a strong correlation between the grades achieved across the two semesters. Figure 7.3 shows the distributions of course grades for the same 485 learners on the two different semesters.

We can observe that very few learners tend to get very high or very low grades and that the majority get about 80 on average in the first semester and about 77 on average in the second semester. A correlation would inform us how each learner's relative standing in the two distributions remains stable over the two semesters.

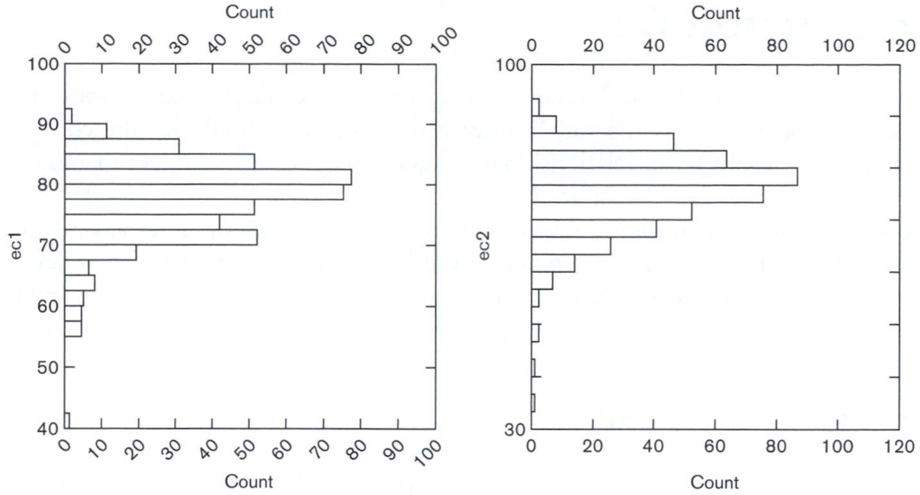

Figure 7.3 The distributions of course grades

To know this, we would first compute the mean and standard deviation for each grade:

$$\frac{\sum x}{n} = \bar{x} \text{ for the 1st grade mean, and } \frac{\sum y}{n} = \bar{y} \text{ for the 2nd grade mean.}$$

Subtracting each learner's grade from the mean of that grade, and summing the squared differences provides the basis for estimating the average variation from the mean on each grade relative to the number of learners, adjusting the fact that the data is a sample from a larger population of learners.

$\sqrt{\frac{\sum(x-\bar{x})^2}{n-1}}$ is the standard deviation (s) for semester 1 and $\sqrt{\frac{\sum(y-\bar{y})^2}{n-1}}$ is the s for semester 2

The two grades are on slightly different scales, so standardizing the grades to a Z score gives each learner's relative standing on each of the grade measures.

$Zx = \frac{x-\bar{x}}{s_x}$ for semester 1 (x) and $Zy = \frac{y-\bar{y}}{s_y}$ for semester 2 (y).

The sum of the products of the two standardized Z scores divided by the adjusted sample size gives the coefficient of correlation between the two grades for the same group of learners:

$$r_{xy} = \frac{\sum(ZxZy)}{n-1}.$$

A correlation can range from 1.0 for a perfect linear relation between an x and a y, through 0, meaning complete independence of x and y, to a –1.0, which would indicate that as x increases, y decreases proportionally.

Extension C2

The assumptions of the product–moment correlation are fairly straightforward. The two variables x and y should both be interval data and be normally distributed. They should also have a linear relationship with each other. Linearity implies that as one variable increases in magnitude, the other should increase positively or negatively correspondingly. A non-linear relation would imply that if one variable increases, the other also increases until some point is reached, and then reverses direction or begins to increase at an accelerated rate. In both cases the relation between the x and y would be non-linear. Graphical and statistical methods can be used to assess non-linearity.

RESEARCH SCENARIO C2

Let us assume that assessment researchers wish to explore the difference between achievement and proficiency. While both achievement and proficiency are measured with the use of instruments devised to assess the capacity of learners to perform particular tasks or comprehend the target language, it is possible to conceptualize achievement as being partly indicative of learners' attitude and motivation to participate in the classroom learning activities that lead to success in the tasks chosen by instructors to instantiate learning. Proficiency, in contrast, can be conceptualized as the sum effect of all previous learning experiences each learner has had, which might include naturalistic exposure to the target language.

Task C2.1

➤ Locate the SPSS data set AchProf.sav. Scroll through it and note the scales of the two semesters of achievement outcomes (ach1 and ach2), as well as the two measures of proficiency (prof1 and prof2). Note that some of the scores are very high or very low. These could indicate that the score data is missing. In such cases, it is important to insert a 'missing' code before any analysis is attempted.

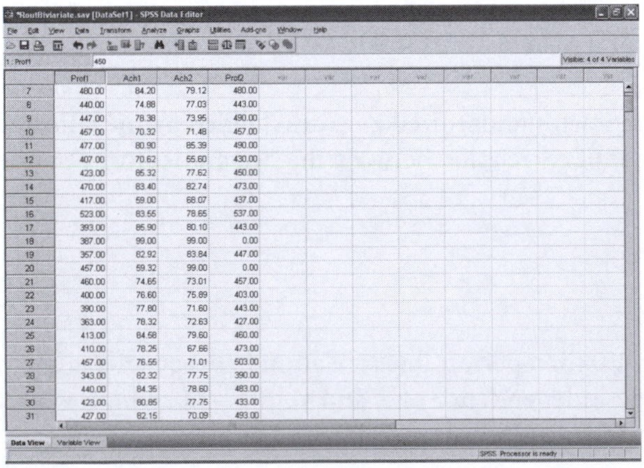

	Prof1	Ach1	Ach2	Prof2
7	480.00	84.20	79.12	480.00
8	440.00	74.88	77.03	443.00
9	447.00	78.38	73.95	490.00
10	457.00	70.32	71.48	457.00
11	477.00	80.90	85.39	490.00
12	407.00	70.62	55.60	430.00
13	423.00	85.32	77.62	450.00
14	470.00	83.40	82.74	473.00
15	417.00	59.00	68.07	437.00
16	523.00	83.55	78.65	537.00
17	393.00	85.90	80.10	443.00
18	387.00	99.00	99.00	0.00
19	357.00	82.92	83.84	447.00
20	457.00	59.32	99.00	0.00
21	460.00	74.65	73.01	457.00
22	400.00	76.60	75.89	403.00
23	390.00	77.80	71.60	443.00
24	363.00	78.32	72.63	427.00
25	413.00	84.58	79.60	460.00
26	410.00	78.25	67.66	473.00
27	457.00	76.55	71.01	503.00
28	343.00	82.32	77.75	390.00
29	440.00	84.35	78.60	483.00
30	423.00	80.85	77.75	433.00
31	427.00	82.15	70.09	493.00

Figure 7.4 Data layout for Achprof.sav

Reprint courtesy of International Business Machines Corporation, © SPSS, Inc., an IBM company

At the bottom left corner of the data sheet two tabs indicate which view is currently open. Click on the Variable View tab to inspect the types scales used and the set up for defining 'missing' data.

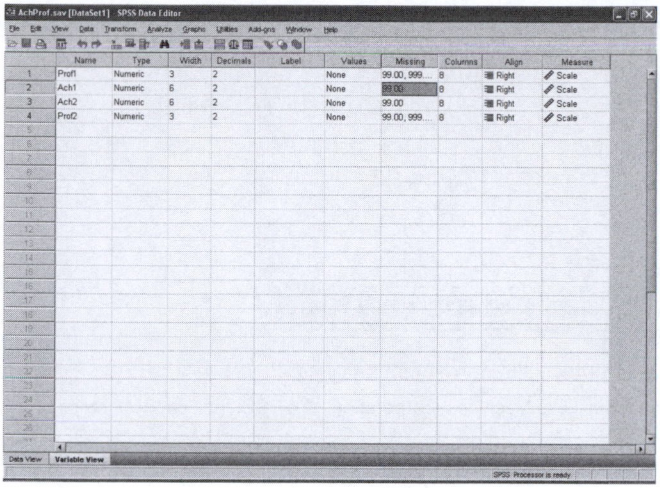

Figure 7.5 Variable view for Achprof.sav

Reprint courtesy of International Business Machines Corporation, © SPSS, Inc., an IBM company

Click on any of the Missing cells and new window will appear. Any range or discrete set of values can be indicated to mean that the data for that cell is missing.

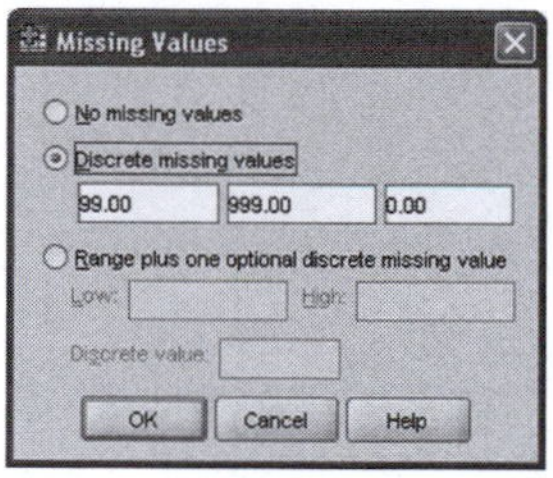

Figure 7.6 Specification of missing values

Reprint courtesy of International Business Machines Corporation, © SPSS, Inc., an IBM company

Once missing data has been identified, the correlation analyses can begin. As in the Ellis (2005) study, it will be useful to examine a pattern of inter-correlations among the four variables. Under the Analysis menu, we will select the Correlate and Bivariate options.

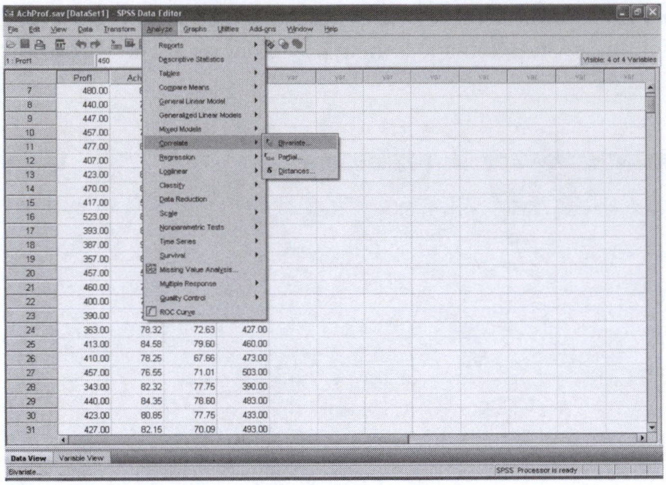

Figure 7.7 Pull-down menu for bivariate correlation analysis

Reprint courtesy of International Business Machines Corporation, © SPSS, Inc., an IBM company

Next, move all four of the variables, two achievement scores and two proficiency scores for the sample in the study into the analysis box. Assuming that the variables are normally distributed and linearly related to each other, we will select Pearson, and a two-tailed test. At this point we have no specific hypothesis to predict if the correlations will be positive or negative, or to what magnitude, so both directions of the possible correlations are plausible.

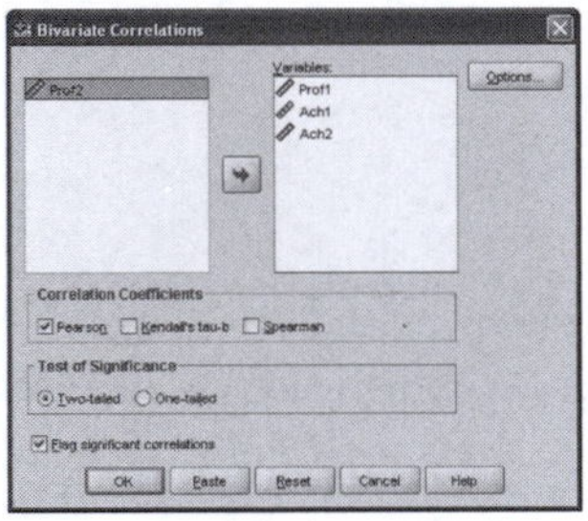

Figure 7.8 Variable selection for correlation analysis

Reprint courtesy of International Business Machines Corporation, © SPSS, Inc., an IBM company

The correlation matrix with the four variables reveals that all of the correlations are significantly higher than zero and are unlikely to be a matter of randomness. It shows that the sample size varies across the sample.

Table 7.1 Matrix of correlations among achievement and proficiency

		Prof1	*Ach1*	*Ach2*	*Prof2*
Prof1	Pearson correlation	1.000	.202**	.248**	.728**
	Sig. (2-tailed)		.000	.000	.000
	N	458.000	439.000	432.000	407.000
Ach1	Pearson correlation	.202**	1.000	.693**	.390**
	Sig. (2-tailed)	.000	.000	.000	.000
	N	439.000	439.000	430.000	405.000
Ach2	Pearson correlation	.248**	.693**	1.000	.386**
	Sig. (2-tailed)	.000	.000	.000	.000
	N	432.000	430.000	432.000	407.000
Prof2	Pearson correlation	.728**	.390**	.386**	1.000
	Sig. (2-tailed)	.000	.000	.000	.000
	N	407.000	405.000	407.000	407.000

** Correlation is significant at the 0.01 level (2-tailed).

Task C2.2

➤ Visually inspect the matrix of correlations and spot which pairs of variables have the highest correlations. Speculate as to why these pairs would be relatively more correlated with each other than with other pairs in the matrix.

Task C2.3

➤ It is often useful to visualize the correlation between two variables. Returning to the two course achievements, each learner's grade outcome in the first semester (Ach1) can be plotted against his or her grade outcome in the second term (Ach2). Using the Graphs menu, scroll down to the scatterplot option.

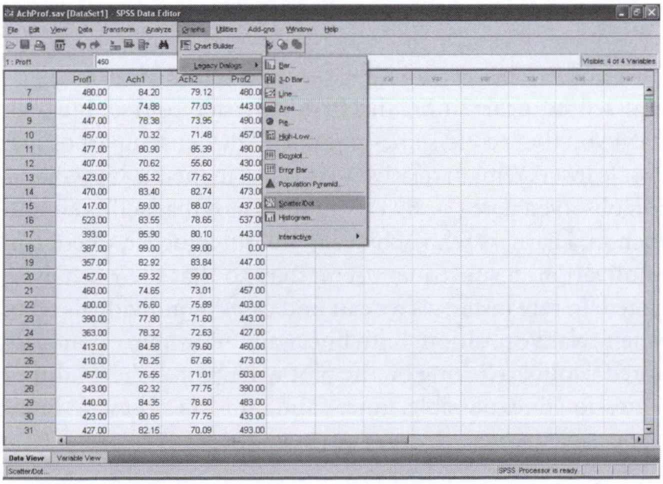

Figure 7.9
Pull-down menu for scatterplot

Reprint courtesy of International Business Machines Corporation, © SPSS, Inc., an IBM company

Select the Simple Scatterplot option and move the Ach2 to the vertical (Y) axis and Ach2 to the horizontal (X) axis in the analysis window.

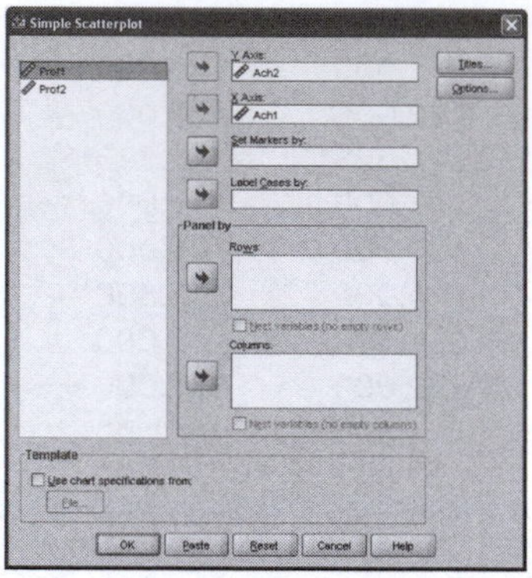

Figure 7.10 Variable selection for Scatterplot display

Reprint courtesy of International Business Machines Corporation, © SPSS, Inc., an IBM company

The resulting scatterplot shows the positioning of each grade. A perfect correlation would find all dots located on a 45-degree angle, which would indicate that grades remained constant in their relative standing, but not necessarily in absolute magnitude.

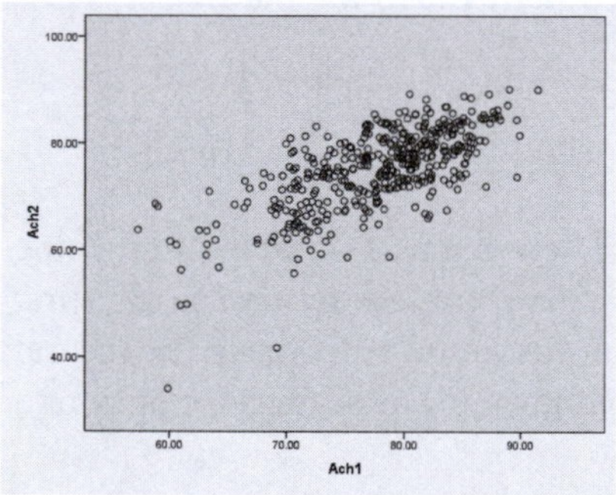

Figure 7.11 Ach 1

The scatterplot often shows outliers, or cases that fall far from the 45-degree angle. For instance, one student scored near 70 on the first semester course, but fell precipitously to just about 43 on the second semester grade. The densest part of the scatterplot shows that most learners remain relatively constant in their achievement outcomes. The correlation observed here (r=.693) would suggest that achievement is a fairly stable phenomenon. Learners who achieve good outcomes in one term tend to maintain their motivation in subsequent semesters so that their achievements are strongly correlated. In rare instances we can find cases of individuals who for some reason change their relative position. Both linear and non-linear trends in a scatterplot can be explored. Double clicking on the plot will open a Chart Editor, which makes different regression lines possible. Linear and non-linear best-fit lines can be added to examine possible trends.

Task C2.4

➤ Ellis used a form of factor analysis to test his hypothesis that the five measures he constructed measure two latent factors: implicit and explicit knowledge. In the AchProf.sav data set, four variables are available for analysis. The correlation matrix in Task C2.2 could suffice for a 'visual factor analysis', although a thorough analysis would require more exploration. To that end, we will reuse the same data set and generate an exploratory factor analysis. We will explore because we do not have an a priori hypothesis about the structure of the interrelations among the variables in the matrix.

First, we need to locate and open the Factor option under the Data Reduction menu.

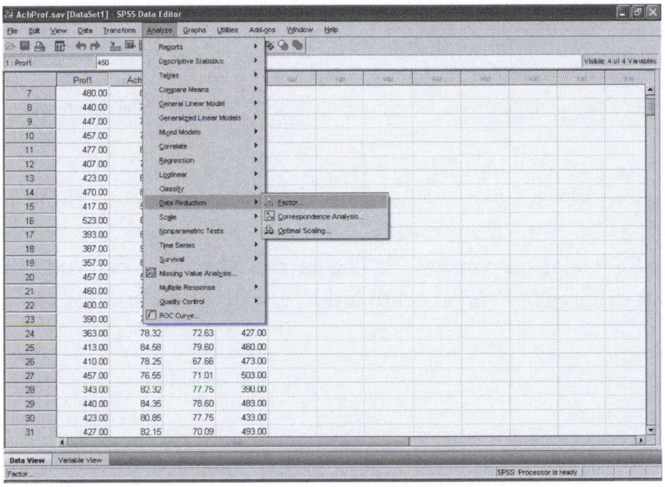

Figure 7.12 Exploratory factor analysis of Achprof.sav

Reprint courtesy of International Business Machines Corporation, © SPSS, Inc., an IBM company

Factor analysis 'reduces' the set of observed variables into a smaller number of latent factors that may be plausible reasons why the variables cohere as inter-correlated subsets. In the present case, there are four measures, but an unknown number of latent variables.

We open the Factor Module and move our four variables into the analysis window.

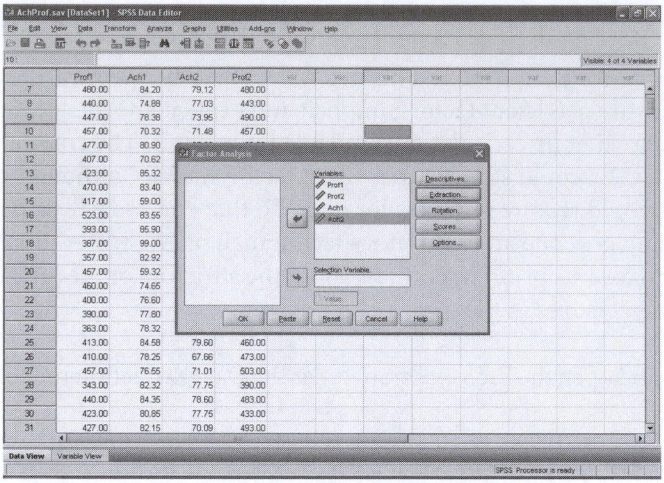

Figure 7.13 Variable selection for exploratory factor analysis

Reprint courtesy of International Business Machines Corporation, © SPSS, Inc., an IBM company

As we are in exploratory mode, we can extract as many latent factors as there is evidence for. The default extraction rule is to let SPSS find as few factors as possible to explain the clusters of correlations observed. The extracted factors can then be rotated to the maximum difference (Varimax) to aid in visual differentiation.

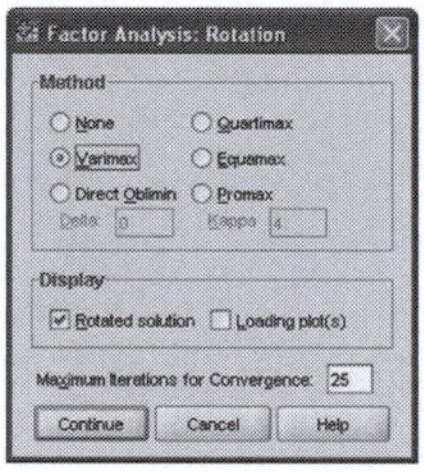

Figure 7.14 Rotation specification

Reprint Courtesy of International Business Machines Corporation, © SPSS, Inc., an IBM Company

For the Achievement and Proficiency data set, there is evidence of two latent variables. Together they account for about 86 per cent of all the variance in the small data set.

Rotated matrix	***Component***	
	Component	
	1	*2*
Prof1	.062	.942
Prof2	.294	.882
Ach1	.905	.153
Ach2	.900	.165

Task C2.5

- Examine the Component matrix and consider what labels would apply to Component 1 and Component 2.

Task C2.6

- Use the correlation matrix above Task C2.2 and create an SPSS Syntax file like the one created to replicate the Ellis study. Run the factor analysis from the syntax module and compare the results to the analysis done in Task C2.4.

Factor analysis has many forms and many options. It is wise to carefully consider which type of factor analysis to use. If a particular theoretical model is to be tested, it has become conventional to use a confirmatory factor model approach instead of the exploratory approach used by Ellis, and in the above example. In the confirmatory approach, the data is compared to what a pre-specified model (see the Chapter 1 section on nomological networks) predicts about the covariance structure of the latent variables. Note that in the exploratory mode, the number and composition of the latent variables are the result of the data analysis. A robust theory is one that makes predictions about the way interrelations among data from the real world will look even before corroborating data is gathered. The research process is then to collect authentic data to compare with the theory about the composition of the constructs, and the covariance structures among them. Mismatches between theory and data are generally taken as criteria for refutation of the theory. If the process is reversed, and theories are constructed post hoc to account for patterns in data, the problem that generally arises is that the data and theory become indistinguishable.

Exploratory factor analysis is generally permissible when there is no clear theory to guide a priori predictions about what the data of the natural world should look like in terms of a nomological network or set of relations among the variables of interest. Factor analysis is thus in general a method for examining questions of relations rather than theories of causation.

Extension C 3

In this chapter we have seen that it is actually a difficult undertaking to ensure precise alignment between the construct being researched and the processes used to research it. Any kind of language proficiency test is in effect a piece of research which attempts to access the construct of a candidate's proficiency (or a component of it) based on their language production.

Task C3.1

- Design a project to test the extent to which 'proficiency' is a stable construct. First identify from your own experience factors which might possibly affect candidate proficiency in a test. One example might be the degree of tiredness of a candidate. Then design a study to see whether such factors do have an impact on candidate proficiency as measured by a common language proficiency test.

Task C3.2

- Design a speaking test in such a way that the interactional styles of different examiners can have no (or negligible) impact on the candidates' scores.

Task C3.3

- Recent trends in speaking assessment increasingly use computerized delivery of tasks and prompts. Many computer-delivered speaking tasks are interlocutor-free and use picture stories, repetition of phrases, and indicators of verbosity to measure speaking. The validity evidence for these tests is that they tend to correlate with live interview ratings. Discuss this criterion for validity and consider how in your view the speaking proficiency construct would optimally be assessed.

Task C3.4

- In this task we consider a different construct, namely that of 'fluency'. Everyone has a common-sense notion of what fluent speech sounds like, but the question is how its characteristics can be identified for use in research.

- You should investigate the construct of 'fluency' by examining learner spoken data. Design a project in which you gather spoken data from learners and devise a system for differentiating different learner levels of fluency. Which characteristics of talk are relevant to evaluating fluency? How might these characteristics be measured?

CHAPTER 8
Mixed-methods studies and complexity

In each of Chapters 2–7 we have compared two studies which approached the same issue using a different methodology. In Chapter 8 we conclude by broadening and diversifying the scope and the perspectives. The main focus throughout the chapter is on how methodologies can be combined in a mixed-methods approach. We consider the impact on language learning research of complexity theory, with its proposal that mixed-methods approaches are suitable to the study of complex systems. In a final section, we consider how fundamental conceptual issues such as validity, epistemology and ontology are conceived through the lenses of the three different methodologies which we have seen employed in Chapters 2–7.

The focus in this chapter is therefore on the following questions. What are the characteristics of a complexity theory approach to research in language learning? How can different methods be combined within a mixed-methods approach? How are fundamental conceptual issues viewed in different methodologies and to what extent are they compatible?

Section A
A1 Complex systems

In this section, the focus is on the characteristics of a complex systems approach. This is followed in Section B by an extract from Larsen-Freeman and Cameron (2008) on how such an approach may be applied to research in language teaching and learning. This approach is very much in its infancy, with Larsen-Freeman's first major article on the subject appearing in 1997. However, since this appears to be the way that research is now moving, it is important for students to understand what is involved.

What does the study of complex systems have to do with language learning and teaching? Language teachers have for countless ages been puzzled by questions like these: Why is it that L2 grammatical development does not always proceed in a straight line, but sometimes stagnates and spurts and even regresses? How can it be that when the same teacher teaches the same lesson to two parallel classes at the same level, with one class the lesson is a triumph whereas with the other it is an abject failure? Why, when you give students specific instructions, do they do something rather different? Why is the IRE pattern ubiquitous throughout the world? A complex systems approach offers a means of understanding why many phenomena in language teaching and learning unfold in a non-linear way.

Read the following characteristics of complex systems (adapted from Seedhouse 2010). Compare these with your own knowledge of language development as a system. Would you say that language development displays a) none of the characteristics of a complex system, b) some of the characteristics of a complex system, c) all of the characteristics of a complex system?

Complex adaptive systems share certain crucial properties:

Self-organization and adaptation of many interacting agents

Coherent, self-organizing clusters at one level combine to form new and different clusters at a higher level. They are adaptive, in that they do not just passively respond to events. For example, the human brain constantly organizes and reorganizes its billions of neural connections so as to make sense of experience.

Non-linearity

In non-linear systems, small changes in the external environment can produce large changes in the system. Non-linear systems express relationships that are not strictly proportional. An example of a non-linear system is the weather, where a minute event can result in major changes to weather systems.

Surface complexity arising out of deep simplicity

Extremely simple systems can generate extremely complex and intricate patterns. This occurs because systems interact with their environment, react to feedback from their environment and feed back on themselves. They are therefore able to self-organize and form new organizations at more complex levels.

Sensitivity to initial conditions

In non-linear systems small inputs can lead to dramatically large consequences and very slight differences in initial conditions can produce very different outcomes.

Complex systems adapt using feedback from the environment and from themselves

Systems receive feedback from their interactions with the environment and organize and adapt themselves accordingly. As the system evolves in time, minute changes amplify rapidly through feedback. So systems starting with only slightly differing conditions rapidly diverge in character at a later stage. This explains non-linearity, or how it is that tiny differences in initial states can produce radically different outcomes.

Complex adaptive systems arise from the interaction of their parts and function as a whole which is more than the sum of its parts

The organization of the complex adaptive systems is created from the non-linear interactions of numerous much smaller elements. So complex adaptive systems cannot, in general, be successfully analyzed by isolating properties or variables that are studied separately and then combining those partial approaches. Instead, it is necessary to adopt a holistic perspective and look at the whole system.

Complex adaptive systems display self-similarity on various scales and levels

The patterns or shapes of complex adaptive systems look similar from different scales, perspectives and levels. This property of endlessly manifesting a motif within a motif is known as self-similarity, which implies that any subsystem of a fractal system is equivalent to the whole system.

A2 Mixed-methods research

In this section, the focus is on how different methods can be combined within a mixed-methods approach.

INTRODUCTION

The growth of interest in mixed-methods research (also known, among other things, as multi-strategy research, multi-method research or just mixed research) over the last decade has been perhaps the most marked trend in approaches to research; in fact, one writer has gone so far as to claim that 'the range and variety of typologies has reached the point where these exercises have become almost too refined' Bryman (2006: 98). Although the products of this new development are thin on the ground in our own area, it seems very clear that mixed-methods research will continue to grow in importance and that an understanding of it will be essential, in our field as elsewhere.

For this reason, we offer an introduction to such research in this section. Of necessity this will concentrate on issues of definition and description, but our intention is not to present an overview of the typologies available or a list of hotly-debated issues; instead we aim to develop an accessible introduction that will not only convey a sense of what mixed-method (henceforth MM) research involves and the options within it, but also serve as a guide to exploring the topic further. Since the terms 'quantitative research' and 'qualitative research' will feature frequently in the discussion, we abbreviate them here to QTR and QLR respectively (the abbreviations that tend to be used for 'quantitative' and 'qualitative' are QUAN and QUAL, which will also feature). We will not review the history of MM, but anyone interested in this will find Johnson *et al.*'s (2007: 113–118) brief overview, beginning with Socrates and Plato, illuminating.

Task A2.1

- Which two of the data collection methods introduced in this book do you think are most likely to feature in mixed-methods research? Why do you think this might be and what might be the dangers involved in combining these methods?

The first and probably most important point to make is that mixing quantitative and qualitative approaches demands an understanding of the conceptual foundations and procedural demands of the approaches chosen. What counts as QLR or QTR should be based on the foundations established in this book and not be merely token nods towards something that might count as qualitative or quantitative (we summarize fundamental conceptual orientations at the end of Section C). For example, dipping into responses to open questions on a questionnaire and grouping these impressionistically does not amount to QLR, any more than QTR boils down to counting the number of times 'high-', 'low-' and 'medium-ability' students ask vocabulary questions in a single lesson and comparing the raw figures. This may seem like obvious advice, but the practice is sufficiently widespread to cause concern among some researchers. Denzin (2010: 420), for example, warns that '[p]ersons who are less familiar with the rich traditions of qualitative inquiry are telling others with the same lack of experience how to do qualitative work.'

In a survey of mixed-methods research, Bryman (2000) found that surveys and qualitative interviews account for the 'vast majority' of such research, something you may have predicted in your response to the above task. The reasons for the popularity of these two forms of data collection are fairly obvious. As we saw in Chapter 4, for example, interviews can play an important part in survey design, so the connection is a natural one. Looked at from a different perspective, qualitative interviews can prompt questions that the researcher decides could be profitably explored using a much wider population. However, the familiarity of the two approaches can bring its own dangers. As we also saw in Chapter 4, qualitative interviewing is very demanding and it is all too easy to settle for a superficial analysis instead of a rigorous process designed to identify key themes. Similarly, survey design has developed sophisticated methods that may not be apparent to a novice quantitative researcher. A good example here is the process of identifying a 'random sample', something that is treated quite casually by some qualitative researchers but which calls for very specific procedures.

DEFINITION OF MIXED-METHODS RESEARCH

Such preliminary considerations aside, the use of MM must be based on an understanding of what the term 'mixed-methods research' represents and what options are available within it. In their analysis of 19 definitions of the term by leading researchers, Johnson *et al.* (2007) demonstrate how considerations such as what is mixed, the timing (i.e. the stage in the research process), breadth, purpose and orientation all inform the nature of the definition offered. These dimensions will be considered below, but the first step must be to settle on a definition that will allow a preliminary point of orientation. Given that Johnson *et al.*'s definition of the term represents a synthesis of so many alternative formulations, there is a strong case for accepting their characterization:

> Mixed methods research is the type of research in which a researcher or team of researchers combines elements of qualitative and quantitative research approaches (e.g. use of qualitative and quantitative viewpoints, data collection, analysis, inference techniques) for the broad purposes of breadth and depth of understanding and corroboration.
>
> (Johnson *et al.* 2007: 123)

Task A2.2

- As you will know from previous chapters, ethnography and CA are both qualitative in their orientation, which means that according to the above definition their combination would not count as mixed-methods research. Reflecting on the differences between them, can you think of any arguments in favour of treating them as mixed methods?

Three things stand out from the above definition. The first is that the term should be reserved for research in which QTR and QLR are combined. In what follows we will adopt the standard position because it is relatively unproblematic. However, there are very strong arguments in favour of not limiting the definition in this way. In your response to the above task, for example, you may have reflected on some quite fundamental differences between CA and ethnography. For example, while CA resolutely refuses to accept the analytic relevance of respondent validation, this is fundamental to ethnography. The CA position is that all the evidence required for analysis is in the talk itself and that retrospective interpretation by any of the participants is not inherently reliable (we will tend to remember the talk from our own point of view and may also have personal reasons for representing something in a particular way), while ethnography is keen to seek participant views, even though it subjects these to careful analytic scrutiny and is careful to treat them as part of a much wider picture. We also saw in Chapter 6 how ethnography draws on aspects of the wider context while CA insists that only those aspects of context made relevant by participants in their talk can be treated as analytically relevant.

These differences reflect quite fundamental differences between the two approaches, and some would wish to argue that when combining them we need to apply the same consideration as those appropriate to MM. This is the position that Morse (2010) takes up in making her case for extending the term 'mixed-methods' research to combinations within QLR. She argues, for example, that CA could be supplemented by focus groups, the former providing 'documentation of dialogue' (a description that many CA researchers would find odd) and the latter 'group experiential data', thus producing a 'QUAL(CA) + *qual* (focus group)' design (2010: 487). She provides an excellent illustration of how this might work in a project designed to investigate the telling of bad news by doctors. Here, CA analysis would be used to understand how the relevant talk was designed, while telephone interviews with patients would be used to determine what they had heard. Morse suggests that the data collected in these ways could be kept separate and combined only in the write-up of results. Her arguments are interesting and in many ways persuasive, though the claim that in such research 'one of the components is complete and forms the theoretical base and the other component supplements the core component' (2010: 491) is slightly problematic in view of the fundamental differences between ethnography and CA identified above (it could be argued, of course, that using interviews is not in itself ethnographic, but then neither is it sanctioned within CA). Nevertheless, the case for describing suitably designed projects within either QTR or QLR as MM research is a strong one and is accepted by many researchers. Mason (2006) for example, argues that it offers a useful way of responding to the challenge of using context, an issue that was highlighted in Chapter 6.

Other aspects are more straightforward. The second point that emerges from Johnson *et al.*'s definition is that 'methods' is not restricted to data collection and analysis but extends to other aspects of the research process such as the perspective of the researcher. Finally, and perhaps more obviously, such research seeks both corroboration and deeper understanding. How this is achieved, however, is a bone of contention in MM. In an editorial that is a model of concision and clarity, Creswell and Tashakkori (2007) identify four different perspectives on this sort of research, which might be summarized as follows:

Method	The focus here is on data collection, analysis and interpretation, setting aside paradigmatic considerations.

Methodological	Here the emphasis is on the whole process of research, from philosophical assumptions through to the presentation of findings. This approach is best exemplified in Teddlie and Tashakkori (2008)
Paradigm	Rejecting the more practical orientation of the above perspectives, in this view what matters most is the philosophical underpinning of the approach.
Practice	This is diametrically opposed to the paradigm perspective, adopting a 'bottom-up' approach which sees the need for mixed methods as emerging during the evolution of a project.

While the authors themselves admit to embracing all these perspectives at one time or another and express no preferences, it is probably fair to say that they would be most sympathetic to the Methodological approach. While recognizing the value of this, the emphasis in what follows will be on the first of their perspectives because of the decision in this book to emphasize the core elements in the research process. While a practice perspective might seem at first sight to suit this orientation, the ad hoc aspects of this make it a poor candidate for consideration here.

Before moving on to the choices facing mixed-methods researchers, it is worth adding a brief note on the concept of *pragmatism*. This is important because it often rears its head in debates about paradigmatic issues in mixed-methods research. Denscombe (2008: 273–4) summarizes the different positions that have been taken up on this matter, but the essential point to note is that the use of the word in this context refers to philosophical positioning and not mere expediency. Whether pragmatism represents a new paradigm to be set next to current paradigms or a radical alternative to these is a matter for debate – but that it represents something foundational is not at issue.

TACKLING A MIXED-METHODS PROJECT

The first and most important requirement for mixed-methods research is a confident grasp of both QLR and QTR, the foundations for which have been laid in this book. Beyond that, two other forms of preparation are advisable. The first is familiarity with all the options within MM, which can be developed by consulting some of the excellent introductions available (e.g. Creswell and Piano Clark 2007, Greene 2007, Teddlie and Tashakkori 2008) and exploring further via relevant journals (e.g. *Journal of Mixed Methods Research*) or papers in Tashakkori and Teddlie's (2003) core collection.

The second form of preparation involves seeking out MM studies with a view to understanding their design and the decision-making involved. Here it can be very helpful to represent in diagrammatic form the design used in the study. Not everyone likes diagrams, but they provide an acid test for MM design: if you are unable to represent your study in visual form then you probably do not have a clear grasp of the steps involved, the elements in it and the relationships among them. The use of diagrams in MM is, in fact, so common that advice is available about how to draw these and some standard notation has emerged. Drawing on earlier work, Ivankova *et al.* (2006) propose 10 guidelines for producing effective diagrams (reproduced in Creswell and Piano Clark 2007). These include fitting the diagram onto a single page, keeping it simple, including a title, employing arrows and boxes, and using concise language.

The notation involved was originally developed by Morse (1991) and reflects core decisions that need to be made in the design of MM studies. One of the decisions, for example, involves the status of the two elements and this is represented by the use of capitals and lower case, so that 'QUAL' with 'quan' would indicate that the qualitative element had greater emphasis in the study than the quantitative one, whereas QUAL with QUAN would represent equal emphasis. The timing of the elements is also captured by the use of symbols: when the two methods are used at the same time the symbol '+' is used, but when the methods are used in a sequence the order of this is represented by using '→'. Finally, brackets are used to indicate that one element is enclosed within another, so 'QUAN(qual)' would indicate that qualitative methods were embedded (some writers use 'nested') within quantitative methods.

In what follows we introduce key considerations in planning and implementing a MM project. In addition to offering you an overview of the process, they will also provide you with the tools you need to interpret studies you read and represent these diagrammatically using the notation just described.

In some respects, MM is no different from other forms of research. Greene's (2006, 2008) oft-cited four domains of MM should by now be familiar to you and require no gloss:

1. Philosophical assumptions;
2. Inquiry logics (the methodological dimension);
3. Guidelines for practice (tools and techniques for data collection, analysis, etc.);
4. Sociopolitical commitments (location of the research within a particular society – interests, power relations, etc.).

Of course, the way these play out in the context of MM is rather more complex than in other forms of research because there are so many dimensions and decision points involved. Inevitably, this has produced a plethora of typologies and no generally agreed position. What follows is not even intended as a general representation of the situation, let alone a definitive position, but it covers the main elements and provides a basic checklist of relevant aspects. It ignores some aspects (e.g. how many strands or phases might be involved) where the basic meaning of these is obvious and it does not attempt to address the complexities of implementation –

for this you will need to consult more extensive treatments such as those indicated above. The resulting list has five elements.

1 *Rationale*

At first blush this seems very straightforward; after all, no researcher would plunge into MM without a clear idea of why they were doing so and what the benefits were likely to be. Put on the spot, then, the researcher should be able to give clear reasons for using MM in this particular case. However, there are a number of reasons why this aspect cannot simply be taken for granted. It is never possible to predict, for example, how research – especially qualitative research – will develop and the researcher needs to be sensitive to unfolding opportunities. In any case, as Bryman notes (2000: 98), the MM aspect might be introduced at any stage in the research process, from question formulation, through data collection and analysis, to interpretation. There are examples where MM are not part of the original design but are introduced only when their potential contribution becomes apparent. In her description of how 'unwanted noise' (scribbled comments etc.) in standardized surveys offered interesting insights and prompted a shift to qualitative analysis, for example, Feilzer (2010) provides an interesting example of qualitative data emerging from a quantitative research tool.

This may well be why Teddlie and Tashakkori (2006: 13) insist that the function of the research study 'is not a design issue, but is related to the function that the results from the study eventually serve'. Nevertheless, at some stage, it will be possible to state clearly the reason for using a MM approach and in many cases this will remain unchanged from the design stage. The following examples from the five studies cited by Creswell *et al.* (2006: 6) provide a good flavour of what such reasons look like:

- Improve an intervention design;
- Develop a model to explain a process;
- Validate quantitative results;
- Develop an instrument;
- Provide a means to examine trends in a national study.

2 *Design*

There is no shortage of advice on this and opinions naturally differ on how best to approach a MM project. However, the classification proposed by Creswell and Piano Clark (2007: 59–79) has the virtue of being both clear and practical (their description includes a table of alternatives which conveys a sense of how cluttered the field is). It relies on a division into four broad categories within which more specific models can be developed: Triangulation, Embedded, Explanatory and Exploratory. What follows is a very brief gloss on these terms; the original provides a more detailed explication of these and variations within them.

Triangulation design	This brings qualitative and quantitative methods to bear on a research problem in a single phase in order to better understand it. Typically, the researcher collects the data separately but at the same time, then brings them to bear on the problem, giving each element equal weight.
Embedded design	In this, one data set plays a secondary role, providing valuable support for the main study. For example, qualitative data might be embedded within an experimental design to develop a treatment (one-phase) or to develop a treatment then to follow up after the intervention (two-phase). The distinguishing feature of this design is that the results of the secondary data type are useful or meaningful only in the context of the other data set.
Explanatory design	This two-phase sequential design begins with a quantitative study which is then followed by a qualitative phase designed to throw light on or build on the quantitative outcomes of the first phase. Quantitative data is normally, though not necessarily, prioritized. A typical example of such research would be a quantitative survey study with a qualitative follow-up designed to explore some of the findings in greater depth or throw light on anomalous results.
Exploratory design	This is also a two-phase sequential model, but here the project begins with qualitative research. It would be useful in research designed to develop and test a new instrument or in order to generalize results to different groups, for example. An example of such research might be a project in which CA has revealed that two different forms of prompt in oral tests produce two very different sorts of response. This can then be investigated quantitatively across different populations to see whether the discovery is generalizable.

3 *Implementation*

As we saw when considering design issues, data can be used either sequentially (as in the explanatory model) or concurrently (as in the triangulation model). The importance of this for project design and planning are obvious, though in two-phase projects it might be necessary to adjust the original plan as the research develops.

4 *Weighting*

This refers to the degree of importance attached to each of the data sets. These might be given equal weight or one might be given priority over the other (as in an embedded design). Although this is something that should be considered at the outset, relationships might change as the research evolves, which is why Teddlie and Tashakkori (2006: 13) insist that the priority of a methodological approach cannot be decided in advance: 'In the real world, a QUAN + qual study may become a QUAL + quan study if the qualitative data become more important in understanding the phenomenon under study, and vice versa.'

Some researchers working in QLR have argued that the qualitative dimension tends to be introduced in only a subsidiary role. Hesse-Biber (2010: 457), for example, provides evidence to support the claim that current mixed-methods practice tends to favour quantitative research. However, these claims have been challenged by a number of researchers working in MM (see, for example, Creswell *et al.* 2006), who insist on the value of QLR and of the primacy of research aims. While it is as well to be aware of this debate, nobody has yet advanced arguments claiming that one approach or another *should* be given primary status and in the absence of such arguments decisions about the relationship between different methods should be informed by the demands of the relevant project.

5 *Mixing*

Within the designs described above, decisions need to be made about how the data are to be brought together. Johnson *et al.* (2007: 125) argue that all mixed-methods research requires 'some form of integration' but the nature of such integration in terms of what alternative approaches might deliver is as yet poorly understood. It is therefore perhaps not surprising to find some scepticism about the ways in which some researchers approach this. Flick (2002), for example, claims that many MM studies end up as 'one-after-the-other', 'side-by-side' or 'dominance' approaches which do not properly respond to the requirement for integration. The temptation to produce two sets of results and draw general conclusions from these therefore needs to be resisted and careful thought should be given to how the different sets might most effectively be exploited.

Different approaches to this have been proposed, though again Creswell and Piano Clark's (2007) characterization represents a fairly standard position, based on three options:

Merged/converged The researcher brings data from both sets together, merging them either at the analysis stage (by consolidating the data or transforming one data type into the other type) or at the interpretation stage after separate analysis.

Connected/linked One set builds on another. The connection occurs when one type of data leads to the need for a different type and it may take different forms (e.g. one form of connection would be selecting participants for qualitative interviews on the basis of survey results).

Embedded/nested One set is embedded within another. This might be done concurrently, or one data set might be collected after the other (sequentially). Hesse-Biber (2010: 457) gives an example of a 'nested' approach where quantitative closed-ended questions were embedded within primarily qualitative in-depth interviews.

There are various ways in which these options might be managed (e.g. using interim results of analyses in one data set to inform analysis in another) or represented (integrated or separate) and the best way of exploring the relevant options is through reading relevant research. However, if you are familiar with both SPSS and NVivo you should find Bazeley's (2003) description of how these can be used together very interesting.

Ultimately, what matters most is that when we adopt a mixed-methods approach we do not see it merely as a question of combining qualitative and quantitative approaches or of following standard models or procedures; instead, we should treat it as an opportunity to explore the potential of different perspectives on the research process. The value of MM, as Greene (2007) observes, lies in its potential to develop a dialogue between different ways of seeing, interpreting and knowing.

Task A2.3

➤ Study the following extracts in terms of the descriptions provided in this section and try to identify what information the author provides about this as a mixed-methods study (e.g. in terms of timing, rationale, etc.). Our interpretation is provided at the start of Extension B2.

This was a two-phase, sequential mixed-methods study (Creswell, 2003) with quantitative survey data being collected first, followed by semistructured qualitative interview data. The survey component of the study was intended to test the hypothesis, derived from the literature, regarding how factors such as group cohesiveness and group norms correlate with individual learners' L2 motivation in terms of self-efficacy and learner autonomy. Semistructured interviews were employed to describe, from the learners' point of view, the role the class group plays in an individual learner's L2 motivation.

(Chang 2010: 135)

Triangulating quantitative survey data with a more detailed illustration from the language learners through interviews allows the researcher to gather qualitative data to 'explain or build upon initial quantitative results' (Creswell and Clark, 2007, p. 71) . . . the aim of this mixed-methods study was for complementarity (discovering different facets of an event), where the researcher looks for elaboration and illustrations in the results of one method and interweaves those results with another method . . . The need to explore the relationship between group processes and L2 motivation from the perspective of language learners led to the necessity of conducting semistructured interviews to address the qualitative research question

(Chang 2010: 136)

Section B
Extension B1

Task B1.1

➤ Read the extract below from: **Larsen-Freeman, D. and Cameron, L. (2008) 'Research methodology on language development from a complex systems perspective,'** ***The Modern Language Journal*** **92(2): 200–213.**

Changes to research methodology motivated by the adoption of a complexity theory perspective on language development are considered. The dynamic, nonlinear, and open nature of complex systems, together with their tendency toward self-organization and interaction across levels and timescales, requires changes in traditional views of the functions and roles of theory, hypothesis, data, and analysis. Traditional views of causality are shifted to focus on co-adaptation and emergence. Context is not seen as a backdrop, but rather as a complex system itself, connected to other complex systems, and variability in system behavior takes on increased importance. A set of general methodological principles is offered, and an overview of specific methods is given, with particular attention to validity in simulation modeling

In this article, we wish to consider ways of researching language development from a complex systems perspective. A complex system is one that emerges from the interactions of its components. The components can be agents or elements. An example of the former would be a flock of birds, which emerges from the interactions of the individual birds that compose it. An example of the latter would be air currents, moisture, and temperature interacting to yield a weather system. Complex systems are often heterogeneous, being made up of both agents and elements. The ecosystem of a forest would include, as component agents, animals, birds, insects, and people; component elements would include trees, winds, rainfall, sunshine, air quality, soil, and rivers. Not only are there many agents and elements in a complex system like an ecosystem, but they are of different kinds.

Some complex systems, such as the stock market, are dynamic and nonlinear. They are dynamic, in that the worth of stocks changes over time, sometimes continuously, both up and down. They are nonlinear, in that at other times, the systems change suddenly and discontinuously. These systems are open to outside influences; in the case of the stock market, it is open to new investments or to changes in regulations. Following a precipitous decline in the stock market, if new investments are forthcoming, the system is said to self-organize, generating new, emergent modes of behavior from the investments that are being made.

Chaos/complexity theory has been used to study complex, dynamic, nonlinear, open systems, including naturally occurring systems, such as the weather and the rise and fall of animal populations. More recently, it has also been applied to human behavior in, for example, the disciplines of economics and epidemiology. Although predator–prey interactions influencing animal populations and the spread of disease are, of course, different in many ways, they have in common dynamical properties of change.

Many of the phenomena of interest to applied linguists can be seen as complex systems as well (Larsen-Freeman, 1997). Applied linguistic complex systems are likely to contain many subsystems, nested one within another. For example, if we see the speech community as a complex system, then it will also have within it sociocultural groups that themselves function as complex systems; individuals within these subgroups can be seen as complex systems, as can their individual brain systems. There are complex systems at all levels, from the social level to the neurological levels. The complexity of a complex system arises from components and subsystems being interdependent and interacting with each other in a variety of different ways.

Because applied linguists deal with complex dynamic systems, we think complexity theory offers a helpful way of thinking about applied linguistic matters (Larsen-Freeman, 1997; Larsen-Freeman & Cameron, 2008). We use complexity theory as an umbrella term to include not only complexity theory, but closely related chaos theory, dynamic(al) systems theory, and complex systems theory. It also relates well and therefore embraces ecological approaches that adopt an analogy between complex ecological systems and human language using/learning systems (Kramsch, 2002;). Although complexity theory has originated in and benefited greatly from work in the natural sciences, there is certainly a material difference between applied linguistics and the natural sciences with respect to objects of inquiry. However, the question we entertain in this article is whether the difference is as clear when it comes to 'methods of inquiry' (Gaddis, 2002, p. 113). To address this question, we will first discuss how complexity theory warrants changes from traditional research that tests hypotheses in order to identify causes for particular events. Then, we will offer some general methodological principles for investigating language development from a complexity theory perspective. Last, we will make some suggestions for how to take extant methods and apply the new principles to them so that they are relevant for a new ontology. Central to all aspects of these discussions is the dynamic nature of complex systems – change and variability become the heart of what is investigated.

Task B1.2

➤ What are the characteristics of a complex system? Which complex systems appear to be associated with language development? What exactly is a complex systems perspective? Which areas of research methodology might be changed if one were to adopt such a perspective?

Methodological principles for researching language and language development

From this complexity theory perspective, certain methodological principles follow. In the complexity approach that we adopt, it is important

1. To be ecologically valid, including context as part of the system(s) under investigation;
2. To honor the complexity by avoiding reductionism, and to avoid premature idealization by including any and all factors that might influence a system;
3. To think in terms of dynamic processes and changing relationships among variables, by considering self-organization, feedback, and emergence as central;
4. To take a complexity view of reciprocal causality, rather than invoking simple, proximate cause-effect links;
5. To overcome dualistic thinking, such as acquisition versus use or performance versus competence, and to think in terms of co-adaptation, soft assembly, and so forth;
6. To rethink units of analysis, identifying collective variables (those variables that characterize the interaction among multiple elements in a system, or among multiple systems, over time);
7. To avoid conflating levels and timescales, yet seek linkages across levels and time scales, and include thinking heterochronically; and
8. To consider variability as central, and investigate both stability and variability in order to understand the developing system.

Modified research methodologies

We now move to consider practical implications of the complexity theory perspective for the empirical investigation of language development, such as measuring the effectiveness of pedagogic interventions or tracking stabilities and variation in learner language. When enacted, some of the methodological principles cited previously will no doubt lead to innovations of which we are currently unaware. Some methods, however, are already in existence with designs that make them useful for investigating complex systems. Other methods will need some modification.

Ethnography

In many ways, qualitative research methods, such as ethnography, would appear to serve the understanding of language as a complex dynamic system well, in that they 'attempt to honor the profound wholeness and situatedness of social scenes and individuals-in-the-world' (Atkinson, 2002, p. 539), by studying real people in their human contexts and interactions, rather than aggregating and averaging across individuals as happens in experimental and quantitative studies. Agar (2004) went further, arguing that ethnography is itself a complex adaptive system, that evolves and adapts as the researcher uses it:

> [It] will lead you to ways of learning and documenting that you had no idea existed when you first started the study. You will learn how to ask the right question of the right people in the right way using knowledge you didn't know existed. You

> will see that certain kinds of data belong together in ways that you would never have imagined until you'd worked on the study for awhile . . . methods 'evolve' as local information about how to do a study accumulates. Ethnography does this. Traditional research prohibits it.
>
> (p. 19)

It is important to note that ethnographers seek emergent patterns in what they study. Agar suggested that ethnography is a fractal-generating process. What ethnographers are looking for are processes that apply iteratively and recursively at different levels to create patterns, variations that emerge from adaptation to contingencies and environment.

One possible modification of ethnographic method, from a complexity theory perspective, however, is the assumption that, when applied effectively, ethnography can produce objectivity. From our perspective, no matter how a researcher tries, total objectivity – a view of matters apart from who he or she is – can never be achieved. A complex system is dependent on its initial conditions, and these conditions include the researcher. Accounts of the 'same' phenomenon will differ when produced by different ethnographers (Aga, 2004). This finding, of course, is not a problem, just a fact.

Combinations of methodologies

Combinations or blends of methodologies would seem to be particularly appropriate to the study of complex systems, allowing different levels and timescales to be investigated. We outline three possibilities.

Discourse analysis and corpus linguistics. Large corpora of language use give us access to stabilized patterns and variability around them. Although we acknowledge that a corpus is a static collection of attested language and cannot show the dynamics of language as it unfolds in use or its future potential, a corpus can serve to some extent as representative of the language resources of members of the speech community where it was collected. We can then combine corpus linguistics with close analysis of actual discourse, to trace the genesis and dynamics of language patterns, such as the conventionalization and signaling of metaphors (Cameron & Deignan, 2006).

Second language acquisition and corpus linguistics. The field of second language acquisition (SLA) needs to make more use of computer-searchable longitudinal corpora for addressing theoretical issues. Myles (2005) advocated the use of Child Language Data Exchange System (CHILDES) tools for SLA research. Mellow (2006) illustrated the impact of large new computerized corpora such as CHILDES and TalkBank on theories of second language learning.

Second language acquisition and conversation analysis. Conversation analysis (CA) attends to the dynamics of talk on the microlevel timescale of seconds and minutes. In a recent special issue of *The Modern Language Journal* (Markee & Kasper, 2004), it was argued that joining a CA perspective on interaction with a long-term view of language development holds great promise. CA offers a rich description of 'the most basic site of organized activity where learning can take place' (Mondada & Pekarek

Doehler 2004, p. 502). If these analyses were to be done with a sufficient density so that retrospective microdevelopmental analyses could be conducted, it would offer another means of connecting synchronic dynamism to its over-time counterpart.

Conclusion

Clearly, each of the approaches just discussed has advantages and drawbacks. CA offers an in-depth view of conversational interaction, but it ignores any insights that a conscious introspection would permit. Corpus linguistics offers rich usage data, but the data are attested; they do not demonstrate the potential of the system. Other approaches, such as brain imaging and neural network modeling, illustrate or simulate the dynamic patterns of brain activity, but do so by isolating the learner's brain from society and from its normal ecology of function. Computer models might be more encompassing in this regard, in allowing for a social interactive dimension, but they, too, involve ecologically reduced ways of representing reality.

We began this article by asking whether the methods of inquiry of the natural sciences would work for applied linguists whose theoretical commitment is to understanding complex, dynamic systems. We have pointed out that different assumptions (e.g., about causality) underlie traditional research methods used in both the natural and the social sciences and have discussed those methods that are perhaps the most suitable for a complexity theory perspective.

What we can aspire to at this point is to entertain the principles we have enumerated earlier in this article while blending and adapting methods, a trend that is increasingly adopted across the social sciences. It should not be surprising that researchers are entertaining the possibility of using multiple blended methods. It is, after all, a pragmatic solution to the demands of a theoretical perspective that seeks to understand the dynamics of change in complex systems.

***The Modern Language Journal* 92, ii (2008) 0026-7902/08/200-213 1.50/0**

Task B1.3

➤ Reflect on your own experiences of language learning and teaching. Identify any phenomena which seem to you to be behave in a non-linear way.

Task B1.4

➤ Do you feel it would be more straightforward for you to conduct your research using a complex systems perspective or a more traditional perspective? Why? Can you see any disadvantages to a complex systems approach to language learning research?

Task B1.5

- The article suggests that combinations of methodologies would be particularly appropriate to a complex systems perspective. Why do you think that is? Which combinations do Larsen-Freeman and Cameron propose?

Task B1.6

> A good application of complexity theory describes the system, its constituents, their contingencies, and also their interactions. Teasing out the relationships and describing their dynamics are key tasks of the researcher working from a complex systems perspective.
>
> (Larsen-Freeman and Cameron 2008: 203)

- To what extent do you think the three approaches we have explored in this book might respond to this? For example, how might the understanding of individuals derived from fieldwork (interviews and observations) combine with the analysis of specific interactions, and both of these with studies aggregating aspects of such behaviour? (You might like to compare your thoughts with the section on second language acquisition and conversation analysis in the Larsen-Freeman and Cameron paper.)

> In many ways, qualitative research methods, such as ethnography, would appear to serve the understanding of language as a complex dynamic system well.
>
> (Larsen-Freeman and Cameron 2008: 206)

- From what you have learned about ethnography in this book, what reasons would you advance in support of this claim? (You might like to check your thoughts against the authors' own development of this statement.)

> Combinations or blends of methodologies would seem to be particularly appropriate to the study of complex systems, allowing different levels and timescales to be investigated.
>
> (Larsen-Freeman and Cameron 2008: 210)

> complexity theorists are interested in understanding how the interaction of the parts gives rise to new patterns of behavior
>
> (Larsen-Freeman and Cameron 2008: 201)

In the first of these quotations Larsen-Freeman and Cameron seem to be suggesting that mixed-methods research is particularly compatible with complexity theory; in the second they are talking more generally. But if the interaction of parts gives rise to new patterns of behaviour, how might this impact on mixed-methods design, where the interaction of parts is fundamental? Most mixed-methods design is linear, even where it accepts that new data or developing analysis might prompt radical revision of the original plan. In the light of complexity theory, to what extent do you think this approach is tenable? Is it time for a radical shift in the way mixed methods are conceived and if so what shape might this take?

Extension B2

In Section A you were asked to look at a description of a research project (Chang 2010) and identify how the author represented it as a mixed-methods study. The following analysis may not correspond exactly to your own, but you should be able to identify at least some points of overlap and, more importantly, see how well the study is positioned.

> This was a two-phase, sequential mixed-methods study (Creswell, 2003) with quantitative survey data being collected first, followed by semistructured qualitative interview data. The survey component of the study was intended to test the hypothesis, derived from the literature, regarding how factors such as group cohesiveness and group norms correlate with individual learners' L2 motivation in terms of self-efficacy and learner autonomy. Semistructured interviews were employed to describe, from the learners' point of view, the role the class group plays in an individual learner's L2 motivation. (p. 135)

Identifies design

Discusses timing

Identifies contributions of each element (which suggests the weighting)

> Triangulating quantitative survey data with a more detailed illustration from the language learners through interviews allows the researcher to gather qualitative data to 'explain or build upon initial quantitative results' (Creswell & Clark, 2007, p. 71) . . . the aim of this mixed-methods study was for complementarity (discovering different facets of an event), where the researcher looks for elaboration and illustrations in the results of one method and interweaves those results with another method . . . The need to explore the relationship between group processes and L2 motivation from the perspective of language learners led to the necessity of conducting semistructured interviews to address the qualitative research question . . . (p. 136)

Provides a rationale for the design

Discusses mixing

Identifies this as an explanatory design (follow-up)

(Chang 2010)

The next task, however, involves a study that is not presented as MM but as a case study, even though it involves both qualitative and quantitative dimensions. This will therefore present a rather more challenging task in terms of description than the above, which was set out as a MM study. Unusually, the appearance of the paper below was followed by a critique published in the same journal, parts of which you will be invited to consider.

Task B2.1

➤ Read the following extract from Basturkmen *et al.* (2004) and try to decide how you might describe it as a MM study. In order to do this you should focus on the two data collection methods described in full here and you will need to know that 'observation' involves the categorization and quantification of features of the lesson (student initiations, teacher elicitations, aspects of linguistic focus such as vocabulary and pronunciation, etc.). Setting aside considerations of mixing methods, you might also consider what criticisms, if any, you might make of the design of this research.

RESEARCH QUESTIONS

Our research questions were as follows:

1 How do teachers practise incidental focus on form?
2 What beliefs do teachers hold about incidental focus on form? To what extent are these beliefs internally consistent?
3 To what extent are teachers' beliefs about incidental focus on form congruent with their observed practices.

Method

Teaching context and participants

This study focuses on the practices of three teachers. It is part of a larger study (Loewen 2002) investigating focus on form in intact classes with different teachers all from the same private language school in Auckland, New Zealand. The full data set consisted of 48 lessons from 12 teachers, from 40 to 65 minutes in length. In recognition of the fact that individuals have their own interpretations of what constitutes communicative teaching, the researcher simply asked to observe lessons that the individual teachers themselves considered to be communicative. No effort was made by the researcher to guide the teachers in their choice of lesson plans. Following the observations, a second researcher interviewed the teachers to elicit their stated beliefs of focus on form in communicative teaching.

In the school there is a set of 'communicative tasks' prepared in-house that teachers can elect to use. During the original observations, the researcher noticed that three teachers used the same communicative task (the Prisoner Task as shown in Appendix A [not included here]). This provides the opportunity to investigate the stated beliefs and practices of these three teachers in relation to their use of the same instructional material. That is, it allows us to compare teachers' practices while keeping the task variable constant. The observational data for this study, then, consists of one lesson for each of the three teachers, using the same task, and in the same school.

The three teachers were all male, native speakers of English. Table 1 shows their experience in teaching ESL, the length of time they had been at the school, as well as their ESL qualifications and the class they were teaching. The teachers are listed in order of teaching experience.

Table 1: Teacher and class information

Teacher	*Teaching experience (years)*	*Time at the school*	*ESOL qualifications*	*Class*	*Number of students*
Steve	15	5 years	Diploma	Upper intermediate level 1	7
Mark	11	4 months	Certificate	Intermediate level 4	8
Rick	1	1 year	Certificate	Intermediate level 3	12

No demographic information, apart from nationality, was gathered from the students; however, students at this school averaged 22 years in age and came to New Zealand to study English for a variety of reasons, including preparation for academic study and professional development (Director of Studies, personal communication). The students participating in the study came from a variety of countries with a majority (over 75 per cent) from Korea, China, Japan, and Taiwan.

Data collection

The study involved a combination of observational and self-report data. The observational component involved observation of the teachers' lessons. The self-report component comprised statements of beliefs about focus on form elicited from teachers through the use of in-depth interviews, cued response scenarios and stimulated recall. These instruments will now be described in further detail.

Observations of lessons

One researcher was present as a non-participant observer in the naturally occurring communicative lessons of the teachers at the school described above. Each lesson was audio-recorded using a wireless clip-on microphone that was attached to the teacher. This arrangement allowed the researcher to record all teacher-student interaction during the class, including talk between the teacher and individuals, pairs, small groups as well as the whole class. The lessons were transcribed in their entirety.

[Introduction to self-report data methods omitted]

(a) *In-depth interview*. The first part of the interview was based roughly around a semi-structured interview protocol. This involved some closed item lead-in prompts that aimed to focus the respondents' attention on the subject at hand. The main items were open-ended. Open-ended items have the added advantage of eliciting ideas expressed in the respondents' own words (Oppenheimer 1992). The principle that guided the design of the interview was to avoid direct questioning in favour of indirect items. For example, we did not ask the teachers what a good communicative lesson should be like, but rather asked them to recall a successful communicative lesson they had recently taught. See Appendix B for sample questions from the in-depth interviews [not included here].

[Details of cued-response scenarios and stimulated recall omitted]

Basturkmen *et al.* (2004: 247–250)

Clearly, any description of this must be provisional since, as the authors note, it is part of a wider study. However, it is immediately clear that the study includes both quantitative (observation) and qualitative data and in this respect it deserves to be considered MM research. The representation of the research questions suggests that this is not embedded research, something borne out in the description that follows, and also implies that equal weighting is assigned to each of the data sets. Although there is no reason why interviews and observation cannot run concurrently, there are obvious advantages in completing observation first (at least on an individual basis), and the stimulated recall can only have followed observation, so we can confidently identify the approach as sequential. It would seem, then, that we can represent the design as follows: QUAN→QUAL. From the research questions and the description of the project, we would expect the data sets to be analyzed and represented separately, and then compared in order to answer the final research question.

Task B2.2

➤ Now read the following criticism of this design and compare it with your own notes. To what extent do you think it is justified (references to parts of the paper not included in the above extract will not be considered)? You might like to evaluate these criticisms in the light of the authors' own claim that Basturkmen *et al.* 'warn of the hazards of researchers' allowing their own views to impinge on their findings (pp. 249–51) but ironically fall prey to this tendency themselves.' (Sheen and O'Neill 2005: 269). Paragraphs have been numbered for ease of reference.

[1] The New Zealand school is private and, therefore, dependent on satisfying the desires of its students who are mainly Japanese and Chinese, who do not adapt well to SCLT mainly because of the dissonance between it and their cultural and academic traditions (Butler 2004; Sakui 2004). Such schools are, therefore, obliged to adopt more traditional grammatical syllabi with the addition of communicative activities which hardly function as examples of SCLT, as becomes clear from the remarks of teachers (pp. 259–62). In fact, those remarks, coupled with the situation in which the teachers find themselves and their natural tendencies to be practical in the face of the problems they face, justify the conclusion that they adopt an eclectic approach.

[2] Support for these claims is as follows: (a) the use of communicative activities is optional (p. 248); (b) a grammatical syllabus (see, for example, p. 267, 'previously taught grammatical structures') is such an important feature that communicative activities are partly seen as a means of practising them (see the remarks of Rick and Steve, p. 267); (c) most importantly, the teachers' approach is not limited to

the constraints of a focus on form. This raises the question as to whether the meaning of this term was established by the interviewers of the teachers. As the authors make no mention of such clarification, it is possible that the teachers and the interviewers were talking at cross purposes in discussing focus on form. Thus, given their eclectic approach, the teachers' responses to interviewers should be interpreted more as expressions of opinions about form-focused instruction rather than about focus on form. Further, their classroom interventions must be seen as different from those entailed in IFF as perceived by the authors because of the context of an explicit grammar syllabus which is a constant source of reference for the teachers. In addition, their various comments indicate that they resort at times to explicit teaching of grammar and vocabulary in communicative lessons.

[3] This point (c) is of crucial relevance as the word 'incidental' may have a fundamentally different meaning in a 'focus on form' as defined in the article and in the understanding of the teachers whose communicative lessons are *not* communicative in the sense established in the article but in the sense of providing opportunities for the practice of grammatical structures. Note here (b) above, and the teacher Rick's mention of his use of 'manipulation' to provoke 'incidental' use of an item (p. 262). Therefore, 'incidental' becomes a term with degrees of meaning including intentionally selecting to do communicative tasks in order to provoke the need to use features of the grammatical syllabus. This casts doubt on the authors' ability to decide what is 'incidental' in their terms and what is not. This, coupled with the ambiguity in the use of the term focus on form, raises serious doubts as to the reliability of the findings of the study.

Sheen and O'Neill 2005: 270

What seems to us to be most striking about this extract is the extent to which the authors allow their own views to 'impinge on their findings'. The first paragraph, for example, contains a number of inferences for which no evidence is provided (our comments are in italics):

- Because the New Zealand school is private it is dependent on satisfying the desires of its students.
  This is a naive, even insulting, view of the nature of language education and one which denies agency to the management and staff of the school. Basturkmen et al. *state that there are a 'variety of reasons' why students attend the school and that these include preparation for academic study. It is not unreasonable to assume that, rather than dictating content on the basis of their own 'desires', such students might trust the school to make appropriate educational decisions.*
- The students are mainly Japanese and Chinese.
  The statement that over 75 per cent are from Korea, China, Japan and Taiwan does not warrant this claim.
- Such students do not adapt well to SCLT because of academic and cultural dissonance.
  The authors quote evidence for this claim, but such essentialist statements should be treated with considerable caution. There is evidence from countries such as China (Zheng and Adamson 2003), Korea (Mitchell and Lee 2003) and Vietnam (Ha 2004) that stereotypical views about resistance to CLT are misguided.

Of the three points (a, b and c) raised in the second paragraph, two are also open to challenge. Although the use of communicative activities is optional, the research focuses on communicative episodes and as trained teachers these participants would be unlikely to find this problematic. Similarly, 'previously taught grammatical structures' cannot be taken to imply a grammatical syllabus, any more than 'previously taught communicative activities' would necessarily imply a communicative syllabus. The third point leads to the observation that the meaning of 'focus on form' may not have been clarified at the start of the interviews, but this ignores the fact that these were open-ended and avoided direct questioning. Beginning by highlighting this aspect as particularly significant might have distorted the data obtained. Nevertheless, Sheen and O'Neill do raise legitimate points about the problem of interpreting 'incidental' and their criticisms point to the need to provide detailed background information in studies of this kind.

In order to allow you the opportunity to get a better sense of how the data were presented and the proposed links established, we will end with extracts relating to one of the participants in the study. First, though, here are Sheen and O'Neill's (2005: 271–272) comments on the classroom extract involved:

> Surely, it is plausible that the teacher's intervention may have been caused by the failure to understand fully both 'thief' and 'theft' and is not *only* concerned with the former as the authors contend. This is supported by the fact that the student does not apparently understand the teacher's question containing the word 'theft' and that the teacher's subsequent interventions are intended to elicit the word 'thief' possibly as a means of enabling the students to understand the word 'theft'. The intervention may have been provoked by a problem of meaning and is, therefore, neither an example of inconsistency nor of concern with the accuracy of meaning of the word 'thief' as is contended (p. 255). Furthermore, it *is* an example of IFF not counted by the authors as both the students immediately concerned and, more importantly, the rest of the class may not have understood either the words 'thief' or 'theft'. Of course, such conjecture could have been obviated had the article provided the necessary context and an appropriate analysis.

Task B2.3

- The following extracts are designed to give you a sense of how quantitative and qualitative data can be represented and brought together analytically. Sheen and O'Neill's comments raise interesting questions about the extent to which exchanges can be extracted from longer passages of talk and what constitutes 'necessary context'. You might like to consider this in the light of the data presented. In terms of what you have learned about CA, you might also like to reflect on the legitimacy or otherwise of inferring mental states (e.g. what a teacher 'wishes') from recordings of interaction. More generally, you could reflect on the effect of space limitations on data presentation, comparing how much can be represented in tabular form with how open-ended interviews are treated (a comparison with an interview study would be revealing in this respect). Our own view is that in the circumstances the authors manage a fair mix of general summary and teacher voice, but you may have different views.

Example 3

Episode		*Characteristics*	*Category*
T:	so if he has committed theft what is he	Type	Teacher-initiated
S1:	um he was in prison for 2 years	Linguistic focus	Vocabulary
T:	yeh that's where he was, what do we call a person who commits theft?	Complexity	Complex
S2:	Thief	Source	Code
T:	Thief	Response	Elicit
S1:	Thief		
T:	Yeh ok		

Example 3 shows the teacher initiating an episode about an item of vocabulary ('thief'). There has been no problem in understanding meaning; however, the teacher wishes to improve the student's ability to use the language accurately (code). The teacher does this by eliciting the form from the students, rather than by providing it for them. The episode is complex as it involves the teacher and students in more than one turn each.

(Basturkmen *et al.* 2004: 254–255)

Mark

The following are the main themes to emerge from the analysis of Mark's beliefs about focus on form:

- Mark referred mostly to pronunciation and vocabulary rather than to grammar in discussing his ideas about communicative instruction. For example, in response to one scenario, Mark emphatically stated 'Pronunciation is important!' He also talked about helping students when they are struggling with vocabulary as a legitimate 'time-out' from actual communication.
- He felt that students should try their best to solve language problems for themselves rather than asking him: 'I do prefer them to work things out' (response to scenario 2). His lack of enthusiasm for student-initiated language queries was revealed again in his response to stimulated recall episode 2: 'If I was asked directly . . . it would be unfair of me not to give them a word . . . so if I am asked directly I suppose I usually give them the answer'.
- Mark saw communication as paramount. He made statements, such as: 'communication is more important than going into linguistic forms', 'I don't like to impede communication unnecessarily (response to scenario 4) and 'I didn't want to stop the communication' (stimulated recall).
- Corollaries of this belief were (1) that time-outs from communication to deal with linguistic form should be as short as possible and unobtrusive; and (2) time should be taken out from communicative activities to deal with issues of language form only when necessary for understanding. He stated 'I will actually allow linguistic form to lie dormant, and I will allow communication to continue. But if I

Table 5 FFE characteristics (Basturkmen *et al.* 2004: 258)

Teacher	*Type*			*Complexity*		*Response*			*Linguistic Focus****			*Source*	
	Reactive	*Student-initiated*	*Teacher-initiated**	*Simple*	*Complex*	*Provide*** *recast*	*Inform*	*Elicititation*	*Vocabulary*	*Grammar*	*Pronunciation*	*Code*	*Message*
Steve	13	16	2	11	20	9	20	2	13	10	6	25	6
	(41.9%)	(51.6%)	(6.5%)	(35.5%)	(64.5%)	(29%)	(64.5%)	(6.5%)	(44.8%)	(34.5%)	(20.7%)	(80.6%)	(19.4%)
Residual	−3.8	3.8		−2.4	2.4	1.6		−1.6	.9	−.6	−.4	−.4	.4
Mark	16	6	4	18	8	15	10	1	12	5	7	19	
	(61.5%)	(23.1%)	(15.4%)	(69.2%)	(30.8%)	(57.7%)	(38.5%)	(3.8%)	(50.0%)	(20.8%)	(29.2%)	(73.1%)	(26.9%)
Residual	.2	−.2		1.9	−1.9	1.8		−1.8	1.4	−2.1	.8	−1.6	1.6
Rick	41	6	3	28	22	29	8	13	13	24	10	45	
	(82%)	(12%)	(6%)	(56.0%)	(44.0%)	(58%)	(16%)	(26.0%)	(27.7%)	(51.1%)	(21.3%)	(90.0%)	(10.0%)
Residual	3.3	−3.3		.5	−.5	−3.0		3.0	−2.0	2.3	−.4	1.8	−1.8
N		98		107			107			100		107	
df		2		2			2			4		2	
χ^2		15.82		6.75			9.08			7.05		3.70	
p		001		.034			.011			.331		.157	

* Teacher-initiated FFEs were not included in the chi-square analysis due to low cell counts.
** Recasts and Informs were combined as Provides for the chi-square analysis.
*** Spelling FFEs ($n = 7$) were excluded from this table.

feel some obstacle is impeding the flow of communication, then I think it is very important to stop' (in-depth interview).

Mark appeared to be inconsistent in his beliefs about error correction. Although he stated a preference for not stopping the flow of communication, he also referred to the importance of helping students with pronunciation and vocabulary. He stated his preference for providing error correction after a communicative activity via some whole-class activity (in-depth interview). However, he also stated a preference for recasting, a technique allowing the teacher to provide linguistic information indirectly and unobtrusively. When presented with examples of recasts in the interview, he stated that this type of response was 'definitely typical of me. . . . Yeah that's typical to actually give them the word without it seeming like I'm giving them the word' (stimulated recall). Elsewhere in the interview, Mark stated a preference for student self-correction (for example in response to scenario 5). One possible explanation for these apparent inconsistencies can be found in his statements of belief about affective variables (for example his appraisal of the class mood and of the confidence of individual students) affecting decision making about whether to do error correction.

The relationship between Mark's stated beliefs and his practice showed a mix of congruence and incongruence. Congruent with his stated beliefs, more of the FFEs initiated by Mark were concerned with pronunciation (29.2 per cent) and vocabulary (50 per cent) than grammar (20.8 per cent). Table 5 shows also that, largely in line with his stated views on student queries about language forms, there were few instances of student-initiated language queries (23.1 per cent) in Mark's lesson. It is also possible that the behaviour of Mark's students in this respect reflects their perceptions of their teacher's attitude to this aspect of focus on form. Additionally, Mark stated that timeouts from communication to deal with language form issues should be as short as possible and unobtrusive. Table 5 shows this belief was reflected in his practice. The FFEs in his lesson were predominantly short and simple (69.2 per cent).

There were also some of Marks' [*sic*] practices that seemed incongruent with his beliefs. Although Mark clearly indicated that he thought he should attend to form only when there was a breakdown in communication, the great majority (73.1 per cent) of the FFEs in Mark's lesson had their source as code, and only 26.9 per cent of the episodes arose because of difficulties in understanding (see Table 5). Also, his actual practice of error correction did not accord closely with his stated beliefs. Table 5 shows that Mark often interrupted the flow of the activity to focus on error correction on the spot (61.5 per cent), whereas he had in fact stated that he believed error correction was best done after the task was finished. He responded to errors with recasts (as indeed he claimed he did), but he rarely used elicitation to allow students to self-correct even though he had indicated the desirability of doing this.

(Basturkmen *et al.* 2004: 260–261)

Section C: Exploration

Preliminary tasks C1

Task C1.1

➢ Revisit the research questions examined in Chapter 1 and other chapters. Consider whether and how these could be answered using a complex systems approach.

Task C1.2

➢ Look at the research studies included in Chapters 2–7 of this book. Decide whether each article is currently compatible with a complex systems approach or not. In the case of studies which are not compatible, consider whether it would be possible to make changes to the research design, replicating the study to make it compatible with a complex systems approach.

Task C1.3

➢ Read Lyster's (2004) study in Chapter 5. Now design a similar study, but employ mixed methods in your research design. This should be set in your own teaching context to answer the following research questions: Which type of error correction is more beneficial to the development of a specific target language structure? What are the characteristics of interaction produced by different types of error correction? How do different types of error correction promote opportunities for the development of the target language structure? How do learners display uptake of the types of error correction?

Task C1.4

➢ Design a mixed-methods study to answer the following research questions: How do the motivations of learners in your teaching context change over the course of one/two years? Identify internal and external factors which might be associated with the changes.

➢ After completing your design, you may wish to read an example of this type of study: Lamb, M. (2007) 'The impact of school on EFL learning motivation: An Indonesian case study, *TESOL Quarterly* 41, (4): 757–780.

Task C1.5

➤ Design a mixed-methods study to achieve the following research aims. Choose a group of learners who have gone to study in a different country and culture. Identify the critical influences on their intercultural adaptation. Examine how these influences impact on them during their stay overseas.

➤ After completing your design, you may wish to read an example of this type of study: Gu, Q., Schweisfurth, M. and Day, C. (2010) 'Learning and growing in a "foreign" context: Intercultural experiences of international students', *Compare: A Journal of Comparative and International Education* 40(1): 7–23.

Conceptual issues C2

In this section, we consider how a number of fundamental conceptual issues are perceived through the lenses of the three different methodologies which we have seen employed in Chapters 2–7. The previous chapters have shown how each of the methodologies has been employed to investigate a range of phenomena, but the descriptions that follow reveal how the same term (e.g. validity) can be interpreted in subtly different ways according to the research orientation adopted. An awareness of such differences is very important in mixed-methods research. Finally, we consider conceptual issues in relation to complex systems approaches.

C2.1 CA METHODOLOGY: CONCEPTUAL ISSUES

In this book we have looked at five CA studies. This section aims to clarify some of the conceptual issues and to position CA in relation to typical social science research methods and concepts such as validity, reliability, generalizability, epistemology, ontology and triangulation[1]. The points made will be exemplified by reference to the CA studies in the collection.

Peräkylä (1997: 206) identifies the key factors in relation to **reliability** as the selection of what is recorded, the technical quality of recordings and the adequacy of transcripts; Ten Have (1999) provides a very detailed account of this area. Another aspect of reliability is the question of whether the results of a study are repeatable or replicable (Bryman 2001: 29), and the way CA studies present their data is of crucial significance here. Many research methodologies do not present their primary data in their publications and hence the reliability of major sections of the researchers' analyses is not available for scrutiny. By contrast, it is standard practice for CA studies to include the transcripts of the data, and increasingly to make audio and video files available electronically via the Web. Furthermore, because CA studies (as exemplified in this collection) display their analyses, they make transparent the process of analysis for the reader. This enables the reader to analyze the data themselves, to test the analytical procedures which the author has followed and the validity of his/her analysis and claims. In this way, all of the analyses of data in this collection are rendered repeatable and replicable to the reader in so far as this is possible. For example, Brown's (2003) procedures are described in such a way that they can be replicated by other researchers. Most importantly, however, the data and the analysis are publicly available for challenge by any reader; in many other research methodologies readers do not have access to these.

We will now consider four kinds of **validity** in relation to qualitative research: **internal, external, ecological** and **construct validity** (Bryman 2001: 30). **Internal validity** is concerned with the soundness, integrity and credibility of findings. Do the data prove what the researcher says they prove or are there alternative explanations? Many CA procedures which seem strange to non-practitioners are based on a concern for ensuring internal validity whilst developing an emic perspective, which reflects the participants' perspective rather than the analyst's. How do CA analysts know what the participants' perspective is? Because the participants document their social actions to each other in the details of the interaction by normative reference to the interactional organizations, as explained above. We as analysts can access the emic perspective in the details of the interaction and by reference to those same organizations. Clearly, the details of the interaction themselves provide the only justification for claiming to be able to develop an emic perspective. Therefore, CA practitioners make no claims beyond what is demonstrated by the interactional detail without destroying the emic perspective and hence the whole internal validity of the enterprise.

External validity is concerned with generalizability or the extent to which the findings can be generalized beyond the specific research context. A typical criticism of qualitative studies is that they are context-bound and therefore weak in terms of external validity. Peräkylä (1997: 214) points out that generalizability 'is closely dependent on the type of conversation analytic research' and indeed there is variation in the generalizability of the studies in this collection. It is sometimes not appreciated that CA studies may analyze on the micro and macro level simultaneously. So, by explicating the organisation of the micro-interaction in a particular social setting, CA studies may at the same time be providing some aspects of a generalizable description of the interactional organization of the setting. This is the case because interaction is seen as rationally organized in relation to social goals (Levinson 1992: 71). CA studies in effect work on the particular and the general simultaneously; by analyzing individual instances, the machinery which produced these individual instances is revealed: 'The point of working with actual occurrences, single instances, single events, is to see them as the products of a "machinery" . . . The ethnomethodological objective is to generate formal descriptions of social actions which preserve and display the features of the machinery which produced them' (Benson and Hughes 1991: 130–131). For example, Koshik's (2002) study (Chapter 2) examines data from eight L2 writing conferences in one US university. However, the pedagogical practice of designedly incomplete utterances, used to elicit knowledge displays in error correction sequences, is widely used in L2 learning contexts around the world. In other words, Koshik is providing a generalizable description of the interactional organization of an interactional/pedagogical practice.

Ecological validity (Cicourel 1973) is concerned with whether findings are applicable to people's everyday life; laboratory experiments in the social sciences can often be weak in terms of ecological validity. CA practitioners typically record naturally-occurring talk in its authentic social setting, attempting to develop an emic, holistic perspective and to portray how the interactants perform their social actions through talk by reference to the same interactional organizations which the interactants are using. Therefore CA studies tend to be exceptionally strong in terms of ecological validity. However, Seedhouse and Almutairi's (2009) study takes place in a laboratory setting, since the digital tabletop technology employed was only available in that location at that time.

In this section we consider **construct validity, epistemology** and **ontology** together. **Construct validity**[2] is a vital concept in a quantitative paradigm (Bryman 2001). However, in an emic paradigm the question is: whose construct is it? Typically, descriptivist linguists look for etically specifiable methods of description, so that an analyst can match surface linguistic features of the interaction to constructs and categories. In an emic perspective, however, we are looking for constructs to which participants orient during interaction, which is not necessarily the same thing. **Epistemologically**, CA is based on ethnomethodology, (for a discussion, see Heritage 1984 and Seedhouse 2004) located (Lynch 2000) in a phenomenological paradigm, which considers that 'it is the job of the social scientist to gain access to people's 'common-sense thinking' and hence to interpret their actions and their social world from their point of view.' (Bryman 2001: 14). Ethnomethodology's **ontological** position can be associated with constructionism or the belief that 'social phenomena and their meanings are constantly being accomplished by social actors'. (Bryman 2001: 18). Hence, CA sees social constructs as being talked in and out of being by interactants. This point might be illustrated by Mori's (2003) study in Chapter 6. If one took a positivistic approach to the talk, one would classify it as a cross-cultural encounter and assume the omnirelevance of interculturality. From a CA perspective, although the participants are Japanese and American, interculturality is not always relevant to their talk. Mori shows how participants sometimes demonstrate the relevance of interculturality in the details of their talk, whilst at other times this is not relevant. The constructs which are revealed by CA are those to which the participants themselves orient during interaction, rather than those which may be pre-specified in a priori fashion by analysts. The knowledge which is created is that of the social world, social phenomena and categories which are talked into being in a sequential environment by the participants themselves. From a broader perspective, CA creates knowledge of how social acts are performed in interaction and of how interaction itself is organized. Ontologically, CA studies that which the interactants themselves make relevant or talk into being. The constructs studied are therefore those which have reality for the interactants.

Given the goals of CA, there is no substitute for detailed and in-depth analysis of individual sequences of interaction; interviews, questionnaires and observations are not able to provide this, which is why **triangulation** and other data-gathering techniques typical of ethnography are not generally undertaken. However, there is currently a movement to integrate CA and ethnography. Auer (1995) and Silverman (1999) have attempted a rapprochement between these two methodological approaches. Silverman's basic argument is that the two approaches are compatible and may be applied to the same instances of talk. An initial CA analysis of *how* participants locally produce context for their interaction can be followed by an ethnographic analysis of *why* questions about institutional and cultural constraints, thus moving from the micro to the macro levels. Auer (1995: 427) points out that data collection procedures in ethnography are eclectic by principle and therefore incorporate CA methods. Another issue of recent interest (e.g. Arminen 2000) has been the extent to which CA analyses of institutional discourse make use of ethnographic or expert knowledge of the institutional setting. Arminen's argument is that CA analysts inevitably do make use of such knowledge and should make as transparent as possible the extent to which their analyses derive from the details of the interaction or from use of ethnographic or expert knowledge. Brown's (2003) study (Chapter 7) employed rater reports in addition to CA. Retrospective verbal reports were collected from four IELTS test raters in order to determine why they had given different ratings to the two interviews. This information would not have been accessible using CA methods, and so triangulation provided vital evidence linking interviewer behaviour to candidate score.

C2.2 ETHNOGRAPHY: CONCEPTUAL ISSUES

One of the outcomes of the so-called 'paradigm wars' which featured in the closing decades of the last century was that qualitative researchers came to recognize that the criteria applying to quantitative research could not be imported into other forms of research without a number of attendant problems. An important step in this process was a paper by LeCompte and Goetz (1982) which demonstrated that replicability, which is fundamental to quantitative research (usually represented as 'post-positivist', 'rationalist' or 'scientific' – the terms tended to be used interchangeably), cannot be applied to ethnography. What emerged from this were new ways of thinking about the terminology that might be employed to ensure rigour in qualitative research.

A key contribution to this debate was provided by Lincoln and Guba, working from the starting point of trustworthiness. They proposed a new set of descriptors deriving from the same underlying concepts as those applying to rationalist research, producing the following equivalences (Lincoln and Guba 1985: 289–331):

Underlying concept	*Rationalist criterion*	*Naturalistic criterion*
truth value	internal validity	credibility
applicability	external validity	transferability
consistency	reliability	dependability
neutrality	objectivity	confirmability

More importantly, they proposed ways in which these naturalistic criteria could be operationalized. Here, they emphasized the need to pay attention to the following features, among others:

- Evidence of long-term experience of the context being studied (*credibility*);
- The adequacy of data from the field, which should involve drawing on different data types, gathered in different ways from different participants (*credibility*);
- The richness of description and interpretation offered (*transferability*);
- The documentation of the research, including records of reflection and decision making according to which the steps of the research process can be reconstructed (*dependability* and *confirmability*).

This description has been taken up and adapted in different ways, producing a range of terms and representations, but the fundamental ideas behind it have remained relatively stable. Instead of generalizability, for example, we are invited to think in terms of **transferability**, which assumes that if description and interpretation are sufficiently rich (Geertz's **thick description** is often used here; see Ponterotto 2006 for a useful exposition of this), the relevance of findings to other settings will be apparent. Similarly, credibility will depend on the extent and nature of exposure to the relevant setting, as well as the **triangulation** of different methods, perspectives, etc. **Dependability** is not a matter of replicability, but of ensuring that details of the situation, participants, etc. are properly documented. This in turn is associated with **transparency**, making the data and the processes of analysis available to those outside the research. For **confirmability** to be possible we need to be aware of the researcher's own standpoint, which demands explicit recognition of the researcher's positioning within the research. This also applies to the ways in which participants are represented. The importance of participant voice has received attention here, but from the perspective of validity or its equivalent it is also important to consider **respondent validation** and issues of **authentication** (see Manning 1997 for a discussion of this and Edge and Richards 1998 for a discussion of authenticity in applied linguistics research).

These issues have received extensive consideration over the years and there are a number of useful contributions addressing the issue of evaluative criteria in qualitative research (e.g. Lazaraton 2003, Long and Godfrey 2004, Freeman *et al.* 2007), but the distinguishing characteristic of ethnographic and ethnographic related research is the place of the researcher at the heart of the research process, a presence that can neither be abstracted from the steps in that process nor adequately represented in theoretical discussion. There have been numerous treatments of conceptual issues in ethnography – some of them of book length – but a genuine understanding of the place of the researcher and of the implications of the different elements in Lincoln and Guba's model can be achieved only through the careful examination of published research and through practice – territory already covered in detail in Chapters 3, 4 and 6.

By comparison with this, the much younger field of mixed methods has received less attention, but Onwuegbuzie and Johnson (2006) identify nine types of validity or legitimation that might be considered in this approach: inside–outside, sample integration, weakness minimization, sequential, conversion, paradigmatic mixing, commensurability, multiple validities and political validity.

C2.3 THE HYPOTHETICAL-DEDUCTIVE APPROACH: CONCEPTUAL ISSUES

As the primary goal of the hypothetical-deductive approach is to empirically investigate hypotheses formulated in light of a particular theory, the adequacy of an investigation depends on sampling, reliability and validity. Of these, validity is the most complex. Validity is a multidimensional concept, with a number of different facets which govern the inferences that can be made about the results of hypothetical deductive research.

Sampling

The generalizability of research devised to test a hypothesis is limited by the sampling frame deployed. Sampling constrains the representativeness of descriptive statements about mean and variance, and is particularly important when causal inference or intervention studies are designed. Two aspects of randomization are important to consider. Random samples are from a defined population. Statistics derived from the random sample ideally generalize to the population from which they come. The second type of randomization is of participants to groups in an intervention study. Experimental designs are by definition based on a complete randomization of all participants to intervention and control conditions. Through randomization, the primary threats to selection bias are neutralized as all moderating variables can be assumed to distribute equally to the different groups formed through the randomization process. With successful randomization, all groups are assumed to be equal other than the impact of the intervention of interest. Quasi-experimental designs, which are usually not fully randomized, can be expected to have less generalizability, and require considerably more design complexity than experiments in order to statistically control for potential moderating variables.

The sampling strategy used in an applied linguistics or language learning research project depends on the intended generalizability. The most common sampling strategy is the convenience sample. Researchers working in an institutional context typically can only recruit study participants from their own institution. Convenience samples only rarely represent the wider population, as educational institutions and the learners situated in them are often the consequence of prior selection and sorting processes. Results of hypothesis testing in studies involving convenience samples are limited to the context in which the study is conducted.

The most typical convenience sample is the use of intact groups which are preformed by processes unknown to the researcher. The groups are normally in class sections which cannot be rearranged for the purposes of research. In such situations, researchers are tempted to assign the intervention to a whole class, and the control condition to another. In such quasi-experimental designs, a number of covariates are needed to ascertain the comparability of the intact groups, and to adjust, if possible, for any pre-existing differences before any causal inference about differences can be made.

When researchers aim to garner broader generalization, effort is made to sample across known strata (Shadish, Cook and Campbell 2002). In such studies, a number of institutions may be involved. The institutions may be known in advance to differ from each other in terms of student ability, parental socioeconomic status, the social capital in the local community and factors such as levels of learner motivation. Researchers may then randomize the individuals within the different institutions to the intervention or control conditions to construct a **randomized block** design. As the contexts are known to differ, the object of interest is focused on any observed differences between the intervention and control conditions independent of the context. Few such studies exist in the applied linguistics literature (cf. Rost and Ross 1991), but are more common in educational intervention research.

An alternative to group-based randomization or stratified sampling is case-control matching. For studies in which the intervention is applied prior to the formation of a counterfactual condition, it is sometimes possible to form a post hoc control group. If the research designers have access to a database of individual difference, biographical or experiential data for all intervention group participants and for others who were not participants, it is possible to generate a **propensity score** for each non-intervention participant. (Rubin, 1997) Assuming there are sufficient numbers of non-participants and useful covariates, each intervention case can be matched to a control who had an equal propensity to be in the intervention group, but who actually was not. Once the matching is successfully done, dependent variable differences between the matched pairs can lead to causal inferences with accuracy approximately equal to quasi-experimental designs.

Reliability

Reliability in the hypothetical-deductive approach to research refers to the consistency of measurement, observation or rating that generates the quantitative variable or categorizations used in the research design. **Reliability** of measures is primarily estimated directly with repeated measures using data collection instruments such as tests, surveys, performances, tasks or rated interviews. A direct correlation between the first and second measure is taken as the evidence of consistency. The correlation reveals the stability in the rank order of the interval-scaled variable. Measures that produce stable rank orders of the attribute or construct are considered reliable.

Repeated measures of tests or surveys are logistically difficult, and are in fact rarely undertaken. For surveys and tests devised to generate scores representing constructs, indirect methods of estimating the reliability of the measurement instruments are the norm. Instrument designers construct tests and surveys to resample each construct several times by posing the same conceptual question in different ways. The expectation is that individual differences in the construct are stable when subsets of like questions correlate with each other strongly. If the set of items on a test or survey generate a score that is a stable indicator of differences between the respondents, the expectation is that the items replicate each other. A simple estimation of internal consistency reliability is the correlation between odd and even items on a test or survey. If the collection of items can be summed to represent a coherent score for each person, the two halves are expected to correlate highly. The **split-half** estimate can be elaborated into multiple parts instead of only odd and even halves. If software such as SPSS, Statistica or Systat is used, all possible parts can be generated to yield an estimate of **Cronbach's Alpha**. The Alpha is a commonly used reliability estimate which in general becomes larger as more items are used on a test or survey. The alpha estimate of reliability also generalizes to ratings given by human judges. To the extent that judges agree in their ranking of tasks or performances such as speech samples, role plays or writing samples, the higher the coefficient alpha is.

The maximum **internal consistency** is 1.0, which is rarely ever reached in real-world instrument making. A reliability of 1.0 would imply that individual differences on the construct measured by an instrument would remain constant if a retest were actually administered. For most applied research, an internal consistency of .80 is considered adequate (see Thompson 2000 for a review of reliability issues). For high stakes instruments such as tests used for admissions decisions the bar is set higher to reliability of .90 or higher.

Validity

Validity is a complex concept in that it refers to the representativeness of the constructs measured by instruments such as tests and surveys, as well as the accuracy of inferences made about data analyses. The validity of interpretations is contingent on sampling and randomization in experimental designs, and the systematic accounting of moderating variables in quasi-experimental designs. Complete validity is only an ideal. Real-world causal inference at best achieves an approximation to validity if all relevant alternative interpretations of research outcomes can be refuted by evidence and study design features devised to counter threats to validity.

The validity of measures used in hypothetical-deductive research falls into subjective and objective categories. The subjective types of validity are interpretive, and depend on expert judgement and cultural expectation. One such type of validity is **face validity.** This kind of validity refers to the apparent representativeness of a measure from the perspective of study participants. If the instrument (a survey or test) does not appear to be an authentic indicator of an identifiable domain, respondents may not take the instrument seriously and thus produce performances or responses that do not represent the construct the instrument designers intend.

The second interpretive validity type is **content validity.** As all tests and surveys need to be representative of one or more constructs by design, the content of the instruments needs to be designed to adequately represent the content domain. Some form of pre-administration moderation is normally called for, and through this process the content of items and tasks can be examined by domain area experts for their thoroughness and homogeneity.

The empirical types of validity are based on data analysis more than impressionistic judgements. Construct validity is predicated on evidence that measures designed to indicate a particular construct do so through patterns of covariance with other measures hypothesized to indicate the same construct. The flip side of this criterion for **convergent validity** evidence is explicit empirical evidence that an instrument does not measure some other construct. The combined convergent and **discriminant validity** evidence, nowadays tested with the use of factor analysis or covariance structure analyses (see Chapter 1 and Ellis's study summarized in Chapter 7), provides empirical support for claims that an instrument measures what its designers claim it measures. Convergent and discriminant validity fit into a **nomological network** such as that outlined in Chapter 1. In the post-positivist approach to research, one that is predicated on critical realism, construct validity is evidenced by coherent patterns of covariance among instruments devised to measure attitudes, abilities, motives, etc. The empirical evidence in this approach is manifested in how individuals respond to instruments such as surveys, or how they perform their competence on instruments such as tests. This approach to construct validity is made evident through recurring structural patterns seen across large and often diverse samples from a population.

A less common type of validity is one which claims a prognostic or predictive capacity. **Predictive validity** evidence can be gathered through group discrimination studies, or by projecting future outcomes. A battery devised to identify individual differences in language learning aptitude, for example, could be validated if the battery successfully differentiated between groups known to have successfully reached a particular level of proficiency, and those who did not. A claim of predictive validity in this case would be predicated on all other moderating variables being controlled so that the putative measures of aptitude are isolated as the only plausible causal factors to discriminate between the two groups. The design complexity involved in such a study is formidable. The projective version of predictive validity must be corroborated through a longitudinal design. If an instrument has predictive validity, individuals with scores above a specific cut score are predicted to achieve some eventual success (Silva and White 1993). The longitudinal design requirement militates against the use of this type of predictive validity. Further, the obvious counterfactual group, those individuals with scores below the cut or selection level often do not experience the same instruction or training as the selected group. This circumstance is common for instance in selection to university or military training. The success rate of the selected group is often the only evidence of predictive validity.

C2.4 DYNAMIC SYSTEMS MODELLING: CONCEPTUAL ISSUES

A growing trend in applied linguistics is the realization that language learning may involve many process that entail non-linear, complex and dynamic processes. Recent research into complexity has deployed metaphorical description of such processes (Larsen-Freeman and Cameron 2009). Dynamic systems models (Bruce and Matthias 2001) provide visual metaphors for complex multivariate processes that can be constructed as hypothetical models or as post hoc reconstructions to illustrate the interrelatedness of factors directly and indirectly influencing a phenomenon.

In an example of acquisition and attrition of proficiency, Ross (2009) illustrates the interplay of socio-economic and community enclosure on individual differences in language learning. The original analysis began as a conventional linear regression model. The dynamic systems version of the model extended the linear system to include variables which make the accumulation of language learning tasks potentially non-linear. Using dynamic systems simulation, potential influences of constraining factors were added to the model to demonstrate instances where both linear and non-linear outcomes would be plausible.

Dynamic systems model simulation can be used to create conceptual or logic models for many applied language learning phenomenon. Motivation, for instance, is a theme that has been well researched in the last three decades. Researchers have in the main used multivariate tools such as factor analysis and linear modelling to account for influences on motivational states as steady-state aspects of individual differences. Recent thinking on motivation appears to be moving from the static interpretation of motivation to one that is more malleable and dynamic (Dörnyei and Ushioda 2009). Empirical research has not quite caught up with the conceptual shifts concerning motivation. In this circumstance, the use of a dynamic systems simulation can provide a tool for concept development which may generate predictive hypotheses that may in the future be amenable to empirical testing.

As an illustration of a dynamic systems simulation, we will consider a model of the inter-relation of motivation and anxiety. Employing dynamic system software (Richmond 1994; Bruce and Matthias 2001), a model with hypothetical variables influencing the dynamics of learning motivation and anxiety is here created.

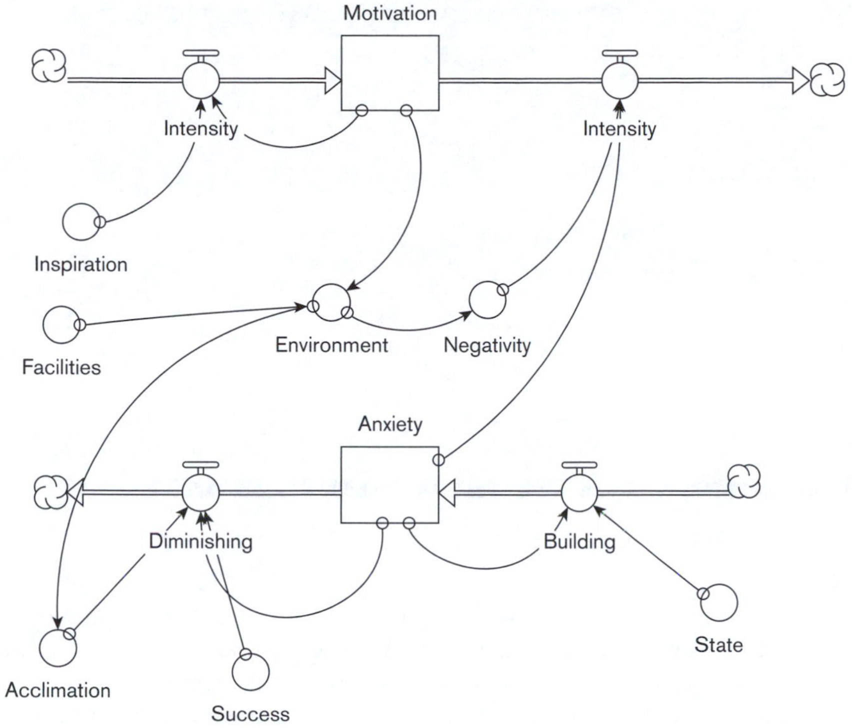

Figure 8.1.1 STELLA model for dynamic motivation

Figure 8.1.1 provides an icon-based representation of the hypothetical model of motivation change. Motivation 'grows' as the product of existing motivational states and inspiration. Motivation dissipates, or drains away as a complex interaction of negativity influenced by the relationship of the learning environment and the facilities afforded to learners.

The lower portion of the diagram shows a parallel process of change in learner anxiety. Here, the growth in anxiety is postulated as a steady state, though it is also possible to make the build-up of anxiety a variable. Anxiety is shown to 'exit' from the rectangular container as it diminishes as a consequence of learner acclimation to the environment, which is postulated to be in a linear relationship with it. Parts of the diagram link motivation dissipation to the volume of anxiety, and the diminishing of anxiety to the relation between acclimation and the learning environment.

The object of interest in such a model with a large number of interacting variables is the dynamics of the two volumes, motivation and anxiety, or perhaps even the conceptually (metaphorically) fluid components labeled intensity or dissipation. Once a model is constructed, hypothetical figures are inserted into the equations level of the simulation.

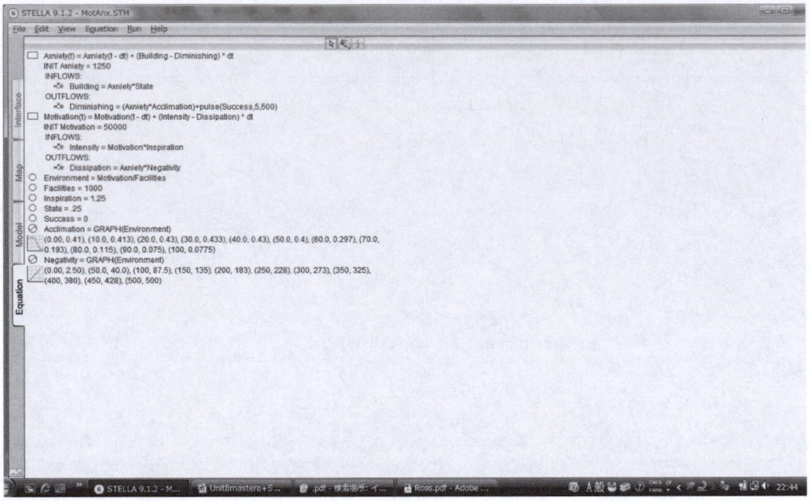

Figure 8.2 STELLA equation model interface

The values of the volumes (motivation and anxiety) and the rates (inspiration, state, success, etc.) can be based on actual 'real world' estimates, or may be initially arbitrary. The estimates (Figure 8.2) can be manipulated to create contrastive simulations to model the effects of changing one component in order to examine the effect throughout the system.

Once the model is constructed and all variables, their relationship and initial starting values are defined in the equations level of the STELLA simulator, the model can be run as a time-series. The simulation plots the projected value of variables of interest of a specified time period in whatever unit of time is of interest.

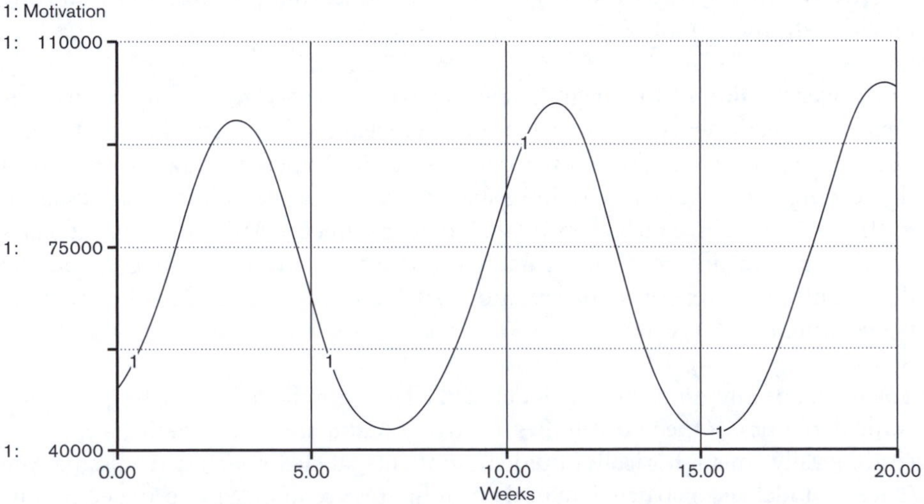

Figure 8.3 Non-linear motivation plot

The volume of motivation is shown in the simulation graph to be oscillating over time. In this hypothetical model, the variation in motivation would be a product of its interaction with changes in anxiety. The apparently dramatic oscillations are perhaps too manic to be realistic; the peaks and troughs are likely to be the artefact of the starting value metrics. The addition of anxiety to the simulation provides a graphic representation of the non-linear interrelatedness between the two variables. Anxiety can covary with motivation positively, which would suggest facilitative anxiety, or motivation and anxiety being in complimentary distribution with each other, which would suggest that growth in one leads to reduction of the other.

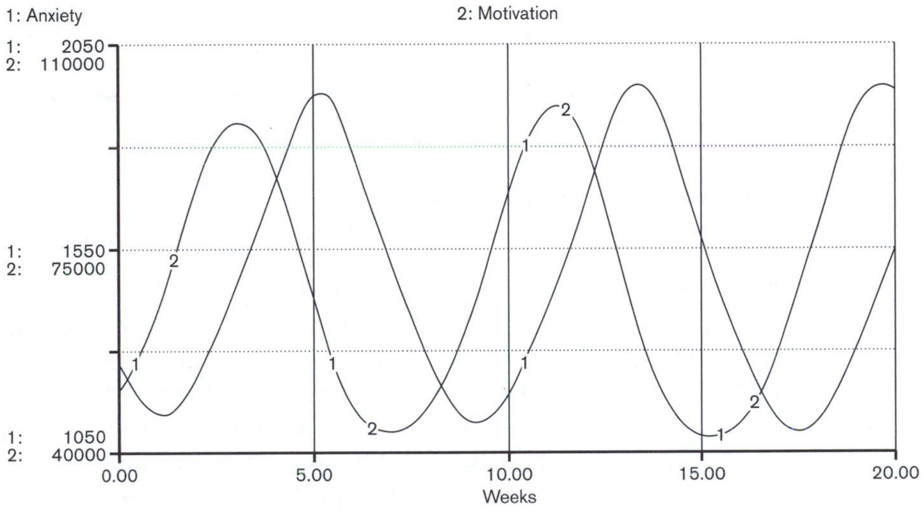

Figure 8.4 Motivation and anxiety oscillation plot

As Figure 8.4 illustrates, anxiety and motivation oscillate in parallel. As anxiety increases, motivation reaches a maximum in each cycle and regresses to a low point before a new cycle starts in tandem. The pattern favours the interpretation that anxiety is facilitative up to a point before motivation 'crashes'.

The relative time frame for a simulation can also be manipulated to project the stability of the interactive non-linear relations between the components. Figure 8.5 illustrates one such projection. The large oscillations between motivation and anxiety are possibly temporary. Projected onto a different time period, the interrelation of anxiety and motivation can be projected outward to gauge the ranges of the oscillations.

Figure 8.5 suggests that the initial large changes in the volume of anxiety relative to motivation would settle down as learners grew increasingly familiar with their new environment. The dynamic system would reach a point of homeostasis or balance between the two psychological phenomena.

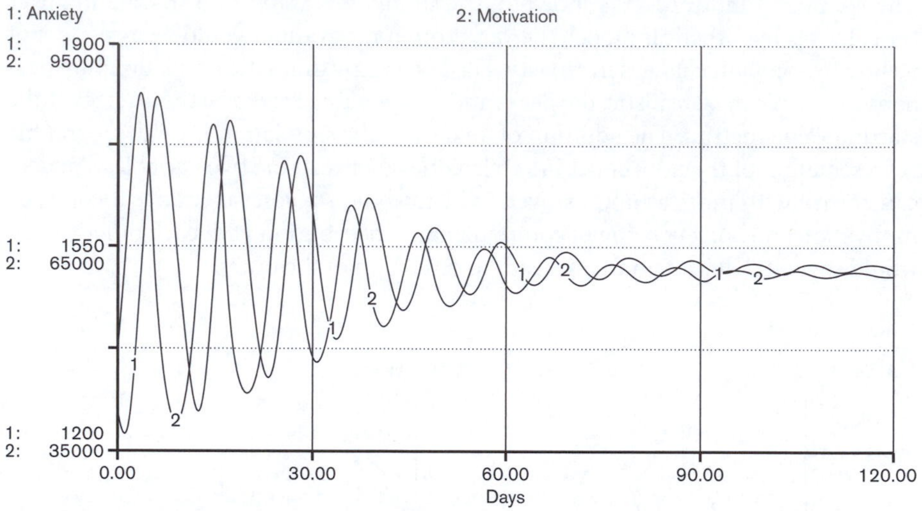

Figure 8.5 Motivation and anxiety projected over time

Dynamic systems simulations can be used as facsimiles of processes that have been well researched through other methodologies. Preliminary models can be modified to include more empirically-grounded measures instead of the initial metrics. Once such plausible systems are identified, simulation can inject hypothetical changes to the system which would be unfeasible in the real world. In domains with little actual empirical research, such as the longitudinal interplay of anxiety and motivation, a dynamic systems simulation can be a boon to concept formation prior to the start of empirical research. As dynamic systems usually begin as visual metaphors for complex processes, they are at best conceptual simulations. They have potential, however, to be corroborated in mixed-methods research in order to investigate whether projected changes occur in the real world. Longitudinal research such as time series designs or longitudinal ethnography can be deployed to check the veracity of dynamic systems simulations.

Task C2.1

- Construct a list of language-learning phenomena that could be part of a dynamic system. Discuss reasons why these phenomena in particular are more likely to be dynamic rather than static.

NOTES

1 The discussion relates to Seedhouse (2005).
2 Construct validity has to do with the question of 'whether a measure that is devised of a concept really does reflect the concept that it is supposed to be denoting' (Bryman 2001: 30).

Glossary of Terms

Action sequence. A first speaker initiates an action which is responded to in some way by a second speaker. This ends when the speakers move to perform a different action or series of actions.

Active listenership. A form of engagement in interviews that stimulates productive talk by focusing on sensitive listening and interaction with the interviewee.

Adjacency pairs. Paired utterances, for example question–answer, greeting–greeting, offer-acceptance.

Adjusted R^2. The amount of variance in a dependent variable adjusted for the number of independent variables entered into a linear regression model. The adjustment penalizes models with many independent variables relative to sample size.

Affiliative. In CA, these moves are ones which bring participants closer together in social terms.

Analysis of variance. A statistical test devised to compare the differences among three or more means of groups formed through a random process. ANOVAs can be one-way (one independent variable, the groups) or factorial, with two or more independent variables hypothesized to interact with the main grouping variable.

Analytic memos. Notes made by researchers for themselves, highlighting analytical discoveries, insights, etc.

Autoethnography. A reflexive form of research and writing that puts the self at the centre of the relevant social context, understanding the broader culture from the perspective of the experiences of the researcher within it.

Axial coding. In grounded theory, organizing the data based on the 'axis' of a category. This involves relating categories to subcategories and making connections between categories. (See also 'grounded theory', open/initial coding', 'constant comparison', 'saturation' and 'theoretical sampling'.)

Backwards elimination. The process of omitting independent variables from a regression model individually, or in sets. Eliminated variables are hypothesized not to affect the size of the model's validity.

Basic themes. A stage in thematic analysis which follows the identification of themes and is used as the basis for developing organizing themes which in turn allows the identification of global themes. (See also 'thematic analysis', 'organizing themes' and 'global themes'.)

Biographical methods. Approaches that seek to understand the life stories of respondents, usually elicited through extended open interviews. In practice, attention is usually also paid to the construction of the narrative and the positioning of the respondent. (See also 'narrative inquiry'.)

Causation. A hypothesis predicated on time-ordered covariance between a casual variable and a dependent variable presumed to be the consequence of it.

Chi-square. A statistical test devised to test the equality of frequencies or tallies of a dependent variable across categories of one or more independent variables.

Complex system. A defining characteristic of a complex system is that its behaviour emerges from the interactions of its components.

Complexity theory. A science which aims to explain the non-linear interactions of microscopic elements in complex systems, or a science of the global nature of systems.

Conditional relevance. In CA, after the first of an adjacency pair, a second is immediately relevant and expectable: this is called conditional relevance. The adjacency pair concept does not claim that second parts are always provided for first parts. Rather, it is a *normative* frame of reference which provides a framework for understanding actions and providing social accountability.

Confirmability. In qualitative research, confirmability depends on researchers making explicit their own standpoint, their positioning within the research. (See also 'transferability' and 'transparency'.)

Constant comparison. In grounded theory, the process by which all elements (codes, categories, themes, etc.) are considered in the light of one another. Specifically, connections between data and conceptualization are maintained by checking one against the other and making adjustments where necessary. (See also 'grounded theory', 'open/initial coding', 'axial coding', 'saturation' and 'theoretical sampling'.)

Construct. An abstract concept operationalized through instruments devised to measure it. Constructs are not directly observable, and are validated through replicable patterns of covariation among variables hypothesized to indicate them.

Context-free and context-sensitive. In CA, there is a context-free machinery which is stated in terms of norms, e.g. one person speaks at a time. People make use of these to orientate themselves in indexical interaction, i.e. we employ them in a context-sensitive way. Similarly, we are only able to interpret the context-sensitive social actions of others because there is a context-free machinery by reference to which we can make sense of them.

Context-shaped and context-renewing. In CA, contributions to interaction are both *context-shaped* and *context-renewing*. Contributions are context-shaped in that they cannot be adequately understood except by reference to the sequential environment in which they occur and in which the participants design them to occur. Contributions are context-renewing in that they inevitably form part of the sequential environment in which a next contribution will occur.

Control group. A group which does not receive an intervention hypothesized to be a causal factor accounting for group differences. The control group serves as the basis of comparison with the intervention/experimental group.

Conversation analysis (CA). The study of the organization and order of social action in interaction by means of the analysis of talk.

Correction. In CA terms, one kind of repair. A CA definition of correction is 'replacement of a trouble item by another item'. This does not necessarily involve anybody committing an error. Repair is the generic term and refers to the treatment of trouble. However, repair does not necessarily involve replacement.

Correlation. The degree to which two variables covary in a systematic manner such that variation in one variable results in variation in another.

Counterfactual. A condition under which an intervention does not apply to an individual or group of individuals. When incorporated into a research design, counterfactuals are synonymous with control conditions or control groups.

Covariance structure analysis. A model designed to test a set of hypothesized relations among latent variables or constructs.

Covariate. A variable whose role is to isolate a source of variation in a dependent variable independently of an intervention or other independent variables hypothesized to covary with the dependent variable. Covariates are often used when groups are not fully formed through randomization.

Cross-tabulation. Tallies of the frequency of a dependent variable across fixed discrete categories.

Culture. 'A fuzzy set of attitudes, beliefs, behavioural conventions, and basic assumptions and values that are shared by a group of people, and that influence each member's behaviour and each member's interpretations of the "meaning" of other people's behaviour.' (Spencer-Oatey 2000: 4)

Degrees of freedom. The number of possible values of a variable given the total number of values the variable can have.

Dependent variable. A variable hypothesized to be affected by other variables incorporated into a study and manipulated by a researcher.

Descriptive statistics. Estimations of the averages, standard deviations or tallies of variables of interest from defined groups.

Designedly incomplete utterances (DIU). A teacher turn which is designed to be an incomplete utterance. It is used to elicit a knowledge display from a student, who is expected to transform it into a complete utterance.

Disaffiliative. In CA, moves which push participants further apart in social terms.

Discourse completion task (DCT). A data collection method in which respondents complete a text using their own judgement as to what is appropriate.

Dynamic model. Linear or non-linear changes among variables interacting over time according to equations postulated to account for a natural phenomenon. Dynamic models are often not empirically grounded, but may be simulations of complex relations among a network of interacting variables.

Embedded correction. According to Jefferson (1987: 95), a correction done as a by-the-way occurrence in the context of a social action

Emic. In CA, the participants' perspective on talk within the sequential environment in which it occurs. More generally, an insider's perspective or data studied from 'within' the relevant system.

Empirical evidence. Overtly recorded data gathered through tests, surveys, observations or interviews. Such evidence may be descriptively summarized, or used in inferential analyses to test hypotheses.

Entry. The process of gaining access to a research site. (See also 'gatekeeper' and 'hierarchy of consent'.)

Ethnography. An approach to studying people's behaviour in groups based on careful observation (often extended to include interviewing) with the object of building up a picture of how the group organizes and understands its activities. Note that 'ethnographic' also tends to be used very loosely to refer to data collection methods associated with ethnography (e.g. interviews and observation) or to qualitative research generally.

Etic. An analyst's rather than a participant's perspective, or data studied from 'outside' the relevant system.

Experiment. A hypothetical-deductive research design in which all independent variables are formed through a random process. The classical model for randomized designs distributes all participants to groups randomly so that all potential moderating variables are equally distributed across groups, thus isolating the effect of the intervention on the outcome or dependent variable.

External validity. The degree to which a study can generalize to a larger population or to similar contexts.

Gatekeeper. A person controlling access to an individual or group. In the process of gaining entry to the field, the researcher may need to negotiate with a number of gatekeepers. (See also 'entry' and 'hierarchy of consent'.)

Generalizability. A claim that descriptive or inferential statistics generalize beyond a specific sample to a larger population from which the sample was taken.

Global themes. The highest level of theme in thematic analysis, often represented as networks. (See also 'thematic analysis', 'organizing themes' and 'basic themes'.)

Grounded theory. Although this is a distinct tradition with recognized procedures and stages in the process of data analysis, the term is often used more generally to refer to an approach in which theory is generated from, or *grounded* in, the data. The process of data collection involves continual adjustment in the light of what has been discovered. (See also 'open/initial coding', 'axial coding', 'constant comparison', 'saturation' and 'theoretical sampling'.)

Hierarchy of consent. A chain of people with whom the researcher may need to negotiate in the process of gaining entry to the research site (e.g. director of education, principal, head of department, teacher). (See also 'entry' and 'gatekeeper'.)

Hypothesis. An a priori statement about expected relations among variables included in a study.

Hypothetical-deductive. Research that tests an a priori hypothesis against the null (no difference or relation) alternative. Observed outcomes are compared to results that could occur by random chance alone. Probability theory is used to deduce if the observed outcomes surpass those possibly arising from random variation.

Independent variable. An ordinal, categorical or interval-scaled variable which is purposely included in the research design and manipulated by the researcher in order to test its effect on or relation to the dependent variable.

Inferential statistics. Statistical tests based on probability distributions generated from random data. Statistical tests that surpass 'critical values' of a statistic given the degrees of freedom support the inference that the observed outcome is unlikely to be the consequence of random variation.

Initial coding. Breaking down the data for the purpose of categorizing, conceptualizing and comparing (also referred to as 'open coding'). (See also 'grounded theory', 'open coding', 'axial coding', 'constant comparison', 'saturation' and 'theoretical sampling'.)

Internal consistency. An estimate of reliability based on the extent of intercorrelation among indicators of a specific construct. Indicators are normally measures such as test items or survey questions. To the extent that indicators correlate highly among themselves, a summation score generated to represent individual differences is expected to be reliable.

Internal validity. A feature of research design that accounts for all plausible variables affecting the outcome or dependent variable. Internal validity subsumes measurement reliability.

Interruption. In CA, when overlap is used to intensify a disaffiliative social action, e.g. disagreement.

Interval variable. A variable on a measurement scale with equal intervals between values on the scale. Interval scales are presumed to be normally distributed.

Intervention. An experimental treatment designed to be given to be administered to a group for the purpose of testing the effect of the intervention compared to a control group, which does not experience the intervention. Interventions are coded as categories of an independent variable.

Interview schedule/interview guide. Used to describe not the timetable for interviews but the plan for the structure of the interview itself. Schedules for open interviews will tend to be minimal, but the more structured the interview, the more detailed the schedule.

Large culture. Culture in the normal sense of a large national or cultural group. The term is used by Holliday in contrast to a small culture, where there is an emphasis on aspects of group cohesion. (See also 'small culture'.)

Latent factor. An unobservable variable identified through a pattern of co-variances among measured variables. Latent factors are the evidence that constructs can be measured.

Life history interview. An interview designed to elicit a life history, sometimes distinguished from 'life story' on the basis that the former is developed collaboratively with the interviewer.

Likert scale. A rating scale with statements or numerical steps representing an order of magnitude ranging from low to high. Likert scales are often used on surveys of attitudes.

Linear regression. A method of testing the relative influence of several competing independent variables on a dependent variable. Incremental changes in an independent variable are hypothesized to result in a corresponding change in the dependent variable controlling for the influence of all other independent variables in the model.

Linguistic ethnography. An approach to research that focuses on the relationship between language and social life, combining the contextual breadth offered by ethnography with the penetration afforded by the detailed analysis of spoken and/or written texts.

Local management system. The mechanism governing turn-taking in conversation. This means that decisions can be made locally by the participants, rather than having the turns allocated in advance, as is the case in a courtroom.

Matched pairs. Matching of each intervention group member with a control group member on all relevant biographical and experiential characteristics. Matched pairs are tested to determine if the intervention cases perform differently from their controls.

Measurement model. A covariance structure hypothesized to indicate a latent construct through the covariances of two or more measured variables assumed to indicate the latent construct or factor.

Meta-analysis. A method to synthesize research empirical research on a particular theme. Research outcomes are pooled and averaged so that a numerical summary can be generated.

Moderating variable. A variable that can potentially affect a dependent variable. Moderating variables not included in a research design may constitute a threat to the internal validity of a study. Potential moderating variables can be controlled if they are accurately measured and incorporated into a research design so that their actual effects can be estimated.

Mono-method bias. A source of possible bias injected into research when all measurements are based on the same method of gathering data. Mono-method bias can emerge when a single method such as self-report surveys are exclusively used.

Narrative inquiry. A form of research that explores the way people understand and represent their lives and experiences in the form of narratives. Data collection is in the form of extended open (or semi-structured) interviews and analysis focuses on meaning making. (See also 'biographical methods'.)

Nominal variable. A type of variable indicating fixed, invariant categories. Nominal variables may be assigned a numerical or categorical representation, though no arithmetic manipulations are possible.

Nomology. A system of replicable relations among measured variables interpreted to indicate a set of general principles hypothesized to govern the relationships among the variables.

Non-linear. A relation between variables such that changes in one variable results in varying patterns of positive or negative change in another.

Non-linear systems. Systems in which small changes in the external environment can produce large changes in the system. Non-linear systems express relationships that are not strictly proportional.

Non-parametric. A category of statistical tests that do not involve group means or standard deviations, but instead compare frequencies or tallies across fixed categories.

Null hypothesis. The 'no difference' baseline against which research outcomes are compared. Test results are compared with outcomes that could arise from randomly generated data. Statistical tests with a magnitude larger than those attributable to randomness provide the inferential basis to reject the null hypothesis.

Open coding. Breaking down the data for the purpose of categorizing, conceptualizing and comparing. Some researchers prefer the term 'initial coding'. (See also 'grounded theory', 'initial coding', 'axial coding', 'constant comparison', 'saturation' and 'theoretical sampling'.)

Open interview. An interview which allows considerable freedom to the researcher in terms of development. In this respect it is very different from the structured interview. Most narrative and biographical interviews tend to be fairly open. (Sometimes called an 'unstructured interview'.)

Organizing themes. A stage in thematic analysis that involves organizing basic themes as the basis for identifying global themes. (See also 'thematic analysis', 'basic themes' and 'global themes'.)

Overlap. Occurs when two or more speakers speak at the same time.

Participant observer. In fieldwork, a situation where the researcher joins the relevant group as a participant (e.g. is employed as a teacher) and observes the group from this perspective.

Post-positivism. An approach to empirical research that acknowledges the fact that scientific research is conducted in a social milieu, with potential bias, motives and incentives of stakeholders. Post-positivists postulate there is a reality external to the bias of researchers, though such biases need to be interrogated.

Probability. The theory that data observations can arise from random variation, as opposed to observations that are systematic and replicable.

QUAL. An abbreviation for qualitative research, which embraces a wide range of inductive approaches.

QUAN. An abbreviation of quantitative research, which subsumes descriptive, inferential, causal and hypothetical-deductive approaches.

Quasi-experimental design. A hypothetical-deductive research design that does not involve complete randomization of all possible moderating variables. The non-randomized variables are incorporated into the design as covariates so that their influence on the dependent variable can be statistically estimated and accounted for before interpretation of the effect of the intervention is attempted.

Random sample. A strategy to create a representative sample from a known population so that descriptive and inferential statistics generated in the research will accurately generalize to the larger population.

Randomization. The process of assigning participants to groups in a manner such that any participant has an equal chance to be in any of the possible groups involved in a study.

Rasch model. A model used to compare estimates of person ability with estimates of task or item difficulty in order to derive response probabilities. The Rasch model is useful in screening items on tests and surveys, and for identifying survey respondents answering Likert-type items in an incoherent or random manner.

Reflexive relationship. A two-way, mutually influencing relationship.

Reliability. A quantitative data analysis that estimates through direct or indirect methods the consistency of test items, ratings, judgements or survey responses on a scale from 0 through 1.

Repair. In CA, repair comes into play whenever there are problems in the accomplishment of talk and may be defined as the treatment of trouble occurring in interactive language use. It is important to distinguish self-initiated repair (I prompt repair of the trouble) from other-initiated repair (somebody else notices the trouble and initiates repair). Self-repair (I correct myself) must also be distinguished from other-repair (somebody repairs the trouble).

Respondent validation. Involving research participants in the process of analysis and representation (e.g. by offering them the chance to comment on the researcher's interpretation of a particular incident or statement).

Saturation. In grounded theory, this is the point where any new data added to a particular category throw no new light on the relevant concepts. At this point the category is said to be 'saturated'. (See also 'grounded theory', open/initial coding', 'axial coding', 'constant comparison' and 'theoretical sampling'.)

Selection bias. A type of bias occurring when groups are not fully formed randomly. Statistical tests on group differences will be biased if groups are formed in such a manner that one or more groups have systematically different means and standard deviations on moderating variables before an intervention is applied.

Selective coding. In grounded theory, the point where a central category (or explanatory concept) is identified, in terms of which other categories can be refined and integrated.

Semi-structured interview. A form of interview that has a definite structure but nevertheless allows researchers considerable freedom in how they allow the interview to develop. Situated between 'structured' and 'open' interviews, this is by far the most common form of interview.

Small culture. A term introduced by Holliday (1999: 248). A social grouping has a small culture when 'there is a discernible set of behaviours and understandings connected with group cohesion.' (See also 'large culture'.)

Social-constructionism. An ontological position which asserts that social phenomena and their meanings are constantly being accomplished by social actors, rather than fixed (Bryman 2001: 18). Also often referred to as constructivism, though some (e.g. Crotty) distinguish between the two.

Specification error. An error of omission in which an important independent variable is left out of a regression model. Inclusion of the omitted variable would increase the model fit and validity of the analysis.

Speech-exchange system. A variety of interaction (e.g. interview or lecturing) with its own identifiable organization of turn-taking, sequence, repair etc.

Standard deviation. A measure of dispersion of scores around a variable's mean. High standard deviations imply group heterogeneity on the measured variable, while a small standard deviation implies group homogeneity.

Standardized regression coefficient. A regression weight ('beta') indicating the proportion of a standard deviation on a dependent variable's scale that changes with one unit change on an independent variable, controlling for all other independent variables in a regression model. Betas are useful for examining the relative influence of competing independent variables.

Statistical significance. A predetermined criterion probability threshold beyond which an inference is made that a statistical test is unlikely to be the result of random chance. Statistical significance does not imply substantive importance.

Stratified samples. Samples chosen from identifiable pre-clustered strata in a known population. Stratified sampling makes it possible to randomize an intervention within each stratum and thus build a basis for generalization across the strata representing the population.

Structured interview. An interview with a pre-determined structure. In practice, there is a degree of flexibility because an interview where all the questions are fixed is best thought of as a spoken questionnaire.

Thematic analysis. A form of analysis based on the identification of themes in a text at different levels. It involves organizing themes in order to reveal underlying patterns and then using these to identify global themes. (See also 'basic themes', 'organizing themes' and 'global' themes'.)

Theoretical sampling. In grounded theory, using emerging theory (from data analysis) to inform further data collection. (See also 'grounded theory', open/initial coding', 'axial coding', 'constant comparison' and 'saturation'.)

Thick description. This expression was originally used by Clifford Geertz but is now common currency. It is used to refer to an account of a particular setting which is rich in detail and embraces different perspectives. The idea behind it is that it is possible to learn a great deal from narrowly-focused observation, provided that the observation is sufficiently penetrating and comprehensive.

Trajectory. There are normally four repair trajectories:

self-initiated self-repair
other-initiated self-repair
self-initiated other-repair
other-initiated other-repair

Transferability. A term sometimes used by qualitative researchers instead of 'replicability' It refers to the proper documentation of the setting, participants, data collection, etc. (See also 'confirmability' and 'transparency'.)

Transition relevance place (TRP). Listeners project when a speaker is going to finish a turn, and the point at which speaker change may occur is known as the transition relevance place or TRP.

Transparency. In qualitative research, this involves making the data and the processes of analysis available to those outside the research. (See also 'confirmability' and 'transferability'.)

Triangulation. Approaching the data from different perspectives in order to get a 'fix' on them. Usually it involves using different data collection methods (e.g. observation and interviews), but it can also include, for example, different researchers.

Trouble. In CA, anything which the participants judge is impeding their communication; a repairable item is one which constitutes trouble for the participants.

t-test. A statistical test designed to compare the mean and standard deviation of two randomly-formed groups on a dependent variable.

Turn-taking. The system by which speakers exchange turns at talk.

Unmotivated looking. In CA, looking at interaction without research questions and being open to discovering patterns or phenomena.

Unstructured interview. Sometimes used instead of open interview. (See 'open interview'.)

Visual ethnography. A form of ethnography which uses contextually situated visual data as a means of understanding particular cultures.

References

Adler, P. A. and Adler, P. (2003) 'The reluctant respondent' in J. A. Holstein and J. F. Gubrium (eds) *Inside Interviewing: New Lenses, New Concerns*: 153–173. Thousand Oaks, CA: Sage.

Agar, M. (2004) 'We have met the other and we're all nonlinear: Ethnography as a nonlinear dynamic system', *Complexity* 10(2): 16–24.

Algarawi, B. (2010) 'The effects of repair techniques on L2 learning as a product and as a process: A CA-for-SLA Investigation of Classroom Interaction', unpublished doctoral thesis, Newcastle University.

American Psychological Association (2009) *Publication Manual*, 6th edn. American Psychological Association.

Anderson, R. W. (1984) 'The one to one principle of interlanguage construction', *Language Learning* 34: 77–95.

Arminen, I. (2000) 'On the context sensitivity of institutional interaction', *Discourse and Society* 11: 435–458.

Atkinson, D. (2002) 'Toward a sociocognitive approach to second language acquisition', *The Modern Language Journal* 86: 525–545.

Atkinson, J. and Drew, P. (1979) *Order in Court.* London: Macmillan.

Atkinson, J. M. and Heritage, J. (eds.) (1984) *Structures of Social Action: Studies in Conversation Analysis.* Cambridge: Cambridge University Press.

Atkinson, P. (1992) *Understanding Ethnographic Texts.* Newbury Park, CA: Sage.

Attride-Stirling, J. (2001) 'Thematic networks: an analytic tool for qualitative research', *Qualitative Research* 1(3): 385–305.

Auer, P. (1995) 'Ethnographic methods in the analysis of oral communication' in U. Quasthoff (ed.) *Aspects of Oral Communication*: 419–440. Berlin: Walter de Gruyter.

Bagnoli, A. (2009) 'Beyond the standard interview: the use of graphic elicitation and arts-based methods', *Qualitative Research* 9(5): 547–570.

Baez, B. (2002) 'Confidentiality in qualitative research: reflections on secrets, power and agency', *Qualitative Research* 2(1): 35–58.

Baker, C. (1997) 'Membership categorization and interview accounts' in D. Silverman (ed.) *Qualitative Research: Theory, Method and Practice*: 130–143. London: Sage.

Ball, S. J.(1990) 'Self-doubt and soft data: social and technical trajectories in ethnographic fieldwork', *International Journal of Qualitative Studies in Education* 3(2): 157–171.

Barbour, R. (2007) *Doing Focus Groups.* Los Angeles, CA: Sage.

Basturkmen, H., Loewen, S. and Ellis, R. (2004) 'Teachers' stated beliefs about incidental focus on form and their classroom practices', *Applied Linguistics* 25(2): 243–272.

Bazeley, P. (2003) 'Computererized data analysis for mixed methods research' in A.

Tashakkori and C. Teddlie (eds) *Handbook of Mixed Methods in Social and Behavioral Research*: 385–422. Thousand Oaks, CA: Sage.

Benson, D. and Hughes, J. (1991) 'Method: evidence and inference – evidence and inference for ethnomethodology' in G. Button (ed.) *Ethnomethodology and the Human Sciences*: 109–136. Cambridge: Cambridge University Press.

Benson, P. (2005) '(Auto)biography and learner diversity' in P. Benson and D. Nunan (eds.) *Learners' Stories: Difference and Diversity in Language Learning*: 4–21. Cambridge: Cambridge University Press.

Bergmann, J. (1992) 'Veiled morality: notes on discretion in psychiatry' in P. Drew and J. Heritage (eds.) *Talk at Work: Interaction in Institutional Settings*: 137–162. Cambridge: Cambridge University Press.

Bialystok, E. (1982) 'On the relationship between knowing and using linguistic forms', *Applied Linguistics* 3(3) (autumn): 181–206.

Block, D. (2000) 'Problematizing interview data: Voices in the mind's machine', *TESOL Quarterly*, 34(4): 757–763.

Block, D. (2006) *Multilingual Identities in a Global City: London Stories.* Basingstoke: Palgrave Macmillan.

Blommaert, J. and Jie, D. (2010) *Ethnographic Fieldwork: A Beginner's Guide.* Bristol: Multilingual Matters.

Bond, M. H., Žegarac, V. and Spencer-Oatey, H. (2000) 'Culture as an explanatory variable: Problems and possibilities' in H. Spencer-Oatey (ed.) *Culturally Speaking: Managing Rapport Through Talk Across Cultures*: 47–74. London: Continuum.

Bond, T. and Fox, C. (2002) *Using the Rasch Model*, 2nd edn. Mahwah, NJ: Lawrence Erlbaum.

Bowen, G. A. (2008) 'Naturalistic inquiry and the saturation concept: a research note', *Qualitative Research* 8(1): 137–152.

Bowles, H. and Seedhouse, P. (2007) *Conversation Analysis and LSP.* Berlin: Peter Lang.

Boyatziz, R. E. (1998) *Transforming Qualitative Information: Thematic Analysis and Code Development.* London: Sage.

Brannan, M., Pearson, G. and Worthington, F. (2007) 'Ethnographies of work and the work of ethnography', *Ethnography* 8(4): 395–402.

Braun, V. and Clarke, V. (2006) 'Using thematic analysis in psychology', *Qualitative Research in Psychology* 3: 77–101.

Breen, M. (1989) 'The evaluation cycle for language learning tasks' in R.K. Johnson (ed.) *The Second Language Curriculum*: 187–206. Cambridge: Cambridge University Press.

British Council (1985) *Teaching and Learning in Focus. Edited Lessons* (4 vols.). London: British Council.

Brouwer, C. E. and Wagner, J. (2004). 'Developmental issues in second language conversation', *Journal of Applied Linguistics* 1(1): 30–47.

Brown, A. (2003) 'Interviewer variation and the co-construction of speaking proficiency', *Language Testing* 20(1): 1–25

Brown, J. D. and Rodgers, I. S. (2002) *Doing Second Language Research.* Oxford: Oxford University Press.

Bruce, H. and Matthias, R. (2001) *Dynamic Models.* Berlin: Springer

Bruner, J. S. (1986) *Actual Minds, Possible Worlds.* Cambridge, MA: Harvard University Press.

Bryman, A. (2000) 'Integrating quantitative and qualitative research: how is it done?', *Qualitative Research* 6(1): 97–113.

Bryman, A. (2001) *Social Research Methods.* Oxford: Oxford University Press.

Bryman, A. (2006) 'Paradigm peace and the implications for quality', *International Journal of Social Research Methodology* 9(2): 111–126.

Bryman, A. (2008). *Social Research Methods*, 3rd edn. Oxford: Oxford University Press.

Burgess, R. G. (1984) 'Autobiographical accounts and research experience' in R. G. Burgess (ed.) *The Research Process in Educational Settings: Ten Case Studies*: 251–276. Lewes: Falmer.

Burgess, R.G. (1989) 'Grey areas: Ethical dilemmas in educational ethnography' in R. G. Burgess (ed.) *The Ethics of Educational Research*: 60–76. New York: Falmer.

Bygate, M., Skehan, P. and Swain, M. (2001) Introduction, in M. Bygate., P. Skehan and M. Swain (eds) *Researching Pedagogic Tasks: Second Language Learning, Teaching and Testing*: 1–20. Harlow: Pearson.

Campbell, D. T., and Stanley, J. C. (1966) *Experimental and Quasi-experimental Designs for Research.* Chicago: Rand McNally.

Carlin, A. P. 2009. 'Edward Rose and linguistic ethnography: an ethno-inquiries approach to interviewing', *Qualitative Research* 9(3): 331–354.

Carr, D. (ed) (2006) *Teacher Training DVD Series* (Set of 15 DVDs). London: International House.

Carroll, D. (2005) 'Vowel-marking as an interactional resource in Japanese novice ESL conversation' in K. Richards and P. Seedhouse (eds) *Applying Conversation Analysis*: 214–234. Basingstoke: Palgrave Macmillan.

Chang, L. Y.-H. (2010) 'Group processes and EFL learners' motivation: a study of group dynamics in EFL classrooms', *TESOL Quarterly* 44(1): 129–154.

Charmaz, K. (2006) *Constructing Grounded Theory: A Practical Guide through Qualitative Analysis.* London: Sage.

Cheng, X. (2000) 'Asian students' reticence revisited', *System* 28(3): 435–446.

Cicourel, A. V. (1964) *Method and Measurement in Sociology.* New York: The Free Press.

Cicourel, A. V. (1973) *Cognitive Sociology: Language and Meaning in Social Interaction.* Harmondsworth: Penguin.

Clark, R. and Gieve, S. N. (2006) 'On the discursive construction of "the Chinese learner" ', *Language, Culture and the Curriculum* 19(1): 54–73.

Cloke, P., Cook, I., Crang, P., Goodwin, M., Painter, J. and Philo, C. (2004) *Practising Human Geographies.* London: Sage.

Clough, P. and Nutbrown, C. (2007) *A Student's Guide to Methodology: Justifying Enquiry.* London: Sage.

Cook, V. (2010) 'Prolegomena to Second Language Learning' in P. Seedhouse, S. Walsh and C.J. Jenks (eds) *Conceptualising 'Learning' in Applied Linguistics*: 6–22. London: Palgrave Macmillan.

Corbetta, P. (2003). *Social Research: Theory, Methods, Techniques.* London: Sage.

Craig, M. and Cook, I. (2007) *Doing Ethnographies.* London: Sage.

Creese, A. (2003) 'Language, ethnicity and the mediation of allegations of racism: Negotiating diversity and sameness in multilingual school discourses', *International Journal of Bilingual Education and Bilingualism* 6(3 and 4): 221–236.

Creswell, J. W. (2003) *Research Design: Qualitative, Quantitative, and Mixed Methods Approaches*, 2nd edn. Thousand Oaks, CA: Sage.

Creswell, J. W. and Piano Clark, V. L. (2007) *Designing and Conducting Mixed Methods Research.* Thousand Oaks, CA: Sage.

Creswell, J. W. and Tashakkori, A. (2007) 'Editorial: Differing perspectives on mixed methods research', *Journal of Mixed Methods Research* 1(4): 303–308.

Creswell, J. W., Shope, R., Piano Clark, V. L. and Green, D. O. (2006) 'How interpretive qualitative research extends mixed methods research', *Research in the Schools* 13(1): 1–11.

Cronbach, L. and Meehl, P. (1955) 'Construct validity in psychological tests', *Psychological Bulletin* 52: 281–302.

Crotty, M. (1988) *The Foundations of Social Research.* London: Sage.
Cryer, P. (2000) *The Research Student's Guide to Success.* Buckingham: Open University Press.
Davis, K. A. (1995). 'Qualitative theory and methods in applied linguistics research', *TESOL Quarterly* 29(3): 427–454.
Day, D. (1998) 'Being ascribed, and resisting, membership of an ethnic group' in C. Antaki and S. Widdicombe (eds) *Identities in Talk.* London: Sage.
DeKeyser, R. (1997) 'Beyond explicit rule learning: Automatizing second language morphosyntax', *Studies in Second Language Acquisition* 19: 195–221.
DeKeyser, R. (2003) 'Implicit and explicit learning' in C. Doughty and M. Long (eds.) *Handbook of Second Language Acquisition.* Oxford, Blackwell.
De Leon, J. P. and Cohen, J. H. (2005) 'Object and walking probes in ethnographic interviewing', *Field Methods* 17(2): 200–204.
Delamont, S. (2006) 'Ethnography and participant observation' in C. Seale, G. Gobo, J. F. Gubrium and D. Silverman (eds) *Qualitative Research Practice*: 205–216. London: Sage.
Delin, J. (2000) *The Language of Everyday Life: An Introduction.* London: Sage.
Denscombe, M. (2008) 'Communities of practice: A research paradigm for the mixed methods approach', *Journal of Mixed Methods Research* 2(3): 270–283.
Denzin, N. K. (2010) 'Moments, mixed methods, and paradigm dialogs', *Qualitative Inquiry* 16(6): 419–427.
DeRidder, I, Vangehuchten, L, and Sesena Gomez, M. (2007) 'Enhancing automaticity through task-based language learning', *Applied Linguistics* 28(2): 309–315.
Dingwall, R. (1980) 'Ethics and ethnography', *Sociological Review* 28(4): 871–891.
Dörnyei, Z. (2001) *Teaching and Researching Motivation.* Harlow: Longman.
Dörnyei, Z. (2003) *Questionnaires in Second Language Research.* Mahwah, NJ: Lawrence Erlbaum.
Dörnyei, Z. (2007) *Research Methods in Applied Linguistics.* Oxford: Oxford University Press.
Dörnyei, Z. and Ushioda, E. (2009) 'Motivation, language identities and the L2 self' in Z. Dörnyei and E. Ushioda (eds) *Motivation, Language Identity, and the L2 Self.* Bristol: Multilingual Matters.
Doughty, C. (2001) 'Cognitive underpinnings of focus on form' in P. Robinson (ed.) *Cognition and Second Language Instruction*: 206–257. Cambridge: Cambridge University Press.
Drew, P. (2004) 'Conversation analysis' in K. Fitch, and R. Sanders, (eds) *Handbook of Language and Social Interaction*: 71–102. Mahwah, NJ: Lawrence Erlbaum.
Duff, P. (1986) 'Another look at interlanguage talk: Taking task to task' in R. Day (ed.) *Talking to Learn: Conversation in Second Language Acquisition*: 147–181. Rowley: Newbury House.
Dwyer, S. C. and Buckle J. L. (2009) 'On the space between: On being an insider-outsider in qualitative research', *International Journal of Qualitative Methods* 8(1): 54–63.
Edge, J. and Richards, K. (1998) '"May I see your warrant, please?" Justifying outcomes in qualitative research', *Applied Linguistics* 19(3): 334–356.
Ellis, A. and Beattie, G. (1986) *The Psychology of Language and Communication*, London: Weidenfeld & Nicolson.
Ellis, C., Kiesinger, C. E. and Tillman-Healy, L. M. (1997) 'Interactive interviewing: Talking about emotional experience' in R. Hertz (ed.) *Reflexivity and Voice*: 119–149. Thousand Oaks, CA: Sage.
Ellis, R. (1984) *Classroom Second Language Development.* Oxford: Pergamon Press.
Ellis, R. (1992) *Second Language Acquisition and Language Pedagogy.* Clevedon: Multilingual Matters.
Ellis, R. (1994) *The Study of Second Language Acquisition.* Oxford: Oxford University Press.
Ellis, R. (1997) *SLA Research and Language Teaching.* Oxford: Oxford University Press.

Ellis, R. (2003) *Task-based Language Learning and Teaching.* Oxford: Oxford University Press.

Ellis, R. (2005) 'Measuring implicit and explicit knowledge of a second language', *Studies in Second Language Acquisition* 27: 141–172.

Ellis, R. (2008) *The Study of Second Language Acquisition*, 2nd edn. Oxford: Oxford University Press.

Emerson, R. M., Fretz, R. I. and Shaw, L. L. (1995) *Writing Ethnographic Fieldnotes.* Chicago: University of Chicago Press.

Erickson, F. (2004) 'Demystifying data construction and analysis', *Anthropology and Education Quartely* 35: 486–493.

Feilzer, M. Y. (2010) 'Doing mixed methods research pragmatically: implications for the rediscovery of pragmatism as a research design', *Journal of Mixed Methods Research* 4(1): 6–16.

Fine, G. A. (1993/2001) 'Ten lies of ethnography: moral dilemmas of field research', *Journal of Contemporary Ethnography* 22: 267–94. Reprinted in A. Bryman (ed.) (2001) *Ethnography*, vol. III: 367–86. London: Sage.

Finger, M. (1988) 'The biographical method in adult education research', *Studies in Continuing Education* 10(2): 33–42. [Appears online as 1989, 11(1): 33–42.]

Flick, U. (2002) *An Introduction to Qualitative Research.* London: Sage.

Fontana, A. and Frey, J. H. (2000) 'The interview: From structured questions to negotiated text' in N. K. Denzin and Y. S. Lincoln (eds) *Handbook of Qualitative Research* (2nd edn): 645–672. Thousand Oaks, CA: Sage.

Freebody, P. (2003) *Qualitative Research in Education: Interaction and Practice.* London: Sage.

Freeman, M., deMarrais, K. Preissle, J. Roulston, K. and St. Pierre, E. A. (2007) 'Standards of evidence in qualitative research: An incitement to discourse', *Educational Researcher* 36(1): 25–32.

Fulcher, G. and Davidson, F. (2007) *Language Testing and Assessment.* Abingdon: Routledge.

Gao, X. (2006) 'Strategies used by Chinese parents to support English language learning: Voices of "elite" university students', *RELC Journal* 37(3): 285–298.

Garfinkel, H. (1984) *Studies in Ethnomethodology.* Cambridge: Polity Press.

Geertz, C. (1973) 'Thick description: Toward an interpretive theory of culture' in C. Geertz *The Interpretation of Cultures: Selected Essays*: 3–30. New York: Basic Books.

Genovese, B. J. (2004) 'Thinking inside the box: The art of telephone interviewing', *Field Methods* 16(2): 215–228.

Gibson, L. (2010) Using email interviews, Realities Toolkit #09 (ESRC). http://www.socialsciences.manchester.ac.uk/realities/resources/toolkits/email-interviews/09-toolkit-email-interviews.pdf [Accessed 11 August 2010]

Glaser, B. G. and Strauss, A. L. (1967) *The Discovery of Grounded Theory: Strategies for Qualitative Research.* New York: Aldine.

Gobo, G. and Diotti, A. (2008) 'Useful resources: ethnography through the internet', *International Journal of Social Research Methodology* 11(4): 357–382.

Goffman, E. (1981) *Forms of Talk.* Oxford: Blackwell.

Golato, A. (2003) 'Studying compliment responses: A comparison of DCTs and recordings of naturally occurring talk', *Applied Linguistics* 24(1): 90–121.

Gonzalez-DeHass, A. R., Willems, P. P. and Holbein, M. F. D. (2005) 'Examining the relationship between parental involvement and student motivation', *Educational Psychology Review* 17(2): 99–123.

Goodwin, C. (1987) 'Forgetfulness as an interactive resource', *Social Psychology Quarterly* 50: 115–131.

Greene, J. C. (2006) 'Toward a methodology of mixed methods social inquiry', *Research in the Schools* 13(1): 93–98.
Greene, J, C. (2007) *Mixed Methods in Social Inquiry*. San Francisco, CA: Jossey-Bass.
Greene, J. C. (2008) 'Is mixed methods social inquiry a distinctive methodology?', *Journal of Mixed Methods Research* 2(1): 7–22.
Grimes, W. (2008) 'Studs Terkel, Listener to Americans, Dies at 96.' *New York Times*, 31 October 2008. <http://www.nytimes.com/2008/11/01/books/01terkel.html?hp> [Accessed 1 November 2008]
Gu, Q., Schweisfurth, M. and Day, C. (2010) 'Learning and growing in a "foreign" context: Intercultural experiences of international students', *Compare: A Journal of Comparative and International Education* 40(1): 7–23.
Gustafson, K. (2009) 'Us and them – children's identity work and social geography in a Swedish school yard', *Ethnography and Education* 4(1): 1–16.
Gwyther, G. and Possamai-Inesedy, A. (2009) 'Methodologies à la carte: an examination of emerging qualitative methodologies in social research', *International Journal of Social Research Methodology* 12(2): 99–115.
Ha, P. L. (2004) 'University classrooms in Vietnam: Contesting the stereotypes', *ELT Journal* 58(1): 50–57.
Hammersley, M. (1980) 'A peculiar world? Teaching and learning in an inner-city school', unpublished doctoral thesis, Faculty of Economic and Social Studies, University of Manchester.
Hammersley, M. (2006) 'Ethnography: problems and prospects', *Ethnography and Education* 1(1): 3–14.
Hammersley, M. and Atkinson, P. (1995) *Ethnography*, 2nd edn. London: Routledge.
Hanneman, G. and McEwen W. (eds) (1975) *Communication and Behavior*. Reading, MA: Addison-Wesley.
Harklau, L. (2005) 'Ethnography and ethnographic research on second language teaching and learning' in E. Hinkel (ed.) *Handbook of Research in Second Language Teaching and Learning*: 179–194. Mahwah, NJ: Lawrence Erlbaum.
Hasan, A.S. (1988) 'Variation in spoken discourse in and beyond the English foreign language classroom: a Comparative Study', unpublished doctoral thesis, University of Aston, UK
Hatch, E. and Lazaraton, A. (1991) *The Research Manual: Research Design and Statistics for Applied Linguists*. Rowley, MA: Newbury House.
Hauser, E. (2005) 'Coding "corrective recasts": The maintenance of meaning and more fundamental problems', *Applied Linguistics* 26: 293–316.
Have, P. ten (1999) *Doing Conversation Analysis: a Practical Guide*. London: Sage.
Hayes, D. (2005) 'Exploring the lives of non-native speaking English educators in Sri Lanka', *Teachers and Teaching* 11(2): 169–194.
Hellermann, J. (2006) 'Classroom interactive practices for literacy', *Applied Linguistics* 27: 377–404.
Heritage, J. (1984) *Garfinkel and Ethnomethodology*. Cambridge: Polity Press.
Heritage, J. (1988) 'Explanations as accounts: A conversation analytic perspective' in C. Antaki (ed.) *Analyzing Everyday Explanation: A Casebook of Methods*: 127–144. London: Sage.
Hesse-Biber, S. (2010) 'Qualitative approaches to mixed methods practice', *Qualitative Inquiry* 16(6): 455–468.
Hofstede, G. (1980) *Culture's Consequences: International Differences in Work-related Values*. Beverly Hills, CA: Sage.
Holliday, A. (1999) 'Small cultures', *Applied Linguistics* 20(2): 237–264.

Holstein, J. A. and Gubrium, J. F. (1995) *The Active Interview.* Thousand Oaks, CA: Sage.

Horowitz, E. (1986) 'Preliminary evidence for the reliability and validity of a foreign language anxiety scale', *TESOL Quarterly* 20: 559–62.

Houtkoop-Steenstra, H. (1997) 'Being friendly in survey interviews', *Journal of Pragmatics* 28(5): 591–623.

Hutchby, I. and Wooffitt, R. (1998) *Conversation Analysis.* Cambridge: Polity Press.

Inui, T. S. (1996) 'Editorial: The virtue of qualitative and quantitative research', *Annals of Internal Medicine* 125(9): 770–771. http://www.annals.org/content/125/9/770.full [Accessed 5 August 2010]

Ivankova, N. V., Creswell, J. W. and Stick, S. (2006) 'Using mixed methods sequential explanatory design: From theory to practice', *Field Methods* 18(1): 3–20.

Jansen, H. (2010) 'The logic of qualitative survey research and its position in the field of social research methods', *Forum: Qualitative Social Research* 11(2): Art. 11. http://www.qualitative-research.net/index.php/fqs/article/view/1450/2947 [Accessed 5 August 2010]

Jefferson, G. (1987) 'On exposed and embedded correction in conversation', in G. Button and J. Lee (eds.) *Talk and Social Organisation*: 86–100. Clevedon: Multilingual Matters.

Jenks, C. J. (2007) 'Floor management in task-based interaction: The interactional role of participatory structures', *System* 35(4): 609–622.

Johnson, E. K., and Golombek, P. R. (2002) *Teachers' Narrative Inquiry as Professional Development.* Cambridge: Cambridge University Press.

Johnson, J. C. and Weller, S. C. (2002) 'Elicitation techniques for interviewing' in J. F. Gubrium and J. A. Holstein (eds) *Handbook of Interview Research: Context and Method*: 491–514. Thousand Oaks, CA: Sage.

Johnson, K. (1995) *Understanding Communication in Second Language Classrooms.* Cambridge: Cambridge University Press.

Johnson, R. B., Onwuegbuzie, A. J. and Turner L. A. (2007) 'Toward a definition of mixed methods research', *Journal of Mixed Method Research* 1(2): 112–133.

Jones, J. (1985) 'Depth interviewing' in R. Walker (ed.) *Applied Qualitative Research*: 45–58. Brookfield: Gower.

Jones, K. (2000) 'A regrettable oversight or a significant omission? Ethical considerations in quantitative research in education', in H. Simons and R. Usher (eds) *Situated Ethics in Educational Research*: 146–161. London: RoutledgeFalmer.

Kasper, G. (2009) 'Locating cognition in second language interaction and learning: Inside the skull or in public view?' *IRAL* 47: 11–36.

Kenny A. J. (2005) 'Interaction in cyberspace: an online focus group', *Journal of Advanced Nursing* 49(4): 414–422.

Kent, G. (2000) 'Informed consent' in D. Burton (ed.) *Research Training for Social Scientists*: 81–87. London: Sage.

Kitano, K. (2001) 'Anxiety in the college Japanese language classroom', *The Modern Language Journal* 85: 549–566.

Kontos, M. (2005) 'Cross-national comparative research with biographical methods: Problems and solutions', paper presented in the Workshop on Comparative Biographical Research, TCRU, Institute of Education, University of London, 24–25 November 2005. http://eprints.ncrm.ac.uk/11/1/MariaKontos-ProblemsSolutions.pdf [Accessed 28 May 2010]

Koro-Ljungberg, M. and Greckhamer, T. (2005) 'Strategic turns labeled "ethnography": from description to openly ideological production of cultures', *Qualitative Research* 5(3): 285–306.

Koshik, I. (2002) 'Designedly incomplete utterances: A pedagogical practice for eliciting

knowledge displays in error correction sequences', *Research on Language and Social Interaction* 35(3): 277–309.
Kramsch, C. (ed.) (2002) *Language Acquisition and Language Socialization: Ecological Perspectives.* London: Continuum.
Krashen, S. (1981) *Second Language Acquisition and Second Language Learning.* London: Pergamon.
Kumaravadivelu, B. (2003) 'Problematizing cultural stereotypes in TESOL', *TESOL Quarterly* 37(4): 709–719.
Kvale, S. (2007) *Doing Interviews.* London: Sage.
Larsen-Freeman, D. (1997) 'Chaos/complexity science and second language acquisition', *Applied Linguistics* 26: 141–165.
Larsen-Freeman, D. and Cameron, L. (2008) 'Research methodology on language development from a complex systems perspective', *The Modern Language Journal* 92(2): 200–213.
Larsen-Freeman, D. and Cameron, L. (2009) *Complex Systems and Applied Linguistics.* New York: Oxford University Press.
Lazaraton, A. (2003) 'Evaluative criteria for qualitative research in applied linguistics: Whose criteria and whose research?', *The Modern Language Journal* 87(1): 1–12.
Lazaraton, A. (2004) 'Gesture and speech in the vocabulary explanations of one ESL teacher: A microanalytic inquiry', *Language Learning* 54(1): 79–117.
LeCompte, M. D. and Goetz, J. P. (1982) 'Problems of reliability and validity in ethnographic research', *Review of Educational Research* 52(1): 31–60.
Lerner, G. H. (2003) 'Selecting next speaker: The context-sensitive operation of a context-free organization', *Language in Society* 32.
Levinson, S. (1983) *Pragmatics.* Cambridge: Cambridge University Press.
Levinson, S. (1992) 'Activity types and language' in P. Drew and J. Heritage (eds.) *Talk at Work: Interaction in Institutional Settings:* 66–100. Cambridge: Cambridge University Press.
Li, S. (2010) 'The effectiveness of corrective feedback in SLA: A meta-analysis', *Language Learning* 60(2): 309–365.
Lincoln, Y. and Guba, E. (1985) *Naturalistic Inquiry.* Beverly Hills, CA: Sage.
Lipton, P. (2004) *Inference to the Best Explanation*, 2nd edn. London: Routledge.
Loewen, S. (2002) 'The occurrence and effectiveness of incidental focus on form in meaning-centred ESL classrooms', unpublished doctoral thesis, University of Auckland.
Lofland, J. and Lofland, L. H. (2004) *Analyzing Social Settings: A Guide to Qualitative Observation and Analysis*, 4th edn. Belmont, CA: Wadsworth.
Long, A. and Godfrey, M. (2004) 'An evaluation tool to assess the quality of qualitative research studies', *International Journal of Social Research Methodology* 7(2): 161–196.
Long, M. H. (1996). 'The role of the linguistic environment in second language acquisition', in W. C. Ritchie and T. K Bhatia (eds.) *Handbook of Second Language Acquisition*: 413–468. New York: Academic Press.
Long, M. H., Inagaki, S. and Ortega, L. (1998) 'The role of implicit negative feedback in SLA: Models and recasts in Japanese and Spanish', *The Modern Language Journal* 82, (3): 357–371.
Lynch, M. (2000) 'The ethnomethodological foundations of conversation analysis', *Text*, 20(4): 517–532.
Lyster, R. (2004) 'Differential effects of prompts and recasts in form-focused instruction', *Studies in Second Language Acquisition* 26: 399–432.
MacIntyre, P. and Gardner, R. (1994) 'The subtle effects of induced anxiety on cognitive processing in the second language', *Language Learning* 44: 283–305.
Mackey, A. (2006) 'Feedback, noticing, and instructed second language learning', *Applied Linguistics* 27(3): 405–430.

MacLure, M. (1993) 'Mundane autobiography: Some thoughts on self-talk in research contexts', *British Journal of Sociology of Education* 14(4): 373–384.
Mallozzi, C. A. (2009) 'Voicing the interview: a researcher's exploration on a platform of empathy', *Qualitative Inquiry* 15(6): 1042–1060.
Manning, K. (1997) 'Authenticity in constructivist inquiry: methodological considerations without prescription', *Qualitative Inquiry* 3(1): 93–115.
Markee, N. (2000). *Conversation Analysis.* Mahwah, NJ: Lawrence Erlbaum.
Markee, N. (2005) 'The organization of off-task talk in second language classrooms', in K. Richards and P. Seedhouse (eds.) *Applying Conversation Analysis*: 197–213. Basingstoke: Palgrave Macmillan.
Markee, N. (2008) 'Toward a learning behavior tracking methodology for CA-for-SLA', *Applied Linguistics* 29: 404–427.
Markee, N., and J. Stansell (2007) 'Using electronic publishing as a resource for increasing empirical and interpretive accountability in conversation analysis', *Annual Review of Applied Linguistics* 27: 24–44.
Mason, J. (2006) 'Mixing methods in a qualitatively driven way', *Qualitative Research* 6(1): 9–25.
Mazeland, H. and ten Have, P. (1996) 'Essential tensions in (semi-) open research interviews' in I. Maso and F. Wester (eds) *The Deliberate Dialogue: Qualitative Perspectives on the Interview*: 87–114. Brussels: VUB Press.
Maybin, J. (2006). *Children's Voices: Talk, Knowledge and Identity.* Basingstoke: Palgrave Macmillan.
Méhan, H. (1979) *Learning Lessons: Social Organization in the Classroom.* Cambridge, MA.: Harvard University Press.
Mellow, J. D. (2006) 'The emergence of second language syntax: A case study of the acquisition of relative clauses', *Applied Linguistics* 27: 645–670.
Merriam, S. B. (1988). *Case Study Research in Education: A Qualitative Approach.* San Francisco, CA: Jossey-Bass.
Miller, G. (1997) 'Towards ethnographies of institutional discourse: proposals and suggestions', in G. Miller and R. Dingwall (eds) *Context and Method in Qualitative Research*: 155–171. London: Sage.
Mishler, E. (1986) *Research Interviewing: Context and Narrative.* Cambridge, MA.: Harvard University Press.
Mitchell, R. and Lee, H-W (2003) 'Sameness and difference in classroom learning cultures: Interpretations of communicative pedagogy in the UK and Korea', *Language Teaching Research* 7(1): 35–63
Mondada, L. and Pekarek Doehler, S. (2004) 'Second language acquisition as situated practice: Task accomplishment in the French second language classroom', *The Modern Language Journal* 88: 501–518.
Mori, J. (2003) 'Construction of interculturality: A study of initial encounters between Japanese and American students', *Research on Language and Social Interaction* 36(2): 143–184.
Morse, J. M. (1991) 'Approaches to qualitative-quantitative methodological triangulation', *Nursing Research* 40: 120–123.
Morse, J. (2010) 'Simultaneous and sequential qualitative and mixed methods designs', *Qualitative Inquiry* 16(6): 483–491.
Murray, R. (2002) *How to Write a Thesis.* Buckingham: Open University Press.
Myles, F. (2005) 'Interlanguage corpora and second language acquisition research', *Second Language Research* 21: 373–391.
Nazari, A. (2007). 'EFL teachers' perception of the concept of communicative competence', *ELT Journal* 61(3): 202–210.

Nespor, J. (2000) 'Anonymity and place in qualitative inquiry', *Qualitative Inquiry* 6(4): 546–69.

Nias, J., Southworth, G. and Yeomans, R. (1989) *Staff Relationships in the Primary School: A Study of Organizational Cultures.* London: Cassell.

Norris, J. M. and Ortega, L. (2000) 'Effectiveness of L2 instruction: A research synthesis and quantitative meta-analysis', *Language Learning* 50: 417–528.

Noy, D. (2009). 'Setting up targeted research interviews: A primer for students and new interviewers', *The Qualitative Report* 14(3): 454–465. http://www.nova.edu/ssss/QR/QR14–3/noy.pdf [Accessed 3 August 2010]

Nunan, D. (2004) *Task-based Language Teaching.* Cambridge: Cambridge University Press.

O'Toole, P. and Were, P. (2008) 'Observing places: using space and material culture in qualitative research', *Qualitative Research* 8(5): 616–634.

Oakley, A. (1981) 'Interviewing women: a contradiction in terms' in H. Roberts (ed.) *Doing Feminist Research*: 30–61. London: Routledge & Kegan Paul.

Oates, C. (2000) 'The use of focus groups in social science research', in D. Burton (ed.) *Research Training for Social Scientists*: 186–195. London: Sage.

Oliver, P. (2003) *The Student's Guide to Research Ethics.* Maidenhead: Open University Press.

Olsen, B. (2006) 'Using sociolinguistic methods to uncover speaker meaning in teacher interview transcripts', *International Journal of Qualitative Studies in Education* 19(2): 147–161.

Omaggio Hadley, A. (1993) *Teaching Language in Context.* Boston: Heinle and Heinle.

Onwuegbuzie, A. J. and Johnson, R. B. (2006) 'The validity issue in mixed research', *Research in the Schools* 13(1): 48–63.

Opdenakker, R. (2006) Advantages and disadvantages of four interview techniques in qualitative research [44 paragraphs]. Forum Qualitative Sozialforschung / Forum: Qualitative Social Research, 7(4), Art. 11. http://nbn-resolving.de/urn:nbn:de:0114–fqs 0604118. [Accessed 11 August 2010]

Palfreyman, D. (2003) 'Expanding discourse on learner development: A reply to Anita Wenden', *Applied Linguistics* 24(2): 243–248.

Palmer, D. K. (2009) 'Middle-class English speakers in a two-way immersion bilingual classroom: "Everybody should be listening to Jonathan right now . . ."' *TESOL Quarterly* 43(2): 177–202.

Paradis, M. (2004) *A Neurolinguistic Theory of Bilingualism.* Amsterdam: John Benjamins.

Paradis, M. (2009) *Declarative and Procedural Determinants of Second Languages.* Amsterdam: John Benjamins.

Pearce, L. (2005) *How to Examine a Thesis.* Buckingham: Open University Press.

Peirce, B. N. (1995) 'Social identity, investment, and language learning', *TESOL Quarterly* 29(1): 9–31.

Peräkylä, A. (1997) 'Reliability and validity in research based on transcripts' in D. Silverman (ed.) *Qualitative Research: Theory, Method and Practice*: 201–220. London: Sage.

Phillips, D.C. and Burbules, N. (2000) *Postpositivism and Educational Research.* Lanham, MA: Rowman and Littlefield.

Pica, T. (1997) 'Second language teaching and research relationships: A North American view', *Language Teaching Research* 1: 48–72.

Pink, S. (2004) 'Performance, self-representation and narrative: Interviewing with video' in C. J. Pole (ed.) 'Seeing is Believing? Approaches to Visual Research', *Studies in Qualitative Methodology* Vol. 7: 61–77. Amsterdam: Elsevier.

Polkinghorne, D. E. (1995) 'Narrative configuration in qualitative analysis', *International Journal of Qualitative Studies in Education* 8(1): 5–23.

Ponterotto, J. G. (2006) 'Brief notes on the origins, evolution, and meaning of the qualitative research concept "thick description"', *The Qualitative Report* 11(3): 538–549.

Potter, J. and Hepburn, A. (2005) 'Qualitative interviews in psychology: problems and possibilities', *Qualitative Research in Psychology* 2: 1–27.

Psathas, G. (1995) *Conversation Analysis.* Thousand Oaks, CA: Sage.

Rababah, G. (2001) 'An Investigation into the strategic competence of Arab learners of English at Jordanian universities', unpublished doctoral thesis, Newcastle University.

Rapley, T. (2001) The art(fullness) of open-ended interviewing: some considerations on analysing interviews', *Qualitative Research* 1(3): 303–323.

Rampton, B. (2002) 'Ritual and foreign language practices at school', *Language in Society* 31(4): 491–525.

Rampton, B., Tusting, K., Maybin, J., Barwell, R., Creese, A. and Lytra, V. (2004) 'UK linguisitic ethnography: A discussion paper'. UK Linguistic Ethnography Forum. http://www.lancs.ac.uk/fss/organisations/lingethn/documents/discussion_paper_jan_05_.pdf (accessed 7 March 2011)

Raudenbush, S. and Bryk, A. (2002) *Hierarchical Linear Modeling*, 2nd edn. Thousand Oaks, CA: Sage.

Richards, K. (1996) 'Opening the staffroom door: Aspects of collaborative interaction in a small language school', unpublished doctoral thesis, University of Aston in Birmingham.

Richards, K. (1999) 'Working towards common understandings: Collaborative interaction in staffroom stories', *Text* 19(1): 143–174.

Richards, K. (2011) 'Using micro-analysis in interviewer training: "Continuers" and interviewer positioning', *Applied Linguistics* 32(1): 95–112.

Richards, K. (forthcoming) 'Engaging identities: Personal disclosure and professional responsibility' in J. Angouri and M. Marra (eds) *Constructing Identities at Work.* Basingstoke: Palgrave Macmillan.

Richmond, B. (1993) 'Systems thinking: Critical thinking skills for the 1990's and beyond', *Systems Dynamics Review* 9(2): 113–133.

Riley, P. (ed.) (1985) *Discourse and Learning.* London: Longman.

Roberts, C., Byram, M., Barro, A., Jordan, S. and Street, B. (2001) *Language Learners as Ethnographers.* Clevedon: Multilingual Matters.

Ross, S. J. (1998) 'Self-assessment in second language testing: a meta-analysis and analysis of analysis of experiential factors', *Language Testing* 15: 1–20.

Ross, S. J. (2009) 'Program evaluation' in M. Long and C. Doughty (eds) *Handbook of Second Language Teaching*, 2nd edn. London: Blackwell.

Rost, M. and Ross, S. J. (1991) 'Learner use of strategies in interaction: Typology and teachability', *Language Learning* 41(2): 235–273.

Roulston, K. (2006) 'Close encounters of the "CA" kind: a review of literature analysing talk in research interviews', *Qualitative Research* 6(4): 515–534.

Roulston, K. (2010a) *Reflective Interviewing: A Guide to Theory and Practice.* London: Sage.

Roulston, K. (2010b) 'Considering quality in qualitative interviewing', *Qualitative Research* 10(2): 199–228.

Rubin, D. B. (1997) 'Estimating causal effects from large data sets using propensity scores', *Annals of Internal Medicine* 127: 757–763.

Runcie, J. F. (1980) *Experiencing Social Research.* Homewood, IL: Dorsey Press.

Russell, L. (2005) 'It's a question of trust: balancing the relationship between students and teachers in ethnographic fieldwork', *Qualitative Research* 5(2): 181–199.

Sacks, H. (1992) *Lectures on Conversation, Volumes One and Two.* Oxford: Blackwell.

Sacks, H., Schegloff, E. and Jefferson, G. (1974) 'A simplest systematics for the organisation of turn-taking in conversation', *Language* 50: 696–735.

Samuda, V. (2001) 'Guiding relationships between form and meaning during task performance: The role of the teacher' in M. Bygate, P. Skehan and M. Swain (eds.) *Researching Pedagogic Tasks: Second Language Learning, Teaching and Testing*: 119–140. Harlow: Pearson.

Sarangi, S. (2002) 'Discourse practitioners as a community of interprofessional practice: Some insights from health communication research' in C. N. Candlin (ed.) *Research and Practice in Professional Discourse*: 95–135. Hong Kong: City University of Hong Kong Press.

Sarangi, S. (2003) 'Institutional, professional and lifeworld frames in interview talk' in H. van den Berg, M. Wetherell and H. Houtkoop (eds) *Analysing Race Talk: Multidisciplinary Approaches to the Interview*: 64–84. Cambridge: Cambridge University Press.

Sarangi, S. (2007) 'Editorial: The anatomy of interpretation: Coming to terms with the analysis paradox in professional discourse studies', *Test & Talk* 27(5–6): 567–584.

Sarangi, S. and Candlin, C. N. (2001) 'Motivational relevancies: some methodological reflections on social theoretical and sociolinguistic practice' in N. Coupland, S. Sarangi and C. N. Candlin (eds) *Sociolinguistics and Social Theory*: 350–388. London: Pearson.

Sarangi, S. and Candlin, C. N. (2003) 'Introduction. Trading between reflexivity and relevance: new challenges for applied linguistics', *Applied Linguistics* 24(3): 271–285.

Sarangi, S. and Hall, C. (1997) 'Bringing off "applied" research in inter-professional discourse studies', paper presented at BAAL/CUP seminar on urban culture, discourse and ethnography, Thames Valley University, 24–25 March.

Schegloff, E.A. (1987) 'Between Micro and Macro: Contexts and Other Connections' in J. Alexander (ed.) *The Micro-Macro Link*. Berkeley: University of California Press.

Schegloff, E.A. (1992) 'In another context' in A. Duranti and C. Goodwin (eds.) *Rethinking Context: Language as an Interactive Phenomenon*: 191–228. Cambridge: Cambridge University Press.

Schegloff, E.A. (2000) 'Overlapping Talk and the Organization of Turn-Taking for Conversation', *Language and Society* 29: 1–63.

Schegloff, E.A. and Sacks, H. (1973) 'Opening up closings', *Semiotica* 7: 289–327.

Schegloff, E.A., Jefferson, G. and Sacks, H. (1977) 'The preference for self-correction in the organization of repair in conversation. *Language* 53: 361–382.

Schmidt, R. (1990) 'The role of consciousness in language learning', *Applied Linguistics* 11(2): 129–158.

Schmidt, R. (1995) 'Consciousness and foreign language learning: A tutorial on the role of attention and awareness in learning' in R. Schmidt (ed.) *Attention and Awareness in Foreign Language Learning*: 1–64. Honolulu: Second Language Teaching and Curriculum Center.

Schmidt, R. (2001) 'Attention' in P. Robinson (ed.) *Cognition and Second Language Instruction*: 3–32. Cambridge: Cambridge University Press.

Scovel, T. (1978) 'The effect of affect on foreign language learning: a review of the anxiety research', *Language Learning* 28: 129–142.

Searle, J. (1969) *Speech Acts*. Cambridge: Cambridge University Press.

Seedhouse, P. (1996) 'Learning talk: A study of the interactional organisation of the L2 classroom from a CA institutional discourse perspective. Unpublished doctoral thesis, University of York.

Seedhouse, P. (2004) *The Interactional Architecture of the Language Classroom: A Conversation Analysis Perspective*. Malden, MA: Blackwell.

Seedhouse, P. (2005) 'Conversation analysis and language learning', *Language Teaching* 38 4: 165–187.

Seedhouse, P. (2010) 'Locusts, Snowflakes and Recasts: Complexity Theory and Spoken Interaction', *Classroom Discourse* 1(1): 5–25.

Seedhouse, P. and Almutain, S. (2009) 'A holistic approach to task-based interaction', *International Journal of Applied Linguistics* 19(3): 311–338.

Seedhouse, P. and Egbert, M. (2006) 'The interactional organisation of the IELTS speaking test', *IELTS Research Reports* 6: 161–206.

Seedhouse, P., Walsh, S. and Jenks, C. J. (eds.) (2010) *Conceptualising 'Learning' in Applied Linguistics.* London: Palgrave Macmillan.

Shadish, W., Cook, D. and Campbell, D. (2002) *Experimental and Quasi-experimental Designs for Generalized Causal Inference.* Boston: Houghton-Mifflin

Sheen, R. and O'Neill, R. (2005) 'Tangled up in form: Critical comments on "Teachers' stated beliefs about incidental focus on form and their classroom practices" by Basturkmen, Loewen and Ellis', *Applied Linguistics* 26(2): 268–274.

Silva, J. and White, L. (1993) 'Relation of cognitive aptitudes to success in foreign language training', *Military Psychology* 5(2): 79–93.

Silverman, D. (1993) *Interpreting Qualitative Data: Methods for Analysing Talk, Text and Interaction.* London: Sage.

Silverman, D. (1999) 'Warriors or collaborators: Reworking methodological controversies in the study of institutional interaction' in C. Roberts and S. Sarangi (eds.) *Talk, Work and Institutional Order*: 401–425. Berlin: Mouton de Gruyter.

Silverman, D. (2005) *Doing Qualitative Research.* London: Sage.

Silverman, D. (2006) *Interpreting Qualitative Data: Methods for Analysing Talk, Text and Interaction*, 3rd edn. London: Sage.

Singer, D. and Willett, J. (2003) *Applied Longitudinal Data Analysis: Modeling Change and Event Occurrence.* New York: Oxford University Press.

Skåreus, E. (2009) 'Pictorial analysis in research on education: method and concepts', *International Journal of Research and Method in Education* 32(2): 167–183.

Skehan, P. (2003) 'Task-based instruction', *Language Teaching* 36: 1–14.

Small, M. L. (2009) 'How many cases do I need? On science and the logic of case selection in field-based research', *Ethnography* 10(1): 5–38.

Smeyers, P. and Verhesschen, P. (2001) 'Narrative analysis as philosophical research: bridging the gap between the empirical and the conceptual', *International Journal of Qualitative Studies in Education* 14: 71–84.

Spence, D. P. (1986) 'Narrative smoothing and clinical wisdom', in T.R. Sarbin (ed.) *Narrative Psychology: The Storied Nature of Human Conduct*: 211–232. New York: Praeger.

Spencer-Oatey, H. (2000) 'Introduction: Language, culture and rapport management' in H. Spencer-Oatey (ed.) *Culturally Speaking: Managing Rapport Through Talk Across Cultures*: 1–10. London: Continuum.

Spencer-Oatey, H. and Franklin, P. (2009) *Intercultural Interaction: A Multidisciplinary Approach to Intercultural Communication.* Basingstoke: Palgrave Macmillan.

Spradley, J. P. (1979) *The Ethnographic Interview.* New York: Rinehart & Winston.

Spradley, J. P. (1980). *Participant Observation.* New York: Holt Rinehart & Winston.

Stenhouse, L. (1984) 'Library access, library use and user education in academic sixth forms: An autobiographical account' in R. G. Burgess (ed.) *The Research Process in Educational Settings: Ten Case Studies*: 211–234. Lewes: Falmer.

Strauss, A. (1987) *Qualitative Analysis for Social Scientists.* Cambridge: Cambridge University Press.

Strauss, A. and Corbin, J. (1998) *Basics of Qualitative Research: Techniques and Procedures for Developing Grounded Theory*, 2nd edn. London: Sage.

Sturges, J. E. and Hanrahan, K. J. (2004) 'Comparing telephone and face-to-face qualitative interviewing: a research note', *Qualitative Research* 4(1): 107–118.

Sukutrit, P. (2010) '*A study of three phases of interaction in synchronous voice-based chat rooms*', unpublished doctoral thesis, Newcastle University.

Taber, K. (2007) *Classroom-based Research and Evidence-Based Practice: A Guide for Teachers.* London: Sage.

Talmy, S. (2010) 'Qualitative interviews in applied linguistics: From research instrument to social practice', *Annual Review of Applied Linguistics* 30: 128–148.

Talmy, S. and Richards, K. (2011) 'Theorizing qualitative research interviews in applied linguistics', *Applied Linguistics* 32(1): 1–5.

Tanggard, L. (2007) 'The research interview as discourses crossing swords. The researcher and apprentice on crossing roads', *Qualitative Inquiry* 13(1): 160–176.

Tanggard, L. (2008) 'Objections in research interviewing', *International Journal of Qualitative Methods* 7(3): 16–29. http://ejournals.library.ualberta.ca/index.php/IJQM/article/view/1827/3449 [Accessed 11 August 2010]

Tarnpichprasert, M. (2009) 'Inside bilingual education in Thailand: staffroom and classroom perspectives', unpublished doctoral thesis, University of Warwick.

Tashakkori, A. and Teddlie, C. (eds) (2003) *Handbook of Mixed Methods in Social and Behavioral Research.* Thousand Oaks, CA: Sage.

Taylor, S. and Beasley, N. (2005) *A Handbook for Doctoral Supervisors.* Abingdon: Routledge.

Teddlie, C. B. and Tashakkori, A. (2006). 'A general typology of research designs featuring mixed methods', *Research in the Schools* 13(1): 12–28.

Teddlie, C. B. and Tashakkori, A. (2008) *Foundations of Mixed Methods Research: Integrating Quantitative and Qualitative Approaches in the Social and Behavioral Sciences.* London: Sage.

Thompson, B. (2002) *Score Reliability.* Thousand Oaks, CA: Sage.

Tjora, A. H. (2006) 'Writing small discoveries: an exploration of fresh observers' observations', *Qualitative Research* 6(4): 429–451.

Toohey, K. (1998) '"Breaking them up, taking them away": ESL students in Grade 1', *TESOL Quarterly*, 32(1): 61–84.

Toothaker, L. (1991) *Multiple Comparisons for Researchers.* Newbury Park, CA: Sage.

Trochim, W., and Donnelly, J. (2007). *The Research Methods Knowledge Base, 3rd edn.* Cincinnati: Atomic Dog Publishing.

Tsui, A. (1995) *Introducing Classroom Interaction.* London: Penguin.

Tusting, K. and Maybin, J. (2007) 'Linguistic ethnography and interdiciplinarity: Opening the discussion', *Journal of Sociolinguistics* [Special issue] 11(5): 575–583.

Van Dijk, T. A. (1999) 'Context models in discourse processing', in H. van Oostendorp and S.R. Goldman (eds) *The Construction of Mental Representations during Reading*: 123–148. Mahwah, NJ: Lawrence Erlbaum.

Van Geert, P. and Steenbeek, H. (in press) 'A complexity and dynamic systems approach to development assessment, modeling and research' in K. W. Fischer, A. Battro and P. Lena (eds) *The Educated Brain.* Cambridge: Cambridge University Press.

Van Lier, L. (1988) *The Classroom and the Language Learner.* New York: Longman.

Van Lier, L. (1989) 'Reeling, writhing, drawling, stretching, and fainting in coils: oral proficiency interviews as conversation', *TESOL Quarterly* 23: 489–508.

Wacquant, L. (2002) 'Scrutinizing the street: Poverty, morality and the pitfalls of urban ethnography', *American Journal of Sociology* 107(6): 1468–1532.

Walford, G. (2005) 'Research ethical guidelines and anonymity', *International Journal of Research and Method in Education* 28(1): 83–93.

Warren, M. (1985) 'Discourse analysis and English language teaching', unpublished master's dissertation, University of Birmingham, UK.

Wasserman, J. A., Clair, J. M. and Wilson, K. L. (2009) 'Problematics of grounded theory: innovations for developing an increasingly rigorous qualitative method', *Qualitative Research* 9(3): 355–381.

Watson-Gegeo, K. A. (1988) 'Ethnography in ESL: Defining the essentials', *TESOL Quarterly* 22(4): 575–592.

Watzlawick, P., Beavin, J. and Jackson, D. (1980) 'The impossibility of not communicating' in J. Corner and J. Hawthorn (eds.) *Communication Studies*: 137–150. London: Arnold.

Wengraf, T. (2001) *Qualitative Research Interviewing*. London: Sage.

Westgate, D., Batey, J., Brownlee, J. and Butler, M. (1985) 'Some characteristics of interaction in foreign language classrooms', *British Educational Research Journal* 11: 271–281.

Whyte, W. F. (1984) *Learning from the Field*. Beverly Hills, CA: Sage.

Willis, D. and Willis, J. (2007) *Doing Task-based Teaching*. Oxford: Oxford University Press.

Willis, J. (1996) A *Framework for Task-based Learning*. Harlow: Longman.

Wolcott H. F. (1994) *Transforming Qualitative Data: Description, Analysis, and Interpretation*. London: Sage.

Wong, J. (2002) '"Applying" conversation analysis in applied linguistics: evaluating dialogue in English as a second language textbooks', *International Review of Applied Linguistics* 40(1): 37–60.

Wooffitt, R. and Widdicombe, S. (2006) 'Interaction in interviews' in P. Drew, G. Raymond and D. Weinberg (eds) *Talk and Interaction in Social Research Methods*: 28–49. London: Sage.

Wright, B. and Masters, G. (1982) *Rating Scale Analysis*. Chicago: MESA Press.

Yin, R. K. (2004) *The Case Study Anthology*. Thousand Oaks, CA: Sage.

Young, R. (2008) *Language and Interaction: An Advanced Resource Book*. Abingdon: Routledge.

Zheng, X. and Adamson, B. (2003) 'The pedagogy of a secondary school teacher of English in the People's Republic of China: Challenging the stereotypes', *RELC Journal* 34(3): 323–337.

Zimmerman, D. H. (1998) 'Identity, context, and interaction' in C. Antaki and S. Widdicombe (eds) *Identities in Talk*: 87–106. London: Sage.

Zuengler, J., Ford, C. and Fassnacht, C. (1998) '*Analyst eyes and camera eyes: Theoretical and technological considerations in "seeing" the details of classroom interaction*', technical report, The National Research Center on English Learning and Achievement, The University at Albany, State University of New York. Available from http://cela.albany.edu/analysteyes/index.html.

Research design flow chart

Chart your research design in this space. Complete the following flow chart to show how you intend to carry out your research project. This will help you to complete your research proposal (see Appendix C, website) and you will be able to check you are following your design as you progress through your project. Insert a timescale showing the dates by which each stage should be completed.

What are the research questions?

↓

How do the research questions relate to the literature?
What is the rationale or justification for doing the research?

↓

What evidence will help provide an answer to this research question?
How will you answer the questions?

↓

What kind of data would provide such evidence?

↓

What's the best way of collecting such data?
What kind of methodology is appropriate?

↓

Write your research proposal – see Appendix C (website) for guidelines

↓

Request permissions and ethical approval. Obtain access to your data source – see Appendix E (website) for guidelines

↓

Gather data – see Appendices D and G (website) for guidelines

↓

Analyze the data and relate them to the research questions

↓

Write up your dissertation or thesis – see Appendix B (website) for guidelines

Index